D1596634

JEWISH

RETHINKING ANCIENT
GROUPS AND TEXTS

CHRISTIANITY
RECONSIDERED

Edited by Matt Jackson-McCabe

FORTRESS PRESS
Minneapolis

BR
195
.J8
J492
2007

JEWISH CHRISTIANITY RECONSIDERED
Rethinking Ancient Groups and Texts

Copyright © 2007 Fortress Press, an imprint of Augsburg Fortress. All rights reserved. Except for brief quotations in critical articles or reviews, no part of this book may be reproduced in any manner without prior written permission from the publisher. Visit http://www.augsburgfortress.org/copyrights/contact.asp or write to Permissions, Augsburg Fortress, Box 1209, Minneapolis, MN 55440.

Scripture quotations, unless otherwise marked, are from the New Revised Standard Version Bible, copyright © 1989 by the Division of Christian Education of the National Council of the Churches of Christ in the USA. Used by permission. All rights reserved.

Scripture quotations in Chapter 9 are from the Revised Standard Version of the Bible, copyright © 1946, 1952, 1971 National Council of the Churches of Christ in the USA. Used by permission. All rights reserved.

Cover image: Drawing of a menorah engraved into a lime floor upon a thick layer of plaster, in a house opposite the Temple of Jerusalem (around 40 BCE), burnt at the destruction of the second temple in 70 CE. Photo © Erich Lessing / Art Resource, NY.
Cover design: Abby Hartman
Book design: Jessica A. Puckett

Library of Congress Cataloging-in-Publication Data
Jewish Christianity Reconsidered : rethinking ancient groups and texts / Matt Jackson-McCabe, editor.
    p. cm.
  Includes bibliographical references.
  ISBN-13: 978-0-8006-3865-8 (alk. paper)
  1. Jewish Christians—History—Early church, ca. 30-600. 2. Judaism—Relations—Christianity. 3 Christianity and other religions—Judaism. 4 Church history—Primitive and early church, ca. 30-600. 5. Bible. N.T.—Criticism, interpretation, etc. 6. Christian literature, Early. I. Jackson-McCabe, Matt A.
  BR195.J8J492 2007
  270.1--dc22

                                                                    2006024554

The paper used in this publication meets the minimum requirements of American National Standard for Information Sciences—Permanence of Paper for Printed Library Materials, ANSI Z329.48-1984.

Manufactured in the U.S.A.

11   10   09   08   07   1   2   3   4   5   6   7   8   9   10

Contents

CONTRIBUTORS

WILLIAM ARNAL is Associate Professor of Religious Studies at the University of Regina, Saskatchewan, Canada. His books include *Jesus and the Village Scribes: Galilean Conflicts and the Setting of Q* (Fortress Press, 2001) and *The Symbolic Jesus* (Equinox, 2005). His articles on Q, the Gospel of Thomas, the Synoptic tradition, the historical Jesus, and theoretical issues in religious studies have appeared in *Harvard Theological Review*, *Journal of Biblical Literature*, *Journal of the American Academy of Religion*, and elsewhere.

WARREN CARTER is Pherigo Professor of New Testament at Saint Paul School of Theology in Kansas City, Missouri. His many publications include *Matthew and the Margins: A Socio-political and Religious Reading* (Orbis, 2000); *Matthew and Empire: Initial Explorations* (Trinity Press International, 2001); *Matthew: Storyteller, Interpreter, Evangelist* (revised edition; Hendrickson, 2004); *John: Storyteller, Interpreter, Evangelist* (Hendrickson, 2006); and *The New Testament and the Roman Empire: An Essential Guide* (Abingdon, 2006).

JONATHAN A. DRAPER is Professor of New Testament at the School of Religion and Theology, University of KwaZulu-Natal, Pietermaritzburg. He has published numerous articles on the *Didache* and edited *The Didache in Modern Research* (Brill, 1996). He is the author (with Richard A. Horsley) of *Whoever Hears You Hears Me: Prophets, Performance, and Tradition in Q* (Trinity Press International, 1999), and editor of *Orality, Literacy and Colonialism in Antiquity* (Society of Biblical Literature, 2004) and, with R. A. Horsley and J. Miles Foley, *Performing the Gospel: Mark, Orality and Memory* (Fortress Press, 2006). He is currently preparing a critical text and commentary on the *Didache* for a new series, *Oxford Early Christian Texts: The Apostolic Fathers,* edited by Paul Foster, Andrew Gregory, and Christopher Tuckett, to be published by Oxford University Press.

RAIMO HAKOLA is Docent of New Testament Studies and postdoctoral researcher at the University of Helsinki. He is the author of *Identity Matters: John, the Jews and Jewishness* (Brill, 2005).

PATRICK J. HARTIN is Professor of Religious Studies and Chair of the Classical Civilizations Program at Gonzaga University, Spokane, Washington. His recent publications on the Letter of James include *A Spirituality of Perfection: Faith and Action in the Letter of James* (Liturgical, 1999); the Sacra Pagina commentary *James* (Liturgical, 2003); and the Collegeville Bible Commentary *James, First Peter, Jude, Second Peter* (Liturgical, 2006).

CRAIG C. HILL is Professor of New Testament and Director of Wesley Ministry Network at Wesley Theological Seminary in Washington, D.C. He is the author of *Hellenists and Hebrews: Reappraising Division within the Earliest Church* (Fortress Press, 1992) and *In God's Time: The Bible and the Future* (Eerdmans, 2002).

MATT JACKSON-MCCABE is Associate Professor and Chair of Religious Studies at Niagara University in Lewiston, New York. He is the author of *Logos and Law in the Letter of James* (Brill, 2001), and founding chair of the Society of Biblical Literature's Jewish Christianity Consultation.

F. STANLEY JONES is Professor of Religious Studies at California State University, Long Beach. He is the author of *An Ancient Jewish-Christian Source on the History of Christianity: Pseudo-Clementine "Recognitions" 1.27–71* (Scholars Press, 1995) and editor, with Simon Mimouni, of *Le judéo-christianisme dans tous ses états* (Cerf, 2001). He is presently preparing a critical edition and English translation of the Syriac *Pseudo-Clementines* for the Corpus Christianorum, Series Apocryphorum (Brepols).

PETRI LUOMANEN is Docent of New Testament Studies at the University of Helsinki and Academy Research Fellow at the Academy of Finland. In addition to articles on Jewish Christianity and Matthew, he is the author of *Entering the Kingdom of Heaven: A Study on the Structure of Matthew's View of Salvation* (Mohr Siebeck, 1998) and co-editor (with Antti Marjanen) of *A Companion to Second-Century Christian "Heretics"* (Brill, 2005).

JOHN W. MARSHALL is Assistant Professor in the Department for the Study of Religion at the University of Toronto. He is the author of *Parables of War: Reading John's Jewish Apocalypse* (Wilfrid Laurier University Press, 2001).

JERRY L. SUMNEY is Professor of Biblical Studies at Lexington Theological Seminary. His many publications include *Identifying Paul's Opponents: The Question of Method in 2 Corinthians* (JSOT Press, 1990); *Servants of Satan, False Brothers, and Other Opponents of Paul* (Sheffield Academic Press, 1999); and (with Thomas Olbricht) *Paul and Pathos* (Society of Biblical Literature, 2001).

ACKNOWLEDGMENTS

Any book, and particularly a book such as this, comes to see the light of day only through the efforts of many people. As the editor of this book I would like to express sincere thanks to all those who contributed to its production, some in obvious and some in more subtle ways. I can unfortunately single out only a few of you by name.

In the first place I must, of course, thank the authors of the chapters for responding positively to the initial idea for the volume and for seeing it through to publication. It has been a genuine pleasure to collaborate with such good-natured individuals, and I have learned a great deal from working with each of them.

I am also very grateful to the folks at Fortress Press for publishing this work, and for the care with which it was brought to print. I would especially like to thank Neil Elliott for his enthusiastic support for the project, and for the ongoing effort and guidance that he, along with Susan Johnson and Jessica Puckett, provided along the way.

I owe thanks as well to Alonza Jackson-McCabe for bringing her technical expertise to bear on the compilation of the volume's considerable bibliography, and to Andreas Randell for producing its indices. Andreas's work was funded by a generous grant from the Niagara University Research Council, for which I am most grateful. Thanks are also due to Samantha Gust and the Interlibrary Loan staff at Niagara University for helping to make some of the research that went into this volume possible.

There are a number of people with whom I have discussed this project over the last few years, and who have provided perhaps more help than they realize. Petri Luomanen was an important conversation partner at a time when I was initially conceptualizing the volume, and Margaret Mitchell, Adela Yarbro Collins, and Brian Bennett (my trusted friend and colleague at N.U.) provided helpful and stimulating sounding boards along the way. I have also benefited from interaction with all of the various participants in the Society of Biblical Literature's Jewish Christianity Consultation.

My most constant and provocative dialogue partners, ever since I first began thinking about the problem of "Jewish Christianity" as a graduate student, have been Chris Mount, Dale Walker, Jim Hanges, and Paul Holloway. I owe many thanks to Chris and Dale in particular for reading my own contributions to the book with great care and saving me from many errors, as well as for attempting to save me from others to which I have stubbornly clung.

My greatest debt, finally, is to my family. The McCabes and the Boysels have continued to offer the unfailing support on which I have relied so heavily over the years, as have the Jacksons. Most especially, though, I owe thanks to A.J. and Jeremy for being patient and encouraging through the many and various distractions this project introduced into our family. I love you both more than I can say.

M.J.-Mc.
February 2007

Introduction

Matt Jackson-McCabe

Since the nineteenth century, the category "Jewish Christianity" has been fundamental to scholarship on the origins and early history of the Christian religion. Though the terminology has varied, scholars have generally assumed that there was a segment of early Christianity—indeed, perhaps even its original, apostolic form—that can be usefully distinguished from others as *Jewish* (or *Judaic*, *Judaistic*, etc.) Christianity. Specific ancient groups and texts, accordingly, are routinely classified as such in the academic literature, presumably to convey something significant about their character.

The reader who comes across such references and wishes to study this ancient Jewish Christianity more systematically may be surprised, given its apparent significance, to find little in the way of introductory books on the subject, let alone up-to-date ones. Although there has been no shortage of specialized studies on this or that aspect of the topic in recent years, books offering broad, synthetic treatments have always been somewhat scarce. In English there have really only been F. J. A. Hort's *Judaistic Christianity* (1894), Jean Daniélou's *The Theology of Jewish Christianity* (revised and translated from the initial French edition [1958] in 1964), and Hans Joachim Schoeps's *Jewish Christianity* (translated from the German original [1964] in 1969).[1] One finds little more in German and French.[2]

There is probably no single explanation for the lack of such books over the last four decades. But there can be little doubt that the tremendous and ever-increasing complexity of the subject has been a major factor. Despite its ubiquity in early Christian studies, Jewish Christianity has always been an ambiguous category. There has never been a uniform terminology employed to name the class; nor is there any consensus regarding its definition, or even the body of data that belongs in it. To begin to see the problem, one need only consider the fact that the ancient phenomena treated by Hort, Daniélou, and Schoeps—the actual texts and groups each one studies— overlap only minimally from book to book.

Hort's *Judaistic Christianity* assumes a distinction between two closely related terms: "Judaic Christianity" and "Judaistic Christianity." Judaic Christianity is not clearly defined, but seems to refer essentially to a historical era, namely, the earliest phase of Christianity, which for Hort represented "a time of transition during which the old [Jewish] order would live on by the side of the new [Christian one], not Divinely deprived of its ancient sanctity, and yet laid under Divine warning of not distant extinction" (1894, 37-38). The term thus functions within a broad reconstruction of Christian origins that is both overtly theological (assuming a providential hand behind the course of Jewish and Christian history) and markedly anti-Jewish (anticipating the final extinction of Judaism as fundamental to the divine plan). In any event, the real interest of Hort's book is not this *Judaic* Christianity, but what he identifies more specifically as *Judaistic* Christianity. A minority movement within the Judaic phase of Christianity, this form of the religion, by "ascrib[ing] *perpetuity* to the Jewish Law," "falls back to the Jewish point of view, belonging naturally to the time before Christ came" (1894, 5 [my emphasis]). Characterized by Hort as a "futile" early Christian "anachronism," this Judaistic Christianity is said to have been confined primarily to the first century, finding only isolated and sporadic revivals in "limited and obscure forms" in the second century and beyond before "at length dying naturally away" (1894, 6). Hort's book thus focuses principally on the first-century New Testament literature—which, however, is said to provide merely indirect testimony to Judaistic Christianity—with only marginal interest in later, extracanonical texts.

Schoeps's book, on the other hand, is devoted to what he calls simply "Jewish Christianity" (*Judenchristentum*). For Schoeps this class is not defined primarily in terms of an approach to the Torah, but connotes a heretical, sectarian form of early Christianity that was distinct from the "Great Church" in both social organization and doctrine, especially christology.[3] Moreover, while its roots lay "in the earliest beginnings of the primitive church," this "Jewish Christianity" is said to have first appeared "as a clearly defined entity" only in the second century (1969, 1; see also 18). Schoeps's study is thus devoted to later, extracanonical works like the fragmentary Nazarene and Ebionite gospels and, above all, the Pseudo-Clementine literature, not the New Testament.

Daniélou's *Theology of Jewish Christianity* has something quite different in mind again. Here Jewish Christianity (*Judéo-christianisme*) is presented as an *orthodox* theology that characterized *Christianity in general* from its beginnings through the middle of the second century. The core data of Daniélou's Jewish Christianity, accordingly, are a wide array of extracanonical texts that are of little or no interest to either Hort or Schoeps. On the other hand, the New Testament texts are (inexplicably) entirely omitted from discussion (contrast Hort), while the Pseudo-Clementine writings are said to be only peripheral to the class (contrast Schoeps).

What, then, *is* Jewish Christianity? And where in antiquity does one find it? Scholars have failed to arrive at any generally accepted answers to these questions, and the result is a fundamental ambiguity surrounding a category that has been elemental to scholarly discourse on the New Testament and early Christianity. As Bruce Malina (1976, 46) observed some thirty years ago, "The label, 'Jewish Christianity', seems to be a rubber bag term, applied to a host of phenomena yet saying nothing with any clarity about the phenomena that would warrant this specific label." This sobering sentiment was echoed at the inaugural meeting of the Society of Biblical Literature's Jewish Christianity Consultation in November 2005 by Magnus Zetterholm, who characterized the current situation as one of almost "complete confusion on what is actually referred to by the term."

In fact, in the intervening decades between Malina and Zetterholm the problem has only become more complicated. The broad reconceptualization of Christian origins that has resulted from recent research on ancient Jewish–Christian relations has led some to question the utility of the category "Jewish Christianity" at all. Some have replaced this category with one called "Christian Judaism," while others consider calling such borderline groups "Christian" at all to be anachronistic and positively misleading.

Even if some agreement could be reached regarding the usefulness and proper delineation of the terms, there remains the perennial problem of identifying the body of data relevant to the category. What particular groups and texts are we talking about here? If ancient reports about groups such as the early Jerusalem community or the Ebionites have rendered their classification as "Jewish Christian" generally noncontroversial,[4] determination of the provenance and tendencies of anonymous and possibly pseudonymous works of ancient literature is a much more complex matter, and thus much more debatable. Specialists in the particular works of literature involved in this discussion not infrequently disagree among themselves regarding the date, location, and proper interpretation of the texts, let alone tackling the broader question of classifying the religious data of antiquity. To put the matter simply, there is not now, nor has there ever been, a generally agreed upon canon of works that constitute definitive examples of Jewish Christianity, Christian Judaism, or any other such category.

In sum, scholarship continues to be informed by the recognition that a segment of the religious movement that would eventually produce (among other things) orthodox Christianity was in some way "more Jewish" than this latter—to the point, in fact, of constituting a distinct class of religion; and, accordingly, individual scholars continue to assign particular ancient groups and works of literature to that class. However, there is little in the way of consensus regarding the basic features that define the class, the particular body of data that manifests it, or how best to construe its relationship to the categories "Judaism" and "Christianity." Seen in this light, the dearth of introductory books on the subject is quite comprehensible. How does one present the general results of scholarship—the traditional role of the survey—on a subject matter that is very much in flux in contemporary study?

The present book was born from the conviction that, precisely because of this lack of consensus, so-called Jewish Christianity represents an important site of study for anyone interested in the historical redescription of Christian origins. The struggle to identify, describe, and classify ancient texts and groups that seem to occupy a borderland between what we normally think of as the distinct religions of Judaism and Christianity brings to the surface a number of issues that are fundamental to study of the New Testament and Christian origins, including the nature of the earliest Christian religion and its relationship to Judaism; the so-called parting of the ways between these two religions; and ultimately the meaning and relation of "Christianity" and "Judaism" as categories within our own contemporary discourse.

The aim of this book is to provide a much-needed orientation to what has traditionally been and is still sometimes called "Jewish Christianity" as it appears in contemporary study. Given what has been said above, however, it should be clear that there can be no question of presenting an exhaustive and systematic treatment of the "assured results of scholarship." This book, rather, has the much more modest aim of providing the reader with a point of entry into this complex and controversial subject by presenting, simultaneously, a representative sample of the ancient texts and groups that have figured prominently in the discussion, and a variety of approaches to the problem of classification found in contemporary scholarship on them.

After an initial chapter that orients the reader to key issues that have historically been involved in the scholarly formulation of categories such as "Jewish Christianity" and "Christian Judaism," the book presents chapters on some of the ancient groups and texts that have frequently been classified in such terms. These chapters were written by specialists in each area who, informed by the best, most recent scholarship on their subjects, examine the rationale for, and the usefulness of, describing them with such terms as "Jewish Christianity," "Christian Judaism," or the like. The contributors were deliberately selected not only for their relevant specializations, but to represent a range of approaches to the broader issue of classification. Together, the chapters put on display concrete examples of the construction and use of such categories in contemporary, critical scholarship on the New Testament and Christian origins. As such, they place in bold relief the range of issues that define the current study of what has traditionally been called "Jewish Christianity."

In keeping with its aim of providing an introduction to its subject matter, this book was written with the general reader in mind. In order to make it accessible to such a reader and useful for university and seminary students, contributors have done their best to avoid overly technical analysis, to focus on English-language scholarship where possible, and to keep endnotes to a minimum. Suggestions for further reading are included at the close of each chapter, and a comprehensive bibliography is provided at the end of the volume.

At the same time, it is hoped that this book will be of interest also to our professional colleagues and that its up-to-date treatments of some of the relevant texts and groups themselves, as well as its emphasis on the broader matter of classification, will provide helpful groundwork for more advanced historical, comparative, and methodological studies on the forms of ancient religion traditionally called Jewish Christianity, and indeed on Christian origins more generally. If it succeeds in bringing into focus the significance of these forms of ancient religion for the study of Christian origins, it will have achieved its purpose.

1. What's in a Name?
The Problem of "Jewish Christianity"
Matt Jackson-McCabe

Scholarship on early Christianity, like all scholarship, involves the ongoing generation of categories for the purpose of organizing and illuminating its data. Scholars group together certain texts, for example, on the basis of common traits deemed especially significant in some respect. Those interested in making a point about recurring forms of ancient thought might class together under the term "apocalypticism" works that, while otherwise quite different, envision an abrupt, radical end to the current world order, supernatural savior figures, or scenarios of final judgment. Works that share a notion that the world was created by a relatively low-order and not altogether good deity, on the other hand, are often grouped together in a category called "Gnosticism." The more generally useful—whether descriptively or ideologically—such categories prove to be, the more widespread their usage in the scholarly literature.[1] Some, indeed, become givens in the discourse of the field, providing the basic lenses through which the raw data of early Christianity are refracted and understood.

This is a natural and necessary part of any analytical work. Lenses, however, can potentially distort as much as they bring into focus. Jonathan Z. Smith (1990, 52) has pointed out that comparison, by its very nature, is an act of "disciplined exaggeration in the service of knowledge."

> It lifts out and strongly marks certain features within difference as being of possible intellectual significance, expressed in the rhetoric of their being "like" in some stipulated fashion. Comparison provides

the means by which *we* "re-vision" phenomena as *our* data in order to solve *our* theoretical problems.

The construction of categories is inseparable from such comparison (J. Z. Smith 2004, 20; cf. Satlow 2005). In the case of "apocalypticism" and "Gnosticism," particular patterns or features that recur in works of ancient literature are emphasized to the point of being identified as core characteristics of distinct classes of ancient religious phenomena. Ancient texts such as *1 Enoch* and the *Gospel of Thomas* are then re-presented as more or less typical examples of those classes. But one must be careful that "disciplined exaggeration" does not become misleading caricature. It is always possible that emphasis on this or that aspect of a given text or set of texts will come at the expense of other aspects that would create different, and perhaps even more adequate, understandings of the category. Michael Allen Williams's observation regarding the category "Judaism" is illuminating in this respect. "Judaism," he writes, "is indeed a tradition that takes observance of law seriously, but to focus only on this feature, and to fail to appreciate variety within Judaism on this question, is to fail to understand Judaism" (1995, 5).

The issue is crucial because the categories we generate have a way of taking over the interpretive process. The classification of a given text immediately creates a range of expectations about it on the part of the interpreter relative to his or her understanding of the category. The reader, that is, will "know" certain things about that text even before actually beginning to read it. To the extent that one's understanding of the category is clear and apposite, such knowledge can in fact be very useful for interpretation. Alert to elements or structural patterns that are the hallmarks of a class, the reader will have a ready-made comparative context in which to make sense of elements of a specific text that might otherwise seem insignificant or obscure. What is more, identification of such typical elements will set in relief those aspects of a given work that are *not* typical, that distinguish it from other members of its class, that make it itself rather than something else. To the extent that one's understanding of the category is problematic, however, the reader may ignore significant features of a text, misinterpret the meaning of others, or even assume the presence in it of things that are not actually there.[2]

A necessary part of any healthy academic discipline, then, is the critical consideration of its own core categories. One will thus find scholars working to clarify what, precisely, categories such as "Judaism" (Sanders 1976; 1977; Neusner 1978; Smith 1988) or "apocalypticism" (J. Collins 1989, 1–32) should be understood to entail, and even whether others, such as "Gnosticism," are so problematic that they should be abandoned altogether (Williams 1996).

Since the nineteenth century, "Jewish Christianity" has been among those categories that function essentially as givens in the field of early Christian studies.[3] Scholars, in other words, have generally taken for granted that there was in antiquity an identifiable phenomenon that should be considered a distinctly Jewish subclass of Christianity, and that some early Christian groups and texts are best understood as examples of it. Remarkably, however, there has been no agreement as to what the particular phenomenon in question actually is, nor, consequently, the specific body of data that manifests it. Despite repeated attempts to clarify the category, contemporary scholars have little or nothing to say with a unified voice regarding the specific features or structural patterns that distinguish Jewish Christianity as a class from other forms of ancient religion. The lack of progress on this matter after more than 150 years of scholarship is at least remarkable; at worst it is symptomatic of a category that is inherently problematic and a field of scholarship in fundamental disarray. Not surprisingly, a number of scholars have recently begun to counsel the abandonment of "Jewish Christianity" as a category that obfuscates more than it illuminates about the origins of the Christian religion.

The aim of the present chapter is to highlight salient aspects of this complicated but important discussion. I shall first distinguish several different, though in practice frequently overlapping, approaches to formulating the category "Jewish Christianity" that have dominated past discussion.[4] I shall then examine the issues that have led some recent scholars to abandon this category in favor of alternatives such as "Christian" or "Christ-believing Judaism." The chapter concludes by identifying the fundamental problems faced by those who would construct and employ such categories, and suggesting a promising direction for future study.

JEWISH CHRISTIANITY AS THE JERUSALEM COMMUNITY

In the course of a defense of his gospel and apostolic status, the self-pro-claimed apostle Paul explains in his letter to the Galatians the nature of his relationship with "those who were already apostles before [him]"(Gal 1:17)—and particularly with the recognized "pillars" of the movement, James "the Lord's brother," Cephas (Peter), and John. On the whole Paul is at pains to demonstrate his fundamental independence from these earlier leaders. He says he did not consult with them at all when he first received his revelatory call to become apostle to the Gentiles (1:15-17); he is em-phatic that he saw no one but Cephas and James during a fifteen-day stay in Jerusalem three years after that revelation (1:18-24); and he implies that he did not explain even to those two "the gospel [he] proclaim[s] among the Gentiles" until a subsequent trip to Jerusalem fourteen years later (2:1-2).[5] Nor, by Paul's account, was his independence significantly compromised even when he finally did submit his gospel to them "to make sure that [he] was not running, or had not run, in vain" over all those years (Gal 2:2).

> On the contrary, when [James, Cephas, and John] saw that I had been entrusted with the gospel for the uncircumcised, just as Peter had been entrusted with the gospel for the circumcised (for he who worked through Peter making him an apostle to the circumcised also worked through me in sending me to the Gentiles) . . . they gave to Barnabas and me the right hand of fellowship, agreeing that we should go to the Gentiles and they to the circumcised. They asked only one thing, that we remember the poor, which was actually what I was ea-ger to do. (Gal 2:7-9 [NRSV])

Paul's account gives the impression that the earliest followers of Jesus in-cluded two distinct spheres of missionary activity, separated along ethnic lines, with each functioning under the leadership of different apostolic fig-ures. It suggests that this arrangement existed de facto within a few years of Jesus' death, at least from the time Paul joined the movement, only to be formally acknowledged roughly a decade and a half later. The extent to which all this reflects the actual social realities of the early Christ movement, on one hand, and Paul's rhetorical concern to shape the Galatians' perception of those realities, on the other, is not immediately clear.[6] Whatever the case, Paul's account of his relationship with the Jerusalem apostles has been a crucial building block in the scholarly construction of the category "Jewish Christianity."

Jewish Christianity commonly refers collectively to the group of communities associated with the missionary efforts of Peter's "gospel for the circumcised." Revolving around Jerusalem, and associated with Jesus' original apostles and perhaps especially his brother James, Jewish Christianity in this sense represents the very earliest Christian communities (see Daniélou 1964, 8; Longenecker 1970, 3–4). As such, it contrasts with the "Gentile Christianity" later spearheaded by Paul and those in his orbit, typically understood to have been centered in Syrian Antioch (see Acts 13–15 and Gal 2:11-14). Given the impression of Peter's and Paul's respective leadership over these separate spheres of activity created especially by Gal 2:7-9, this dichotomy between "Jewish" and "Gentile" Christianity is also sometimes formulated in terms of "Petrine" and "Pauline" Christianity (classically Baur 1963 [= 1831]; more recently Goulder 1994).

The most pressing issue facing those who conceive of Jewish Christianity in this way is the identification of relevant data. The central criterion for inclusion in the category is of course direct social-historical connection to the Jerusalem community and its leaders. Works written by Peter, James, or John would obviously be included in the class. So too would any community, with its texts, that lived under the umbrella of the Jerusalem group and its mission. But the fact that a given work bears the name of Peter, James, or John is no guarantee that it was produced by that figure, nor even within the Jerusalem community at all. The early Christians display a clear penchant for creating pseudonymous works of literature: texts that effectively identify the beliefs and concerns of some later group with those of the apostles by means of fictive claims of apostolic authorship. No serious scholar believes that the canonical Letter of James, the *Protevangelium of James*, and the *Apocryphon of James* were all produced within the Jerusalem community, let alone by James himself. Nor is it conceivable that Peter or John actually wrote all of the works that bear their names.[7] The problem, of course, is determining which if any of these works are actually authentic.

Where such determinations are not driven by a theological or nostalgic tendency to trust the canonical ascriptions, they inevitably involve a judgment regarding the extent to which a given work exemplifies characteristics that one, on other grounds, associates with the "Jewish Christianity" of the Jerusalem group. And while some scholars would argue for the authenticity of one or another of these works, there is presently no single text that a general consensus of scholars would attribute to the early Jerusalem community.

Making matters more complicated is the fact that the Jerusalem community per se had ceased to exist by 70 CE when the city was destroyed at the climax of the Jewish war with Rome. The historical value of later stories about the community migrating more or less en masse to Pella just before the outbreak of the war is unclear.[8] Thus when one sees reports from subsequent centuries about ethnically Jewish communities, such as the Ebionites and Nazarenes, who combined interest in Jesus with traditional Jewish practices, their historical connection to the Jerusalem community is not immediately obvious. Surely they would have claimed as much; but then so too would a number of other groups with quite different characteristics. The same mentality that gave rise to pseudonymous works of literature also produced spurious genealogies that sought to link communities of subsequent generations directly to the Jerusalem community and its leaders. Where "earliest" and "apostolic" are taken to mean "true" and "genuine," Christians were (and are) quick to establish lines of descent between their own communities' teachings and one or more of the original apostles—and to deny the competing claims of others.[9]

The establishment of an accurate genealogy of the Jerusalem community has thus been a central preoccupation of scholarship on Jewish Christianity. Where nineteenth-century scholars, flush with confidence, produced elaborate genealogies of a half-dozen or more varieties of Jewish Christianity descending from the original Jerusalem community (e.g., Ritschl 1857, 248 n. 1; Lightfoot 1972 [1865], 318–46), subsequent scholarship has generally been characterized by more modest aims and at any rate less-complicated classification schemes (though see the tentative suggestion in S. G. Wilson 1995, 143–58). The most basic question is whether *any* of the second-century groups or texts represent direct historical descendants of the Jerusalem community. Johannes Munck (1959–60; see also 1965), for example, argued that the Jerusalem community effectively ended in 70 CE, leaving no direct descendants; "all later Jewish Christianity," he said, thus represented more or less spontaneous developments within "the Gentile-Christian church" (1959–60, 114). Accordingly, Munck introduced a simple distinction between "primitive" or "apostolic" Jewish Christianity, identified with the Jerusalem community, and the "later" or "post-apostolic" forms that, on his view, were entirely unrelated to it.

As in the case of texts attributed to James, Peter, and John, attempts to establish lines of descent from later groups and literature to the early Jerusalem community ultimately depend on the extent to which one finds traits associated with the Jerusalem community in the later evidence. There is, it must be noted, potential for circularity here; for the location of texts and groups within a genealogy of the Jerusalem community will assume some prior notion of the character of that community's religion, while determination of the nature of their religion will depend largely on the texts and groups that are linked to it. In any event, this genealogical approach to Jewish Christianity depends in practice on establishing a morphology of the class.

MORPHOLOGIES OF JEWISH CHRISTIANITY

Jewish Christianity has not always been conceived simply in terms of the Jerusalem community and its lines of descent and influence. When Munck classified certain writings and groups under "later" or "post-apostolic Jewish Christianity," he did not intend in any way to associate them with the Jerusalem community. On the contrary, he classified them as such only because they were characterized by traits typically associated with Christianity in combination with those typically associated with Judaism—and in spite of his central argument that they had no significant connection to the Jerusalem group whatsoever. Munck's work thus exemplifies an altogether different approach to the category. Here "Jewish Christianity" is not simply another name for the communities and texts within the orbit of the

Christ movement in Jerusalem, but a more general category of phenomena of which the Jerusalem community is but one example (even if, in Munck's work, the privileged one). In this more generic sense, the term "Jewish Christianity" purports to identify a class of early Christian groups and texts that can be usefully distinguished from others owing to their possession of certain formal features, regardless of genealogy. Historical lineage becomes entirely secondary to morphology, as one possible explanation of patterns of formal similarity and difference that are observable in any case. Indeed, if one begins by defining the class in terms of morphological traits, the extent to which the Jerusalem community itself exhibits those traits, and thus belongs in the class at all, becomes an open question (e.g., J. E. Taylor 1990, 316).

When the category is approached in this way, the primary issue becomes identifying the particular feature or set of features that warrant inclusion in the class. Typically this has come in the form of attempts to isolate the specific Jewish features that constitute an identifiable subclass of Christianity; that is, of clarifying what is especially Jewish about *Jewish* Christianity.

There is from the outset a certain ambiguity inherent in the term, since "Jewish" can indicate an ethnic descent, a religious character, or both. Thus while Jewish *Christianity* is most naturally taken as descriptive of a distinct class of religion, Jewish *Christian*, as applied to a person, may simply indicate something about her or his ethnic extraction. Oddly enough, then, depending on one's use of the terms, "Jewish Christians" may or may not have anything to do with "Jewish Christianity."[10] Scholars have thus periodically suggested the employment of different terms to distinguish Christians of Jewish descent from people of any descent who practice a particularly "Jewish" form of Christianity (see Ritschl 1857, 105, citing Schliemann 1844; R. Murray 1974). Such proposals, however, have found little traction.

It is in any case the religious sense of the term "Jewish Christian" that has been most important in reconstructions of early Christianity. But this limitation scarcely resolves the matter. It is clear by all accounts that early Christian groups and texts in general are characterized by distinctly Jewish features. Most if not all, for example, relied on the Jewish scriptures for understanding humanity's place within a created order, whatever their evaluation of the Jewish deity. The issue, then, is identifying the specific Jewish feature or features that justify the isolation of *some* such texts and groups as a separate, Jewish subclass of Christianity.

Three quite different types of answers to this question are found in the scholarly literature. As often as not, and especially in the older literature, they are embedded in larger attempts to reconstruct the genealogy of the Jerusalem community and its importance for the emergence of catholic Christianity. In fact, the different morphologies of Jewish Christianity often reflect competing reconstructions of the nature and historical origins of the Christian religion more generally. While each has enjoyed a certain popularity at some point in the history of scholarship, none of these delineations of Jewish Christianity has ever achieved anything like the kind of consensus that leads to uniform usage of the term across the field. Not surprisingly, conclusions regarding the particular groups and texts that belong in the class have also been widely divergent.

Particularism

It has been common over the history of scholarship to identify Christianity fundamentally with universalism. Christianity, in other words, is frequently portrayed as a religion that by its very nature transcends the national, ethnic, and cultural limitations—in sum, the particularism—said to characterize other religions of the world. On this view, Christianity arose, more specifically, in conscious opposition to a particularistic Jewish religion said to have characterized the society in which Jesus and his earliest followers lived. From this vantage point, Jewish Christianity has sometimes been conceptualized as a segment of the early Christian movement that, due to its fundamental misunderstanding of the universalistic essence of the religion, continued to emphasize Jewish particularism alongside faith in Jesus.

This approach characterizes the work of F. C. Baur, the nineteenth-century New Testament scholar and early church historian who is largely responsible for making the category "Jewish Christianity" a fixture in the scholarly imagination of Christian origins. Over his career, Baur argued relentlessly that earliest Christianity was divided into two bitterly opposed camps, Jewish Christianity and Pauline (Gentile) Christianity, and that the catholic Christianity that ultimately emerged at end of the second century represented a synthesis of these two factions.[11]

According to Baur's reconstruction (1878, 1:24–37), the roots of both factions could ultimately be traced to Jesus himself. Jesus' unique and original contribution, he said, was a certain "moral consciousness" that, oriented around a person's inner disposition rather than external acts, transcended all religious or national barriers. While Jesus, Baur said (1:32), was no doubt aware that his teaching implied a fundamental antagonism toward Judaism, he felt "that it was unnecessary . . . to set forth the antagonism of the principle expressly . . . sure that, as the spirit of his teaching came to be understood and realized, it would be worked out to all the results which it necessarily involved." What is more, Jesus, ironically, couched his universalistic teaching in the patently nationalistic idiom of Jewish messianism, in this way forcing a fundamental choice on the Jewish people: "the whole nation [was] called on to declare whether it would persist in that traditional Messianic belief which bore the stamp of selfish Jewish particularism, or if it would accept such a Messiah as he was" (1:41).

According to Baur, it was this presentation of a fundamentally universalistic message in traditionally particularistic language that sowed the seeds for division among Jesus' followers after his death. Some of Jesus' followers, effectively mistaking the husk for the kernel, focused on "the national side of his appearance, and attach[ed] themselves to it so firmly as never to surmount the particularism of Judaism at all" (1:49). The result "was simply a new and stronger form of the old Messianic expectations," the "only difference" being that this group believed that the messiah had already come. Apart from further development, then, "[t]he Christian faith would have become the faith of a mere Jewish sect, in whose keeping the whole future of Christianity would have been imperilled" (1:43).

Ironically, it was according to Baur precisely those most closely associated with Jesus during his lifetime—the apostles (including Peter and John), as well as Jesus' brother James—who failed to grasp the full import of their master's teaching. Within the early Jerusalem community led by James, Peter, and John (see Gal 2:9), however, arose a liberal, hellenized circle that began to give more forceful expression to the universalism of Jesus' message—and, in the process, to make more explicit the antagonism to Judaism that that message (according to Baur) had originally implied. When these "Hellenists" were persecuted for their views, they withdrew to Antioch, leaving Jerusalem entirely to the conservative "Hebraists," led by the apostles (1878, 1:44–46; cf. Acts 6:1—8:1). While Jerusalem thus became the seat of a particularistic Jewish Christianity, Antioch would become the seat of a universalistic Gentile Christianity, with the newly converted Paul as its chief advocate and most penetrating expositor. Indeed, to the extent that it was this erstwhile persecutor of the Hellenist Christians who would finally give a full, clear voice to Jesus' universalistic message, Paul's conversion amounted to a "new beginning" of Christianity (1878, 1:46).

Apart from a short-lived truce struck during a rare visit by Paul to Jerusalem, the relationship between the universalistic Gentile Christianity he led and the particularistic Jewish Christianity led by the original apostles was, as Baur reconstructed it, basically antagonistic. Rejecting Paul's claims of revelation and apostleship, the Jerusalem apostles supported a counter-mission that attempted to undermine both the personal authority and the universalistic gospel of Paul, and to bring his Gentile converts under the yoke of Jewish law. For his part, Paul accused Peter and the others of hypocrisy and redoubled his efforts to establish his own teaching as the true gospel. That the hostility between these two factions lasted well beyond the lives of the apostles was clear to Baur from later reports concerning the Ebionites, who were characterized, among other things, by a stark rejection of Paul. It gradually subsided as both sides began to make overtures toward some manner of reconciliation. The end result was a new synthesis of Pauline and Jewish Christianity in the religion of catholic Christianity.

With this comprehensive reconstruction of Christian origins in place, the research agenda of Baur and his followers, known collectively as the Tübingen School, was essentially set. The crucial questions brought to any early text were, first, the category to which it belonged (Jewish Christianity or Pauline Christianity) and, second, whether it showed the sort of tendency toward reconciliation with the opposing faction that would imply a later date. With the data thus classified, reconstructing early Christian history was primarily a matter of charting the various developments within Jewish and Pauline Christianity that led from their initial opposition to their final synthesis.[12]

The reconstruction of Christian origins proposed by Baur and the Tübingen School was not, to say the least, universally accepted. Among other things, the notion of a fundamental and enduring rift between Paul and the Jerusalem apostles was widely rejected, and with it the idea that an interplay between Jewish and Pauline Christianity was the (or even a) crucially formative aspect of early Christianity through the second century. On the other hand, to the extent that they shared Baur's core conviction regarding the fundamental contrast between Christian universalism and Jewish particularism, even those scholars who rejected his historical reconstruction continued to find it useful to classify Christian groups or texts characterized by Jewish particularism as a distinct category within Christianity.

Adolf von Harnack, whose astounding body of work on early Christianity was itself immensely influential in the early twentieth century, illustrates this well. "Original Christianity," for Harnack (1961 [1896], 1:287, 288), represented "the creation of a universal religion on Old Testament soil," "the religion of Israel perfected and spiritualized." As such, it "took possession of the whole of Judaism as religion." Harnack thus rejected as entirely misleading the use of the term "Jewish Christianity" to describe the simple Christian appropriation of Jewish discourse or practice, as some have been inclined to use it (see below). "Wherever the universalism of Christianity is not violated in favour of the Jewish nation," he wrote, "we have to recognize every appropriation of the Old Testament as [simply] Christian," not *Jewish* Christian. The latter term

> should be applied exclusively to those Christians who really maintained in their whole extent, or in some measure, even if it were to a minimum degree, the national and political forms of Judaism and the observance of the Mosaic law in its literal sense, as essential to Christianity . . . or who, though rejecting these forms, nevertheless assumed a prerogative of the Jewish people even in Christianity. (1:288–89)

Harnack thus approached the data of early Christianity with the same core assumptions as Baur had regarding its basic nature and its relationship to Judaism: Christianity was an essentially universalistic religion, while Judaism was a particularistic—or, in Harnack's favored terminology, "national"—one.

The former thus stood in fundamental opposition to the latter.[13] Indeed, for Harnack (1961 [1896], 1:289), Jewish Christianity is to be contrasted not with Gentile Christianity but with "the Christian religion" itself "in so far as [the latter] is conceived as universalistic and anti-national in the strict sense of the term." Much as for Baur, then, Jewish Christianity for Harnack represented the compromise of a supposed Christian universalism through a particularistic assumption of Jewish privilege.

The similarities, however, end there. Though sharing Baur's theoretical definition of the class, Harnack came to radically different conclusions regarding who and what was to be included in it, as well as regarding its significance within the historical development of Christianity more generally. Influenced by Albrecht Ritschl's alternative reconstruction of early Christian history (see immediately below), Harnack (1986 [1957], 179) held that Peter and the other apostles, though not without struggle, ultimately affirmed the validity of Paul's universalistic gospel. Given Harnack's strict identification of Jewish Christianity with Jewish particularism, this would seem to call into question the extent to which Peter and the Jerusalem community belong in the class at all. Harnack is in fact oddly silent about the Jerusalem apostles in the chapter on Jewish Christianity in his *History of Dogma*;[14] and he is in any case elsewhere (1908, 1:61) quite explicit that once Peter (with the rest of "the primitive apostles") began associating with Gentile Christians as a result of an agreement with Paul, he "ceased to be a 'Jewish Christian.'" On the other hand, to the extent that Paul "neither could nor would believe in a final repudiation of [Israel as] God's people" (see Rom 11:25, 29), he himself, at least "[i]n this sense . . . remained a Jewish Christian to the end" (1908, 1:65).

In Harnack's view (1961 [1896], 1:295 n. 2; cf. 288), finally, there are no surviving texts that merit inclusion in the category: "No Jewish Christian writings," he asserts, "have been transmitted to us, even from the earliest period." In the end, the actual data relevant to the category are effectively reduced to later reports of Ebionites and similar groups and the few extant fragments of their Gospels (1:295-96 n. 2). It is perhaps not surprising, then, that Harnack (1:290) flatly rejected the notion that Jewish Christianity had any significant impact on the development of catholic Christianity.

Although common assumptions regarding the essential nature of Christianity and Judaism led Baur and Harnack to the same theoretical

definition of a Jewish Christianity, their accounts of it as an actual historical reality differed sharply owing to differing interpretations of specific
early Christian texts and varying reconstructions of the development of
the early Christian religion more broadly. Both scholars found it useful in
principle to group together Christian groups or texts that exemplified Jewish particularism as a separate class of Christianity. The questions, though,
were (1) the extent to which Peter and the Jerusalem community actually
belonged in the class; (2) which surviving texts, if any, belonged in the
class; and (3) how significant Jewish Christianity was within the historical
development of Christianity more generally.

Practice

The conclusion that the earliest apostles had a principled resistance to universalism was not widely shared outside of Baur's Tübingen School. Unlike Harnack though, most scholars still found it illuminating to describe
the early apostles and the Jerusalem community as Jewish Christian, even
apart from the issue of particularism. The end result was an alternative definition of the category "Jewish Christianity" and, with it, a more complex
taxonomy of the class. The particularistic Jewish Christianity of Baur and
Harnack became, in effect, one species of a larger, more complex category
whose members were marked by something other than Jewish particularism. For a number of scholars, that something is a distinct form of religious
practice, specifically, observance of Jewish law.

The second edition of Albrecht Ritschl's *Die Entstehung der altcatholisch-
en Kirche* [*The Emergence of the Ancient Catholic Church*] (1857), presented
as a direct challenge to Baur's reconstruction of Christian origins, stands
at the head of this reformulation of the category. According to Ritschl, the
particularistic Christian movement opposed to Paul was not the great historical force that Baur had made it out to be. It originated not with the
apostles but as a small, Pharisaic segment of the early Jerusalem community (see Acts 15:5). Though Ritschl acknowledged that the earliest apostles
did observe the Torah, he argued that they did not do so for the same reasons these Pharisaic Christians did. While the latter remained convinced

that no one could enter into the new covenant without being simultaneously party to the old covenant between God and the Jewish people, the
apostles, he said, held no such view; they, like Paul, believed that entrance
into the new covenant depended solely on faith in Christ (1857, 147). In
principle, then, they were indifferent to the Torah. They simply observed
the laws that governed their nation; they had no *religious* reason to do so,
much less to require such observance of non-Jews (128-29; cf. 125, 141,
147). They were in this respect, Ritschl said (125), simply following the
example of Jesus.

Ritschl's historical reconstruction amounted to a reconceptualization of
the category "Jewish Christianity." This new formulation was more complex
than that of Baur and Harnack, as signaled by Ritschl's introduction of a
series of technical distinctions between seemingly closely related terms, the
different nuances of which are somewhat difficult to reproduce in English.
"Jewish Christianity" (*Jüdische Christenthum*) was the name he gave to the
overarching category to which belonged texts and groups marked not by
particularism but simply by their combination of Christian faith and Jewish practice (e.g., 1857, 248). The compound term "Judaeo-Christianity"
(*Judenchristenthum*), on the other hand, was used with reference to those
who believed that *"the law that God gave through Moses is also the essence
of Christianity"* (106, his emphasis); who assumed, in other words, the basic
"identity of Judaism and Christianity" (107).[15] This class approximated what
Baur and Harnack had identified simply as "Jewish Christianity" (see esp.
Harnack 1961 [1896], 1:288–89, cited above). Different from each of these
were those aspects of early Christianity that could be described more generally as "Judaic" (*judaistisch*), which is to say influenced in a more general way
by the postclassical Judaism of the Second Temple period. Such influence
included things like apocalypticism, and the term was thus broad enough to
include elements of Paul's theology as well as that of catholic Christianity.[16]

What Ritschl in effect created was a taxonomy of Jewish Christianity that
directly reflected his own reconstruction of ancient Judaism and Christian
origins. The resulting genealogy was summarized in the form of a family tree (1857, 248 n. 1). The general category "Jewish Christianity" now
included both universalistic (apostolic) and particularistic (Pharisaic) varieties, both of which were found in the early Jerusalem community. Each

of these, moreover, was said to have given rise to further Jewish Christian groups in subsequent centuries. Specifically, the second-century group the church fathers called the Nazarenes were said to descend from the early apostles, while the Ebionites (in Pharisaic and, subsequently, Essene varieties) descended from the early opponents of Paul. The early Christian literature was then classified according to this scheme, with particular texts assigned to specific groups within the taxonomy.

Though Ritschl held that both varieties of Jewish Christianity existed into the second century and beyond, he argued further against Baur that neither was particularly influential in the development of catholic Christianity. On the contrary, they became increasingly isolated and insignificant as a result of the Jewish wars of the first and second centuries. Jewish Christians in general thus had little or no impact on the formation of the catholic Church, which was essentially a Gentile phenomenon.

Ritschl's analysis had a broadly formative influence on scholarly discussion of Jewish Christianity through the Second World War (Luedemann 1989, 14–18) and, if more indirectly, beyond. While it is fair to say that scholars today are generally more reticent to establish elaborate genealogies of Jewish Christianity than were Ritschl and his immediate successors, and though the particular texts Ritschl identified are not universally acknowledged as being relevant to the category, the use of the term "Jewish Christianity" to denote groups or texts that combine veneration of Jesus with practice of Jewish law remains very common. Some of the most significant scholarship on Jewish Christianity over the last half-century has argued in favor of precisely this definition of the category, regardless of genealogical matters (e.g., Simon 1996 [1986]; Strecker 1988; Luedemann 1989; Mimouni 1992; Paget 1999). More generally, Ritschl's division of this Jewish Christianity into universalistic (apostolic) versus particularlistic (judaizing) varieties became commonplace (e.g., Lightfoot 1972 [1865]; Hort 1894; McGiffert 1897). This distinction was inevitably correlated with further (and frequently apologetic) dichotomies such as original/later, mainstream/fringe, Great Church/sectarian, and orthodox/heretical (e.g., Munck 1959–60; 1965; Quispel 1968; Schoeps 1969, 1–37; Riegel 1978).

The crucial questions for those who would approach the category in this way are: (1) How much Torah observance is required for inclusion in the category? (2) Which specific groups and texts actually reflect the type of observance that counts as Jewish Christian? (3) Does a given example represent a universalistic or particularistic variety of Jewish Christianity? Regarding the first question, Paul's position on the law often seems to be at least an implicit point of reference (see Ritschl 1857, 106); that is, any approach to observance beyond Paul's simple "love of neighbor" formulation (see Rom 13:8-10) is approaching Jewish Christianity. Marcel Simon (1965, 7–8; 1975, 56–57) suggested using the so-called apostolic decree regarding Gentile observance (see Acts 15) in an analogous way, while others have been content to work with a more fluid approach to the matter (e.g., Jones 1995, 164 n. 21; Paget 1999, 241). How one answers the second and third questions will of course be a function not only of one's answer to the first, but of one's negotiation of the detailed argumentation generated in connection with specialized studies of the relevant texts and groups. Does the Letter of James evidence the type of Torah observance that is said to count as Jewish Christianity? Does the book of Revelation? If so, a Jewish Christian text of what variety? Naturally, the specific understanding of the wider body of data that belong in the category will vary from scholar to scholar depending on how these specific questions are answered.

Discourse

An additional layer of complexity was added to the discussion of Jewish Christianity with the publication of Hans Joachim Schoeps's *Theologie und Geschichte des Judenchristentums* [*Theology and History of Jewish Christianity*] (1949), a condensed version of which was later translated into English under the title *Jewish Christianity: Factional Disputes in the Early Church* (1969). Like those examined in the previous section, Schoeps accepted in principle the distinction between what he called "moderate," or "Great Church" Jewish Christians who accepted Paul's mission and the "extremist" Pharisaic *cum* Ebionite group that insisted that Gentiles, too, observe the Torah.[17] He argued, however, that this latter group was marked not merely by their stance on proper Christian practice, but by a distinctive theology: specifically, a conception of Jesus' role as True Prophet and Messiah that was at odds with the christology of the "Great Church." Schoeps's aim was to explicate this distinctly and definitively "Jewish Christian" theology.

Jean Daniélou then set out in his *Theology of Jewish Christianity* "to do for orthodox what Schoeps ha[d] already done for heterodox Jewish Christianity" (1964, 10 n. 21). Daniélou argued that orthodox Jewish Christianity, too, was characterized by a recognizably distinct theology, and his book aimed to reconstruct it. Richard Longenecker subsequently sought, in *The Christology of Early Jewish Christianity*, to work out what he took to be, more specifically, "a unity of basic christological conviction" (1970, 7) characteristic of the earliest Jewish Christian community over its first one hundred years.

Particularly as a result of Daniélou's book, which undoubtedly ranks among the most influential works on the subject written in the history of scholarship, a host of scholars began to radically reconceptualize Jewish Christianity as a category of Christian groups and texts marked simply by a recognizably Jewish discourse.

Daniélou's work on Jewish Christianity was undertaken as part of a more broadly conceived, three-volume study called *The Development of Christian Doctrine before the Council of Nicaea*. The starting point of this larger project is a dogmatic assumption that a divine revelation of transcendent truth stands as the ultimate origin of Christianity. Theology is construed by Daniélou as the (logically, though not necessarily temporally) subsequent human response to that revelation; theology gives revelation verbal expression and interprets it in terms provided by the interpreter's culture (1964, 1–5; cf. 9–10; compare 1973, 1–3; 1977, xiii–xvi). Accordingly, while recognizing other possible definitions, Daniélou organized his study of Jewish Christianity around a conceptualization of the category that he took to be "of the highest importance for the historical study of Christian doctrine" (9), namely, Jewish Christianity as "*the expression of Christianity in the thought-forms of Later Judaism*" (10, his emphasis); "a type of *Christian thought expressing itself in forms borrowed from Judaism*" (9, his emphasis).

Daniélou's work constituted a significant reconceptualization of Jewish Christianity along the lines of what Ritschl had earlier distinguished specifically as Judaic (*judaistisch*) Christianity.[18] Inclusion in the category required neither particularism nor practice; nor did it imply Jewish ethnicity, nor even social ties to any Jewish community. The "Jewishness" of Jewish Christianity on this approach consists solely in the use of forms of discourse derived from Jewish culture. Formulated as such, Jewish Christianity is contrasted with neither Pauline nor Gentile Christianity; indeed, Paul himself is included under Daniélou's version of the category, as could be certain Gentiles (1964, 9). Instead, it stands in contrast to later expressions of Christian theology in terms generated within other cultural complexes, such as the "Hellenistic" and "Latin" Christianities that provided the subjects of the second and third volumes, respectively, of Daniélou's larger study of ante-Nicaean theology. The primary division within Jewish Christianity, moreover, no longer turned on a distinction between universalism and particularism. The key issue now was orthodox versus heterodox doctrine, particularly with respect to christology (see 1964, 7–9; further 55–85).

With the category conceived in this way, the data of Jewish Christianity change drastically. Any text could now be identified as Jewish Christian provided it met at least some of three criteria (1964, 11): (1) an early date, since "[t]he Jewish Christian period [i.e., the period in which Christian theology was being expressed primarily in "thought-forms" provided by Jewish culture] extends from the beginnings of Christianity to approximately the middle of the second century"; (2) a literary genre reflective of the conventions of "Later Judaism"; and (3) the presence of Jewish ideas (especially apocalypticism). The class thus now included a broad assortment of extracanonical literature that did not count as Jewish Christian in earlier approaches to the category (see 1964, 11–54).[19] At the same time, some of the groups and texts most typically associated with the category, like the Ebionites and the Pseudo-Clementine literature, became only marginally significant for (true) Jewish Christianity (1964, 55).[20] Indeed, in the wake of Daniélou, the term "Jewish Christianity" could be reserved specifically for "the historically perceived orthodox Christianity that undergirds the ideology of the emergent Great Church" (Malina 1976, 49). How far from Baur and Harnack the category had come!

Though Daniélou's study of Jewish Christianity has not gone without criticism (esp. R. A. Kraft 1972; more recently, Luedemann 1989, 25–27; Paget 1999, 737–39), its influence has been considerable. At the end of the 1980s, more than forty years after the publication of its initial, French edition, Gerd Luedemann (1989, 29) found Daniélou's approach to the category to be the dominant one in scholarship, criticized or not. Even a scholar such as Marcel Simon, who remained an advocate of a practice-oriented definition, endorsed Daniélou's analysis, suggesting only one main revision: that Daniélou's category be termed "Semitic Christianity" (*christianisme sémitique*) in order to distinguish it from the "Jewish Christianity" (*judéo-christianisme*) marked by Torah observance (Simon 1975, 66).

Daniélou's work spawned a number of such attempts to bring clarity to an increasingly confusing subject through suggestions of distinct technical terms corresponding to various Jewish phenomena within early Christianity—much as Ritschl had done more than a century before. In addition to Simon's distinction between "Semitic" and "Jewish Christianity," one finds schemes in which terms such as "Jewish Christianity," "Judaeo-Christianity," "Judaic Christianity," "Judaistic Christianity," "Hebrew Christianity," "Hebraistic Christianity" and "Christian Judaism" emerge as signifiers of distinct classes of ancient phenomena (R. Murray 1974; 1982; Malina 1976; Riegel 1978). But as competing scholars generate different sets of terminology, different analytical distinctions, and even varying delineations of the terms used in common, these efforts have scarcely had the desired effect. None has proved compelling enough to become generally accepted in the field. Moreover, as a host of closely related terms are used to describe a diverse—and indeed sometimes mutually exclusive—range of ancient phenomena, the proper subject matter of Jewish Christianity has only become more obscure.

More than a century and a half after Baur succeeded in establishing "Jewish Christianity" as a fundamental category in the study of the New Testament and Christian origins, scholars have made little progress toward articulating a clear and generally accepted understanding of what that category entails, and thus why it should be considered analytically useful. One scholar, while lauding Daniélou's work as having "taken a step which had to be taken sooner or later," declared that the term "Jewish Christianity," after Daniélou, had become "impossible to define . . . because it proved to be a name that can readily be replaced by 'Christian'" (Klijn 1973–74, 426). Another has referred to it as "a rubber bag term, applied to a host of phenomena yet saying nothing with any clarity about the phenomena that would warrant this specific label" (Malina 1976, 46). If, despite these sobering assessments, neither of these scholars is prepared to abandon the category,[21] it is perhaps not surprising that others have been less sanguine.

JEWISH CHRISTIANITY OR (CHRISTIAN) JUDAISM?

One occasionally finds in the older scholarship a passing suggestion that at least some of the phenomena typically called "Jewish Christianity" might be more properly classified as forms of Judaism. This seems to have occurred especially where the Judaism/Christianity dichotomy was construed as one between particularism and universalism, and in such cases it generally came with a normative edge. To the extent that a group or text was understood to exhibit particularistic sensibilities, its classification as (true) Christianity was seen as questionable. Thus, as we have already seen, Baur (1878, 43) remarked that, to the extent that Jewish Christianity represented "simply a new and stronger form of the old [particularistic] Messianic expectations," it amounted to "a mere Jewish sect, in whose keeping the whole future of Christianity would have been imperilled." Harnack (1961 [1896], 289) is more explicit: "To this [particularistic] Jewish Christianity is opposed, not Gentile Christianity, but the Christian religion, in so far as it is conceived as universalistic and anti-national in the strict sense of the term." A similar line of reasoning led F. J. A. Hort (1894, 5), who in the wake of Ritschl distinguished between a universalistic "Judaic" Christianity and a particularistic "Judaistic" one, to suggest that the latter "might with at least equal propriety be called Christian Judaism."[22]

Apart from such musings, though, the category has generally been construed by scholars, and mostly unreflectively so, as a subclass of Christianity. Two critical if typically unspoken assumptions undergird this notion of a Jewish *Christianity*. The first is that, even if the name itself had not yet been coined, a religion that can usefully be distinguished from Judaism as Christianity was in fact in existence immediately in the wake of Jesus' death, if not already within his own lifetime. The second is that those ancient groups who seem from our perspective to sit on the borderline between Judaism and Christianity are nonetheless better understood as examples of the latter. Serious questions have been raised regarding both of these assumptions in recent scholarship.

A new ideological context, coupled with stunning discoveries of previously unknown ancient texts, has led to a fundamental reconceptualization of early Judaism and early Christianity in scholarship over the last half-century. The supersessionism and self-conscious opposition to Judaism that have typically characterized Christianity throughout its history, and not least in the influential German New Testament scholarship of the nineteenth and early twentieth centuries, were cast in a profoundly disturbing light by the Holocaust. The tragic consequences of Nazi Germany's radical anti-Semitism inspired a broad re-thinking of the nature and relationship of these two religions on the part of historians and theologians alike in postwar scholarship. For students of early Judaism and Christian origins, this work was aided by the fortuitous discovery of the Dead Sea Scrolls in the 1940s and 1950s. The literature contained in these scrolls gave scholars in-depth access to a sectarian Jewish viewpoint contemporary with Jesus and his followers and posed a sharp challenge to the earlier scholarly tendency to view first-century Judaism through the lens of later rabbinic texts. With a new appreciation for the diversity of Second Temple Judaism, scholars took interest in other previously known but generally neglected Jewish works of the period. The so-called Old Testament Pseudepigrapha were collected and newly translated (Charlesworth 1983; 1985) and, along with the works of Philo, Josephus, and the so-called Apocrypha, became the focus of intensive research. The tendency of previous scholars to view "late" or "intertestamental" Judaism as a relatively static—and indeed, in apologetic Christian scholarship, stagnant and lifeless—religion gave way to a picture of a vibrant, creative, and highly diverse "early Judaism."[23] Indeed, as the notion of a normative, proto-rabbinic Judaism in the Second Temple period evaporated, scholars began speaking instead of early *Judaisms*.

The discovery of the Nag Hammadi library in 1945, along with the publication of a new German edition (1963) and English translation (1971) of Walter Bauer's *Orthodoxy and Heresy in Earliest Christianity* (now complete with an appendix "On the Problem of Jewish Christianity" by Georg Strecker) did much the same for Christianity. Bauer's brilliant critique of the traditional notion that Christian heresies represented late developments that broke with a singular, original orthodoxy became foundational for a new generation of scholars who began speaking routinely, as with Judaism, of early *Christianities*. As notions of Judaism and Christianity as essentially stable, monolithic religions broke down, the issue was no longer how "Judaism" and "Christianity" related to one another in antiquity, but how any given Christian group related to any given Jewish one.

Particularly important for the question of Jewish Christianity in all this has been the realization that much of what has traditionally been associated with Christianity in particular was actually characteristic of other first-century Jewish movements as well. The Dead Sea sect, for example, viewed the Jewish scriptures much as Jesus' followers did: as veiled prophesies that predicted the coming of their own teacher and their own community. (The two groups even singled out some of the same passages for this purpose, e.g., Isa 40:3; compare 1QS 8:12-16 with Mark 1:1-3 and par.; John 1:23). In a related move, members of this sect also viewed themselves as exclusive participants in a "new covenant" initiated by God with his elect (e.g., CD 6:19; 8:21; 19:33-34; 1QpHab 2:3; compare 2 Cor 3:6; Heb 8:8; 9:15; Luke 22:20 and par.; cf. Jer 31:31-34). Nor were Jesus' followers the only Jews of the period who claimed to have crucial new prophecies, or to have found the messiah (Horsley and Hanson 1985; Gray 1993). Such similarities have raised anew, though on very different and less normative grounds, the fundamental question of classification hinted at already in the works of Baur, Harnack, and Hort. If all of these other movements are simply regarded as parts of a diverse first-century Jewish landscape—that is, as early Judaisms—why should Jesus' followers be viewed as a separate religion, as "Christianity"?

The commonsense answer might seem to come from our knowledge of subsequent history. It is after all quite clear that the evolution of the movement that sprang up around the figure of Jesus would ultimately produce a recognizably distinct species of religion. But one must always ask whether a category developed in and appropriate for a later era might not distort more than it illuminates an earlier one. To continue the biological metaphor, if *Australopithecus africanus* is considered an ancestor of the modern human, calling it *Homo sapiens* for that reason would nonetheless create a very misleading impression of its character. There is in fact virtually universal agreement in contemporary scholarship that calling Jesus himself "Christian" would confuse more than it would clarify about the religion he espoused. At what point, then, does the employment of the category become useful to describe the religion of Jesus' followers?

This question has become all the more pressing in light of recent research into the so-called parting of the ways, which has made it quite plain that the emergence of Christianity as a religion recognizably distinct from Judaism was the result of historical processes that were slower, more irregular, and generally more complex than traditionally envisioned (e.g., Boyarin 1999; 2004). The complexity of the matter as understood in contemporary scholarship is telegraphed immediately in titles like *The Partings* [plural!] *of the Ways* (Dunn 1991) and *The Ways That Never Parted* (Becker and Reed 2003), as well as in studies that emphasize close social-scientific analysis of specific historical and geographical locations over sweeping generalizations about a supposed historic split between "Judaism" and "Christianity" (Zetterholm 2003). In short, barring some move to a dogmatic claim of divine revelation (à la Daniélou), the particular point(s) in history and the particular setting(s) in which the historian can begin to speak usefully of Christianity as a class of religion distinct from Judaism are no longer as immediately obvious as they once seemed. And if this is the case with Christianity in general, how much more so Jewish Christianity!

A number of recent scholars have in fact begun to suggest that Jewish Christianity is a malformed category that scholarship would be better to abandon altogether; that, as in the case of Jesus himself, it is anachronistic and positively misleading to classify some, at least, of his earliest followers in terms of anything other than Judaism. This point has given rise to a more insistent and thoroughgoing employment of the classification "Christian Judaism" that was used only sporadically and suggestively over a century ago by Harnack and Hort (e.g., Saldarini 1994). Others have argued that the term "Christian" in any form is so laden with connotations of a later era that even "Christian Judaism" would inevitably obscure the nature of the religion of the texts or groups in question (e.g., Marshall 2001). This concern has spawned a variety of alternative terms such as "Jesus-movement" (Gager 2000, viii), "Jesus-believing Jews" (Zetterholm 2003, 6 and n. 21),

"Christ-believers" (Nanos 2002a, 20 n. 5), and "apostolic Judaism" (Nanos 2005), each of which is intended to portray its subject more squarely and fully as an example of first-century Judaism, while avoiding any false expectations generated by association with the later religion of Christianity.

Whether employing the adjective "Christian" or not, however, this new approach suffers from some of the same basic problems that have plagued the more traditional formulations. There is no more agreement among these scholars about the criteria that allow one to distinguish "Christian (or Jesus-believing, etc.) Judaism" from "Christianity," or regarding the specific body of data relevant to the category, than there has been in the case of Jewish Christianity. For some, the class is conceptualized broadly enough to describe, in a manner reminiscent of Daniélou, virtually all Christ-believing groups and literature up to a certain period in the history of the religion. Bruce Chilton and Jacob Neusner (1995) include the entire New Testament (with the partial exception of Hebrews) under "Christian" or "New Testament Judaism." Daniel Boyarin (1999, 20), on the other hand, uses "Christian Judaism" as "an intentionally startling name" for all varieties of Christians up to the fourth century.[24] Gabrielle Boccaccini (1991) goes even further: not only was Christianity one among many Judaisms of antiquity, but it has never ceased being anything other than a species of Judaism. For Boccaccini, then, "Christian Judaism" and "Christianity" are entirely coterminous categories (1991, 19). Others, on the other hand, take a more restricted approach to the category, suggesting only that this or that *specific* ancient work should be classified in terms of (Christian) Judaism, thus implying that some particular segment of the Christ movement remained a Jewish sect even as the new religion of Christianity was emerging around it. Thus, Anthony Saldarini (1994) singled out the Gospel of Matthew in this respect, while John Gager (2000, viii) mentions Paul, Revelation, the Letter of James, and the Gospels of Mark and John. It is interesting in any case to note that a number of recent studies have argued that the apostle Paul in particular—precisely the figure that earlier scholarship took to be quintessentially "Christian" while emphatically *not* "Jewish Christian"—is better understood in terms of Judaism than Christianity (see Gager 2000).

It should be emphasized that this new approach to classifying the early followers of Jesus, while an increasingly important trend in contemporary scholarship, has not yet succeeded in establishing itself as *the* discourse of the field. If the category "Jewish Christianity" has come under serious attack, it has by no means been wholly displaced in the academic literature, where a significant segment of scholarship has simply carried on with the traditional coinage in one or another of its uses (e.g., Jones 1995; Mimouni 1998). And at least one scholar has employed "Jewish Christianity" and "Christian Judaism" side by side, to distinguish two separate classes of early Christian religion (Malina 1976; so too, apparently, Gager 2000, 58, 62; cf. Gager 2003).

Problems and Prospects

The study of so-called Jewish Christianity has come to a critical crossroads. To be sure, despite its widespread employment over the history of the critical study of the New Testament and Christian origins, the category has always been beset with fundamental problems. To the extent that the term is taken to be synonymous with the Christ movement in Jerusalem and, by extension, the results of what Paul portrays as Peter's missionary "gospel for the circumcised" (see Gal 2:7), the basic problem is one of data. Quite differently than in the case of Paul and his "gospel for the uncircumcised," there are no texts that can be attributed without controversy either to the Jerusalem group itself or to any community resulting directly from its missionary efforts. What is more, the historical fate of the Jerusalem community after the destruction of the city in 70 CE, and thus the relevance for it of reports concerning later groups like the Ebionites and Nazarenes, are not obvious. Of course, individual scholars do argue for or against both the authenticity of works attributed to the Jerusalem "pillars" and lines of descent from the Jerusalem community to one or another later group; such arguments, however, will always be based on some perception of formal similarities and differences between the Jerusalem community and the text or group in question. As a practical matter, then, morphology must in this case precede genealogy.

The morphological approach to the category, however, comes with its own set of complications. In the first place, it raises the possibility of members of the class with no direct genealogical connection to the Jerusalem community: groups that exhibit key formal features associated with the latter for reasons other than direct historical connection to Peter's supposed missionary sphere. Indeed, whether the Jerusalem community itself belongs in the class will now depend on the extent to which it is understood to exhibit the feature or features that one, on other grounds, associates with the category. Most basically, this approach requires one to articulate precisely what those particular formal features are: the specific trait or range of traits that allow one to identify a member of the generic category "Jewish Christianity." And it is precisely here that most of the confusion surrounding the category begins. Scholars have been unable to generate anything like a consensus on this crucial question, and the result is a highly ambiguous term, the definition of which and the data associated with which vary—sometimes radically—from study to study.

Some variation is to be expected, given the fact that any such category is ultimately the artificial construction of a scholarly imagination. As noted at the outset of this chapter, Jonathan Z. Smith's point about comparison is applicable to the formation of categories as well. Classification, too, provides a "means by which *we* 're-vision' phenomena as *our* data in order to solve *our* theoretical problems" (J. Z. Smith 1990, 52). In a very real and important sense, then, Jewish Christianity is a scholarly invention—one that is in fact continually re-created, reconceptualized, and redefined even as the ancient data themselves remain essentially unchanged.[25] What is more, it has become clear from the preceding survey that approaches to Jewish Christianity are always embedded in, and expressive of, broader theories regarding the nature, origin, and historical development of Christianity. As theoretical and ideological contexts vary—from Baur to Ritschl to Daniélou to post-Holocaust scholarship—Jewish Christianity itself is "re-visioned" accordingly. In this sense, then, one might answer the question What is Jewish Christianity? by saying that it is nothing more and nothing less than what any scholar says it is for the purposes of his or her study (see Satlow 2005, 293, 295). And if different scholars inevitably bring different theoretical interests and problems to bear on the data, it is only natural that their respective constructions of Jewish Christianity will likewise vary.

To acknowledge this fact, however, is not to deny that some measure of consistency in terminology across the field of early Christian studies is desirable. Much less is it to suggest that all categories are created equal. While interpretive categories such as "Jewish Christianity" are products of scholarly invention and reinvention, they are generated within the context of a shared academic discourse, by a scholarly community that depends on common technical vocabulary to communicate, let alone to progress. Categories, then, "need not, and should not, be completely random" (Satlow 2005, 294).[26] Indeed, in Smith's view (2000, 239; cf. 2004, 28–32, 197–98), the aim of comparative study includes not only redescription of the data in question, but a "rectification of the categories in relation to which [the exempla] have been imagined." Progress, in other words, should involve a "recursive sharpening of a category" in order to give it greater descriptive or theoretical utility.[27]

From that perspective, very little progress has been made in the study of Jewish Christianity. The category has become elastic to the point of being unhelpful, and it is no small wonder that a number of recent scholars have begun openly to question its utility. Indeed, the variation in its usage within the scholarly literature goes far beyond that of categories such as "apocalypticism," "Judaism," or even (ancient) "Gnosticism." There is disagreement not only about definition, but even regarding the core body of data covered by the class. In any given study, the designation "Jewish Christianity" may be used with reference to a very small and relatively insignificant segment of the Christian movement, or to Christianity in general through the first century or centuries of its history; with reference to some form of practice regardless of discourse, or to some pattern of discourse regardless of practice; with exclusive reference to "heterodox" forms of Christianity, or to "orthodox" forms; as including every work in the New Testament, or including none of them.

The present trend, evident in a number of recent works, to reassert a narrow, practice-based approach that identifies Jewish Christianity as Christ belief combined with Torah observance is an understandable reaction to this problem of elasticity (Strecker 1988; Luedemann 1989; Taylor 1990; Mimouni 1992; Jones 1995, 164 n. 21; Paget 1999; cf. S. G. Wilson 1995, 143–59). I do not believe, however, that this move is the way toward real progress in either the historical redescription of Christian origins or the rectification of the categories employed for that purpose, and for two

interrelated reasons. First, it does not adequately address the basic problem highlighted by post-Holocaust scholarship, namely, the rationale for
including any given ancient group or text within the class "Christianity"
rather than "Judaism." Second, inasmuch as it identifies the category with
a single and essential trait, it represents a methodologically problematic
approach to classifying historical phenomena.

Among the most pressing problems identified by post-Holocaust scholarship on Christian origins has been one of classification; specifically, the
use of the category "Christianity" in distinction from "Judaism" to describe
groups and texts in the first centuries of the Common Era. Succinctly put,
the problem is this: Given that early Judaism itself encompassed a wide
variety of subspecies in antiquity, many of which exhibited traits analogous
to those of Jesus' followers, on what basis, and in what particular historical
setting(s), can one begin to speak of groups that venerated Jesus as belonging to a class other than Judaism, that is, to Christianity? For the traditional
Christian imagination, this problem is easily resolved by appeals to authentic revelation and divine providence; and this move is in fact evident
in some scholarship (so, as we have seen, Daniélou; cf. Longenecker 1970,
9–10). Nonetheless, such an appeal is entirely out of bounds for the proper historian of religion who—regardless of his or her personal beliefs—is
methodologically constrained (to borrow Bruce Lincoln's phrase [2005,
8]) to analysis of "things temporal and terrestrial." The practice-based approach to Jewish Christianity seems to assume that veneration of Jesus is
sufficient for this purpose (Simon 1996, 241; Strecker 1988, 311; Mimouni
1998, 69–70; cf. Munck 1959–60, 107; Longenecker 1970, 6). But since veneration of prophets, teachers, and messiahs is also characteristic of some
early Judaisms, this only begs the question. Why should we understand
attachment to *this* hero to constitute a religion that is something other than
Judaism when we do not do so in the case of others?

The quick classification of any group or text that shows interest in Jesus
as "Christianity" glosses over a set of complex issues that would seem to be
crucial to the whole enterprise of the historical redescription of Christian
origins.[28] Exactly how and why did veneration of Jesus come to be associated, eventually at any rate, with the formation of a class of religion recognizably distinct from Judaism? What specific morphological traits separate this

class from all of the various forms of Judaism, and where, when, and under what particular circumstances can one observe these traits emerging?

A more fundamental problem with the practice-based definition comes to light when one considers contemporary studies on method and theory in classification (J. Z. Smith 1988; 1990; 1996; 2000; Needham 1975). Smith in particular has shown that any attempt to isolate a single trait as the hard core of a given class of religion is inherently problematic for the historian; for inasmuch as religions are subject to change over time, there is "neither a theoretical basis nor an empirical warrant for the assumption that any given ancestral trait would persist in any given descendant." Drawing on models of classification found in the biological sciences, he has thus proposed a "self-consciously *polythetic* mode of classification which surrender[s] the idea of perfect, unique, single differentia" and views classes instead in terms of *sets of traits*, many of which are possessed by many members of a class, but with no single one necessary or, of itself, sufficient for inclusion (1988, 4). Daniel Boyarin (1999; 2003; 2004) has brought analogous models from linguistic and cultural studies to bear on the specific problem of clarifying the complex relationship of Judaism and Christianity in late antiquity. On this approach, members of classes are imagined, as Boyarin (2003, 74) puts it, as "points on a continuum" rather than as carriers of a single, definitive trait. If one were to arrange members of a given class so that those with most traits in common were placed nearest each other, in fact, those furthest from one another might have few or even no features in common (Boyarin 2003, 78-79, 83-84; cf. J. Z. Smith 1988, 4).

Viewed from this perspective, the practice-based definition of Jewish Christianity appears problematic on two scores: it effectively identifies Christianity with veneration of Christ alone; and it conceptualizes a subclass of Christianity (*Jewish* Christianity) in terms of another singular trait, namely, Torah observance. There is of course in principle nothing to hinder one from grouping together for comparative purposes Christ believers who enjoin certain forms of Torah obedience. Indeed, this would undoubtedly prove very useful for clarifying how the Torah functions over a range of texts and groups in different times and places. But to saddle an analytical distinction like "Torah-observant Christ believers" with the designation "Jewish Christianity," particularly given the tremendous ambiguity surrounding that term, would be to sacrifice clarity and precision for the sake of what, in the end, amounts only to a needless tautology. The comparative study of such a trait represents an important precursor to the construction of properly polythetic categories, but not its end. The classification of any given text or group as a subclass of Christianity or Judaism would ultimately require an explicit and transparent reasoning based on a nuanced articulation of an *array* of such traits, ideally encompassing matters of both discourse and practice, as well as social identity and institutional structures.[29] Quite apart from any specific conclusions regarding classification, such an approach would thus engender a more subtle and sophisticated redescription of the social and religious realities of antiquity than traditional, essentialist approaches to Judaism, Christianity, and so-called Jewish Christianity allow.

Both Smith and Boyarin emphasize that the study of the borderline cases that inevitably result from such a polythetic approach to classification can be especially productive in the larger attempt to think through the construction of the categories in question (J. Z. Smith 1988, 4; Boyarin 2003, 66). The ancient groups and texts that have given rise to categories like "Jewish Christianity" and "Christian Judaism" represent precisely the type of borderline cases that these scholars have in mind. Inasmuch as they exhibit in combination traits associated with *either* Judaism *or* Christianity as these categories are typically conceived, they challenge us to rethink received wisdom about the boundaries that define and separate these classes and the extent to which appeal to them is helpful for the historical redescription of religions in antiquity. For that reason, if no other, the texts and groups that challenge our normally dichotomous use of the categories Judaism and Christianity represent a particularly fertile field of investigation for historians of religion.

SUGGESTED READINGS

Baur, Ferdinand Christian. 1878 [1863]. *The Church History of the First Three Centuries*. 3d edition. Translated by Allan Menzies. 2 vols. London: Williams and Norgate. Translation of *Kirchengeschichte der drei ersten Jahrhunderte*. Tübingen: L. F. Fues, 1863.

Boyarin, Daniel. 2004. *Border Lines: The Partition of Judaeo-Christianity.* Divinations: Rereading Late Ancient Religion. Philadelphia: University of Pennsylvania Press.

Daniélou, Jean. 1964. *The Theology of Jewish Christianity.* Vol. 1 of *The Development of Christian Doctrine before the Council of Nicaea.* Translated by John A. Baker. London: Darton, Longman & Todd; Chicago: Henry Regnery.

Horrell, David G. 2000. "Early Jewish Christianity." Pages 136–67 in vol. 1 of *The Early Christian World.* Edited by Philip Esler. 2 vols. London and New York: Routledge.

Hort, Fenton John Anthony. 1894. *Judaistic Christianity: A Course of Lectures.* Cambridge and London: Macmillan.

Klijn, A. F. J. 1973–74. "The Study of Jewish Christianity." *New Testament Studies* 20:419–31.

Luedemann, Gerd. 1989. "A Survey of the Research on Jewish Christianity as a Means of Formulating the Problem." Chapter 1 (pages 1–32) of *Opposition to Paul in Jewish Christianity.* Translated by M. Eugene Boring. Minneapolis: Fortress Press.

Paget, J. Carleton. 1999. "Jewish Christianity." Pages 731–75 in *The Cambridge History of Judaism.* Vol. 3, *The Early Roman Period.* Edited by W. Horbury, W. D. Davies, and J. Sturdy. Cambridge and New York: Cambridge University Press.

Schoeps, Hans Joachim. 1969. *Jewish Christianity: Factional Disputes in the Early Church.* Translated by Douglas R. A. Hare. Philadelphia: Fortress Press.

Simon, Marcel. 1996 [1986]. *Verus Israel: A Study of the Relations between Christians and Jews in the Roman Empire AD 135–425.* Translated by H. McKeating. The Littman Library of Jewish Civilization. Oxford: Oxford University Press. Repr., 1996.

Smith, Jonathan Z. 1988 [1982]. "Fences and Neighbors: Some Contours of Early Judaism." Pages 1–18 in *Imagining Religion: From Babylon to Jonestown.* Chicago: University of Chicago Press. Repr., 1988.

Wilson, Stephen G. 1995. *Related Strangers: Jews and Christians 70–170 C.E.* Minneapolis: Fortress Press.

Part I: Groups

2. The Jerusalem Church
Craig C. Hill

Who is a Jew? What makes someone a Christian? No simple, enduring answers exist to such questions, in part because no single person or group is in a position to enforce its definition. If one is excommunicated from a particular church, one can always find (and, barring that, start) another church. Ought practitioners of Christian Science to be called Christians? Are today's Messianic Jews truly Jewish? It all depends on whom one asks.

I teach in a seminary that is theologically, as well as racially and culturally, diverse. It is by no means easy to say what is held in common by all of our students and faculty. Certainly, the great majority identify themselves as Christians, although they do not all mean the same thing by it. If, entirely for the sake of argument, one were to classify as "Christian" only those who accept the Apostles' Creed, then a somewhat smaller but still significant core would qualify. But even within that select group, there would be substantial disagreement as to the meaning of phrases such as "conceived by the Holy Ghost" and "the resurrection of the body," and a sizable percentage would dismiss "he descended into hell" entirely. As a result, it is unlikely that all members of this group would regard all others as at least equally Christian.

Defining Judaism and Christianity is rather like trying to identify by sight the colors red and orange. It is not difficult to spot a deep red or orange, but distinguishing between the two colors at their border is another matter. What appears a reddish orange to one might seem an orangish red to another.[1] Similarly, at what point would a Jew's ideas about Jesus make him or her a Christian? And would someone inhabiting this border region be a Christian Jew or

39

a Jewish Christian—or neither? Any such labeling is bound to be somewhat artificial and arbitrary. Among other reasons is the simple fact that humans tend not to think, much less to behave, according to clear and consistent, neat and tidy categories. Instead, they are, in practice if not in principle, tolerant of a considerable amount of self-inconsistency and ambiguity. The attempt to classify religious belief and practice, especially at the boundaries, is thus an inherently limited and often frustrating exercise. Adding to this complexity is the theological taxonomist's own bias. What is at stake in the identification? It is altogether understandable that Jewish and Christian scholars might disagree as to the appropriateness of the category "Christian Judaism," to mention only the most obvious example.

The problem becomes even more acute when we ask about the definition of Judaism or Christianity, much less Jewish Christianity, in the first and second centuries. Contemporary debates over the question of "normative Judaism" illustrate this point perfectly. The evidence is never what we would like—primary-source data are severely limited—and, even here, more goes on under the table than is usually admitted. To cite a parallel example, disputes over the distinction between Christianity and Gnosticism often serve as thinly disguised arguments over the shape and boundaries of present-day Christian faith. Those who disparage and those who defend early orthodox criticisms of Gnosticism, such as those of Irenaeus, usually have a personal stake in the outcome of that dispute. Defining a religion is not a value-neutral enterprise.

Little wonder, then, that the terms "Jewish Christian" and "Christian Jew" are employed so variously and loosely in both scholarly and popular writing. To attempt a definition is to invite criticism. Indeed, since no universally agreed upon characterization of either Judaism or Christianity exists, it goes without saying that defining "Jewish Christianity," or any other such hybrid, to the satisfaction of all is quite impossible.

Desirable as they might be, we do not require globally accredited definitions. The more modest and attainable goal is relative clarity about our own use of such terminology, especially at the center of its meaning (that is, not attempting to adjudicate every border dispute). When we speak of Jewish Christianity, to what, at least in general, might we refer?

A little more ground clearing is necessary, however, before answering that question. The first point concerns the choice of terminology, namely, my own preference for the phrase "Jewish Christianity" over "Christian Judaism." In part, this is a retrospective judgment that takes into account the eventual split between the two religions. Just as important, it factors in the existence of Gentile Christianity, whose legitimacy was formally recognized by the Jerusalem church. (Gentile Christians were not considered Jews, so "Judaism" is not the overarching category.) That having been said, it appears likely that early Christ-believers in the Jerusalem church continued to regard themselves as Jews (see below).

I said that this exercise is not value-neutral, so it is important to acknowledge my own perspective. I am Christian, which means in this case that I am not inclined to think that first-century Jews who believed some quite extraordinary things about Jesus (e.g., that he was resurrected and so vindicated as Messiah) were either misguided or that their views were in essential conflict with the historic faith of Israel.[2] At the same time, I have profound respect for Judaism and abhor Christian supersessionism, that is, the notion that the church has taken over the place of Israel. Therefore, on neither count do I see "Jewish Christian" as an oxymoron. I would seek neither to de-Judaize nor to de-Christianize the faith of a James or a Peter. This is in contrast to a great many (often Christian) writers of the past two centuries, who seem bent on one or the other agenda. In the first instance, the Jerusalem church is regarded as having been too Christian to be Jewish; in the second, it is thought too Jewish to be Christian. The assumption in either case is that one could have been truly Christian only to the extent that one was not authentically Jewish.

On a popular level, it is the first approach that dominates. Christians such as James and Peter, both leaders of the Jerusalem church, are thought to have thrown off the shackles of their Jewish past. It is not difficult to see in this view an uncritical retrojection of modern Gentile Christianity onto the primitive church. Issues more characteristic of Judaism, such as the restoration of Israel (a concern repeatedly mentioned in the description of the Jerusalem church in Acts 1–3), are therefore ignored. The opposite approach, more common in scholarly circles, is to regard figures such as Peter and, especially, James as *too* Jewish, and therefore sub- or pre-Christian. Christianity instead is the product of the Hellenistic church (ironically, those who did not have the benefit—or, apparently, the distraction—of having known Jesus), especially the apostle Paul.

Hence, "Jewish Christianity" becomes secondary, problematic, and largely dismissible—except, that is, as a foil, the source of whatever one finds distasteful in early Christianity.

Jacob Jervell, among others, rightly protested against such construals of Christian origins (1980, 13–38). Jewish believers in Christ, especially in the church of Jerusalem, were indeed a "mighty minority" who exercised formative and lasting influence on the development of Christian theology. In my judgment, the recovery of the Jewishness of early Christianity on the part of a number of major scholars is the greatest accomplishment of modern New Testament scholarship, albeit one that has yet to win the field. Anti-Jewish bias is still much in evidence, not least in the continued depreciation of the Jerusalem church.[3] The New Testament itself strongly attests to the foundational role of Jerusalem Christianity, but one would scarcely know it when reading many contemporary New Testament studies, which look everywhere but the obvious place in their quest for the fountainhead of Christian theology. Doubtless, this is because the Jerusalem church does not give them what they want—a primordial (and therefore primary) nonchristological "Christianity." Instead of focusing on the group of early believers whom we can name and about whom we have some solid evidence, they postulate otherwise unknown and conveniently anonymous groups of believers ("Galilean Jesus followers," "Q Christians," etc.) (see Allison, 1997) whose views are invariably similar to those of their modern discoverers. At stake, of course, is the identity of Jesus, whom we know only indirectly, that is, through his effects. One's church history is thus the primary effect for which one's historical Jesus is adequate cause. Those who wish to hold onto their good opinion of Jesus but who do not like the shape of Jerusalem Christianity[4] are thus bound to locate for Jesus some other, more desirable historical consequence.

But the evidence for the primacy of the Jerusalem church is exceedingly strong, not least in the New Testament's most important historical source, the Pauline epistles.[5] Paul's letters are not only the earliest New Testament writings, they are the New Testament's only undisputed primary sources. They were written by a leading church figure who knew many other Christian leaders, including the "pillar" Jerusalem apostles (Gal 2:18—3:14). Moreover, Paul's letters contain earlier Christian traditions that Paul himself "received" from "those who were in Christ before me" (Rom 16:7; e.g., in 1 Cor 11:23-26 and 15:3-7). If we want to know about the beliefs and practices, movements and controversies in earliest Christianity, Paul is by a wide margin our most important source.

In his seminal study *Paul and Power*, Bengt Holmberg argued convincingly that while Paul disagreed with the Jerusalem apostles on some points, he was never fully independent of their authority (Holmberg, 1980, 9–56). At the "Jerusalem Conference" (Gal 2:1-10; Acts 15:6-29), Paul and Barnabas submitted for the apostles' approval the Antiochene practice of admitting uncircumcised Gentiles. Wrote Paul, "I laid before them . . . the gospel that I proclaim among the Gentiles, in order to make sure that I was not running, or had not run, in vain" (Gal 2:2). Paul himself recognized the authority of the Jerusalem church to validate—or even to invalidate—his gospel.

The exceptional status of the mother church is confirmed in the subsequent "Antioch incident" (Gal 2:11-14). At stake were the conditions surrounding mixed table fellowship, a matter not settled by the earlier council in Jerusalem. A delegation from the Jerusalem church succeeded in convincing the Antiochenes ("even Barnabas" [Gal 2:13]) that Jewish believers as Jews ought to continue to observe food laws, a perspective with which Paul vehemently disagreed. It appears that Paul lost the argument and soon departed, abandoning Antioch as his missionary base. While Paul could claim an equal calling and status (his slant on the Jerusalem agreement [Gal 2:7-8]), it is clear that he did not possess authority equal to that of either Peter or James. In Galatians, he was in the awkward position of simultaneously asserting independence and admitting subordination. Holmberg finds a similar dynamic at work in the collection for the church of Jerusalem; however Paul might spin the story, he is fulfilling the request of the Jerusalem leaders (Gal 2:10) and admitting its propriety (Rom 15:27) (Holmberg, 1980, 54).

Paul's acknowledgment of the primacy of the Jerusalem church is evident in numerous other passages, for example, 1 Cor 11:16 and 14:34, where "we see the apostle correcting practices in the Corinthian church with regard to the 'practice' (*synētheia*) of the Jewish Christian church" (Holmberg 1980, 50). A similar appeal is found in 1 Thess 2:14, which commends the character of the "churches of God in Christ Jesus which are in Judea." Paul's description of his own ministry in Rom 15:19 ("from Jerusalem and as far around as Illyricum," echoed in Jesus' commission in Acts 1:8, "Jerusalem . . . to the ends of the earth") shows how unselfconsciously he thought of Jerusalem as the source of the gospel. The same idea is present in Paul's description of the collection in Rom 15:25-27:

> At present, however, I am going to Jerusalem in a ministry to the saints; for Macedonia and Achaia have been pleased to share their resources with the poor among the saints at Jerusalem. They were pleased to do this, and indeed they owe it to them; for if the Gentiles have come to share in their spiritual blessings, they ought also to be of service to them in material things.

It is worth underscoring the fact that Paul considered the Jerusalem "saints" (note also the repeated use of the term in 2 Corinthians 8–9) to be fully Christian. Nowhere in Paul's correspondence is there evidence of a disagreement with the Jerusalem church over christology. Contention arose instead over the application of shared beliefs to concrete practice, primarily with respect to the observance of the Jewish law. According to Larry Hurtado,

> We have no hint that the Judaizing advocates who caused problems for Paul in Galatia made any issue of the pattern of devotion to Jesus that they encountered in the Galatian churches. Surely, had they done so, Paul would have responded as vigorously as he does in his Galatian epistle on the questions of circumcision and his own apostolic legitimacy. (Hurtado 2003, 166)

As we have already seen, Paul not only regarded the Jerusalem believers as Christians; he esteemed them as those to whom his Gentile believers were spiritual debtors. The same idea might be present in 2 Cor 8:14, another collection text, which mentions the "abundance" (*perisseuma*) of the Jerusalem church that can supply the want of the Corinthians.

The priority of the Jerusalem apostles is underscored also in Paul's account of the resurrection in 1 Cor 15:3-11, where he places himself last within a closed group of apostles commissioned by Christ. The only other persons named explicitly are Peter (Cephas) and James, both associated with the Jerusalem church, as were "the twelve" in v. 5. The legitimacy of these same Jerusalem leaders is assumed in all of Paul's other references to them (e.g., 1 Cor 3:22 and 9:5).

That the Jerusalem church held a uniquely important and authoritative place in earliest Christianity is also plainly evidenced in Acts. The earliest circle of believers is ordered by the resurrected Jesus to remain in Jerusalem (1:4), where the first Christian proclamation occurs (chaps. 2–7). As in Gal 2:1-10, it is to Jerusalem that a delegation from the church of Antioch goes for a definitive ruling on the question of Gentile admission. Similarly, it is to James and the elders of the Jerusalem church that Paul presents himself in Acts 21. This list could be extended considerably, but the point should be obvious: in Acts, Christianity begins and remains centered in Jerusalem.

The difficulty here is not in understanding Acts but in accepting Acts as a historical source. The attitude of scholars toward the book varies enormously. For some, it is little more than a latter-day Christian fantasy that can tell us nothing reliable about church origins, at least prior to Paul's conversion. But the picture of primitive Christianity in Acts correlates far too well with Paul's epistles (without, it should be added, demonstrating any knowledge of those letters) to be dismissed out of hand.[6] Acts is a complex, multi-layered book, and there is no single, uncomplicated answer to the question of its historicity. Nevertheless, where Acts converges with Paul, as it frequently does, it ought to be taken seriously as a historical source.

JEWISH CHRISTIANS

It would be possible to call the members of the Jerusalem church "Jewish Christians" and mean by it only that these were Christian believers whose ethnic identity (to use a modern category) was Jewish. That would be little different from saying that someone is an Irish athlete or an African American singer. These designations tell us something specific about the person but nothing particular about the form of athletics or the type of singing. Few people speak of Jewish Christianity in this sense. Instead, the qualifier

"Jewish" is substantive: a Jewish Christian is one whose self-understanding, beliefs, and practices are substantially both Jewish and Christian.

Bearing in mind all of the caveats set out at the beginning of this essay, how might we test the "Jewish" half of the Jewish-Christian label when applied to the Jerusalem church? One way forward is to consider a few key features of Judaism that appear not to have been widely incorporated into (or, at least, sustained by) Gentile Christianity. If Jerusalem believers retained common and important elements of Judaism not generally carried over into Gentile Christianity,[7] we might indeed be justified in calling them Jewish Christians. With respect to first-century Palestinian Judaism, I would suggest the following three criteria: belief in the election and hope for the restoration of Israel, obedience to the law of Moses, and reverence for the temple.[8]

Israel

One important datum about the Jerusalem church is the simple fact of its location. Following the crucifixion of Jesus, and despite repeated local persecution (1 Thess 2:14-16; Acts 4:1-22; 5:17-42; 6:11—7:60; 8:1-3; etc.), a group of leading apostles stayed in Jerusalem (Gal 2:2). This must have been a deliberate choice and is suggestive of the attitude toward which all other relevant evidence points, namely, that these persons believed themselves called to lead Israel to eschatological repentance and faith.

That the Jerusalem church saw itself as undertaking a mission to the whole Jewish people is evident in Paul's account of the Jerusalem Council in Gal 2:1-10:

> [W]hen they saw that I had been entrusted with the gospel for the uncircumcised, just as Peter had been entrusted with the gospel for the circumcised (for he who worked through Peter making him an apostle to the circumcised also worked through me in sending me to the Gentiles), and when James and Cephas and John, who were acknowledged pillars, recognized the grace that had been given to me, they gave to Barnabas and me the right hand of fellowship, agreeing that we should go to the Gentiles and they to the circumcised. (vv. 7-9)

The necessity of a mission to "the circumcised" appears to have been assumed by all parties. The only question concerned the legitimacy of a corresponding outreach to Gentiles.

Important corroborating evidence is found in Paul's meditation on the fate of Israel in Romans 9–11 (see especially 9:1-5; 11:25-32). Paul's impassioned rhetoric was prompted by the apparent failure of the church's mission to Israel. Not coincidentally, Romans was composed on the eve of Paul's final trip to Jerusalem. Paul himself believed in the election of Israel ("the gifts and calling of God are irrevocable" [11:29]), and thought that Israel's current rejection of Christian faith could not mean its abandonment by God (11:11-15, 25-32). Ultimately, "all Israel will be saved" (Rom 11:26). It is hard to believe that Paul's perspective was *more* Jewish than that of the Jerusalem church on this point.

The evidence of Acts aligns well with Paul. The program of Acts is laid out in 1:6-8, which includes the disciples' final question, "Will you at this time restore the kingdom to Israel?" From the perspective of Luke-Acts, this is not an illegitimate inquiry. For forty days, the disciples have been instructed by the resurrected Jesus "about the kingdom of God" (Acts 1:3), a theme echoed near the conclusion of Luke's Gospel: "beginning with Moses and all the prophets . . . [he] interpreted to them the things about himself in all the scriptures" (Luke 24:27); Jesus "opened their minds to understand the scriptures" (Luke 24:45). The reader is meant to understand Acts 1:6 as an informed question; in other words, these are not the bumbling Markan disciples. Jesus answers, "It is not for you to know the times or seasons that the Father has set by his own authority." The clear implication is that Israel will indeed someday be restored.[9] The disciples are not chastised for their incomprehension. Instead, Jesus refocuses their attention on their immediate mission: "but you will be my witnesses . . . ."

The only other reference to eschatological *restoration* comes in 3:19-21, in a speech of Peter directed to "You, Israelites" (3:12 NRSV):

> Repent therefore, and turn to God so that your sins may be wiped out,
> so that times of refreshing may come from the presence of the Lord,
> and that he may send the Messiah appointed for you, that is, Jesus,

who must remain in heaven until the time of universal restoration that
God announced long ago through his holy prophets.

The phrase "universal restoration" (or "restoration of all things") is tak-
en over by Luke from Mark 9:12 and is a paraphrase of the famous Jewish
restoration text Mal 4:5-6 (also in Luke 1:17).[10]

According to Acts, the preaching of the Jerusalem church is intentionally directed toward the whole people of Israel. For example,

> Therefore let the entire house of Israel know with certainty that God has
> made him both Lord and Messiah, this Jesus whom you crucified. (2:36)

> [L]et it be known to all of you [in Jerusalem], and to all the people of
> Israel, that this man is standing before you in good health by the name
> of Jesus Christ of Nazareth, whom you crucified, whom God raised
> from the dead. (4:10)

> God exalted him at his right hand as leader and savior that he might
> give repentance to Israel and forgiveness of sins. (5:31)

> "Did you offer to me slain victims and sacrifices forty years in the
> wilderness, O house of Israel?" (7:42)

> You know the message he sent to the people of Israel, preaching peace
> by Jesus Christ—he is Lord of all. (10:36)

It is interesting that the language as well as the themes of the early
speeches in Acts reflects this perspective. For example, in the New Testament only Acts 3:22 (Peter's speech) and 7:37 (Stephen's speech) make use
of Deut 18:15, the promise of a prophet like Moses. The same is true of a
small collection of distinctively Jewish titles for Jesus, including "the Righteous One" (*ho dikaios*), for example, in 3:14; 7:52; and 22:14. Another example is the use of *pais*, meaning "child" or "servant," as in Acts 3:13: "The
God of Abraham, the God of Isaac, and the God of Jacob, the God of our
ancestors has glorified his servant [*pais*] Jesus, whom you handed over and

rejected in the presence of Pilate, though he had decided to release him." According to Hurtado,

> [T]he only cases in the New Testament where people directly refer to Jesus as God's *pais* (i.e., not in biblical quotations) are in Acts. . . . I contend that it becomes clear that these applications of *pais* to Jesus carry a specifically Israel-oriented and royal-messianic connotation. The Lukan nativity account has two other relevant occurrences, both in passages that celebrate eschatological blessings in Israel, which in the narrative are connected to the birth of Jesus. (Hurtado 2003, 191)

The Law

That members of the Jerusalem church strove to keep the Jewish law is a relatively uncontroversial point. This is clear enough in Acts, where the Jerusalem Christians are shown to follow a high standard of legal observance (e.g., Acts 21:20). As Stephen G. Wilson concluded in his helpful book *Luke and the Law*, Luke "viewed living according to the law as a natural and appropriate way of life for Jews and Jewish-Christians." "[T]here is no conflict in living according to the law, indeed doing so zealously, and being a Christian" (S. G. Wilson 1983, 114–15, 102). This is in accord with the evidence from Paul's epistles, especially Paul's account of the Antioch incident in Gal 2:11-14. Interestingly, it is a perspective close to that of Matthew's Gospel (e.g., Matt 5:17-20), which itself might have been composed in Antioch a few decades later (Brown 1997, 212).

Points of contention concern the Jerusalem church's attitude toward Gentiles and the possibility that one group, the "Hellenists" (Acts 6:1), might have taken a more radical stance toward both the law and the temple. I have written extensively about both of these matters elsewhere, and so will offer only the briefest summary here.[11]

In both accounts of the Jerusalem Conference (Gal 2:1-10 and Acts 15:6-29), the Jerusalem church, led by James, accepted the Antiochene practice of admitting uncircumcised Gentiles. It is highly unlikely that they regarded this decision as a violation of the law of Moses. The incoming of Gentiles was an eschatological hope anticipated, in particular, in the latter chapters of Isaiah. Unfortunately, these and similar passages did not specify the conditions for their acceptance. Whether it came as an immediate or a later result of the Jerusalem Conference, the Jerusalem Decree of Acts 15:28-29 probably reflects the eventual policy of the Jerusalem church (Hill 1992, 113). It is instructive that Gentile believers are essentially held to the comparatively lenient standards reserved for "resident aliens," rules that focused on sexual morality and the avoidance of idolatry and the eating of blood (e.g., see Lev 17:8-14 and 18:24-30). Doubtless, this is the point of James's statement in Acts 15:21, "For in every city, for generations past, Moses has had those who proclaim him, for he has been read aloud every sabbath in the synagogues." In other words, their expectations concerning Gentiles were wholly within the law.[12]

The notion that the "Hellenists," a subgroup within the earliest Jerusalem church, criticized both the law and the temple is a highly persistent but poorly founded hypothesis. It is based in large part on a misreading of Stephen's speech in Acts 7:2-53. Critics argue that Stephen's "false" accusers (6:13) were in fact telling the truth: Stephen had indeed spoken blasphemous words against the law and the temple. Confirmation is then found in the speech itself, which they regard as both anti-Moses and anti-temple. But the speech is neither; on the contrary, it offers, in the first instance, an extraordinarily high estimate of both Moses and the law. The fault instead lies with the Jewish people, who "received the law as ordained by angels, and yet have not kept it" (7:53). Likewise, error is not found with the temple itself but with the Jews, whose obduracy would result, as it did before, in the temple's destruction.[13] The specific charge is that Stephen preached that "Jesus of Nazareth will destroy this place [the temple]" (6:14). Assuming a post-70 dating of Acts, the inaccuracy and irony of this accusation would be obvious to readers: Jesus himself did not destroy the temple. Instead, its destruction was the fault of the Jews themselves. That is why Amos 5:25-27, quoted in Acts 7:42-43, is changed to "I will remove you beyond Babylon." (The original text of Amos reads "Damascus.") The mention of Babylon here links Jewish rejection of Moses with the destruction of the first temple, which explains how, from Luke's perspective, the rejection of Jesus, the second Moses (Acts 7:37), leads to the tragedy of 70 CE. In other words, Luke wishes to show that it is the Jews themselves who are guilty of blasphemy against Moses and the temple.[14]

Criticism of the law arose precisely as we would have expected, that is, as an eventual consequence of the Gentile mission. It is instructive that the Jerusalem Conference, which took up this matter, did not occur until about the year 50 CE. In any event, few if any scholars believe that an anti-law faction long endured within the Jerusalem church. The evidence instead is that the Jerusalem Christians continued to observe the law of Moses. It is worth adding that this fact does not mean that they were hidebound religious conservatives; instead, it means that they were Jewish.

The Temple

Our only evidence concerning the attitude of the Jerusalem Christians toward the temple is found in Acts, where reverence toward the temple appears as a consistent feature of the church's piety. The temple served as an appropriate place to gather (2:46; 3:21), to pray (3:1) and to preach and teach (5:20, 42)—even, according to the author of Acts, for Paul himself (21:26; 22:17; 25:8).

This is true despite the fact that the Jerusalem church's opposition was centered in the temple leadership (e.g., Acts 4:1; 5:22-26; 7:1; 9:1), as had been the opposition to Jesus. Corroborating evidence comes from the Jewish historian Josephus, who in *Antiquities* 20.200 recounts the death of James, the leader of the Jerusalem church, at the instigation of the high priest Ananus the Younger. Interestingly, Ananus was the brother-in-law of Caiaphas, who was high priest at the time of Jesus' and then Stephen's death.

The association of the Jerusalem Christians with the temple thus parallels their deliberate choice to remain in Jerusalem, and it suggests strongly that they saw themselves as being in mission to Israel.

In sum, on the basis of their view of Israel, the law, and the temple, three core Jewish symbols, it appears likely that the Jerusalem Christians remained, in their own eyes at least, faithful Jews. In that sense, they might properly be called *Jewish*. But were they "Christian"?

JEWISH CHRISTIANS

For the sake of testing the Jewishness of the Jerusalem church, we looked briefly at three substantial elements of Judaism not generally carried over into Gentile Christianity. A similar test might be applied to the Christian half of the Jewish-Christian label. What most clearly differentiated early Christian faith and practice from (non-Christian) Judaism?

In his masterful study of christology, *Lord Jesus Christ: Devotion to Jesus in Earliest Christianity*, already quoted above, Larry Hurtado argues persuasively that "cultic veneration of Jesus" was the distinguishing feature of earliest Christianity.[15] He lays out a wide range of beliefs and practices, such as "calling upon the name" of Jesus, expectation of "the day of the Lord [Jesus]," prophecy in the name of Jesus, prayer directed to Jesus, and baptism in Jesus' name, which comprise an astonishingly early "devotional pattern of early Christian groups [that] has no real analogy in the Jewish tradition of the period" (Hurtado 2003, 31).

Hurtado's primary foil is Wilhelm Bousset's influential *Kyrios Christos*, which distinguished between "a supposedly original ethicizing piety of Jesus (and the primitive 'Palestinian' community of Jesus followers) and the 'Christ cult' of the 'Hellenistic' Christian community," a distinction that "permitted him [Bousset] to posit an ideal, original Christian piety with which he could more comfortably associate himself as a liberal Protestant of his time" (Hurtado 2003, 10; 11–12). As we have already noted, this remains a commonplace strategy among both specialist and popular authors on Christian origins. Hurtado cites several contemporary examples, including Burton Mack, who considers "the Christ-cult as a regrettable shift from what he calls the 'Jesus people' of Jewish Palestine, for whom . . . Jesus was by no means Messiah, Lord, or recipient of devotion, but simply a Cynic-like sage, an inspiring exponent of clever sayings and a carefree lifestyle" (2003, 16).[16]

One must strain at evidential gnats while swallowing camels to maintain such a characterization of Jesus' earliest Jewish followers.[17] As Hurtado abundantly documents, "the most influential and momentous developments in devotion to Jesus took place in early circles of Judean believers. To their convictions and the fundamental pattern of their piety all subsequent forms of Christianity are debtors" (2003, 216).

The most important evidence is again found in the Pauline epistles, which contain numerous references and allusions to the beliefs of Paul's Jewish Christian predecessors and contemporaries, especially in Jerusalem. Among these are the accounts of the Lord's Supper and the resurrection in 1 Cor 11:23-36 and 15:1-11 respectively, traditions that Paul said he had "received." Both accounts have Jewish (e.g., "new covenant" in 11:25 and "according to the scriptures" in 15:3) as well as Christian (e.g., "Lord Jesus" in 11:23 and "Christ died for our sins" in 15:3) elements, and both are frequently associated by scholars with the Jerusalem church. That linkage is especially likely in the case of 1 Corinthians 15, which, as we have already seen, focuses on the appearances of the resurrected Jesus to the leaders of the Jerusalem church. The authority and apparent ubiquity of the Lord's Supper tradition are also best accounted for if it originated in Jerusalem.

Numerous other passages appear to contain pre-Pauline formulae (e.g., Rom 1:3-4, 1 Thess 1:10, Phil 2:6-11), all of which are decidedly Jewish-Christian in character. Similarly, many of the titles used by Paul for Jesus (e.g., "Christ," "Son of God," "Lord") were already traditional and therefore routinized and uncontroversial, and each of these evidences a Semitic background. An especially important example is Paul's use of the Aramaic *marana tha* ("Our Lord, come!") in 1 Cor 16:22. (Compare the use of *Abba* in Gal 4:6 and Rom 8:15.) Calling upon the name of Jesus is an extraordinary but nevertheless common feature of early Christian piety (see, e.g., 1 Cor 1:2, where Christians are universally described as "all those who call upon the name of our Lord Jesus Christ"). The likeliest origin for *marana tha* is, of course, Judean Christianity, both because of the use of Aramaic and because the term was so well established as to require no translation for a Greek-speaking audience.

Lars Hartman argues convincingly in his *"Into the Name of the Lord Jesus": Baptism in the Early Church* that Christian baptism also arose within early Judean, and specifically Jerusalem, Christianity as an adaptation of the practice of John the Baptist, who alone had previously associated it "with conversion and repentance in a critical, eschatological perspective" (Hartman 1997, 31). Christian practice of baptism was early and widespread, facts that again point to its origin in the mother church:

There are good reasons to believe that from the beginning entrance
into the early church normally meant that the neophyte was baptised.
This is self-evident to Luke in Acts, and other independent traditions
point in the same direction: the Johannine (John 3.5), the Matthean
(28.19), and, before these, Paul and those Christians before him and
contemporary with him, of whom he bears indirect witness in his letters (e.g. Rom 6.3). When asking how early the first Christians baptised, it is useful to remember that Paul takes it as a matter of course
that he himself was baptised (1 Cor 12.13). (Hartman 1997, 29)

Numerous other arguments for the Christian character of the Jerusalem
church can be advanced on the basis of the Pauline epistles, but three in
particular stand out. The first was discussed earlier in this essay, namely,
Paul's own regard for the Jerusalem Christians *as* Christians. The legitimacy (indeed, the primacy) of their faith is frequently stated and everywhere assumed by Paul (see, e.g., Gal 1:23, where Paul reports the response
of the churches in Judea: "The one who formerly was persecuting us is
now proclaiming the faith he once tried to destroy"). The second argument
concerns the persecution of the church in Jerusalem by Jewish authorities.
As we have already seen, this opposition is evidenced in a range of sources,
including Paul, Acts, and Josephus. Although the specific reason(s) for persecution cannot be known, the existence of such conflict supports the conclusion that members of the Jerusalem church held views that were both
distinctive and objectionable. Finally, there is the argument from silence.
Had Paul known—as he certainly would have, had it been the case—that
the Jerusalem church did not share in the practice of "Christ-devotion," it
is beyond comprehension that he would have failed entirely to mention
it. "In all of Paul's letters cultic devotion to Christ is presupposed," and
Paul shows no knowledge of any controversy on this point either within or
among the Christian groups with which he was associated, including the
church of Jerusalem (Hurtado 2003, 136).

It should go without saying that the evidence of Acts dovetails on these
points with that of the Pauline epistles. The church begins and is then head-
quartered in Jerusalem. Titles known from Pauline and other sources, such as
"Christ" and "Lord," are applied to Jesus. Other, more distinctive titles with a

Jewish-eschatological cast, such as "leader," "prophet like Moses," and "servant/ child," are also employed (Hurtado 2003, 178). Additionally,

> Judean circles are described as baptizing adherents "in the name of Je- sus" (e.g., 2:38) and believers are referred to as "all those who invoke your [Jesus'] name" (9:14). Both expressions refer to invoking Jesus' name in cultic actions. Moreover, ritual use of Jesus' name is an important feature of other religious practices attributed to Judean Christians, such as heal- ing and exorcism (e.g., 3:6; 4:29-30). (Hurtado 2003, 175)

Obviously, the author of Acts, like Paul, believed that the Jerusalem Christians practiced "cultic veneration of Jesus" and so, on that basis, might fairly be called Jewish *Christians*.

CONCLUSION

By and large, modern authors have been content to refer to members of the Jerusalem church as Jewish Christians. As we have seen, however, that designation can mean entirely different things to different people. In this essay, I have suggested a small experiment, a way of testing both halves of the Jewish-Christian label, by isolating and then applying what is distinc- tive and common (though not necessarily universal, which would in any case be impossible to prove) to Judaism and to Christianity as separate religions. The result with respect to the Jerusalem church is affirmative: Je- rusalem Christians were substantially *both* Jewish and Christian. They did not see themselves as having departed from Judaism; nevertheless, their faith and practice were shaped decisively by a remarkably high estimate of Jesus, whose veneration is unparalleled elsewhere in Judaism. Some non- Christian Jewish contemporaries, such as the pre-Christian Paul, probably already regarded this as an untenable stance—in effect, a self-contradic- tion. From this perspective, there is no point talking about Jewish Chris- tianity; the category simply cannot exist. But there is a lot to be said for defining a religion from the vantage point of its adherents, and it is beyond reasonable doubt that the Jerusalem Christians continued to regard themselves as Jews.

The attempt to define a religion is fraught with difficulty. I have attempted in this essay to avoid some of those problems by staying close to at least one central meaning of the phrase "Jewish Christian" and not attempting to account for every nuance and exception. I offered three criteria concerning the Jewishness of the Jerusalem church, namely, its attitude toward Israel, toward the law, and toward the temple. But what about a Christian, such as Paul, who was born a Jew but who might pass only one or two of these tests? (I judge that one capable of living "outside the law" [*anomos;* 1 Cor 9:21] no longer shares a typical Jewish perspective on legal observance.) Is Paul rightly regarded as a Jewish Christian? As this example illustrates, comprehensive answers to questions of religious identity remain elusive.

SUGGESTED READINGS

Hartman, Lars. 1997. *"Into the Name of the Lord Jesus": Baptism in the Early Church.* Studies of the New Testament and Its World. Edinburgh: T & T Clark.

Hill, Craig. 1992. *Hellenists and Hebrews: Reappraising Division within the Earliest Church.* Philadelphia: Fortress Press.

———.2002. "Restoring the Kingdom to Israel: Luke-Acts and Christian Supersessionism." Pages 185–200 in *Shadow of Glory: Reading the New Testament after the Holocaust.* Edited by Tod Linafelt. New York and London: Routledge.

Holmberg, Bengt. 1980. *Paul and Power: The Structure of Authority in the Primitive Church as Reflected in the Pauline Epistles.* Philadelphia: Fortress Press.

Hurtado, Larry W. 2003. *Lord Jesus Christ: Devotion to Jesus in Earliest Christianity.* Grand Rapids and Cambridge: Eerdmans.

Jervell, Jacob. 1980. "The Mighty Minority." *Studia Theologica* 34:13–38.

3. PAUL AND CHRIST-BELIEVING JEWS WHOM HE OPPOSES

Jerry L. Sumney

Almost immediately after Paul's letters were written, some understood them to be texts that opposed Judaism or at least any sort of Christian practice that included Torah observance.[1] Even in Paul's lifetime (it seems) and the immediately succeeding generation, some thought Paul opposed Torah observance for all believers in Christ (see Acts 21:21). Such an understanding of Paul and what he wrote against has been dominant throughout the history of the interpretation of his letters. This view has dominated modern critical scholarship just as it did early readings of Paul. F. C. Baur's *Paul the Apostle* advocated this view with such power in 1845 that it continues to retain adherents. But even for those who recognize that his reconstruction of the early church is too simple to account for the literary and historical data from early Christians, Baur's scheme has set the agenda and the terms of the discussion about the shape of the early communities of Christ-believers.

Baur argued that there were only two types of early Christians: Jewish Christians, with Peter as their leader, and Gentile Christians, with Paul as their leader. For Baur, all those whom Paul opposes in his letters are Jewish Christians. These Jewish Christians remain Torah observant and require this observance of all who would be part of the Christian community. These Jewish Christians are legalists who also fail to see the universalistic elements of the gospel Paul proclaims.[2]

While this understanding of Paul's letters and the early church has wielded extraordinary power, its problematic nature is apparent even in those Baur designates as the leaders of the opposing movements. Naming Paul, the Jew who was a Pharisee, the leader of Gentile Christianity signals this scheme's incongruity with history. Even Baur acknowledges that some Pauline letters provide no evidence that the issue is Torah observance. Still he insists that those who require Torah observance of all Christians must be the target of Paul's polemic because that is who Paul opposes everywhere and always. Despite these and other problems, interpreters continue to use this model to understand Paul and others who believe in Christ in the first century.[3]

The texts of the Pauline letters demand a more nuanced understanding of the situations they address and the diversity of the early church. Over twenty years ago Raymond E. Brown proposed a more complex model for thinking about the diversity found within "Jewish Christianity" and "Gentile Christianity" (Brown 1983). He argued that there were at least two different theologies within each of these branches.

Such recognitions of diversity have become more common in the years that followed that essay, and yet there are problems even with the terms used in these designations. Perhaps the first issue is the word "Christianity." For many readers that term denotes a movement with set institutional structures such as those that developed in later decades and centuries (see Gaston 1984, 61–62). But in the mid-first century, no single type of organizational or governing structures functioned in all churches. So in order to refrain from imposing anachronistic models of the church, this essay will avoid that term when speaking of those with whom Paul interacted.

Even the term "Christian" can be problematic because the evidence we have from the mid-first century indicates only that people outside the movement spoke of those in the church as "Christians," not that church members claimed this name for themselves. Yet when Acts 11:26 says that the believers were first called Christians in Antioch, it seems clear that they accept the language—whether they first coined it, reluctantly accepted it, or enthusiastically embraced it. Acts also puts the name in the mouth of Agrippa. Here Acts' Paul accepts it as a designation without repeating the word (26:28-29). But this is not a term Paul uses in his letters to speak of those in his churches or those he opposes.[4] However, by the time 1 Peter is written (around the end of the first century), that writer uses "Christian" to describe the letter's readers (4:16).[5] Given the acceptance of the term by the late first or early second century, this term is a satisfactory designation for those in the early church if we use it without suggesting that a fully formed institutional entity is in view. But because the term is absent from the Pauline corpus, this essay will most often use "Christ-believer" as the designation for those who are members of the early church in its various manifestations.

Not only are the foregoing terms for Christ-believers problematic, but even the designation "Gentile" presents problems. That translation of *ethnē* glosses over the sort of designation this term is. *Ethnē* is the Jewish category for all non-Jews, just as "barbarian" is the Greek term for all non-Greeks.[6] It simply throws together all people who are not Jewish, as though they derived their identity from being non-Jewish. Of course, that is not the case. Non-Jews throughout the Roman world would have distinguished themselves in many ways from other ethnic, racial, and regional groups. Thus, adopting the language of opposing Jews and Gentiles means that all identities are subsumed under the category of non-Jew and Jew. From within identity as Jews, this creates an important boundary, even as it inappropriately reduces the diversities among these others. Starting with these categories from outside Jewish identity can lead to a similar glossing over of differences and categorizing that often results in skewing our understandings of the settings of early Christ-believers. It also sets Jews apart from all others in a way that exaggerates their differences in comparison with other ethno-religious groups and so may contribute to anti-Semitism. So we must be careful to limit the use and meaning of "Gentile" as well.

The diverse settings of the Pauline churches and the multiple forms of Judaism practiced in the first century make it unlikely that any reconstruction of the early church that finds only two types of early Christ-believers—those who agree with Paul about the way Gentile believers should relate to the Torah and a united front of those who do not—is adequate to account for the evidence of his letters. Since this inadequacy is only increased when interpreters a priori identify those who oppose Paul as "Jewish Christianity," we need to look again at the evidence. When we begin without the presupposition that all those Paul opposes belong to a single group, his letters manifest diverse sets of problems that his churches faced. Moreover, not all those with whom Paul disagreed opposed Paul, and they certainly did not all define themselves as people who opposed Paul or his teaching (see Sumney 1999, 303–19).

Among the undisputed Pauline letters, there are at least two in which his primary purpose in writing is to oppose other teachers (2 Corinthians and Galatians) and two in which teachings he opposes come into clear focus (Philippians and Romans). We will concentrate on 2 Corinthians and Galatians because they give us more data and because they give evidence for two different sorts of groups of Christ-believing Jews whom Paul opposes. As we will see, it may be more appropriate to refer to the opponents of 2 Corinthians as Christ-believers who are also Jews, while it is better to refer to those Paul opposes in Galatians as Jews who are also Christ-believers; that is, the primary identity of the former group is their faith in Christ, while the latter group retains Jewishness as its primary identity. Neither group stops being Jewish, but how they position that aspect in their self-understanding seems to be different.

2 CORINTHIANS

While some interpreters argue that it is a single letter (e.g., Matera 2003, 29–32), most commentators see the canonical 2 Corinthians as a composite of multiple letters. Among the various hypotheses about the number of letters in 2 Corinthians, I will work with the view that chapters 1–7 are a single letter (which may have included ch. 8 as well), rather than dividing out 2:14—7:1 as another separate letter. I will also assume that chapters 10–13 are a single letter that was written a few months after 1–7.[7]

The basic issue that leads Paul to vehemently oppose the teachers who are wooing the church at Corinth is that of the way the Spirit manifests itself in the lives of apostles.[8] The other teachers argue that the Spirit enables them to live powerful and successful lives; lives that impress those around them and so draw others to the God who provides such power, strength, and dominance. They claim that the Spirit lifts them above the troubles of the world that others experience and makes them impressive speakers who perform miracles and claim places of commanding leadership over the Christian community. As superiors in relation to other Christ-believers, these teachers, who claim the title "apostle," assume authority over the church and demand rights and privileges among the other Christ-believers, including a salary and public deference. They also clearly claim that the Spirit makes them authoritative teachers whom the Corinthians should acknowledge.

To advocate such a theology of ministry, leadership, and authority, these teachers must oppose Paul's form of ministry and his manner of life within his churches. They argue that his experiences of hardships and difficulties, along with his refusal to accept financial support from the Corinthians, were evidence that he did not possess the measure of the Spirit they possessed and thus he could not legitimately claim the office of "apostle." These teachers seek to depose Paul as apostle of the church in Corinth and take that position for themselves—significantly redefining what it means to be an apostle both for the apostle and for the church.

Paul rejects these teachers in no uncertain terms. Sometimes he chides the Corinthians for listening to them (e.g., 11:19); sometimes he makes fun of the claims those teachers make (e.g., 10:12-13; 11:21-29; 12:11); and sometimes he makes fairly direct comparisons between himself and the other teachers (e.g., 3:1; 12:12). Paul argues that they have misunderstood what it means to be an apostle and what the Spirit provides in an apostle's life. He argues that their understanding of ministry and apostleship violates the gospel of the crucified and risen Christ.

We may enhance our understanding of what it meant to be both Jewish and a believer in Christ by taking note of one particular aspect of this controversy over leadership in the Corinth: the claims these other teachers make about their ethno-religious heritage. The church at Corinth was composed mostly of non-Jews, but it included some members who were ethnically Jewish. Paul's greeting to "all the saints in the whole of Achaia" indicates that he is addressing all Christ-believers, both Jews and Gentiles. The presence of Prisca and Aquila (1 Cor 16:19; Rom 16:3; cf. Acts 18:1-3) demonstrates that Paul includes Jews among the Christ-believers he addresses in the Corinthian setting, even as the church is composed predominantly of Gentiles. This seems to mirror the makeup of most of Paul's congregations.[9]

There is no good evidence that the controversy over leadership in Corinth involved questions about whether Gentiles should adhere to more of the Torah than they were already doing or to adhere to it differently. Paul does compose an extended comparison between the ministry of

Moses and his own ministry, which included the claim that Paul's ministry was superior to Moses' because the covenant Paul serves provides more direct access to the presence of God (3:1-18). But this discussion gives no hint that what Paul proposes is controversial. In fact, it serves as a proof of his contention that God has equipped him for apostleship and supports him in that work (see Furnish 1984, 226, 243; Sumney 1990, 96–99; Hurtado 1999, 52). Beyond this passage, nothing in the letter of chapters 1–7 indicates that the controversy involves the relationship of Christ-believers to non–Christ-believing Jews, Judaism, or the Torah.

The dispute between Paul and the Corinthians that was evident in the earlier letter of 2 Corinthians 1–7 has escalated by the time he writes the letter of chapters 10–13. In 10–13 Paul's comments are sharper, with more rebuke of the Corinthians and more irony in his treatment of the other teachers. It is only in this more polemical letter that we learn something about the ethno-religious identity of the other teachers. In a section of this letter commonly called the "Fool's Speech" (11:1—12:13), Paul matches the claims of his rivals—though this is often done by claiming what they would reject and so reframing the criteria for claiming to be an apostle.

In 11:21b-23 Paul recites a list of qualifications that his rivals claim. Paul says that since they "boast" in these things, he will also boast in them, even though it is acting like a fool to do so. According to these verses, the other teachers claim to be "Hebrews," "Israelites," "descendants of Abraham," and "servants of Christ." Paul asserts that whatever claim his rivals have to these identities, he can match or better that claim. Part of the evidence for his claim to be authentically Jewish is that he has submitted to the authority of the synagogue to give him thirty-nine lashes. Some interpreters argue that each element of this list of self-designations points to a particular aspect of Jewish identity. Some go so far as to assert that the designations cumulatively point to the Jerusalem apostles (e.g., Barrett 1973, 292). But there is no indication that Paul has turned his attention away from the teachers who are actually present in Corinth in order to make a comment about the Jerusalem apostles. Other interpreters see these titles in a very different light, arguing that they point to Hellenistic Jews (e.g., Friedrich 1963, 181–86; Georgi 1986, 49–60, 73-82 [cf. 1964, 63–81]). It is probably best to see the three designations of Jewish identity as somewhat synonymous.

Even if there were nuances of differences among these titles, the basic point is that they emphasize their Jewish identity (Plummer 1915, 319–20; Bultmann 1985, 214; Furnish 1984, 534).

The interesting feature for the present inquiry is that Paul, his rivals, and the Corinthian church all see being Jewish as a persuasive element of a claim to authority within the church. Were his rivals not using Jewish identity as a way to assert authority, Paul would not need to match their claims to it. Paul gives no hints about why being Jewish is accorded this status. We may speculate that the Jews among the Christ-believers know Scripture better than others, have more experience of worshiping God and of avoiding worship of other gods, and understand more about the connection between the God of Israel and moral behavior. Beyond this, Paul himself, the founder of their community, was Jewish, to say nothing of the ethno-religious identity of Jesus and the Twelve. Furthermore, Paul clearly claims in Romans that there are advantages to being Jewish and that Gentiles are indebted to Jews because it is through them that the gospel is proclaimed among the Gentiles (e.g., 1:16; 3:1-2; 9:4-5). In their own setting, the local leaders in the Corinthian churches may have been predominantly Jewish, and some of the members of these churches would still be associated with a synagogue. That connection might well increase the authority of anyone who claimed Jewish heritage. Paul says nothing that would let us know which of these, if any, are the reasons the Corinthians would accede to those who claim identity as Jews.

Yet it seems that Jewish identity was an important part of what made these rival teachers genuine competitors for the loyalties of the Corinthian churches. As we have noted, there is no good indication that these teachers differ from Paul in how they want the Corinthian Gentile Christ-believers to relate to the Torah or the non–Christ-believing Jewish community. The only issues Paul takes up with these rivals are the modes of leadership that are compatible with the gospel and how the Spirit operates in the lives of apostles. Since Paul does not raise other issues, he appears to view these issues related to leadership as the most important in his struggle to recall the Corinthians to the understanding of Christian life he had taught them. In view of the importance he assigns to the proper relationship of Gentile Christ-believers to the Torah, we can be relatively sure that the absence of any explicit comments on this topic means that it was not an issue in the

Corinthian controversy. The absence of this issue makes the power of the claim to authority on the basis of Jewish identity puzzling. It is the assumption that Gentile Christ-believers perceive that Jews have more and deeper experience of God because of their background of lived experience with God (perhaps both personal and ancestral) that best explains the deference the Corinthians seem to accord to Christ-believing Jews.

Even if this hypothesis is incorrect, it remains certain that Jews retained important aspects of their ethno-religious identity as Jews, and non-Jews of various sorts retained important aspects of their former identity after joining the Pauline community. Both groups retain these identities even in a community in which Paul claims the ancestors of Israel for his non-Jewish converts (see 1 Cor 10:1-5, in which Paul speaks of "our ancestors" when referring to the story of the exodus). On the other hand, he can also tell this church that circumcision and uncircumcision are both "nothing" (1 Cor 7:17-20).

Paul can make these assertions about the community of Christ-believers because he subsumes both Jews and Gentiles under the category of Christ-believer. Believing in Christ has become the primary identity marker for the church; Christ-believing is the identity that has soteriological significance. Still, former identities are not eradicated or so diminished that they are without importance. They remain part of who the person is, though now those differences are reevaluated in light of being "in Christ." Thus, being Jewish does inform the way one lives and how that person is understood by fellow Christ-believers.

When these rivals of Paul claim Jewish identity as a mark of authority, the Corinthians accept that claim, and Paul does not dispute it. In this setting, Jewish Christ-believers from outside Corinth are able to influence this predominantly non-Jewish church in part because they are Jewish. There is no argument about borders between Jews and non-Jews who believe in Christ, only the recognition that being Jewish has some persuasive value among Gentile Christ-believers. No neat division between "Jewish Christianity" and "Gentile Christianity" can account for this situation at Corinth. It is the more primary identity as those "of Christ" that binds the Christ-believers together. It is because that identity is recognized as central that the debate about internal authority structures may proceed as it does in 2 Corinthians. However, the centrality of that identity is the focus of the debate when we turn to Galatians.

GALATIANS

There is fairly broad agreement among interpreters that the teachers Paul opposes in Galatians advocate circumcision. After this basic agreement, interpreters disagree about the motivation for the demand (e.g., for salvation or perfection or acceptance by non–Christ-believing Jews) and how much more Torah observance the teachers advocate. Interpreters also disagree about whether the opposed teachers know they are teaching something different from what Paul teaches and whether they reject Paul's apostleship.

In addition to clearly urging the Galatian non-Jewish Christ-believers to accept circumcision, the teachers also seem to encourage them to observe some holy days from Judaism (4:8-10). Such demands do not necessarily signal that these teachers want to turn the Galatians away from Paul. In fact, 5:11 indicates that they contend that Paul also teaches that non-Jewish Christ-believers need to be circumcised. Given this, it is unlikely that these teachers oppose or reject Paul's apostolic position or authority. However, these teachers urge observance of the Torah for Gentile Christ-believers in a way that is different from Paul. They and Paul may understand differently the relationship between the Torah and Gentile Christ-believers.

Unfortunately, Paul does not tell us what those teachers claim that the Galatian Gentiles would gain from observing the Torah in the way they advocate. Perhaps they see it only as an accommodation to the non-Christ-believing Jews that allows the church more integration with the synagogue, or to Christ-believing Jews who are experiencing difficulty in the synagogue because of their closer association with nonobservant non-Jews who have begun to make surprising claims about their place within the people of God.[10] Such associations of Christ-believing Jews with Christ-believing Gentiles who are not becoming proselytes could cause non-Christ-believing synagogue members problems because the Romans had granted Jews exemptions from participation in the civic cults and other activities that would violate their faith. If non-Jewish others began to exercise such prerogatives in the name of the exemptions allowed the synagogue, this behavior could endanger those privileges, particularly if some in the broad society began to object to the nonparticipation of Gentile Christ-believers (Tellbe 2001, 24–69; Nanos 2002b, 316). So these teachers may encourage this sort of Torah observance for the non-Jewish Christ-believers for reasons that are more practical than theological.

Whatever the other teachers think their teachings do or do not imply, Paul sees important theological issues at stake. He thinks that accepting their demands means that the Galatian non-Jewish Christ-believers forfeit their standing with God that is attained through Christ. His arguments against these teachers reveal some important things about his understanding of Christian identity and its relationship to other elements of his congregants' self-definitions. Though the Galatian teachers did not recognize it, the differences in practice that they advocate reveal a difference between themselves and Paul on the crucial matter of the most basic identity of Christ-believers.

Paul thinks that a central issue in the balance is the most fundamental definition of the Christ-believing community. The shape of Paul's argument suggests that he is the one who supplies this frame for the question. Both his narratives and his more direct arguments contribute to this impression. Though there is no consensus concerning the interpretation of the Antioch incident (2:11-14, 15-21) or the Jerusalem Conference (2:1-10) as Paul recounts them, we may discern some important things about Paul's view of Christian identity from them.

We must not assume that the issues at the Jerusalem Conference were precisely those Galatians opposes. Rather, Paul recounts that episode because he sees it, in some important way, as analogous, not necessarily exactly the same as, the problem he addresses in the letter. As Paul presents the outcome of this meeting, the leaders of the Jerusalem church recognize both his mission to the Gentiles with a gospel that does not include circumcision and Peter's mission to Jews with a gospel that includes circumcision (and presumably full Torah observance). Notably, Paul uses the term "gospel" (*euangelion*) only once, in 2:7, while the reader must supply the second "gospel." Perhaps Paul was a bit reluctant to declare that there are two gospels. But even this passing acknowledgment of a mission so different that it can be spoken of in this way is surprising in light of the vehemence of 1:6-9, where Paul declares that if anyone preaches a gospel to the Galatian churches that is different from the one Paul had already preached, that person is accursed. So within a small space Paul both acknowledges a second gospel and says that any gospel other than the one he proclaimed to the Galatians brings a curse. The best explanation for how Paul could make both affirmations is that the gospel he preached is the only one appropriate for the Galatian Gentile Christ-believers, but not the only gospel that brings people into contact with the saving work of Christ. Peter's proclamation has the same core and brings its hearers to an existence "in Christ," but it is appropriate only for Jews. The important point for our study is that there is something more foundational than the difference between these two gospels; there is something that allows the mutual recognition and support of these two different missions. That fundamental is a shared understanding of the work of Christ as that which makes one right with God. This shared understanding entails the creation of a community that grounds its most foundational identity in the act of God in Christ (see Dunn 1991, 76–77). This identity takes into itself those who are Jews and those who are Gentiles. As Paul will argue, it must not mean that Gentiles simply join the Jewish community.

Christ-believing had been central for group identity in Jerusalem before this conference (Horrell 2002, 316; Hurtado 1999, 51–53; Holmberg 1998, 416–19). But they had not recognized the significance of this core identity because there was less tension between their identity as Christ-believers and their identity as Jews when all (or nearly all) Christ-believers were Jewish. In this situation, all Christ-believers are already both "in Christ" and in the Mosaic covenant. Belief in Christ might even have clarified some things in the Mosaic covenant, so the relationship between the two was very compatible. But once the number of Gentile Christ-believers begins to grow, questions arise about the relationship between these two religious convictions and the communities in which each is central. Such questions demand attention because these Gentiles are not proselytes and are not moving toward proselyte conversion. The Antioch church, especially after the mission of Barnabas and Paul to Gentiles, brings this matter to a head because it includes so many Gentiles. When Jewish dominance is clear, questions about identity are not so problematic. But when the number of Gentiles equals or surpasses the number of Jews in churches outside Palestine, the questions of identity loom large and demand answers.

With clear hindsight, we know that the Jerusalem accord did not take sufficient account of situations that would develop (and already existed in

Antioch) in which a single community of Christ-believers included adherents to the "gospel of circumcision" (a gospel recognized by Paul in Gal 2:7-10) and to the "gospel of uncircumcision." Paul's account of the Antioch incident chronicles the dispute that followed in the wake of the decision in Jerusalem not to require Gentiles to observe the Torah as Jews observe it. Peter comes to Antioch and apparently finds the Gentile Christ-believers to be accommodating enough in their practices regarding food and drink to allow him, an observant Jew, to share a table with them. Since there were different views of appropriate ways for Jews to eat with Gentiles in this period (see Bockmuehl 1999, 164–79), it is not surprising that Peter ate with them or that a dispute about this matter arose. However, the meaning Paul assigns to the actions of Peter and those "from James" shows that Paul sees something about the nature of the church's identity at stake.

Paul argues in Gal 2:15-21 that the faithful death of Christ is the basis for righteousness in the Christian community. Anything that competes for status at this foundational level must be rejected, and Paul understands the separation of Jews and Gentiles in the church at table (whether this is for the Eucharist or a common meal) to be admitting a competing foundation for salvation—even if "those from James" and the Galatian teachers do not.

One of the reasons table fellowship is such an important issue is what it signals. This is not simply a matter of how carefully some Christ-believing Jews adhered to a particular understanding of halakah on food. As anthropologists note, table fellowship is an important statement and reinforcement of social boundaries (see Holmberg 1998, 398 for bibliography and discussion of this). Refusing to admit a person to table draws a clear social boundary that places the excluded person outside the group. Whom one eats with makes a statement about group identity. While all people have competing identities, some identities are more central and take precedence when they come into conflict with others and this ordering may change in varying settings. In the first-century setting, Jews had to think about how their identity as residents of a city (which would have included some elements of religious celebration) related to their religious identity. Furthermore, for some Jews challenges to rules about table fellowship may have been understood as challenges to their understanding of the covenant between God and Israel (so Dunn 1991, 109–11, following Neusner).

It seems likely that at Antioch, the question has to do with how Jewish identity related to identity as a Christ-believer. Those "from James" seem to think that, in the context of the gathered Christ-believers, identity as Jews remains the more fundamental identity for them in relation to Christ-believing. This does not mean that Peter or those "from James" want to require Gentiles to be circumcised or to adhere to more food regulations (Nanos 2002b, 317). Rather, separation at table embodied an understanding of their primary identity that made Christ-believing, (or better, being "in Christ") secondary to their identity as Jews. A number of interpreters draw the distinction between Paul and the Jerusalem church's theology along these identity lines (Chilton 1999, 259–63; McKnight 1999, 129). Such an understanding of the theology of James and the Jerusalem church rests on thin evidence, and much of it from Acts. It is difficult to evaluate how accurately Luke portrays James's or Jerusalem's theology. Still, such a description is plausible for that church in its early days. Whether that remains the view of James in particular or of the majority of Christ-believers in Jerusalem when Paul writes Galatians is less certain.

It is subordinating belief in Christ or membership "in Christ" to membership in the Mosaic covenant that Paul will not accept. It may well be that Peter and Barnabas had not thought about the matter in these terms. After all, the terms of the Jerusalem agreement (whether in Acts or in Galatians) allow for either of these rankings of primary identity.

In the light of the various ways Second Temple Judaism envisioned the admission of righteous Gentiles into the eschatological kingdom (see Fredricksen 2002, 244–47), early Jewish Christ-believers could easily have invited Gentiles to become "righteous Gentiles" without a fundamental rethinking of their own Jewish identity.[11] It is not really a question of whether or how to observe Torah, but of the center of the "definitive covenant community" (the expression is from N. H. Taylor 2002, 589). In a profound sense, Paul is redrawing the group boundary; the primary boundary is no longer drawn in relation to the covenant with Moses, but in relation to being "in Christ" (see Horrell 2002, 318–20). Those "from James," it seems, took a very different view on this matter. For them, the primary covenant community is that of Israel. Gentiles are then joined to this community of the renewed covenant in this eschatological time through the work of Christ (see Gaston 1984, 69–70).

It may well be that the teachers Paul opposes in Galatians had a much less theological agenda than what we have attributed to "those from James" and Paul in relation to the Antioch incident. After all, Paul brings up that incident to demonstrate that he had always rejected the practices the Galatians are being urged to adopt. That is, this episode makes it clear that Paul had never preached or allowed Gentile Christ-believers to accept circumcision as part of their identity or practice as Christ-believers. Perhaps the teachers influencing the Galatian churches only want the Christ-believers to be able to associate more freely with non-Christ-believers in the synagogues or are worried about local reaction to Gentile Christ-believers claiming the prerogatives granted to Jews without committing themselves fully to the Jewish community. Paul, however, sees other things at stake. Whatever the theological agenda, or lack of theological agenda, the Galatian teachers have, Paul invests their demands with deep theological meaning. Given Paul's own previous experiences, including his arguments with colleagues and other Christ-believers, a call for the circumcision of non-Jewish Christ-believers must be rejected. He must reject this suggestion because, for him, acceptance of circumcision means that the Gentile recipient commits himself to the wrong definitive covenant community. For Paul, that primary identity must be "in Christ," with other identities being subsumed within that understanding of one's self and one's relationship with God.

PHILIPPIANS 3

Philippians 3:2-11 also suggests that Paul has reoriented his primary identity and redefined the definitive covenant community.[12] In this passage Paul explicitly compares his membership in the covenant community of Israel with life "in him [Christ]" (v. 9). Because Paul is speaking polemically, warning the Philippians not to accept teaching that requires circumcision for Gentiles and so includes incorporation into the Mosaic covenant, he uses extravagant language that devalues his identity and practice as a faithful, Torah-observant Jew. Not only are his statements polemical, they are also comparative, again with the intent of making the view he is rejecting as unpalatable as possible.

He argues in these verses that the Philippians must not commit themselves to the Mosaic covenant because they have something more valuable. What they have "in Christ" is so valuable that Paul is willing to reevaluate the privileges he has previously held as a participant in the covenant community of Israel. He exchanges that primary identity for an identity in Christ. This passage shows that Paul's religious commitment has undergone a significant shift, a shift that requires him to change his understanding of his Jewish identity and that moves him into a new religious community (Segal 1990, 113–17; N. H. Taylor 2002, 587–89, following Gaventa and Segal). The discourse of Philippians 3 is what Boyarin labels "disidentification" (Boyarin 1999, 125). Thus, even while Paul remains within Judaism, he defines himself over against it.

In less polemical settings (particularly in Romans 9–11) Paul makes it clear that the things he says he has given up in Philippians 3 are valuable. Even in Philippians 3 they are a genuine loss (v. 7). It is the comparative nature of the Philippians passage that is instructive for our discussion. In opposition to teachers he has encountered who require non-Jewish Christ-believers to be circumcised and so identify themselves more closely with the practice of the synagogue by becoming proselytes to Judaism, Paul argues that the most important element of his religious identity is being in Christ—and that this is the category that has soteriological significance. Still, Christ-believers remain either Jews or non-Jews, just as they remain either female or male. But the meanings of these other identities are relativized. These other identities continue to influence and even determine how one lives out the gospel, but for Paul they all remain secondary to and are subsumed under that central identity of being "in Christ."[13]

Synthesis

Our brief survey of Paul's letters shows that there was considerable diversity among those who claimed identity as both Jews and Christ-believers. The opponents of 2 Corinthians seek to establish their place as authoritative teachers and apostles in part on the basis of being Jewish. There is no indication in 2 Corinthians that Paul disagrees with them on matters that concern community identity, soteriology, or even christology. The basic issue concerns the manner of life the Spirit inspires in apostles and leaders. These traveling teachers oppose Paul's apostolic authority at Corinth, but apparently not because they want to draw the boundaries of the church in a different way. They take advantage of the presumed privilege of being Jewish among these mostly Gentile Christ-believers, but there is no reason to think that they ask the Corinthians to associate more closely with the Jewish community and Torah observance or that that they claim any soteriological advantage over Gentiles.

We encounter in 2 Corinthians Christ-believing Jews who seem to draw their central identity from their relationship to Christ, who grants them the Spirit that they emphasize in their self-presentations. This does not mean they have forfeited their Jewish identity or that it is without value. Just the opposite is the case. Gentile Christ-believers respect and honor the Jewish identity of these teachers. Unfortunately, the texts give no clear indication of why the Corinthians see being Jewish as advantageous. We may speculate that it has to do with their heritage and life experience as those who worship only the God of Israel. First Corinthians makes it obvious that the Corinthian church needs help as it thinks about how it should function as a group and how members should negotiate their lives in the broader, pagan world. Jews had faced many of the kinds of situations that the Christ-believers now encounter. Christ-believers who are Jewish can offer the wisdom and experience of that religious heritage which is inseparably a part of the proclamation of Christ.

Not only do they have the tradition and the experience of the Jewish community to offer, but Christ-believing Jews also bring a familiarity with scripture that few non-Jews could claim. Again, Christ-believing Jews know techniques of interpretation and application of scripture that the new churches need if the Bible is to serve as a guide for their beliefs and practices. Paul's letters themselves are witness to the importance of scripture in the Pauline churches. He often draws on scripture, sometimes using interpretive techniques that appear in other Jewish writers, to argue for his positions. So the superior knowledge of scripture that Jewish members possess may contribute to Christ-believing Gentiles' readiness to accept Jewish identity as an element of a claim to authority.

Finally, Paul himself retains some prerogatives for Jews in Romans. He affirms that it is advantageous to be Jewish and that the gospel continues to be for "Jews first, and also for the Greeks" (e.g., 1:16). What Paul denies is that there is soteriological (or ecclesial) advantage to being Jewish. So as Paul asserts that it is advantageous to be Jewish, it is not surprising that his Corinthian converts find Jewish identity significant when evaluating claims to authority.

The disagreement that prompted Paul to write 2 Corinthians is not related to his opponents' identification of themselves as Jews. Although Paul does not put his Jewish identity forward as a reason to accept his leadership—except when he must match the claims of his rivals—he does not seem to view such a use of Jewish identity as a violation of the gospel. So here are Christ-believing Jews, a group that may rightfully be called a Christ-believing Jewish group of traveling preachers (a movement) that preaches to and interacts fully with predominantly Gentile churches. These roving preachers seem to define the Christian community in much the same way that Paul does. So even though he has serious disagreements with them, those disagreements do not involve the place of Torah-observance or the relationship between Christ-believing Jews and Christ-believing Gentiles.

Perhaps we could label these opponents of Paul Christ-believing Jews. We would put them together with Paul in this category. The designation of Christ-believing Jews would stand for those who understand their primary religious identity to be determined by being "in Christ" and retain their Jewish identity, with perhaps varying halakah of Torah observance. (As is evident from Romans 14, Paul has room within the category of Christ-believer for Jews with differing ideas about how to observe the Torah.)

When we look to Galatians and Philippians, the Christ-believing Jews Paul opposes in those letters are rather different from his opponents in Corinth. Though some have argued that those urging circumcision on Gentile Christians are not themselves Christ-believers (Nanos 2002a), it seems more likely that Christ-believing Jews would wield enough influence to evoke the response we find in Galatians. Furthermore, Paul's response seems clearly intra-Christian, as he assumes with no argument the importance of attachment to Christ as necessary for a right relationship with God.

Since Nero can distinguish between Jews and Christ-believers within a decade or so of the writing of Galatians and Claudius may have done so earlier in the Edict of Claudius, it is more probable that the distinction was clear within the community, though that distinction did not necessarily entail a complete separation between Christ-believers (Jewish and non-Jewish) and Jews who did not adopted belief in Christ. Perhaps the Christ-believing Jews who urge circumcision for Gentiles want to maintain closer ties to the synagogue than some other Pauline churches had. Or perhaps some synagogues in Galatia are disturbed at the way the Christ-believers include Gentiles and so pressure the Christ-believers to require conformity with more of the Torah if those non-Jewish Christ-believers want to claim the civic privileges accorded Jews.[14] At least it seems that those urging circumcision want to enable easier association with the broader Jewish community for Christ-believing Gentiles, Gentiles who would have abandoned worship of other gods and would have adopted the basic morality of Judaism. In comparison with others Paul mentions, those urging circumcision in Galatia may be fairly theologically innocent. They may see Gentile circumcision as a relatively insignificant concession considering the ways that the non-Jewish Christ-believers had already separated themselves from their cultural, civic, and familial environments.[15] If this is the case, they are thinking within a different paradigm from that in which Paul works, whether they recognized it or not. In any case, they do not think their proposal will disturb Paul or violate his theology. Paul's understanding of circumcision as formal admission into the Mosaic covenant, however, requires him to reject the Galatian proposal as a violation of the gospel.

Perhaps those whom Paul opposes in Galatians had been less reflective about the meaning of circumcision than Paul thought they should be. Or perhaps more likely, they had not been forced to think carefully about the relationships among their various identities and what that might mean for their understanding of the work of Christ and the place of non-Jews within the people of God. But Paul had been required to give extensive thought to these questions and so rejects their proposal with a vehemence and for reasons they would not have expected. When they did give thought to these issues, some individuals may have begun or joined the movement that Paul opposes in Philippians 3.

Those whom Paul opposes in Philippians 3 seem to value membership in the Mosaic covenant in a way that makes it more important for one's religious identity than faith in Christ.[16] In this way, they appear to hold much the same view that "those from James" embodied in Paul's account of the Antioch incident. It may be that these visitors to Antioch represent well the early theological outlook of the Jerusalem church and some of its leaders—though perhaps not Peter, since he associated with the mixed congregation freely before the visitors arrived. But Paul has fundamental differences with the outlook he opposes in Antioch.

The Christ-believing Jews who demand separation from Gentiles at table make being Jewish their primary religious identity. Paul, however, finds participation "in Christ" to be the proper decisive religious and covenant identity. So in an important way he has redefined "the people of God." Interpreters who are reticent to speak of Paul's experience of the risen Christ as a conversion are correct to point out that Paul does not abandon Judaism when he becomes a Christ-believer and the apostle to the Gentiles. However, it is too simple to say that his experience and call did not change his understanding and evaluation of his Jewish identity. Significant aspects of that identity were reevaluated and reinterpreted. As Segal notes, Paul's experience of the risen Christ leads him "to change commitments from one religious community to another" (1990, 117). The change in Paul does not take him out of Judaism, but it makes faith in Christ the defining element of his religious identity. Within the eschatological community "in Christ," he remains a faithful Jew. The difference between Paul and "those from James" is that for the latter faith in Christ does not reorient their identity to the extent that this faith reoriented Paul's.

What is really at issue between Paul, on the one hand, and those who demanded that Jews eat separately from Gentiles in Antioch and those who advocated Gentile circumcision (Philippians 3), on the other, is not Torah observance. Rather it is the question of which religious identity is definitive. Paul has redefined the boundaries of the primary covenant community so that being Jewish is a subcategory within the sphere defined by Christ-believing. These Christ-believing Jews who oppose his mission continue to define the boundaries of the covenant community primarily in terms of the Mosaic covenant, with Christ-believing a subcategory within the sphere of that covenant.[17] In this understanding, Christ is interpreted within the Mo-saic covenant. This does not mean that non-Jews cannot share in the escha-tological kingdom of God. As we have noted, some Jewish apocalyptic writ-ers saw a place for righteous Gentiles in God's kingdom. But they remain in a secondary position. If non-Jews want to join fully the people of God they must convert to Judaism and so become members of the definitive cove-nant community. Such an understanding of the place of non-Jews motivates those Christ-believing Jews who call for Gentile circumcision in Philippians 3 and probably those who caused the separation at table in Antioch.

The first Christ-believing Jews of the Jerusalem church probably gave little thought to the relationship between membership in the Mosaic cov-enant and the church. The earliest Christ-believers would have understood the resurrection of Christ as evidence that God had indeed worked through him. But such a conviction would not necessarily involve rethinking the covenant beyond Jeremiah's promise of the covenant written on the heart (Jeremiah 31). But as the Christ-believing mission moved out of Judea and as they continued to think about what it meant to claim that the death of Jesus was "for us" (see the early confession in 1 Cor 15:3-4), some signifi-cant discontinuities also became apparent. Still, it would seem most natu-ral to maintain the temporal and soteriological priority of Israel.[18] These earliest Christ-believers had no cause to attend to the question of the place of Gentiles until there were enough Gentile converts who were not from among God-fearers that the issue of the community's identity forced itself upon them. It is those who continue to understand Christ solely within the Mosaic covenant who oppose the Pauline mission and so represent a type of Christ-believing Jew that is fundamentally different from the Christ-believing Jew Paul.

This understanding of the community created "in Christ" is so different from Paul's that it affects nearly every aspect of the ways Jews and non-Jews relate to one another and to the Torah.[19] Again, the foundational difference is the question of what creates the definitive boundary or what constitutes the covenant community. If it remains the Mosaic covenant, renewed as promised in the prophets of Israel, then non-Jews must convert to Judaism to be full members of the covenant community. If the primary identity of members of the covenant community is that of believing in Christ, then non-Jews remain non-Jews and Jews remain Jews with these identities relativized but not eradicated. They are not eradicated because whether one is Jewish or Gentile continues to define in important ways how one embodies the gospel in the conduct of one's life.

Denise K. Buell and Caroline Johnson Hodge are among those who argue that in one way or another Paul brings the Gentiles into Judaism or into Israel. Buell and Hodge envision Paul making the ethnic designator "Judean" fluid enough to include Gentiles who believe in Christ. According to them, Christ brings a "kinship for Gentiles with Israel" that is based on both Jews and non-Jews possessing the Spirit (2004, 245). Their observations about the elasticity of ethnicity are important, as is their recognition that Paul "constructs a myth of collective identity" for Christ-believing Gentiles (2004, 246). But they underestimate the eschatological change Paul claims for both Jews and non-Jews who believe in Christ.

Buell and Hodge also too easily conflate being Jewish or, in their terms, adopting a "Judean identity" (2004, 247) with claiming Abraham as one's ancestor. For Paul, non-Jewish Christ-believers are not simply "gentiles affiliated with Israel" (2004, 249), they are a part of a "new creation" (2 Cor 5:17) that includes the nations. Pamela Eisenbaum (2003) emphasizes the ways that patrilinear societies have flexible ethnic or genealogical identities, but recognizes the difference between claiming Abraham as one's ancestor and adopting Jewish identity. She notes that in Jewish tradition Abraham is sometimes seen as the ancestor of both Jews and the nations.[20] Thus, the connection to Abraham can bring kinship for all "in Christ" without in some way identifying non-Jewish Christ-believers as Jewish. It is the eschatological act of God in Christ that initiates the new creation and the new identity for Christ-believers, both Jewish and non-Jewish. Paul's ways of relating these identities is eschatological, complex, and nuanced—so much so that it is difficult to grasp or to live out. Yet he demands that the church live its identity as the new creation not just in the eyes of God but also in the context of the gathered body of multiethnic Christ-believers. In this setting, living as Christ-believers takes precedence over all other identities.

If we designate as "Christ-believing Jews" those Christ-believing Jews who agree with Paul about the primary identity of Christ-believers and the central definition of the covenant community, then we may want to designate those he opposes in Philippians and "those from James" as Jewish Christ-believers. The latter expression would then indicate that their primary religious identity is Jewish; that is, they are most fundamentally faithful adherents to the Mosaic covenant. Their belief in Christ, then, functions within that sphere of identity.

Our study indicates that there was no single way—or even only two ways—of being a Christ-believer and Jewish in the first century. How Christ-believers understood the mission and work of Christ in relation to Israel and Gentiles varied significantly. There is enough variation among Christ-believing Jews that a single designation for them is misleading, particularly if that label's central function is to distinguish them from Paul or from Pauline churches. Serious theological issues divided Paul from some other Christ-believers, but sometimes those on his side would have been Jews and sometimes Gentiles and probably nearly always a mixture of the two.

The issues Paul addresses in 2 Corinthians demonstrate that questions about relations between Jews and non-Jews were not always the central concerns for his churches. It seems that many Jews who came to believe in Christ accepted Paul's understanding of the reorientation of identities that such belief involved. Many other matters about Christian belief and practice—structures of leadership (1 and 2 Corinthians), the significance of spiritual experiences (1 Corinthians and Colossians), or the meaning of persecution (1 Thessalonians), among other things—occupied the churches when they were not focused on the distinctions among believers based on whether they were Jewish or not. So it is far too simple and even incorrect to divide the Christ-believers of Paul's day into Jewish/Jerusalem Christianity and Gentile/Pauline Christianity. Regional similarities probably existed among Christ-believers, but such regional groupings were not monolithic. Indeed, they often included substantive and debated differences, only some of which involved the meaning of being Jewish or of being non-Jewish once incorporated into Christ.

The ways interpreters have used the label "Jewish Christianity" over the last 150 years provides another reason to leave it behind. Not only does it imply a kind of uniformity of Christ-believing Jews that did not exist (particularly when interpreters see the label's primary purpose to be identifying opposition to Paul and his mission), but it has also been used to characterize those in that group as legalists. It has been a mistake to identify full Torah observance as the central issue that separated Paul from those who demand circumcision for non-Jewish Christ-believers. The real issue is that of identity. Torah observance was a central expression, but only an expression, of an understanding that Paul finds inadequate for the way belief in Christ shapes religious identity. Calling non-Jews to accept circumcision and so full conversion to Judaism represents an understanding of Christ-believing that retains the view that membership in the Mosaic covenant is the central religious identity of God's people. It is this relationship among religious (or ethno-religious) identities that Paul rejects, arguing that Christ-believers have reoriented their religious identities so that all other self-definitions are secondary in relation to membership "in Christ."[21] Even though the explicit topic is often the Torah, the heart of the issue in Philippians 3, in the Antioch incident, and in Paul's response to the Galatian situation is what constitutes the definitive covenant community and so what defines one's primary religious identity.

Perhaps one of the reasons we continue to struggle to understand the place of Paul's churches in relation to Judaism is that we frame the question in terms of ideal types. It seems that in Paul's letters we have internal group discourse about identity as a new identity emerges. We hear the conversation at what Homi Bhabha calls a site of "hybridity." Paul's multi-ethnic Christ-believing community "exceeds the frame of the image" and so requires a renegotiation of identities (Bhabha 1994, 49). Paul and his fellow Christ-believing Jews must construct a new self-understanding, an understanding that draws elements from multiple sources to create something different from any of its predecessors.

The term "Jewish Christianity," because of its anachronism and its inaccuracy, is an imprecise and misleading label. No single understanding of the nature of the Christ-believing community existed among Christ-believers who were Jewish. If we allow the first word of the label to represent the most formative element of their religious identity, then Paul and other Jews who make Christ-believing central might be called "Christ-believing (or Christian) Jews," while those who make the Mosaic covenant central might be called "Jews who are Christ-believers (Jewish Christ-believers)," or perhaps better "Jews who also believe in Christ." These labels are not as handy or felicitous as some, but they are more accurate, provided we do not assume that all those within these rather broad categories agree on other issues.

Suggested Readings

Bockmuehl, Markus. 1999. "Antioch and James the Just." Pages 155–98 in *James the Just and Christian Origins*. Edited by Bruce Chilton and Craig A. Evans. Novum Testamentum Supplements 98. Leiden: Brill.

Dunn, James D. G. 1991. *The Partings of the Ways between Christianity and Judaism and Their Significance for the Character of Christianity*. Philadelphia: Trinity Press International.

Eisenbaum, Pamela. 2003. "Paul as the New Abraham." Online: http://www.thepaulpage.com. Accessed January 18, 2003.

———. 2004. "A Remedy for Having Been Born of Woman: Jesus, Gentiles, and Genealogy in Romans." *Journal of Biblical Literature* 123:671–702.

Fredriksen, Paula. 2002. "Judaism, the Circumcision of Gentiles, and Apocalyptic Hope: Another Look at Galatians 1 and 2." Pages 235–60 in *The Galatians Debate: Contemporary Issues in Rhetorical and Historical Interpretation*. Edited by Mark Nanos. Peabody, Mass.: Hendrickson.

Hurtado, Larry W. 1999. "Pre-70 CE Jewish Opposition to Christ-Devotion." *Journal of Theological Studies* 50:35–58.

Nanos, Mark. 2002a. *The Irony of Galatians: Paul's Letter in First-Century Context*. Minneapolis: Fortress Press.

Saldarini, Anthony J. 1998. "The Social World of Christian Jews and Jewish Christians." Pages 115–54 in *Religious and Ethnic Communities in Later Roman Palestine*. Edited by Hiyam Lapin. Bethesda: University of Maryland Press.

4. Ebionites and Nazarenes

Petri Luomanen

Early Christian heresiologists painted stereotyped pictures of the Ebionites and the Nazarenes as Christians who erroneously followed Jewish laws and customs. Therefore, these two groups have frequently served as the best examples of ancient Jewish Christianity. Nevertheless, a closer look at the evidence reveals that groups characterized as "Ebionite" or "Nazarene" often differed considerably from each other—some of them being more "Jewish" than others. The following discussion will cast light on some of the characteristic differences among these groups, paying special attention to the question of whether it is feasible to call them Jewish Christian.

The Ebionites and the Nazarenes are known only from the writings of the church fathers who present short summaries of their teachings and quotations of their writings, usually in order to confute what they considered to be heresy. The Ebionites appear for the first time in Irenaeus's *Adversus haereses*, written around 180 CE. In order to find the first description of the "heresy" of the Nazarenes, we must turn to a work authored some two hundred years later, Epiphanius's *Panarion* (ca. 386 CE). The *Panarion* also contains the richest ancient description of the Ebionites. Because Epiphanius was writing at the end of the fourth century, he was able to use all the information about the Ebionites collected by his predecessors (Irenaeus, Hippolytus, Tertullian, Pseudo-Tertullian, Origen, and Eusebius), which he supplemented with many details obtained from his contemporaries.

It is not possible in the present context to deal with all the church fathers who referred to the Ebionites. Therefore, I have chosen to focus on Epiphanius's *Panarion*, comparing it with the earliest information available, Irenaeus's *Adversus haereses*. This will make it possible to sketch an overview of how the information about the Ebionites developed from the second to the fourth century CE, and to ask whether this development in the descriptions might mirror actual changes in the character of the Ebionite movement.

In the case of the Nazarenes, there are only two church fathers whose information provides a practicable starting point: Epiphanius and Jerome. These two fathers were contemporaries and knew each other very well. Furthermore, they both lived for a long time in Palestine, which makes their information about Jewish Christianity especially interesting. Although we have good grounds for believing that they both had some personal contacts with Jewish Christians, it is also clear that their information is heavily biased and needs to be assessed in the light of their personal history and their position as representatives of "mainstream" Christianity.

The Ebionites' and the Nazarenes' possible relation to the early Jerusalem community has often been debated. Over the history of research, both have been assessed as genuine successors of the early Jerusalem community. F. C. Baur argued that the Ebionites were not originally a heretical sect but successors of the very first Jewish Christians in Jerusalem. The Nazarenes, for their part, represented a later phase of Jewish Christianity, which had developed from its strictly anti-Pauline stance to a more lenient attitude toward the Gentiles (Baur 1966 [1860], 174, 174 n. 1). Among contemporary scholars, Gerd Luedemann (1996, 52–56) and Michael D. Goulder (1994, 107–13) have argued for similar views. On the other hand, Albrecht Ritschl (1857, 152–54) already argued against Baur that strict Jewish Christianity with its anti-Paulinism could not be considered the dominant current in first-century Christianity. In his view, the Nazarenes, who accepted the apostle Paul, were the successors of the early Jerusalem community. Ray A. Pritz (1988, 28, 82, 108–10) has presented a similar interpretation.[1] According to him, the history of the Nazarenes can be traced back to the early Jerusalem community, while the Ebionites came out of a split among the Nazarene ranks around the turn of the first century.

Any solution to this problem is bound to be speculative because there is a hundred-year gap in the historical sources that explicitly deal with the Jerusalem community and the Ebionites (from Acts to Irenaeus's *Adversus haereses*). In the case of the Nazarenes, the gap is still longer, about three hundred years. Although the main intention of the present chapter is to discuss the Jewish-Christian profile of the Ebionites and the Nazarenes at the end of the fourth century, it will become clear in the course of the discussion that I find the Ebionites better candidates than the Nazarenes for being the successors of the Jerusalem community. I have argued elsewhere in detail (Luomanen 2005a) that the separate sect of the Nazarenes was mainly Epiphanius's own creation, invented to help him protect his own version of Christianity against judaizers. As far as Epiphanius's and Jerome's information contains historically reliable data about the Nazarenes, it only suggests the presence of Syriac/Aramaic-speaking Christians who may occasionally have followed some Jewish practices but whose theological ideas barely differed from the formative Catholic tradition. Thus, the Nazarenes seem to have been Jewish Christian only in the narrow sense of being Christians who were of Jewish origin and spoke a Semitic language. In general, the groups that the church fathers called Ebionites were more Jewish in character, although there is also variation among them.

The church fathers' descriptions of the Ebionites and the Nazarenes often differ considerably and we cannot always be sure if they are really describing the same historical group. Therefore, in the course of the following discussion, I shall always specify whose Ebionites and Nazarenes I am discussing. I shall first introduce my approach to defining early Jewish Christianity and then discuss Epiphanius's Ebionites[2] and their relation to Irenaeus's Ebionites. After that, I move on to Epiphanius's Nazarenes, and finally to Jerome's Nazarenes.

Jewish-Christian Profiles

The concept of Jewish Christianity is inherently modern because it presumes two distinct religious bodies, Judaism and Christianity, which were less clearly separated from each other in antiquity than they are today. On the other hand, it also suggests an overlap of these categories in a way that is less common today. This makes the term both elusive and generative. While the term is not found in ancient sources, it is useful historically because it directs attention to the way our modern categories "Judaism" and "Christianity" overlapped in some ancient communities.

The present chapter is not based on any conclusive definition of Jewish Christianity. A predetermined definition of Jewish Christianity—be it broad or narrow—seems inappropriate because the multifaceted character of both ancient Judaism and Christianity is generally acknowledged today. In scholarly discourse, this is often indicated by the plurals "Christianities" and "Judaisms." Consequently, it is likely that there was not just one Jewish Christianity but several Jewish Christianities.

Acknowledging this possibility, I will approach Jewish Christianity in this chapter from an analytical point of view, looking for *indicators of Jewish Christianity* in the church fathers' characterizations of the Ebionites and the Nazarenes. Specifically, I will call attention to the following points, which map out ideas and practices that are today commonly connected to either Judaism or Christianity:

1. Are characteristically Jewish practices such as (Jewish) circumcision, the Sabbath, and purity laws observed?
2. Are characteristically Jewish ideas such as Yahweh as the only God, the temple as Yahweh's abode, or the Torah, maintained?
3. What is the pedigree of the group/person? Jewish or not?
4. What is the role of Jesus in the worship and ideology of the community? Is Jesus considered to be a Jewish prophet, or is he more a divine being, worshiped as *Kyrios* ("Lord"), an equal to God?
5. Is baptism in the name of Jesus (or the triune God) an entrance rite to the community?
6. To what extent are these or other issues important for inter- or intra-group relations? What roles do they play in defining the borders and identity of the group in question?

A discussion of these indicators will yield a *Jewish-Christian profile* that will show to what extent a group has characteristics that are today associated with either Judaism or Christianity. [3] The last point also enables one to make a distinction between simple Jewish-Christian inclinations, which might characterize several Jewish and Christian communities, and independent Jewish-Christian movements that stick so devoutly to some of their own border-marking practices and ideas that they become socially distinguishable from other Jewish and Christian movements. These questions, which tap into the border marking of communities, are particularly significant in the case of the Ebionites and the Nazarenes, who are described as distinct groups by the church fathers, especially Epiphanius.

EPIPHANIUS'S EBIONITES

Epiphanius was born in Palestine near modern Gaza around 315 C.E. He probably had Christian parents and was first educated in local monasteries. He later moved to Egypt to complete his education but came back to Palestine in his twenties and founded a new monastery in Eleutheropolis. He was the head of that monastery for about thirty years until he was elected bishop of Salamis in Cyprus in 367. About ten years later, he completed a major work against heresies, the *Panarion*, in which he describes and confutes eighty Jewish and Christian heresies. The name of the work, *Medicine Chest* in English, characterizes its main intent: in Epiphanius's view, the heresies represented poisonous doctrines that threatened the Christians of his day, and his intention was to provide the antidotes.

Epiphanius believed that a person called Ebion founded the "heresy" of the Ebionites. Modern scholars generally agree, however, that the person is fictive. In reality, the name of the movement seems to be derived from the Hebrew word *'ebyon*, which means "poor." Irenaeus did not yet know about a person called Ebion. That name was introduced by Tertullian and Hippolytus but, by Epiphanius's time, the existence of a person by that name seems to have been taken for granted. Because heresies were usually thought to have been introduced by actual persons, the genesis of the Ebionites was made to conform by being traced back to the activity of a person called Ebion.

Epiphanius's refutation of the Ebionites (*Panarion* 30) is the richest ancient source on the Ebionites available. Together with the passage on the Nazarenes (*Panarion* 29), this material amounts to a full-blown history of the Jewish-Christian "heresy" from the times of the early Jerusalem community to Epiphanius's day. Earlier heresiologists had described the heresies of Cerinthus[4] and the Ebionites successively, but Epiphanius placed the Nazarenes between these two, claiming that Ebion, whom he identifies as the originator of the Ebionite heresy, was originally one of the Nazarenes. As we shall see below, this whole history mainly serves Epiphanius's polemical interests and has little or nothing to do with the actual course of events.

In the *Panarion,* Epiphanius was able to use all the information provided by his predecessors, especially by Irenaeus, Hippolytus, Origen, and Eusebius. In addition, he had some knowledge about Ebionites who were his contemporaries, and he was able to quote passages from their literature.[5] Epiphanius presents quotations from a Gospel they used and refers to their *Acts of Apostles* as being different from the canonical one. Epiphanius also states that the Ebionites used "Clement's so-called *Circuits of Peter*" (*Periodoi Petrou; Pan.* 30.15.1), "though they corrupt the contents and leave a few genuine items, " as well as the *Ascents of James* (*Anabathmoi Iakōbou; Pan.* 30.16.7), which is "full of nonsense." Modern scholars connect these writings to sources that stand behind the present Pseudo-Clementine *Recognitions* and *Homilies.*[6] At some points, Epiphanius obviously quotes the *Book of Elchasai* as well. (I will deal with the *Pseudo-Clementines* and the *Book of Elchasai* in more detail below.)

Much of what Epiphanius reports about the Ebionites is consistent with the accounts of his predecessors, Irenaeus, Hippolytus, Origen, and Eusebius:[7]

1. Christ was believed to be the seed of man, Joseph (*Pan.* 30.2.2).
2. The Ebionites adhere to the law, circumcision, Sabbath, and other Jewish (and Samaritan) practices (*Pan.* 30.2.2; 30.26.1–2).
3. The Ebionites use the Gospel of Matthew, calling it "according to the Hebrews" (*Pan.* 30.3.7; 30.13.2).
4. The Ebionites are anti-Pauline (*Pan.* 30.16.8–9).

At the same time, the profile of Epiphanius's Ebionites clearly differs from those of the earlier reports because of all the new information Epiphanius provides. He presents a number of new details about the Ebionite beliefs and practices that are not found in the earlier sources:

1. Ebion, the alleged founder of the movement, was originally a Samaritan (*Pan.* 30.1.3, 5; 30.2.3)

2. Ebionites are careful not to touch a heathen (*Pan.* 30.2.3).

3. They had to purify themselves after having intercourse with a woman (*Pan.* 30.2.4).

4. They also practiced other lustrations several times a day, fully clothed (*Pan.* 30.2.5; 30.15.3; 30.16.1).

5. They forbade virginity and chastity even though they had earlier boasted of virginity (*Pan.* 30.2.6; cf. no. 16 below).

6. In Epiphanius's view, they maintain contradictory views of Christ: Some of them say that (a) Adam is Christ (Pan. 30.3.3), while others claim that (b) Christ is eternal and has appeared several times in history—to Abraham and others—in the guise of Adam's body, and that he was finally crucified, raised, and returned to heaven (Pan. 30.3.4–6). Some of them may also say that (c) Christ went into Jesus (*Pan.* 30.3.6; see also *Pan.* 30.16.4).

7. Epiphanius presents quotations from the Ebionites' Gospel, arguing that the Ebionites have mutilated the Gospel of Matthew (*Pan.* 30.13.2, etc.).

8. They detest Isaiah, Jeremiah, Ezekiel, Daniel, Elijah, Elisha, Samson, Samuel, David, Solomon, and all the prophets (*Pan.* 30.15.2; 30.18.4–5; 30.18.9).

9. They abstain from food prepared from meat (*Pan.* 30.13.5; 30.15.3; 30.18.7; 30.22.3–5).

10. They accept baptism in addition to their daily purifications (*Pan.* 30.16.1).

11. They celebrate the Eucharist annually with unleavened bread and water only (*Pan.* 30.16.1).

12. They believe that Christ came to abolish sacrifices (Pan. 30.16.5) and that James, the brother of Jesus, preached against the temple and sacrifices (Pan. 30.16.7).

13. They claim to have received their name, "Ebionites" ("poor," from the Hebrew word *'ebyon*), when their ancestors delivered their property to the apostles (*Pan.* 30.17.2–3; cf. Acts 4:34–35).

14. They have invocations and lustrations to help those stricken by sickness or bitten by a snake (*Pan.* 30.17.4–5; also in the *Book of Elchasai*).

15. Like Elchasai, they picture Christ as a huge invisible figure, ninety-six miles long and twenty-four miles wide (*Pan.* 30.17.5–7; also in the *Book of Elchasai*).

16. Young Ebionite men are coerced by their teachers to marry (*Pan.* 30.18.2; cf. no. 5 above).

17. The Ebionites have synagogues, governed by archisynagogues and elders (*Pan.* 30.18.2–3).

18. They do not accept the entire Pentateuch (*Pan.* 30.18.7–9).

In addition, Epiphanius transmits some new (fictitious) stories that illustrate the Ebionites' anti-Paulinism. For instance, the Ebionites explained that Paul's antipathy toward the law and circumcision was caused by his unfortunate love affairs. According to this account, Paul was originally of Greek parentage. He went to Jerusalem and fell in love with the daughter of the high priest. In order to get the girl, he became a proselyte and had himself circumcised. However, because he still could not get the girl after all his trouble, he became angry and wrote against circumcision, the Sabbath, and the Jewish law (*Pan.* 30.16.8–9).[8]

Because many of the new ideas and practices attributed to the Ebionites are paralleled in the literature that Epiphanus was using as his sources, it is not clear at the outset how many of these ideas can be attributed to Epiphanius's contemporary Ebionites. Thus, a critical assessment of Epiphanius's sources and information is necessary before it is possible to sketch a picture of the religious profile of Epiphanius's Ebionites. I will do this by proceeding from "clearly Ebionite" evidence and sources to "possibly Ebionite" ones. The information Epiphanius received from his contemporaries and the fragments he quoted from the "Gospel of the Ebionites"[9] will provide the basic "clearly Ebionite" information. A critical assessment of Epiphanius's "possibly Ebionite" information—his references to Pseudo-Clementine and Elchasaite sources—will add some important details to the profile. Since the resulting overall profile of Epiphanius's Ebionites will be clearly different form the profile of Irenaeus's Ebionites, I will close the section by discussing whether it is possible to regard Epiphanius's and Irenaeus's Ebionites as representatives of the same Ebionite movement.

Contemporary Reports

There are four ideas in Epiphanius's description that are not easily attributable to written sources but seem to be based on his own knowledge of contemporary Ebionite practices. First, the Ebionites claimed (falsely, in Epiphanius's view) to have received their name when their ancestors gave their property to the apostles (*Pan.* 30.17.2–3; cf. Acts 4:32–37). This claim is not found in earlier reports nor in the extant fragments of Ebionite literature, so it would seem that Epiphanius received this information from the Ebionites themselves.[10] Because Epiphanius is forced to deny the validity of the Ebionites' own etymology of their name, it is also clear that the name was a self-designation and not merely one used by outsiders. Second, the way Epiphanius describes the Ebionites' therapeutic lustrations suggests that he was informed about their practices (more on this below). Third, information about Ebionite synagogues and leaders has an authentic ring. The same applies, finally, to the report about their teachers coercing young males to marry.

Moreover, while the Ebionites' abstinence from meat and their critical attitude toward the Prophets can be found in their literature (the "Gospel of the Ebionites" and the *Pseudo-Clementines* in particular), Epiphanius also reports contemporary disputes between him (or his fellow Christians) and the Ebionites concerning these particular issues:

> When you ask one of them why they do not eat meat they have nothing to say, and foolishly answer, "Since it is produced by the congress and intercourse of bodies, we do not eat it." Thus, according to their own foolish regurgitations, they are wholly abominable themselves, since they are results of the intercourse of a man and a woman. (*Pan.* 30.15.4; the translations of *Pan.* 29 and *Pan.* 30 follow F. Williams 1987 throughout unless otherwise noted.)

> Nor do they accept Moses' Pentateuch in its entirety; certain sayings
> they reject. When you say to them, of eating meat, "Why did Abraham
> serve the angels the calf and the milk? Why did Noah eat meat, and
> why was he told to by God, who said, 'Slay and eat?' Why did Isaac and
> Jacob sacrifice to God—Moses too, in the wilderness?" he will not be-
> lieve that and will say, "Why do I need to read what is in the Law, when
> the Gospel has come?" "Well, where did you hear about Moses and
> Abraham? I know you admit their existence, and put them down as
> righteous, and your own ancestors." Then he will answer, "Christ has
> revealed this to me," and will blaspheme most of the legislation, and
> Samson, David, Elijah, Samuel, Elisha and the rest. (*Pan.* 30.18.7–9)

The answer given in the first quotation would seem to imply a very as-
cetic lifestyle because it suggests that all sexual intercourse is prohibited.
However, if the information about the Ebionites' obligation to marry is
correct, as it seems, then the Ebionites' abstinence concerned only food
and drink. Nevertheless, their rejection of meat was more fundamental
than that described in the Pseudo-Clementine sources, which prohibited
only the foods listed in the Apostolic Decree (Acts 15:19–20, 29; cf. *Rec.*
4.36.4; *Hom.* 7.8.1).[11]

The second quotation, which seems to question the validity of all Mosaic
law, is very problematic in the light of the traditional information about the
Ebionites' strict observance of Jewish laws. Nevertheless, Epiphanius's reference to the Ebionites' selective use of the Pentateuch is in harmony with
the fact that he also connects Ebion to the *Samaritans*, who were famous
for accepting only their own version of the Pentateuch as their religious
literature. In the beginning of *Pan.* 30, Epiphanius claims that Ebion was
originally a Samaritan (*Pan.* 30.1.3; 30.2.2–3) before he came in contact
with the Nazarenes (*Pan.* 29.7–8; 30.2.7). He also describes the Ebionites'
relations to the Gentiles and their purifications after sexual intercourse in
terms similar to what he had earlier used for describing the Samaritans.
Furthermore, when he refers to the Ebionites' observance of the Sabbath,
circumcision, and the law—practices traditionally attributed to the Ebionites in the heresiologies—he is careful to record that the Ebionites also
observed other things, just like the Jews and the Samaritans. Thus, it seems

clear that, in Epiphanius's view, the Ebionites accepted only the Pentateuch, but even that selectively—just like the Samaritans. The second quotation also suggests that the law is not studied in its own right because it is clearly overshadowed by Christ's revelation (cf. *Rec.* 1.58.2–6). As compared with the earlier tradition about the Ebionites, this kind of attitude results in a significantly different Jewish-Christian profile, but it coheres so well with Epiphanius's overall view of the contemporary Ebionites that we have no reason to doubt its historicity. Epiphanius's Ebionites discarded the Prophets and used even the Pentateuch selectively.

The "Gospel of the Ebionites"

Epiphanius presents quotations from the "Gospel of the Ebionites" that are not known from other sources, mostly in order to illustrate ideas that he considered typically Ebionite. They are therefore just as important as the contemporary reports as a source for ideas typical of Epiphanius's Ebionites.

According to Epiphanius, the Ebionites dropped the genealogies at the beginning of Matthew's Gospel because they did not accept virginal conception. He quotes the beginning of the "Gospel," which indicates that it opened with the description of Jesus' baptism by John (*Pan.* 30.1.5; 30.14.3). In Epiphanius's view, the Ebionites thought that Christ came into Jesus in the form of a dove at his baptism. This, indeed, accords with the wording of their Gospel, which states that the "Holy Spirit in the form of a dove which descended and *entered into* him" (*Pan.* 30.13.7; 30.14.4). On the other hand, Epiphanius claims that the Ebionites denied Jesus' being man on the basis of his saying: "These are my brethren and mother and sisters, these that do the will of my Father" (*Pan.* 30.14.5). The passage harmonizes the wordings of corresponding canonical passages (cf. Matt 12:47-50 and parr.), but in practice, its contents do not differ from them.[12] Thus, the key question is how the Ebionites themselves interpreted the passage. In my view, the Ebionites probably did not find any contradiction between this passage and their own ideas about Jesus' natural way of birth. Rather, it was Epiphanius, who had found the passage in the "Gospel of the Ebionites" and saw his opportunity to turn the tables on the Ebionites by pointing out that even their own Gospel indicates that Jesus did not have human brothers or sisters.

Epiphanius also finds examples of the Ebionites' abstinence from meat in their Gospel. They have changed John the Baptist's diet from *locusts* to *honey cakes* (*Pan.* 30.13.4–5) and they have made Jesus say that he does "*not* earnestly desire to eat meat" with the disciples at Passover (*Pan.* 30.22.4–5). One passage also indicates that Jesus chose the twelve apostles for a testimony to Israel (*Pan.* 30.13.2–3). The most significant information about the contents of the gospel, however, is a statement by Jesus that is unparalleled in the Synoptic Gospels: "I came to abolish the sacrifices, and if ye cease not from sacrifice, wrath will not cease from you" (*Pan.* 30.16.5). The idea that Jesus, the True Prophet, came to abolish the sacrifices is central to the *Pseudo-Clementines*. In this regard, it is clear that the "Gospel of the Ebionites" agreed with them.

The Pseudo-Clementine Sources

It is generally assumed that Epiphanius had access to Pseudo-Clementine sources underlying the present *Homilies*, *Recognitions*, and the introductory letters attached to these. Scholars have been able to reconstruct Pseudo-Clementine sources partially, but we cannot be sure about the relation of these modern reconstructions to the sources that were available to Epiphanius (*Circuits of Peter* and *Ascents of James*; see above). Therefore, we can only compare the modern reconstructions with the information Epiphanius probably derived from his own Pseudo-Clementine sources—keeping in mind that inconsistencies may indicate either (a) that Epiphanius's sources were not identical with the modern reconstructions or (b) that Epiphanius's Ebionites simply interpreted their own Pseudo-Clementine sources freely. Nevertheless, the similarities we will find between the modern reconstructions and Epiphanius's evidence will help us to refine the picture of Epiphanius's Ebionites and make understandable why Pseudo-Clementine literature was in use in the Ebionite community/communities.

In their present state, the Pseudo-Clementine *Homilies* and *Recognitions* are two reeditions of an earlier source that is usually called the *Basic Writing*.

A general outline of the *Basic Writing* can be deduced from parallel passages contained in the *Recognitions* and the *Homilies*. Scholars also largely agree that one section in the *Recognitions*, *Rec.* 1.27–71, is based on an independent source, but there is no consensus about the possible original title of the writing. Some think that this section of the *Recognitions* (*Rec.* 1.27–71) may indeed have preserved the *Ascents of James,* which Epiphanius ascribes to the Ebionites in *Pan.* 30.16.7 (Van Voorst 1989). On the other hand, it has been pointed out that the content of *Rec.* 1.27–71 does not cohere with Epiphanius's characterization of the *Ascents* (Jones 1995, 146–48). For instance, Epiphanius attributes to James much more severe and outspoken criticism of the temple and sacrifices than what is found in James's speeches in *Rec.* 1.27–71. For the sake of convenience, I will simply refer to this section of the *Recognitions* as *Rec.* 1.27–71.[13] Though *Rec.* 1.27–71 clearly forms an entity of its own, scholars think that it had become integrated in the *Basic Writing* before the *Basic Writing* was used by the editors of the *Recognitions* and the *Homilies* (Jones 1995, 118–25).

The similarities between ideas attributed to Epiphanius's Ebionites and the *Basic Writing* (including *Rec.* 1.27–71) include speculations about Christ's position over the angels (*Pan.* 30.3.4; 30.16.4; cf. *Rec.* 2.42.5; 1.45.1–2),[14] his pre-Christian appearances to Abraham and the patriarchs (*Pan.* 30.3.3; 30.3.5; *Rec.* 1.32.4–33.2; cf. *Hom.* 8.10), and speculations about Adam as a prophet and one that was anointed (*Pan.* 30.3.3,5; *Rec.* 4.9, par. *Hom.* 8.10; *Rec.* 1.47.1–4).[15] The Pseudo-Clementine *Basic Writing* also discusses food regulations and lustrations and forbids sharing meals with unbaptized Gentiles because of their impurity (*Rec.* 1.19.5 par. *Hom.* 1.22.5; *Rec.* 7.29.3–5 par. *Hom.* 13.4.3–5; *Rec.* 7.36.4 par. *Hom.* 13.11.4; cf. *Rec.* 2.71.2). According to Epiphanius, the Ebionites shared the same concerns, but their policy was even more stringent. They forbade the eating of meat altogether and did not want any physical contact with Gentiles under any circumstances. The *Basic Writing* also prohibits sexual intercourse during menstruation. In this regard, Epiphanius's Ebionites may have been more lenient, since they refer only to the obligation to wash after intercourse (*Pan.* 30.2.4). The fact that Epiphanius explicitly mentions baptism, in addition to the daily lustrations, as an Ebionite practice also finds a parallel in *Rec.* 1.39.2.

Theologically, the most significant similarities between the Ebionite ideas and the *Basic Writing* are Christ's criticism of the sacrificial cult and a rejection of the Prophets. In this regard, the Ebionites' position especially resembles the views presented in *Rec.* 1.27–71. Epiphanius quotes the list of the patriachs that the Ebionites accepted in *Pan.* 30.18.4: "They acknowledge Abraham, Isaac and Jacob, Moses and Aaron—and Joshua the son of Nun simply as Moses' successor, not as of any importance. But after these they acknowledge no more of the prophets. . . ." This corresponds to the salvation-historical story line depicted in *Rec.* 1.27–71. The positive part of the history from creation to Moses' death is closed with a reference to Joshua, who was nominated as the commander of the people by Moses (*Rec.* 1.38.1). A decline follows the death of Joshua, resulting in the building of the temple in the place of the house of prayer (1.38.4). In this salvation-historical scheme, there is no need for the Prophets because the coming of the True Prophet was sufficiently anticipated by Moses himself. The history continues by referring to the coming of the appropriate time when the True Prophet announced by Moses appeared (*Rec.* 1.39.1). Epiphanius undoubtedly found the scheme "from Moses to the True Prophet" in his Pseudo-Clementine sources, which must have been closely related to *Rec.* 1.27–71. Moreover, as we saw above, Epiphanius's Ebionites had also actively resorted to this scheme in debates about the validity of the Law and the Prophets.

The Ebionites' emphasis on the superiority of the gospel and Christ's revelation over Mosaic law also find parallels in *Rec.* 1.27–71, where one of the apostles, Bartholomew, argues for the superiority of Christ as follows: "For what Moses was, a prophet, Jesus is, too; but what Jesus is, the Christ, Moses is not. Thus, what Moses is, Jesus is, too, but what Jesus is, Moses was not" (*Rec.* 1.59.3). According to Bartholomew, there is no need of prophetic witness for Christ either: "For it is not right for one to receive faith in the greater and more excellent one through the witness of lesser ones. Rather, through the witness of the greater and more excellent one, one will know the lesser ones" (*Rec.* 1.59.6). The Ebionites' comments in the dispute quoted above ("Why do I need to read what is in the Law when the Gospel has come?" and "Christ has revealed this to me") are in full accord with these ideas.

Nevertheless, *Rec.* 1.27–71 also records views that are more conservative in regard to the Prophets. In particular, James the archbishop (Jesus' brother) points out that the Prophets are in agreement with the Law.

Furthermore, he recommends the Books of Kings and lists many proofs that show that Jesus was Christ and that he fulfilled everything predicted about him (*Rec.* 1.69.1–3). This view is clearly more irenic than the Ebionite interpretation of the history of salvation, which rejects the Prophets, focuses only on Moses, and submits even him to Christ.

At the same time, despite their arrogance toward the pentateuchal stories, the Ebionites seem to have been more outspoken regarding some indicators of Judaism than the community where *Rec.* 1.27–71 was produced. According to Epiphanius, for example, the Ebionites did not want to touch the Gentiles under any circumstances. In addition, the Ebionites called their meeting places "synagogues" and their leaders had the same titles as among other Jews. They also observed the Sabbath and practiced circumcision. These practices are not explicitly attested in *Rec.* 1.27–71.[16] These features too, then, indicate that *Rec.* 1.27–71, in its present form as part of the *Recognitions*, does not totally cohere with the views of Epiphanius's Ebionites.[17]

Despite the difference, there is such fundamental agreement among the Pseudo-Clementine sources (especially *Rec.* 1.27–71), the "Gospel of the Ebionites," and Epiphanius's description of the Ebionites that there has to be a connection between them. The idea that Jesus came to abolish the sacrifices and that the temple was destroyed because people were reluctant to cease sacrificing is unique within the early Christian tradition, making its appearance both in *Rec.* 1.27–71 and the "Gospel of the Ebionites" hardly coincidental (Bauckham 2003, 168). Epiphanius's Ebionites and *Rec.* 1.27–71 also share marked anti-Paulinism.

The Book of Elchasai and Elchasaite Missionaries

Epiphanius's description of the Ebionites' beliefs has similarities with the *Book of Elchasai*, and there is one point where he brings forth clear evidence for the Ebionites' actual use of the book:

> When one of them falls ill or is bitten by a snake, he gets into water and
> invokes the names in Elxai—heaven and earth, salt and water, winds

and "angels of righteousness" as they say, bread and oil—and begins to
say, "Help me, and rid me of my pain!" (*Pan.* 30.17.4)

The *Book of Elchasai* has not survived but its basic contents can be deduced from references in Hippolytus, Eusebius, and Epiphanius (for an
overview of the book, see Luttikhuizen 2005). It was originally Jewish,
probably written by a Mesopotamian Jew around 116 CE, during Trajan's
Parthian war. The book predicted an apocalyptic war in the near future,
"when three years of the reign of the emperor Trajan are again completed,"
and it promised that those who took an oath in front of seven witnesses not
to sin any more would be saved at the last judgment. The protection was
provided by a huge angel, whose measurements were given in detail. The
angel was connected to, or perhaps even named, the "Hidden Power" (*Pan.*
19.2.2; Aramaic *hayil kesai* > Elchasai). The huge angel-like figure was also
known as Christ and "Great King"—at least in the version that was available to Epiphanius—but Epiphanius was not able to say if the author was
referring to "our Lord Jesus Christ" or to someone else (*Pan.* 19.3.4). This
comment also indicates that there was nothing specifically Christian in the
contents of the book.

The Gerard Luttikhuizen, who has studied the *Book of Elchasai* extensively (Luttikhuizen 1985; 2005), argues that the book was later used by Transjordanian
and West-Syrian Jewish Christians, who applied the oaths and witnesses of
the book to their purification rites and baptism(s). We learn from Hippolytus
that one representative of this branch of Jewish Christianity was Alcibiades,
from Apamea in Syria, who preached in Rome around 230 CE. Similar "Elchasaite" Jewish-Christian missionaries were also known in Caesarea some ten
to twenty years later when Origen referred to them in his sermon on Psalm
82 (Eusebius, *Hist. eccl.* 6.38). Hippolytus's report on Alcibiades' activities suggests that the rites prescribed for those afflicted by diseases and animal bites
were not described in the *Book of Elchasai* itself, although the oaths of these
rites were sworn in the form—and in front of the witnesses—described in the
book. Obviously, their intention was to call forth the protection of the "Hidden
Power"/Christ. Alcibiades is said to have written instructions on how to use
the oaths, incantations, and lustrations of the book as remedies for major sins,
animal bites, and sicknesses (Hippolytus, *Haer.* 10.14.3–15.1).[18]

Epiphanius connects the *Book of Elchasai* to both the Transjordanian area and the area south and east of the Dead Sea, since this is where he locates the Ossaeans (*Pan.* 19), the Ebionites (*Pan.* 30), the Nazarenes (*Pan.* 29), and the Sampsaeans/Elkeseans (*Pan.* 53)—all of whom are said to have used the *Book of Elchasai*. Since Epiphanius was born in Palestine and had led a monastery there for three decades, it is not unwarranted to assume that he had some knowledge of the basic tenets of the Transjordanian religious movements. It is likely that some ideas derived from the *Book of Elchasai* were also circulating there among different syncretistic Jewish and Jewish-Christian (Ebionite) movements.[19] Furthermore, because the activity of Elchasaite Jewish-Christian missionaries is attested in Rome, Apamea (Alcibiades' hometown), and Caesarea, it seems natural that at some point the Ebionites in Cyprus were also familiarized with these practices. Ships regularly sailed from Cyprus to both Caesarea and Seleucia, the city from which the Apamean Alcibiades most probably embarked when he headed to Rome (cf. Acts 13:4-12; I will come back to this hypothesis at the conclusion of this section). Thus, the most plausible explanation for Epiphanius's use of the *Book of Elchasai* in his description of the Ebionites is that he acquired the book from the Ebionites in Cyprus, along with the Pseudo-Clementine sources (which he called the *Circuits of Peter* and the *Ascents of James*), the Ebionites' *Acts of Apostles* and (excerpts from) the Gospel used by the Ebionites.

Several pieces of data indicate that the Elchasaite missionaries resembled the traditional Irenaean picture of the Ebionites more than Epiphanius's Ebionites did. According to Origen (according to Eusebius, *Hist. eccl.* 6.38), the Elchasaites were anti-Pauline and made *selective* use of every part of the Old Testament and the Gospels. Irenaeus's Ebionites were also famous for their anti-Paulinism, and such "selective use" of the Old Testament might go a way toward explaining his characterization of their interpretation of the Prophets as "careful/curious" (see Irenaeus, *Haer.* 1.26.2). Selective use of the Gospels may also indicate that the Elchasaites were using a Gospel harmony comparable to the "Gospel of the Ebionites." Hippolytus, for his part, states that Alcibiades, the Elchasaite missionary in Rome, required men to be circumcised and to live according to the law. He also taught that Christ was born like all the other men (in conjunction with his Adam christology; Hippolytus, *Haer.* 9.14.1). Undoubtedly, on the basis of these beliefs alone—if he had not made use of the *Book of Elchasai*—Alcibiades would have been as easily called an Ebionite. We also learn from Epiphanius that the *Book of Elchasai* ordered all people to turn their faces to Jerusalem while praying (*Pan.* 19.3.5). This practice was already connected to the Ebionites by Irenaeus.

Although none of these descriptions matches Irenaeus's description of the Ebionites in every detail, it is possible to see in them the central Ebionite ideas dispersed among the various representatives of the Elchasaite missionary movement. This justifies the hypothesis that the Jewish *Book of Elchasai* was received by some "traditional Ebionites" who adopted some new ideas from it and initiated a relatively extensive missionary activity, traces of which can be found both in Rome and in Caesarea. In these cities they had no success—apparently because other forms of Christianity had the upper hand—but they were welcomed by other Jewish-Christian communities that had "heretical" views about the Jewish canon of scriptures (Epiphanius's Ebionites).

The Profile of Epiphanius's Ebionites

In the last analysis, the extent to which the Ebionites really agreed with all that was written in the literature Epiphanius received from them remains an open question. Nonetheless, the substantial agreement between Epiphanius's contemporary information about the Ebionites and the information paralleled in their literature enables us to draw an overall picture of the Ebionites' religious profile.

On the one hand, the Jewish Christianity of Epiphanius's Ebionites is characterized by adherence to customs that traditionally have been boundary markers between Jews and Gentiles: circumcision, purity laws and Jewish institutions (synagogue, leadership, marriage). On the other hand, their ideology and interpretation of scriptures had features that were more Samaritan than Judean in nature, and they had adopted rites and incantations based on the revelation of a "Hidden Power" whom they probably interpreted as the Christian Christ, but who is not attested in the scriptures that "mainstream" Judaism and Christianity had begun to regard as authoritative by the end of the fourth century.

The profound character of the break with Jewish traditions represented by the Ebionites' attitude toward the temple and sacrificial cult has perhaps not always been fully recognized by scholars. Epiphanius's Ebionites did not simply criticize the performers or performance of the temple cult but considered the cult itself only a temporary arrangement made because Moses was not able to root out all at once the people's inclination to sacrifices. For this reason, Moses announced the coming of a prophet who would complete the task. If, as Epiphanius reports, the Ebionites portrayed James as attacking the temple cult, this also surely implies a radical reinterpretation of traditions connected to him: James "the Just" is usually depicted as one who frequently visited the temple, and who was held in high esteem among his Jewish compatriots (Eusebius, *Hist. eccl.* 2.23).

A clear indicator of the Christian character of the Ebionites' doctrine is the central role attributed to the "eternal Christ" (*Rec.* 1.43.1). Indeed Adam, the patriarchs, and Moses have earned their place in the history only through his authority and his presence with them. Christian baptism also had a key role in their religious system, since it was instituted to replace sacrifices. At the same time, the Ebionites' rejection of sacrifices probably also had larger implications for their christology and their interpretation of the Eucharist. This kind of theology would seem to exclude any reference to Jesus' sacrificial death in the Eucharist.[20] This is very much in line with the fact that they only used water in their eucharistic meals: since the Ebionites found blood abhorrent, they paid more attention to purifications with water in their religious rites. The Ebionites' Christ, in sum, was a pre-existent divine being, but he did not come to the world to sacrifice himself or to give his life as a ransom for many. Instead, he had a prophetic task.[21]

From Irenaeus's Ebionites to Epiphanius's Ebionites?

The name "Ebionites" as an obvious self-description, anti-Paulinism, and reverence for Jerusalem are the three features that most clearly connect Epiphanius's Ebionites to the earlier Irenaean tradition about the Ebionites. There also seems to be a significant point of contact with respect to specific ritual practice. Because sacrifices were abhorrent to Epiphanius's Ebionites, we have every reason to accept his report that they celebrated the Eucharist with unleavened bread and water only. This practice is not unique in early Christianity, but it certainly is distinctive and coheres with Irenaeus's report that the Ebionites "reject the commixture of the heavenly wine and wish it to be water of the world only" (Irenaeus, *Haer.* 5.1.3; trans. Klijn and Reinink 1973).[22]

There are also, however, a number of features in the religious profile of Epiphanius's Ebionites that are not included in the earlier reports. Were such features simply not mentioned by earlier heresiologists, or were they in fact peculiar to the form of the Ebionite movement known to Epiphanius? To what extent do they suggest significant development in Ebionite belief and practice in the centuries between Irenaeus and Epiphanius?

Among the new features found in Epiphanius's account, for example, are speculations about Christ's preexistence (*Pan.* 30.16.3), his being created and set over the angels (*Pan.* 30.3.4; 30.16.4), and his pre-Christian appearances in and to Adam and the patriarchs (*Pan.* 30.3.3; 30.3.5). Although these kinds of ideas are not explicitly attested in earlier descriptions of the Ebionites, they do have a certain consistency with the basic tenets of the christology of the Irenaean Ebionites. Irenaeus's description implied that the Ebionites' view of Christ was *similar to* that of Cerinthus and Carpocrates.[23] That would mean that, in the Ebionite view, Christ entered Jesus in (or after) baptism. It is precisely these beliefs that we meet in Epiphanius's Ebionites, only in a more elaborate form: Christ took on Jesus' body, but this was not the first time he had done such a thing; he had in fact done the same thing several times in the course of history.

A number of differences, however, seem much more significant. The oaths and magical incantations attested in the *Book of Elchasai* and in the rites that the Ebionites themselves performed together with the christological speculations lend Epiphanius's Ebionites a more syncretistic outlook when compared to the earlier heresiologists' views. Moreover, Epiphanius's Ebionites' rejection of the temple and sacrifices as well as the Prophets represents not only, as noted above, a clear break with Jewish traditions; it is also the most significant feature that does not cohere with the Irenaean tradition about the Ebionites. The key question here is whether, in spite of this break, the Epiphanian Ebionites can still be regarded as representatives of the same movement that Irenaeus attacked two centuries earlier. It is hard to believe that all the similarities would be incidental results from the judaizing tendencies of two unrelated Christian groups. Are we then to assume a development from Irenaeus's Ebionites to Epiphanius's Ebionites?

In general, religious movements are rather conservative in their attitude toward scriptures honored in their tradition. If necessary, new scriptures may be adopted and old ones updated, reedited, and reinterpreted, but they are seldom discarded if they have, at some point, reached a highly valued position. This kind of patching characterizes human cognition in general: rather than starting all over from scratch, new information is integrated into the existing cognitive structures and old structures are modified only to the extent necessary.[24] Therefore, it is hard to believe that a community that had interpreted the Prophets "carefully" or "curiously"—as Irenaeus's Ebionites did (*curiosius exponere* [Irenaeus, *Haer.* 1.26.2])—would suddenly have dropped them and resorted only to the use of the Pentateuch. Another type of development is more believable. The Jewish-Christian profile of Epiphanius's Ebionites would be a predictable result of the reception of Christian missionaries by Jews (or Samaritans) whose religious canon consisted mainly (or only) of the Pentateuch. If inclined toward the Christian message, they might accept Christ as the prophet predicted by Moses but would probably be less willing to enlarge their collection of scriptures if the understanding of the new message did not require it.

According to Acts, the Hellenists of the early Jerusalem community commenced a missionary activity among the Samaritans after the execution of Stephen (Acts 8:4-7; 11:19-20). If this activity really resulted in conversions among the Samaritans (as is indicated in Acts), then the religious profile of these "Samaritan-Hellenistic" Christians would be likely to resemble the profile of Epiphanius's Ebionites[25]—even more so if these Hellenists also understood themselves as "poor"[26] and hated Paul not only because of his liberal interpretation of the law but because he had been involved with the execution of Stephen (Acts 7:57—8:1). Thus, we may have to reckon with the possibility that, from very early on, there may have been at least two types of Ebionites: (1) Hebrew/Aramaic-speaking Ebionites (= Irenaeus's Ebionites?)

who shared James the Just's positive attitude toward the temple, used only Matthew's Gospel, and accepted all the prophets; and (2) Hellenistic-Samaritan Ebionites (= Epiphanius's Ebionites) who totally rejected worship in the temple, used only the Pentateuch, and, carrying with them the memory of Stephen's execution, perceived Paul as one of their major opponents.

In the last analysis, Epiphanius—the great *doctor confusus* of early church history—may have been on the right track when he concluded that the Ebionites of his day had adopted their ideas from the Samaritans and from a certain Elchasai. Whatever the real history of Epiphanius's Ebionites, it is perfectly clear that, in Epiphanius's view, they had adopted ideas that showed them to have strayed away not only from correct Christian doctrine but also from what he considered genuinely Jewish traditions.

Epiphanius's Ebionites had such a clear and independent Jewish-Christian profile that they must have distanced themselves from other Christian communities as well as from other Jewish communities. They thus represent an independent branch of *Jewish Christianity*. At the same time, their Jewish-Christian profile appears to be so unique that it raises the question whether they should also be given a name of their own. Because they seem to have called themselves Ebionites, it would be natural to call them simply Epiphanius's Ebionites in order to keep in mind that they differed considerably from the Ebionites known to earlier church fathers. Another possibility would be to call them Samaritan-Elchasaite Christians. In any case, it seems that to label these Ebionites simply as Jewish Christians would not do justice to some of their very distinctive beliefs.

Epiphanius's Nazarenes[27]

Epiphanius was able to provide an explanation for the genesis of the Ebionite movement he was familiar with by assuming that Ebion, whom he imagined to be the founder of the heresy, must have been a Samaritan and that his movement must have been influenced by Elchasai later on. Nevertheless, he was faced with yet one more problem: How to account for the earlier descriptions of the Ebionites? According to earlier church fathers, the Ebionites did not have such peculiar ideas and practices as the Ebionites of his day. Furthermore, in order to defend his interpretation of Christian doctrine, Epiphanius would also have to deal with the more conventional form of the Jewish-Christian heresy so that no one would be deluded by teachers who were not quite as strange as his own Ebionites, but still tried to combine Christianity with Judaism in an inappropriate way. Epiphanius found a lacuna to be filled in his history of the heresies. He filled it with the Nazarenes.

When Epiphanius started to write his history of "Jewish-Christian" heresy before the time of Ebion, he had two major problems to solve. The first problem was what to call the earliest phase of the heresy. Because the ideas of "earlier Ebionites" were quite different from the contemporary ones, it was necessary to have a special name for them. This would enable him to devote a separate chapter to them in the *Panarion,* including a refutation of their typical beliefs. In Epiphanius's own historical setting, the term "Ebionites" was so closely attached to the movement that was also active in Cyprus that he was not able to change their name. Therefore, it was the earlier phase of the Jewish-Christian movement that needed to be renamed. The second problem was that he did not have any sources available because his predecessors had only dealt with the Ebionites. He only had his creative imagination and two descriptions of the earliest phases of Christianity: Acts and Eusebius's *Ecclesiastical History.*

Epiphanius knew from his predecessor's writings (Tertullian, *Marc.* 4.8; *Onom.* p. 138, 24–25) and from Acts that, at the outset, all Christians were called Nazarenes. However, Acts 24:5 also suggested to him that in the time of the apostles, there was also a "heresy of the Nazarenes" because the high priest Ananias's attorney, Tertullus, accused Paul of being the leader of this group. Epiphanius makes it clear that, in reality, Paul had no part in this heresy. The application of the title "leader of the heresy of the Nazarenes" to Paul illustrated the malice of his Jewish opponents, and Paul accepted the name Nazarene only because it had also been borne by Jesus himself (*Pan.* 29.6.3). Epiphanius must have concluded from this information that the term "Nazarenes" would be the most appropriate name for the first schismatic Christians (on this, see also the beginning of the next section).

I have elsewhere presented in detail the evidence that shows that Epiphanius's description of the genesis of the sect of the Nazarenes and their central beliefs is based on his creative use of Eusebius's *Ecclesiastical History* and Acts (Luomanen 2005a). In the present context, there is only space for a summary of the essential points of the evidence.

A comparision of *Pan.* 29 with Eusebius's *Ecclesiastical History* and Acts reveals that Epiphanius explicitly quotes these two descriptions of the earliest phases of the Christian movement at a number of points. His dependence on Eusebius's *Ecclesiastical History* is clear at least when he discusses Mark's preaching in Egypt (*Pan.* 29.5.4; cf. *Hist. eccl.* 2.16); Philo's Thereapeutae (*Pan.* 29.5.1–3; cf. *Hist. eccl.* 2.17); James as the first bishop (*Pan.* 29.4.1–4; cf. *Hist. eccl.* 2.23); and the flight from Jerusalem (*Pan.* 29.7.8; cf. *Hist. eccl.* 3.5.3). He also explicitly refers to Acts several times: Jesus was called a Nazarene (*Pan.* 29.5.6; *Pan.* 29.6.7; cf. Acts 2:22); the Apostolic Decree (*Pan.* 29.8.6; cf. Acts 15:28-29); the "leader" of the Nazarenes (*Pan.* 29.6.2; cf. Acts 24:5); Paul's "Nazarene confession" (*Pan.* 29.6.4; cf. Acts 24:12-14).

A more detailed comparison also reveals that when Epiphanius makes an attempt to determine the beginning of the heresy more precisely, he is using the same vocabulary as Acts 15:24 when it refers to the activity of conservative Jewish Christians who came from Jerusalem and caused confusion in Antioch:

> for a short time after the Savior's ascension and after Mark had preached in Egypt, some again seceded [*tines exelēlythasi palin*]. They were called the followers of the apostles, indeed, but I think that they were the Nazarenes whom I am describing here. They are Jews by birth and they dedicate themselves to the law and submit to circumcision. (*Pan.* 29.5.4; my translation)

> Since we have heard that some [*tines*] of us have come [*exelthontes*, literally "went out"] and confused you. . . . (Acts 15:24)

Even more important is the observation that the wording in Epiphanius's description of the actual "conversion" of the Nazarenes is influenced by Acts' story about the conversion of one of the first Christian heretics, Simon Magus:

> When they heard Jesus' name and *saw the* divine *signs that happened through the hands of the apostles they* also *believed* in Jesus. (*Pan.* 29.5.6; my translation)

> *Simon* also *believed* and was baptized . . . and when *he saw the signs* and great miracles *that happened* he was amazed . . . and when he saw that *through* the laying on *the hands of the apostles*. . . . (Acts 8:13, 18)

Many scholars have also found marked similarities between Epiphanius's description of the doctrines of the Nazarenes and Acts' picture of the teaching of the early Jerusalem community. Some scholars (Pritz 1988; de Boer 1998) have interpreted these similarities as evidence of the Nazarenes' historical connection to the early Jerusalem community.

> One need make only a quick comparison with the opening chapters of Acts to see that these basic doctrines had a place in the teaching of the earliest Jerusalem church: the resurrection of the dead (Acts 2:24, 32; 3:15; 4:10); God is the creator of all things (4:24); and belief in one God and his child (*pais*) Jesus Christ (3:13, 26; 4:27, 30). To this point we do not have anything that would differentiate the Nazarene church from the primitive church. (Pritz 1988, 44)

This line of reasoning, however, is problematic in two respects. First, from a historical point of view, it is clear that Acts presents Luke's interpretation of the life and doctrines of the early Jerusalem community. Therefore, if there is a perfect match between *Pan.* 29.7.3 and Acts, it is questionable how much this reveals about the Nazarenes' relation to the early Jerusalem community. Second, in the light of Epiphanius's use of Acts as a source for *Pan.* 29, it is more believable that the similarities are there because Epiphanius picked them up from Acts.

Besides Eusebius's *Ecclesiastical History* and Acts, Epiphanius seems to have had no sources from which he could have derived information about the Nazarenes. His intention was to provide a prehistory for the Ebionites who were his contemporaries, and he accomplished this by tracing evidence of the activities and beliefs of conservative Jewish Christians in Acts and in Eusebius's *Ecclesiastical History*. However, there was a thing that the *doctor confusus* was not sure about: whether or not the Nazarenes would have believed in the virginal conception (*Pan.* 29.7.6). Epiphanius's ignorance in this matter causes serious difficulties for those scholars who think that the Nazarenes were a clearly definable sect in their own right, and that they differed from the Ebionites precisely because of their belief in the virginal conception.

The Jewish-Christian profile Epiphanius created for the Nazarenes is perfect in the sense that it combines exemplary Jewish features with exemplary Christian characteristics, derived directly from the early Jerusalem community. In contrast to the Ebionites, who rejected the Prophets and part of the Pentateuch, the Nazarenes "use not only the New Testament but the Old Testament as well, as the Jews do. For unlike the previous sectarians [Jewish sects in the *Panarion*], they do not repudiate the legislation, the prophets, and the books Jews call 'Writings'" (*Pan.* 29.7.2). He summarizes their position as follows: "They are different from Jews, and different from Christians, only in the following. They disagree with Jews because they have come to faith in Christ; but since they are still fettered by the Law—circumcision, the Sabbath, and the rest—they are not in accord with Christians" (*Pan.* 29.7.5). This short characterization would function as a simple definition of Jewish Christianity for modern scholars as well. It is no wonder because this is what Epiphanius was aiming at: a description of Jewish Christianity in its simplest, stereotypic form. With a picture like this, it was easy to condemn all the attempts to mix Christianity with characteristically Jewish practices and ideas: "In this section, too, my brief discussion will be enough. People like these are refutable at once and easy to cure—or rather, they are nothing but Jews themselves" (*Pan.* 29.9.1).

Social psychologists have long known the importance of stereotypes in the creation and maintenance of social identities. Recently, Philip Esler has fruitfully applied these insights—the so-called *social identity approach*[28]— to the study of Paul's letters (Esler 1998; 2003). Heresiologies are also perfect objects for such sociocognitive analyses, since they were written and used precisely for the kinds of purposes that the social identity approach is designed to expose: categorization of outgroups, accentuation of differences between the ingroup and the outgroups, and the search for subjective cognitive coherence. Epiphanius's Nazarenes are a prime example of an identity-building stereotype that has very little to do with reality but perfectly serves border marking and the building of a positive group identity.

JEROME'S NAZARENES

In *Pan.* 29, Epiphanius devotes an enormous amount of energy and space to a discussion of the kinds of names that were applied to the first Christians: how the heretical Nazarenes differed from the "orthodox" Nazarenes; how the term "Nazarene" is not to be confused with the Nazirites or with the pre-Christian sect of the Nasoreans; and that, besides Nazarenes, the Christians were for a short while also called Iessaeans.[29] These terminological clarifications indicate that the term "Nazarenes" was not commonly used as a title of "heretical" Jewish Christians before Epiphanius wrote his *Panarion*. However, once the point of reference for the term "Nazarenes" was fixed in the *Panarion*, it worked very well among Greek and Latin-speaking Christians because no contemporary, "orthodox" Christian group bore that name in Latin or Greek. After Epiphanius, several authors in the West used the term, but usually referring to Jewish-Christians in general, so that it became synonymous with "Ebionites." Yet we know that before and after Epiphanius in the East, the cognates of the term Nazarenes were commonly used to denote Christians in general among Syrians, Arabs, Persians, and Armenians.[30] It follows that, once we move over to the sphere of Semitic Christianity in the East, we have to reckon with the possibility that the term "Nazarenes" was used to denote Christians whose beliefs and practices were not clearly "heretical." As a matter of fact, it seems that Jerome's Nazarenes provide an example of one such group.

Jerome was born in Stridon in 347 or 348 CE. He had Christian parents and he received his education in Rome. He made his first trip to the East in 372. Originally he had planned to go to Jerusalem, but illness prolonged his stay in Antioch and finally made him give up the plan. Instead, he tried the life of a monk in Beroea (374/375–377). Most scholars assume that if Jerome really met Nazarenes, whose Gospel he started to quote ten years later, it must have happened here. Jerome returned to Rome in 383 in the company of two bishops: Epiphanius, with whom he stayed in regular contact afterwards, and Paulinus. After the death of Pope Damasus in 384, Jerome entertained hopes of becoming his successor. However, he was not elected and he headed again to Jerusalem, where he arrived in 385. After a short trip to Alexandria, Jerome settled in Bethelem in 386. He founded a monastery and spent the rest of his life there.[31]

Jerome's information about the Nazarenes can be classified into three main categories: (1) quotations from a Gospel used by them; (2) occasional references to Nazarene beliefs and practices in connection with the treatment of other topics, as in his letter to Augustine; and (3) explicit descriptions of Nazarene biblical exegesis in Jerome's *Commentary on Isaiah*.

The "Gospel of the Nazarenes"

In his *Illustrious Men*, Jerome boasts that the Nazarenes gave him an opportunity to make a copy of the "original" Hebrew text of the Gospel of Matthew:

> The Hebrew itself has been preserved until the present day in the library at Caesarea which Pamphilius the martyr so diligently collected. From the Nazoreans who use this book in Beroia, a city of Syria, I also received the opportunity to copy it. (*Vir. ill.* 3; trans. Klijn and Reinink 1973)

At first glance, these references seem to give an eyewitness report of a Hebrew Gospel. However, the number of quotations Jerome actually presents in his writings is very limited, and it can be proved that some of them were in fact gleaned from the writings of his predecessors (Origen in particular). Therefore, scholars have long thought that, in practice, Jerome was working with fragments of Jewish-Christian Gospels, only some of which derived from Syrian Christians living in the neighborhood of Beroea. The reconstruction of the "Gospel of the Nazarenes" thus requires that the "genuine" quotations be picked out from materials of very diverse origin. In my own analysis of the fragments, I have argued that Jerome received from the Nazarenes only a collection of anti-rabbinic passages from the Gospel of Matthew. The style and content of these passages closely resembled the passages quoted from the Nazarenes' *Isaiah Commentary*. Nevertheless, Jerome's references to the Gospel that was used by the Nazarenes are not very fruitful in a discussion about the Nazarenes' religious profile because most of the remarks are very brief and contain very little information about the practices and beliefs of the people who transmitted these materials. Since the reconstruction is hypothetical and does not add much to the information that can be gained from the Nazarenes' *Isaiah Commentary*, I will not discuss the details of the "Gospel of the Nazarenes" here.[32]

From our point of view, it is important to note that, although Jerome exaggerated the amount and quality of materials he received from the Nazarenes, scholars largely agree that he did have some connections with Christians in the vicinity of Beroea. It also seems clear that these Christians were called Nazarenes. The crucial question is what kind of Nazarenes these were. Were they the kind of "heretical" Jewish Christians that Epiphanius had sketched in his *Panarion*? Or were they simply Christians who spoke a Semitic language and were therefore regarded as "outsiders" by the western fathers? The character of these Nazarenes can be best assessed on the basis of their exegesis of Isaiah. But before moving to that evidence, I will first look briefly at one of Jerome's more general references to the "Nazarenes." This reference has often been regarded—erroneously, in my view—as crucial evidence for the Nazarenes' doctrines.

Jerome's Letter to Augustine

Compared to Epiphanius, Jerome's attitude toward Christians called Nazarenes is much more positive. His critical comments are usually aimed at Ebion and the Ebionites; but on one occasion he does seem to criticize the Nazarenes. This is in his letter to Augustine in 404 CE, in which he attacks Augustine's interpretation of Paul's and Peter's conflict in Antioch (cf. Gal 2).

> If this [i.e., Augustine's interpretation] is true, we shall fall into the heresy of Cerinthus and Hebion, who believe in Christ and for this only have been anathematized by the fathers, because they mixed the cer-

emonies of the Law with the Gospel of Christ and in this way they confess new things while they did not cut loose from the old. What shall I say of the Ebionites who claim to be Christians? Until now a heresy is to be found in all parts of the East where Jews have their synagogues; it is called "of the Minaeans" and cursed by Pharisees up to now. Usually they are named Nazoreans. They believe in Christ, the Son of God born of Mary the virgin, and they say about him that he suffered and rose again under Pontius Pilate, in whom also we believe, but since they want to be both Jews and Christians, they are neither Jews nor Christians. (Jerome, *Epist.* 112.13; trans. Klijn and Reinink, 1973)

This quotation is the only place where one might see an explicit reference to the Nazarenes' belief in virginal conception. However, scholars who draw such conclusions about the Nazarenes on the basis of this passage seldom pay attention to its overall context and, more specifically, to the way Jerome develops his case against Augustine. First, it is to be kept in mind that Jerome's overriding interest is to confute Augustine's interpretation of the Antioch incident. Jerome's and Augustine's disputation had a long and complicated prehistory, and Jerome's reputation as a biblical scholar was at stake.[33] His aim is to confute Augustine, not to describe the details of the doctrine of the Nazarenes. Second, it is clear that the terms "Ebionites," "Minaeans," and "Nazarenes" are used interchangeably in this passage. Jerome does not make any distinction between the Ebionites and the Nazarenes, but seems to use both terms as titles for Jewish Christians in general. It is probable that the term "Nazarenes" was added to the passage only because this title, together with the term "Minaeans," appeared in the "curse" of the Jewish *Eighteen Benedictions* prayer.[34] Jerome wanted to show that Augustine's position is "cursed," but because "Ebionites" are not mentioned in the prayer, he has to bundle the Ebionites together with the Minaeans and the Nazarenes. Third, the reference to virginal conception appears to be part of a quotation from an early Christian creed. Thus, this passage does not necessarily have anything to do with specifically Nazarene doctrine (if there even was one—which I doubt). Jerome only quotes the creed in order to make clear that even if one has the correct doctrine but tries to combine Christianity with Judaism (as Augustine does, in Jerome's view), he is cursed. Therefore, one should not build any concept of the character of the Nazarenes on this passage.

Exegesis of Isaiah

In his *Commentary on Isaiah*, Jerome presents several passages from the Nazarenes' exposition of the Book of Isaiah. In contrast to Epiphanius's musings about the "Nazarenes" in *Panarion* (29), these passages offer a glimpse of the views of Christians who certainly were called Nazarenes.

One thing immediately stands out from these passages: the Nazarenes fiercely opposed the rabbinic movement. The criticism and slander are so obvious that there is no doubt that the Nazarene communities were separated from synagogues that were more or less connected to the rabbinic movement. According to the Nazarenes' commentary,

> Shammai then and Hillel were born not long before the Lord, they originated in Judea. The name of the first means scatterer and of the second unholy, because he scattered and defiled the precepts of the Law by his traditions and *deuterōseis*. And these are the two houses who did not accept the Saviour who has become to them destruction and shame. (*Comm. Isa.* 8.11–15 [interpretation of Isa 8:11-15]; trans. Klijn and Reinink 1973)

The quotations also indicate that the Nazarenes were versed in Semitic languages (Aramaic and Hebrew in particular), which suggests that they may have been Jewish converts (Luomanen 2005a, 302–4). This raises the question about their Jewish-Christian profile. In addition to language and (possible) pedigree, are there also other indicators of their Judaism?

In his commentary, Jerome introduces the Nazarenes as the ones "who accept Christ in such a way that they do not cease to observe the old Law" (*Comm. Isa.* 8.11). What exactly this means is unclear. How Jewish would the Nazarenes had to have been, and which parts of the Jewish law would they have had to obey, in order to become classified as ones who "do not cease to follow the Law"? Given Jerome's anti-Semitic bias, the degree of Jewishness need not have been very high. Compared to the bulk of the information about the Ebionites, it is interesting to note how unreservedly Jerome's Nazarenes accepted Paul.

> The Nazoreans whose opinion I have set forth above, try to explain this passage [Isa 9:1] in the following way: When Christ came and his preaching shone out, the land of Zebulun and the land of Naphtali first of all were freed from the errors of the Scribes and the Pharisees and he shook off their shoulders the very heavy yoke of the Jewish traditions. Later, however, the preaching became more dominant, that means the preaching was multiplied, through the Gospel of the apostle Paul who was the last of all the apostles. And the Gospel of Christ shone to the most distant tribes and the way of the whole sea. Finally the whole world which earlier walked or sat in darkness and was imprisoned in the bonds of idolatry and death, has seen the clear light of the gospel. (*Comm. Isa.* 9.1; trans. Klijn and Reinink 1973)

In my opinion, this acceptance of Paul indicates that the Nazarenes did not strictly follow Jewish laws and customs.

The total rejection of Jewish traditions can be seen also in the following passage, which equates the following of the traditions with a Gentile nation's worship of idols:

> For the rest the Nazoreans explain the passage [Isa 8:19-22] in this way: When the Scribes and the Pharisees tell you to listen to them, men who do everything for the love of the belly and who hiss during their incantations in the way of the magicians in order to deceive you, you must answer them like this. It is not strange if you follow your traditions since every tribe consults his own idols. We must not, therefore, consult your dead about the living ones. On the contrary God has given us the Law and the testimonies of the scriptures. If you are not willing to follow them you shall not have light, and darkness will always oppress you. (*Comm. Isa.* 8.19-22; trans. Klijn and Reinink 1973)

The last passage that Jerome quotes also targets the nonbelieving Israelites as a whole, not just the scribes and the Pharisees as their leaders:[35]

> The Nazoreans understand this passage [Isa 31:6-9] in this way: O sons of Israel who deny the Son of God with a most vicious opinion, turn to him and his apostles. For if you will do this, you will reject all idols which to you were a cause of sin in the past and the devil will fall before you, not because of your powers, but because of the compassion of God. And his young men who a certain time earlier fought for him, will be the tributaries of the Church and any of its power and stone will pass. Also the philosophers and every perverse dogma will turn their backs to the sign of the cross. Because this is the meaning of the Lord that his will take place, whose fire or light is in Sion and his oven in Jerusalem. (*Comm. Isa.* 31.6–9; trans. Klijn and Reinink 1973)

This passage reveals a viewpoint that is nothing short of the formative Catholic view: the Jews are expected to convert and accept the apostolic faith. In order to do so, they will have to abandon their worship of idols, which, as shown above, is equated with Jewish traditions. Consequently, the young men of Israel, who earlier had fought with the devil against the Christians, will become tributaries of the church. Finally, the conclusion of the passage also indicates that, despite its sharp criticism of the scribes and the Pharisees, the Nazarenes' exposition was also attacking the "philosophers" and other "perverse dogmas." Thus, the Nazarenes guarded their dogmatic frontiers much like the church fathers themselves: against the nonbelieving Jews as well as against Gentile philosophies.

A remarkable parallel to the Nazarenes' position can be found in the *Didascalia Apostolorum* (*DA*), which confirms that the Nazarenes' interpretation exemplified a typically Syrian attitude toward the early rabbis.[36] *Didascalia Apostolorum* makes a clear distinction between the First Law that binds the Christians (Moses' Ten Commandments) and the Second Legislation (*deuterōsis*; cf. *deuterōseis* in Jerome, *Comm. Isa.* 8.11–15) with which the Jews were bound after they had fallen into idol worship (Exodus 32). Consequently, obedience to this Second Legislation is equated with *idol worship* and described as a *heavy burden* and a *hard yoke* in contrast to the First Law, which is described as a *light yoke* and equated with the *"Law and the Prophets,"* which Jesus has come to fulfill according to Matt 5:17.[37] Obviously, Jerome's Nazarenes and the *Didascalia Apostolorum* had a similar view of the Second Legislation.

The Profile of Jerome's Nazarenes

In light of Jerome's passages and similar views presented in the *Didascalia Apostolorum*, it is difficult to picture Jerome's Nazarenes as a strict, law-observant sect separated from the formative Catholic church. The Christians from whom Jerome received the expositions unreservedly accepted Paul and his mission to the Gentiles. They also leveled criticism at the Jewish nation and people as a whole. The Jews were required to repent/convert, and this did not presuppose the maintenance of a particular Jewish identity or aim at the reestablishment of a traditional Jewish covenantal relationship, as one would expect if a person who still had a Jewish self-understanding repented. Instead, the Jews were expected to adopt a Christian identity by becoming subjects of the apostles.

Overall, Jerome's Nazarenes—as far as their beliefs can be reconstructed from their exegesis of Isaiah—exemplify such clear Christian self-understanding that I would not label them Jewish Christian. The sole basis for doing so would be the fact that they were versed in Semitic languages and might have been ethnic Jews. Jerome's Nazarenes clearly sided with Catholic Christianity; nothing of the idea of a *tertium quid* between Jews and (other believing) Christians, which seems to characterize the ideology of the Pseudo-Clementine *Basic Writing*, can be found in Jerome's Nazarenes (see Jones 2005, 329–32; and in the present volume chapter eleven, esp. pp. 288-97). These Nazarenes may simply have been *Syriac Christians* who perhaps had some sympathy toward Judaism—enough to render them suspicious in the eyes of the overtly anti-Jewish Jerome and his compatriots—but who no doubt felt themselves to be Christian, and thus should be classified as such by modern critics.

CONCLUSION

Historians are always faced with the challenge of bridging the gap between present and ancient realities. This cannot be reasonably accomplished without using concepts that are—at least provisionally—understandable to modern readers. In this regard, the concept of Jewish Christianity fares relatively well, since most people today have some sort of idea what "Judaism" and "Christianity" are about and what the "mixture" of these categories might involve. Things become problematic only if these kinds of provisional ideas—whether of a scholarly nature or common sense—are not adjusted and refined according to the object of study.

In this chapter, the category of Jewish Christianity was qualified by drawing attention to the indicators of Jewish Christianity in the groups that the church fathers had labeled Ebionite and Nazarene. The discussion revealed a variety of Jewish Christianities even here.

The Jewish Christianity of Irenaeus's Ebionites involved obedience to Jewish laws (including circumcision), anti-Paulinism, rejection of Jesus' virginal conception, reverence for Jeruselem (direction of prayer), use of Matthew's Gospel, Eucharist with water, and possibly the idea that Christ/Spirit entered Jesus at his baptism. Irenaeus's Ebionites are not easy to locate because Irenaeus wrote in the West (Lyons) and was unlikely to have had personal contacts with the Ebionites. Thus his characterization probably reflects only the literary,[38] western view of the Ebionites at the end of the second century.

Some two hundred years later, the Jewish Christianity of Epiphanius's Ebionites was characterized by similar basic ideas and practices: obedience to Jewish laws, anti-Paulinism, reverence for Jerusalem, Eucharist with water, and distinction between Jesus and the Spirit/Christ who entered him at baptism. These similarities suggest a connection between Irenaeus's and Epiphanius's Ebionites. However, the explicit rejection of the temple and its cult, the idea of the True Prophet and the (selective) acceptance of the Pentateuch only, show that Epiphanius's Ebionites were not direct successors of Irenaeus's Ebionites. Because it is not easy to picture a linear development from Irenaeus's Ebionties to Epiphanius's Ebionites, and because the Samaritans seem to link Epiphanius's Ebionites with the Hellenists of the early Jerusalem community, I am inclined to assume that Epiphanius's Ebionites were in fact successors of the Hellenistic "poor" of the early Jerusalem community, and that Irenaeus's Ebionites were successors of the Hebrews (see Acts 6–8) of the same community. The common connection to the Jerusalem community would thus explain the similarities.

The Jewish-Christian profile of the Elchasaite missionaries as they were described by Origen and Hippolytus would cohere with the assumption that these missionaries were originally "ordinary" Ebionites (of the Irenaean type) who had adopted a Jewish apocalyptic book and interpreted its "Great power" as the Christian Christ. On the other hand, the *Book of Elchasai* was also adopted by the Epiphanian Ebionites. Both types of Ebionites were accepting of the message of the book because of their interest in water rites and the distinction they made between Christ and Jesus.

The religious profile of Epiphanius's Nazarenes was ingeniously developed by the church father himself because he also needed a category of pure "Jewish Christianity" in his *Panarion*. The Ebionites of his day had too many peculiar beliefs and practices to serve as the only example of a "heresy" that tried to combine Judaism with Christianity.

Jerome had probably learned from Epiphanius that Christians who were "too Jewish" could also be called Nazarenes. Nevertheless, the profile of Jerome's own Nazarenes remains fuzzy. On the one hand, he used the term interchangeably with "Ebionites," referring to Jewish Christians in general. On the other hand, he had met Syriac Christians who were called "Nazarenes" and had acquired from them two anti-rabbinic collections: explanations of some chapters of Isaiah and a hand-picked collection of anti-rabbinic passages from the Gospel of Matthew. Judging from the basis of these collections, the religious profile of Jerome's Nazarenes includes mainly Christian elements. The Nazarenes had a clear Christian self-understanding and were pro-Pauline. Thus, they differed considerably from both branches of the Ebionites. Since the Nazarenes used Hebrew/Aramaic Gospels and their commentaries involved wordplays with Hebrew/Aramaic script, it is probable that they were of Jewish pedigree. In light of their pro-Pauline statements, it seems unlikely that their Jewishness would have gone much beyond that.

Categorization is one of the most elementary functions of human cognition. Since our brains are incapable of processing millions of unrelated details simultaneously, we are bound to categorize, to form simplified pictures of ourselves and of the reality to which we are related. Consequently, the unknown features of the past will become understandable only if we are willing to qualify our robust initial categories. In this chapter, I have argued that although the category of Jewish Christianity is a modern one, it can serve as a reasonable starting point for the discussion of ancient "Jewish Christianity." Furthermore, by using the *indicators of Jewish Christianity* as the necessary qualifiers, I hope to have been able to bring the reader a bit closer to the realities of the people whose religiosity consisted of a mixture of elements we today classify as either Jewish or Christian. In any case, the discussion should have made it clear that the ancient authors were as bound by categorizing as we are. Their categories of "Ebionites" and "Nazarenes" hardly fare better than our "Jewish Christianity"—both call for further clarification.

Suggested Readings

Bauckham, Richard. 2003. "The Origin of the Ebionites." Pages 162–81 in *The Image of the Judaeo-Christians in Ancient Jewish and Christian Literature*. Edited by Peter J. Tomson and Doris Lambers-Petry. Wissenschaftliche Untersuchungen zum Neuen Testament 158. Tübingen: Mohr Siebeck.

Häkkinen, Sakari. 2005. "Ebionites." Pages 247–78 in *A Companion to Second-Century Christian "Heretics."* Edited by Antti Marjanen and Petri Luomanen. Supplements to Vigiliae Christianae 76. Leiden: Brill. 2005.

Jones, F. Stanley. 1995. *An Ancient Jewish Christian Source on the History of Christianity: Pseudo-Clementine "Recognitions" 1.27–71*. Society of Biblical Literature Texts and Translations 37, Christian Apocrypha Series 2. Atlanta: Scholars Press.

———. 2005. "Jewish Christianity of the Pseudo-Clementines." Pages 315–34 in Marjanen and Luomanen. 2005.

Klijn, A. F. J., and G. J. Reinink. 1973. *Patristic Evidence for Jewish-Christian Sects*. Novum Testamentum Supplements 36. Leiden: Brill.

Luedemann, Gerd. 1996. *Heretics: The Other Side of Early Christianity*. Translated by John Bowden. Louisville, Ky.: Westminster John Knox.

Luomanen, Petri. 2005a. "Nazarenes." Pages 279–314 in Marjanen and Luomanen. 2005.

———. Forthcoming. "The Nazarenes' Gospel and Their Commentary on Isaiah Reconsidered." In *Bringing the Underground to the Foreground: New*

Perspectives on Jewish and Christian Apocryphal Texts and Traditions. Proceedings of the Apocrypha and Pseudepigrapha Section of the Society of Biblical Literature International Meeting Held in Groningen, The Netherlands, July 25–28, 2004. Edited by Pierluigi Piovanelli. Bibliothèque de l'Ecole des hautes études, Sciences religieuses. Turnhout: Brepols.

Luttikhuizen, Gerard P. 1985. *The Revelation of Elchasai: Investigations into the Evidence for a Mesopotamian Jewish Apocalypse of the Second Century and Its Reception by Judaeo-Christian Propagandists.* Texte und Studien zum antiken Judentum 8. Tübingen: Mohr Siebeck.

———. 2005. "Elchasaites and Their Book." Pages 335–64 in Marjanen and Luomanen. 2005.

Marjanen, Antti, and Petri Luomanen, eds. 2005. *A Companion to Second-Century Christian "Heretics."* Supplements to Vigiliae Christianae 76. Leiden: Brill.

Pritz, Ray A. 1988. *Nazarene Jewish Christianity: From the End of the New Testament Period Until Its Disappearance in the Fourth Century.* Leiden: Brill.

PART II: TEXTS

5. THE Q DOCUMENT
William Arnal

The text rather mysteriously known as "Q" is a lost document that served as the basis and source of much of the sayings material in the Gospels of Matthew and Luke. Its existence was first hypothesized in the nineteenth century as part of the solution to the "Synoptic Problem," the question of the literary relationship of the first three canonical Gospels, Matthew, Mark, and Luke. Once it had been established that the Gospel of Mark was the earliest of these three "Synoptic" Gospels and served as the primary narrative source for Matthew's and Luke's story lines, the question remained what relationship Matthew and Luke had to each other. The editorial and literary procedures of Matthew and Luke seem incoherent and rather senseless if either was working from the other. Thus most scholars of the Gospels have concluded that Matthew and Luke used Mark as their primary narrative source, and did so *independently* of each other.

These conclusions, however, create a problem. Matthew and Luke *share* approximately 230 verses—mostly sayings of Jesus and John the Baptist—that do *not* appear in Mark and so could not have been drawn from that common source. And if neither Matthew nor Luke copied from each other, neither one could have derived these sayings from the other. We are therefore essentially *forced* to hypothesize a common source, used independently by Matthew and Luke analogously to their use of Mark, to account for this shared material. The extent and wording of this now-lost source can be reconstructed by isolating and comparing stories and sayings shared by Matthew and Luke but absent from Mark. This reconstructed text is now known as "Q," probably from German *Quelle* ("source"). It is also referred to as the Synoptic Sayings Source, the Sayings Gospel, and the Q Gospel. The conclusion that Matthew and Luke independently made use of both Mark and a now-lost Q is known, reasonably enough, as the Two-Source Hypothesis.[1]

Strictly speaking, the Two-Source Hypothesis does not require the common source of Matthew and Luke—Q—to be a written source, or a single source. Q could, in principle, be just a convenient designation for a heterogeneous body of diverse oral traditions and/or short, separate, written sources. When, however, one analyzes those 230 or so shared verses of Matthew and Luke—the double tradition—it becomes clear that they exhibit a literary, stylistic, and theological coherence that strongly suggests that the original Q was in fact a real, written, and single document (Kloppenborg 1987, 42–51). Thus, while it is true that Q is a hypothetical document, inferred from the literary patterns of the Synoptic Gospels rather than actually found in the form of an ancient manuscript, that does *not* mean that Q never existed as a document. And since Q can be reconstructed from the double-tradition with some confidence, it is perfectly responsible to inquire into its character, theology, literary history, and the people it represented.[2]

Recent work on Q has made tremendous strides. It is now generally conceded that Q was indeed a single, written document composed in Greek (Kloppenborg 1987, 51–64; Kloppenborg Verbin 2000, 72–80; Robinson 2000, xxxiii; 2002, ix–x; Tuckett 1996a, 83–92). Its extent and wording correspond roughly to that of the Matthean-Lukan double tradition. Its original sequence is more closely approximated by Luke than by Matthew (Kloppenborg 1987, 64–80; Kloppenborg Verbin 2000, 88–91; Koester 1990, 133), with the consequence that Q passages are most frequently referred to by Lukan versification (that is, e.g., Q 7:35 refers to the Q text lying behind Luke 7:35 and its Matthean parallel, which in this case happens to be Matt 11:19). Most scholars locate the composition of Q in the Galilee or southern Syria (Arnal 2001, 159–64; Hoffmann 1982, 331–34; Horsley 1995a, 71; Kloppenborg Verbin 2000, 171–75; Lührmann 1969, 88; Mack 1993, 48–49; Sato 1994, 177; Tuckett 1996a, 102–3; Uro 1987, 21–22; Vaage 1994, 1, 3). The date at which the final version of Q was composed is more controversial. Some insist on a very early date (e.g., Arnal 2001, 165–68; Theissen 1991, 203–34), others date the bulk of the document to the 60s of the first century (e.g., Lührmann 1969; Kloppenborg Verbin 2000, 86–87); and some even suggest that Q was composed after the destruction of the temple in 70 CE (e.g., Hoffmann 1982; Myllykoski 1996). For most purposes, it is probably safest to conclude, with Christopher M. Tuckett (1996a, 102), that Q can only be situated within the broad time span of 40–70 CE.

The genre of Q has been recognized as that of antique wisdom literature, comparable to such texts as the biblical book of Proverbs or the *Gospel of Thomas* (Robinson 1971; Kloppenborg 1987; A. Kirk 1998). More controversially, Q's literary history and development have been traced by several scholars (Schultz 1972; Kloppenborg 1987; Jacobson 1992; Allison 1997). It is of course exceptionally difficult to reconstruct the literary history of a document that is no longer extant, and some scholars dismiss as impossible the very idea of doing so (especially Meier 1994, 180–81). Q, however, has proved surprisingly amenable to redaction-critical analysis, and such analysis has suggested that the document grew in a series of discrete stages. The predominant redaction-critical hypothesis, and the one assumed in what follows, is that of John S. Kloppenborg, who suggests that Q as a document progressed through three distinct stages (Kloppenborg 1987; Kloppenborg Verbin 2000). The first layer was a written collection of inversionary wisdom sayings in the form of argumentative and tightly organized clusters of proverbs and aphorisms ascribed to Jesus (e.g., Q 6:27-49; see Kloppenborg 1987, 171–245). The second stratum comprised the addition of polemically oriented materials to the original text, frequently units in the form of *chreiai* (that is, short narrative frames around a pithy cluster of sayings, e.g., Q 11:14-23; see Kloppenborg 1987, 102–70), as well as the expansion of some of the aphoristic clusters to reflect the new interest in polemical and judgmental motifs (e.g., the addition of Q 10:12-15 to the original Q version of the "mission speech" [Q 10:2-11, 16]). The third layer comprised the addition of Q's extended temptation narrative (Q 4:1-13) and a handful of nomistic glosses (i.e., Q 11:42c; 16:17; see Kloppenborg 1987, 152). These layers or stages in Q's development will be referred to henceforth as Q^1, Q^2, and Q^3.[3]

The Text and Its Ideas

As is the case with any ancient writing, Q's ideology and view of Jesus must be understood on their own terms. Unfortunately, scholars of ancient Christianity historically have tended to view the movements of Jesus people as more or less unified and as deriving from a single, earth-shattering experience or insight, the usual candidate being the supposed resurrection of Jesus. Hence, frequently a Pauline-style "kerygmatic" theology of Jesus' atoning death and salvific resurrection is taken as the sine qua non of all ancient followers of Jesus and their documentary remains. Applied to Q, this tendency has at times meant a refusal to see in Q a coherent or self-sufficient ideological statement, instead finding in the erstwhile document a secondary collection of hortatory material that supplements and assumes the passion kerygma (classically Dibelius 1935, 233–65; see the discussion of this point in Tödt 1965, 238–39). Heinz Eduard Tödt, however, in his study of the terminology of the "Son of Man" in the Synoptic tradition, was able to show that this characterization was inadequate to Q, which in fact had an independent and distinctive theology of its own (1965, 246–74). In spite of some recent efforts to turn back the clock (e.g., Hultgren 1994; Hurtado 2003; Pearson 2004), this approach to Q as an independent theological entity in its own right has come to dominate most scholarship on the document since Tödt.

The First Stage of Q's Composition (Q¹)

Predictably, the theology of Q developed as the document itself was expanded. Proceeding from Kloppenborg's stratification, the document's first layer and earliest written stage (Q¹) presents Jesus as a teacher of unusual wisdom and exhorts obedience to his radical teaching and emulation of the lifestyle that accompanies that teaching (see Q 14:26-27; 17:33). This image of Jesus is not especially exalted, at least by the standards of other christological schemata. Jesus is of course presented as and presumed to be critically important *as a teacher*. His teaching merits not only preservation but active propagation. Living by this teaching is the only way properly to follow Jesus, and the only way to prevent ruin:

> Why do you call me "master, master," and not do what I say? . . . Everyone who hears my words and does not act on them is like a person who built their house on sand; and the rain fell, and the torrents came, and the winds blew and beat against that house, and it fell; and its fall was great. (Q 6:46, 49)

Implicitly, Jesus is the only source of this critically important teaching. Yet, beyond the content of the teaching—which itself is promoted by active persuasive techniques, not simply appeals to authority, divine revelation, or even the ordinary "religious" motifs of ancient Judaism—Jesus is in theory not qualitatively different from any other teacher; he is not explicitly invested with any supernatural qualities or unique titles. Kloppenborg adds that "Q¹ also lacks oracular appeals; the voice of God is not heard nor does Jesus speak as a prophet" (Kloppenborg Verbin 2000, 199). Jesus stands—here as in later stages of Q—as a *primus inter pares*, the most important exemplar of activity (in this case, wisdom teaching) that others can and do undertake as well, including those actually responsible for Q.

While it is clear that the Q materials ascribed by Kloppenborg to the document's first stage are not apocalyptic, many commentators are disposed to characterize the ideological slant of this material as "eschatological" (see, e.g., Kloppenborg 1987, 173; Koester 1990, 150–62; Tuckett 1996a, 141–61; Allison 1997, 5–6, and many others), the "imminent" or even "realized" expectation of the kingdom of God motivating the unconventional wisdom of Jesus' teaching. As Ron Cameron has argued, however, the term "eschatology is now applied so indiscriminately to virtually anything and everything, that the term works solely as a 'magic wand,' to signal the uniqueness of the New Testament and the incomparability of Christian origins" (Cameron 1996, 240; cf. Georgi 1985). Others, such as Burton Mack and Leif Vaage, have argued that, by *analogy* with the more or less contemporary Cynic school, the message of the earliest version of Q was a rather ordinary type of social criticism, calling into question the transparency and self-evident nature of cultural norms (see Mack 1993; Vaage 1994). Such a view helps account both for the use of the wisdom genre to communicate its ideas, and for the unusual, inversionary, or radical nature of that wisdom's content. Whether advancing an "eschatological" or a Cynic-like understanding of Q's rhetoric, many scholars see in Q—and especially its earlier layers—evidence of "wandering charismatics" and "radical itinerants," individuals who practiced what they preached (or, in terms of the agenda behind the composition of Q, preached what they practiced) by undertaking a voluntarily homeless and impoverished life in order both to live and to preach the kingdom of God (so classically Theissen 1978). Arnal, by contrast, denies the cogency of the itinerancy hypothesis and instead proposes that Q's "inversionary" wisdom is actually an effort on the part of sedentary Galilean "village scribes" to criticize a new social order that is disenfranchising them (Arnal 2001). However interpreted, the basic message of this layer of Q is the immediacy of divine providence.

The Second Stage of Q's Composition (Q²)

The ideological stance of the second stage of Q's development is rather easier to identify. It is to this stage that the entirety of Q sayings with an apocalyptic orientation belong. Combined with threats about the future "days of the Son of Man" (e.g., Q 12:40; 17:24, 26, 30) is widespread castigation of "this generation" by Jesus (e.g., Q 7:31-35; 11:29-32, 49-51; 13:29, 34-35) as well as by John the Baptist (e.g., Q 3:7-9; cf. 7:33). Since the ground-breaking work of Dieter Lührmann (1969), these motifs have been recognized as one of the redactional organizing principles of Q, which offers polemic against "this generation" and invokes judgment against it (see also A. Kirk 1998, 14–16; Kloppenborg 1987, 166–70; Kloppenborg Verbin 2000, 201–6; Koester 1990, 149–55; Tuckett 1996a, 165–207; Uro 1987, 162–72; and many others). This set of motifs—drawn from the Deuteronomistic tradition, which emphasizes Israel's need for repentance and threatens catastrophic judgment if that repentance is not forthcoming—is what provides Q with its literary unity (Jacobson 1994, 109–14) and theological center. In Kloppenborg's work, this polemical and Deuteronomistic orientation, invoking apocalyptic threats to underscore the need for repentance, characterizes the redaction—the second layer—of Q. The call to heed Jesus' teachings issued in Q¹ has been ignored, and so the purveyors of the Q material retreat into condemnation of those who have rejected their original message.

In this redactional material, the claims made for Jesus are much more explicit and exalted. Jesus is still a teacher, and the contents of the document still recount his words; but in addition there is substantial and trenchant consideration given to Jesus' status, now exceptionally lofty. His wisdom and prophecy are greater than those of Solomon and Jonah (Q 11:31-32). He is the Coming One (*erchomenos*) proclaimed by John the Baptist (3:16b; cf. 7:18-23) and heralded by scripture (implicitly, Q 13:35). In some fashion, this presaged Coming One, and so Jesus himself, is identified with an apocalyptically conceived Son of Man (see Q 7:34; 11:30). Most strikingly, Q asserts that one's response to Jesus will dictate how one is judged by God: "Anyone who acknowledges me in public, the Son of Man will also acknowledge before the angels of God. But whoever denies me in public will be denied before the angels" (Q 12:8-9). The absolute uniqueness of Jesus, and his status as a Son of God, is affirmed most extravagantly in Q 10:22-24:

> Everything has been entrusted to me by my Father, and no one knows the son except the Father, nor does anyone know the Father except the son, and to whomever the son chooses to reveal him. Blessed are the eyes that see what you see! For I tell you, many prophets and kings wanted to see what you see, and did not see it, and to hear what you hear, and did not hear it.

The appropriate response to Jesus is now more than one's response to a wise teacher. Jesus both initiates the final judgment in his preaching of it and will himself enact that judgment as the coming Son of Man: "I have come to cast fire upon the earth, and how I wish it were already kindled. Do you suppose that I have come to give peace on earth? I have not come to give peace, but a sword" (Q 12:49-51). One is not simply to obey his teaching but is required also to "acknowledge" him, and moreover this requirement is a prerequisite for divine recognition (Q 12:8-9, quoted above). Yet the exaltation of Jesus' status in this redactional stage of Q should not be overstated or conflated with more developed or kerygmatic notions of Jesus' role. Jesus' unique vocation is still expressed in terms of, and embodied in, his words; he remains primarily a teacher. Jesus is to be "acknowledged" but not worshiped; he is still nowhere described as the "Christ," and his character as God's son is expressed in terms of what he *reveals* to his disciples (Q 10:21-24). Jesus does perform miracles in this stratum of Q material (7:1-10; 11:14; cf. 7:22), but these miracles are not emphasized as Jesus' primary task, serving instead to illustrate Jesus' proclamation of the kingdom (Q 11:20; cf. 10:9) or his authority (7:1-10, 22). The miraculous dimension in all three of these texts is rather unde-veloped, serving simply as an occasion for polemical observations (i.e., 7:9; 7:23; 11:19; cf. 10:13). In 7:1-10, the focus is the *request* for a miracle (cf. 11:29, where another such request is denied) and the subsequent conversation; the miracle itself is narrated almost as an afterthought (7:10, which is only uncertainly ascribed to Q). In 7:22, Jesus refers to miraculous healing events as evidence of his identity, but these events are not actually narrated. Indeed, Jesus does not even explicitly indicate that he is the one who has performed such actions. Q 11:14 describes an act of exorcism in a single verse, which then becomes the occasion for a negative reaction to Jesus, and Jesus' critical response. In no instance does Q seem to have an interest in miracles as such, and although it takes for granted Jesus' reputation as a healer, it does not develop this motif or treat it as central to his agenda. Nor are Jesus' healings unique: the Q people themselves are enjoined to heal the sick as part of *their* proclama-tion and demonstration of the kingdom of God (10:9, perhaps 10:13). The consistency with which references to miracles—whether those of Jesus or his followers—are harnessed to the polemical denunciation of those who have failed to repent suggests that the entry of the miraculous into this secondary stratum of Q was undertaken precisely *because* of the polemical potential of such references.

Jesus' death by crucifixion, so central to the Pauline kerygma, is nei-ther narrated nor explicitly reflected upon. It does seem to be taken for granted as early as Q¹ (see Q 14:27), but there it is conceived not as a salvific act or in any way unique; it stands instead as an example of re-solve to be emulated (see esp. Seeley 1991; 1992; cf. also Arnal 1997, 210–13). Interestingly, this view of Jesus as one among many who suffer for God's will is carried over into Q², there being conceptualized in terms of his placement among those who have, throughout Israel's epic history, proclaimed repentance, from Abel (Q 11:51) to John the Baptist (3:7-9), and subsequently to the Q people themselves (6:22-23; 10:10-12): "Even at the main redactional phase (Q2), where christological statements are more in evidence, these remain embedded in a broader strategy of defending the ethos of the Q group and threatening those who are seen as opponents" (Kloppenborg Verbin 2000, 392). In short, the fate of Jesus is an aspect of the *collective* experience of rejection on the part of divine Wisdom's emissaries; thus is Jesus' death assimilated to and deployed within the framework of Q's Deuteronomistic theology, and its singular, once-and-for-all character is not asserted. One's response to those who continue Jesus' message is more determinative of one's ultimate fate than is any historical connection to Jesus' own death: "Whoever hears you hears me, and whoever rejects you rejects me, and whoever rejects me rejects him who sent me" (Q 10:16; see also Tuckett 1996a, 108, 211–12). The same is true of Jesus' resurrection. It is not referred to explicitly, and in this case we cannot assume that Q knows of the belief in Jesus' resurrection by other Jesus people. The implication of belief in Jesus' return as Son of Man or Coming One (see esp. Q 13:35), is that he does not or will not remain dead; nonetheless, the language of resurrection is not applied to Jesus at all, and instead "the Q people may have regarded Jesus' death as the death of a just man or a prophet whom God had assumed [into heaven], pending some future eschatological function. This accounts for the fact that Q accords Jesus' death no special salvific significance, but jumps immediately to Jesus' return as the Son of Man (11:49-51; 13:34-35)" (Kloppenborg Verbin 2000, 378). The assumption into heaven of the righteous man is, again, not unique to Jesus; it is part of the apocalyptic vindication of all of the righteous. When resurrection language is used in Q, it is applied not to Jesus but to figures from Israel's epic past: "the Queen of the South will be raised (*egerthēsetai* in both Matthew and Luke) at the judgment. . . . Ninevite men will arise (*anastēsontai* in both Matthew and Luke) at the judgment" (11:31-32). What we have here is a notion of collective universal resurrection of the just and the wicked, to be vindicated or condemned at that final moment. The personalized, unique character of the resurrection of Jesus is nowhere to be seen, just as the individual, exceptional, and salvific notion of his death is absent.

The Third Stage of Q's Composition (Q³)

The third stage of Q's composition comprises only the addition of the temptation narrative (Q 4:1-13) and two nomistic glosses, one at 11:42c ("without neglecting the others [i.e., tithing]"), and the other at 16:17 ("it is easier for heaven and earth to pass away than for one iota or one serif of the law to fall"; see Kloppenborg 1987, 250–53; Kloppenborg 1990; Kloppenborg Verbin 2000, 212–13). The form and function of the temptation story are consonant with Q's genre as wisdom literature and its characterization of Jesus as a teacher: "The temptation story demonstrates the reliable moral character of its principal character and shows behavior consistent with the teachings that will follow" (Kloppenborg Verbin 2000, 375). What stands out about this story is its unusual interest in scriptural exegesis and its understanding of scripture as law. The story also rehabilitates the temple, which is now, in contrast to Q² (cf. Q 11:51; 13:35), understood to be a holy place where angels dwell (Q 4:9-10; see Kloppenborg Verbin 2000, 212). The two glosses to already extant (in Q²) material that are attributed to Q³ share with the temptation account this otherwise absent exegetical and nomistic orientation. Q 11:42c, interrupting the logic of the Q⁽²⁾ woes against the Pharisees, seems to be an effort on the part of this tertiary redactor to avoid potentially antinomistic readings of these woes. The "original" (Q²) version castigates (and caricatures) the Pharisees for, allegedly, "tith[ing] mint and dill and cumin, and giv[ing] up justice and mercy and faithfulness, but these are what it is necessary to do" (Q 11:42a, b). Lest such lampooning suggest that tithing itself be rejected, the Q³ redactor then adds, by way of clarification: "without giving up those" (i.e., it is necessary to practice justice and mercy and faithfulness, but without neglecting tithing, either, in spite of the apparent contrast [Q 11:42c]). Likewise, Q 16:17 follows a saying that could, conceivably, be understood to consign Jewish Torah to the past: "The law and the prophets were until John. From then on, the kingdom is violated and the violent plunder it" (Q 16:16). Thus, the Q³ redactor, to ensure that this saying *not* be interpreted in such a fashion, added verse 17: "But it is easier for heaven and earth to pass away than for one iota or one serif of the law to fall." This final redaction of Q does not alter the document very much, but does illustrate an increasingly nomistic orientation among Q's tradents.

In general, Q's ethos is scribal at every stage of its development, and its image of Jesus is, accordingly, that of a sage, even when he is ascribed other honors as well. Nowhere is Jesus presented as the Christ/Messiah; nowhere are his death and resurrection understood as unique or salvific. Q's basic development appears to have begun with the articulation and attribution to Jesus of a basic behavioral message framed in terms of scribal wisdom but unorthodox in its content. Subsequent developments within the self-perception of the group propagating this message and in its understanding of Jesus seem to have been dictated by the failure of its initial message (see Arnal 2004). Viewing its countercultural agenda as having been somehow rejected (most likely, ignored), the people responsible for Q's earliest written layer turned inward, using the Deuteronomistic view of history to rationalize the rejection of their message and to inflate the authority of those who promoted that message—John the Baptist, Jesus, and perhaps more importantly, the Q people themselves, who are now emissaries of the Coming One/Son of Man. At its final stage of development as an integral text, Q continues and enhances its interest in inflating the authority of Jesus as a sage, as well as developing its own scribal interests in a more nomistic and scriptural direction, trends already seen in the transition from Q^1 to Q^2. Q thus affords us a remarkable insight into a group of ancient Jesus people otherwise unknown to us, a group whose origins and activity derive from the same locale as Jesus himself, a group of people whose "primitive" view of Jesus as a sage seems innocent of the distinctively "Christian" aspects of the Pauline kerygma. Moreover, as a result of its identifiable layers, Q also provides us a window on the changes and development that ancient views of Jesus underwent over time, as well as insight into some of the reasons for these changes.

Classifying Q

The question this volume aims to explore is that of "Jewish Christianity" or "Christian Judaism." This issue is foremost and fundamentally one of

classification: both the classification of "religious traditions," their boundaries and characteristics, and, more problematically, the question of what
type of classification the term "Judaism" really refers to. This latter question
is more basic and must be addressed first. The problem is, of course, that
the term "Jew" is even today used to refer to an *ethnic* identity (that is, an
identity related to national, linguistic, or cultural placement or ancestry)[4],
and, quite distinctly, to a *religious* identity (that is, an identity due to voluntary participation, via belief and practice, in a certain kind of distinctive
ideological discourse). The one need not imply the other; one can be of
Jewish descent and wholly irreligious or be a devout convert to Judaism
without being of Jewish descent. Self-identification as a Jew, consequently,
may be akin to asserting that one is, say, Italian, or it may be more akin to
asserting that one is, say, Muslim; or both types of assertions may be intended. The same potential duality appears in Hellenistic-Roman antiquity:
one may be of Jewish descent without adhering to any significant aspects
of Jewish "religion"; conversely, one may be of Gentile descent, but wholly
committed to multitudinous aspects of Jewish religious practice. So in asking whether Q is a "Jewish" document, we are actually asking two distinct
questions that should not be conflated: one about the ethno-cultural background of the people responsible for the document, and the other about
the ideological commitments expressed in it. Of course this same distinction does *not* apply to most of the earliest forms of what eventually became
Christianity, which as a *new* movement in a syncretistic and multicultural
hellenized world, was not based on particular ancestral traditions and did
not imply consistently any particular ethnic affiliation. In the first century
(and apparently for some time afterward), one could be a Jew, both ethnically and ideologically, and adhere to the beliefs of the Jesus people (see the
excellent discussion of one such group in Saldarini 1994); conversely, one
could adhere to the beliefs of the Jesus people without being Jewish. Thus,
in exploring the Jewish identity of Q, we will need to ask both about ethnic affiliation and about ideological affiliation, as distinct questions; but in
exploring the classification of Q among the Jesus people, only the ideological question need be asked. Second-century apologetics notwithstanding,
there was no Christian *ethnos*.

     This clarification brings us to the next problem, that of classifying and defining religious traditions. Even once we have set aside the ethno-cultural question, there is no single agreed-upon method for defining belonging to *religious* traditions. Such classification may, for instance, proceed by positing a single necessary and sufficient index of belonging to a given tradition, and then may assess whether a group of people, or a text, or any cluster of phenomena, possesses this index.[5] While such a procedure remains the usual way of *thinking about* religious classification, it is almost impossible to apply in any consistent way. Under the influence of Paul's obsession with circumcision as an identity index, for instance, many commentators would regard circumcision of the penis as a fundamental litmus test of Jewish identity, particularly in antiquity. It turns out, however, on further consideration, that circumcision is neither necessary nor sufficient for ancient Jewish identity. At least half of all observant Jews are uncircumcised—women. One may, therefore, be an observant Jew without circumcision, and hence this index is not *necessary* to Jewish identity. Nor is it a *sufficient* index of Jewish identity, since non-Jews may be circumcised for a variety of reasons, both in antiquity (e.g., Egyptian priests) and today (as a common medical procedure). At the conceptual level, any definition of a religious tradition that proposes such singular criteria for classification, or which views any criterion as a necessary one, is essentialistic at the very least, implying that there is only one way of participating in a given culture, and at worst is normative, suggesting that there is only one particular *correct* way to do so.

Jonathan Z. Smith (1988, 4), by contrast, in a persuasive essay on defining Judaism, has proposed a polythetic classification of religious traditions, and of Judaism in particular, in which:

> a class is defined as consisting of a set of properties, each individual member of the class to possess "a large (but unspecified) number" of these properties, with each property to be possessed by a "large number" of individuals in the class, but no single property to be possessed by every member of the class. If the class contained a large population, it would be possible to arrange them according to the properties they possessed in common in such a way that each individual would most

closely resemble its nearest neighbor and least closely resemble its farthest. The probability would be high that the individuals at either extreme would scarcely resemble one another, that is, they would have none of the properties of the set in common.

As Smith shows, there is no single, absolutely consistent index of Jewish religious identity, but rather there are a range of common markers of adherence, especially—but not exclusively—various forms of identification with the synagogue assembly. Being a religious Jew is not established by any single belief or practice, nor does identification as Jewish necessarily bring with it any such singular conviction or inclination. Instead, Jewish identity should be coordinated with possession of a "large number" (more than would be possessed by non-Jews) of such identity markers.

Without in any way prescinding from Smith's general suggestion here, I note that perhaps the easiest way to assess belonging to any particular *ideological* grouping is to inquire how the person or group identifies *itself*[6]—especially once we have set aside reified understandings of particular religious traditions, and of "religion" itself. In other words, the most straightforward and useful way to identify, say, a Jew, is to ask the person: "Are you a Jew?" The basic point made by Smith, however, that such identity need not require or imply *any single* index of belonging, remains absolutely valid.[7] One can go further: the *absence* of a sufficiently "large number" of the normal attributes of the class among individuals identifying themselves as belonging to that class should lead us to call into question the honesty, sufficiency, or utility of the informant's self-identification. Moreover, identification in terms of the nomenclature of "Judaism" and "Christianity," and treating these categories as equal and mutually exclusive entities, "is a major historical anachronism and category error" (Saldarini 1994, 2).[8] As a result, we will have to seek other ways of identifying claims to belonging in the classes of "Judaism" and the scattered movements that eventually developed or coalesced into later "Christianity" at a time in which these particular labels either were not used, or at least were not the standard way of indicating adherence to the particular cultural entities in question. In the case of the first century, the term "Christianity" is actively misleading, and I will instead prefer the term "Jesus people" or "Jesus movements" to denote that wide-ranging class of first-century ideological discourses that appealed to the figure of Jesus. At least one important indication of an implicit claim or self-understanding of belonging to either Judaism and/or the Jesus people is the phenomenon of the *recognition* of other people and groups. For instance, various of Paul's comments (see, e.g., Gal 1:22; 2:1-10; 1 Cor 3:5-9; etc.) make it quite clear that—regardless of tensions, disagreements, and conflicts—he sees himself and his *ekklēsiai* as of a piece with a larger movement inclusive of other individuals and groups who are not directly related to Paul himself or his churches (e.g., the leaders in Jerusalem, James, Peter/Cephas, Apollos, even the "false brothers" of Gal 2:4). This is implicitly but effectively a *claim* (true or not) to membership in a larger and distinct (in Paul's mind) movement, without the term "Christian" ever being used. This phenomenon of recognition will serve as my primary basis for identifying *self-claims* to a particular ideological identity in the absence of the terminology of "Judaism" and "Christianity."

Q and the Jesus people

The degree to which Q belongs in the larger category of "Jesus people"—in the sense of adherence to a distinctive ideological discourse exemplified variously by Paul, the Gospel writers, and so on—is surprisingly limited, in spite of Q's manifestation of a *few* of the criteria by which a group or document may be thus classified. Of course if by such a classification one refers either to a group constituted by the belief that Jesus is the Christ/Messiah, or to a group both organizationally and ideologically ancestral to later orthodoxy, then Q definitely does *not* belong. Such definitions, however, are prejudicially restrictive and theoretically unjustifiable. Even in terms of Smith's polythetic approach to classification, however, Q's belonging among the Jesus movements remains somewhat ambiguous. There are some features in Q that are typical of other Jesus people at roughly the same period, but fewer of them than one typically finds among those other groups.

    The most obvious index of belonging to the Jesus movements is an interest in or concern with the figure of Jesus. One need not belabor the point that this trait is most certainly present in Q, and indeed at all levels of the document's development. Regardless of how his presentation may change, Jesus is the *topic* of this document from the start. The sayings, with very few exceptions, are those of Jesus;[9] the accusations and challenges to which Q polemically replies are leveled against Jesus (e.g., Q 7:34-35; 11:15, 16, 29); it is Jesus who disputes with—and defeats—the devil (4:1-13). Relatedly, Q, like many other sources for the Jesus movements, does not simply regard Jesus as important: it invests him with titles having some sort of distinctively "religious" or supernatural significance. In the case of Q, the titles are "Son of God" (Q 4:1-13; 10:21-22)[10], and "Son of Man" (Q 6:22; 7:34; 9:58; 11:30; 12:8, 10, 40; 17:24, 26, 30), as well as Q's own distinctive term, "the Coming One" (*erchomenos* [3:16; 7:19-20; 13:35]). It is notable that what we have here is not simply the application of any old title to Jesus; two of the three titles used by Q for Jesus—Son of God and Son of Man— are very common in other first-century sources as well. Q also, famously, evinces an interest in John the Baptist, a feature found in several, but not nearly all, first-century writings concerned with Jesus, as well as in non-Christian sources (Josephus, *Antiquities* 18.116–19). Q likewise appears to take it for granted that the divine being to which it refers is the God of Israel, the God of the Hebrew Bible, and that he is to be worshiped more or less exclusively (see, e.g., Q 4:5-8).[11] And, like both Paul and the canonical gospels, Q treats the Hebrew scriptures as (among other things) a source of predictions about or references to the present time (e.g., Q 7:27; 4:10-11).

Finally, a rather distinctive feature of the ancient discourse of both Paul and the Gospel writers is the use of fictive kinship language, particularly the designation "brother" (*adelphos*) for one's comrades. This is an attribute that *may* be present in Q. The term "brother" is used in at least two locations in Q, but its import is not entirely clear. Q 6:41-42 refers to removing the beam from one's own eye before removing the splinter in the eye of one's brother; in this saying the other person is referred to as "brother" (*adelphos sou*) four times in Luke and three times in Matthew (7:3-5). And Q 17:3, similarly, exhorts forgiveness if "your brother" (*adelphos sou*) sins against you. Since both of these texts derive from the first layer of Q, which does not seem to have a strong sense of sectarian identity, while the term "brother" appears to be absent from Q's second layer, which does promote such a sensibility, I am not convinced that we have here the use of fictive kinship language to denote group members. Nonetheless, in neither of these texts does the "brother" *appear* to be a biological brother, so it probably should be conceded that Q does use fictive kinship language, albeit not necessarily identically to the way Paul, for example, uses such terminology.

Turning to the other side of the ledger, Q seems to *lack* almost as many indices of the ancient Jesus movements as it possesses—and rather important ones at that. One striking instance is Q's complete failure to conceptualize Jesus in terms of the *kerygma* of death and resurrection, as discussed above. The reference to the cross in Q 14:27 is so vague that it cannot even be demonstrated that it refers to Jesus' particular mode of execution; it most certainly does not present Jesus' death as a unique salvific act. Nor is there any reference in Q to Jesus as "Christ" (*christos*), perhaps the most distinctive of the titular honors attributed to Jesus by Paul, the Gospel writers, and later Christians. Also lacking in Q but apparently distinctive of several different groups of ancient Jesus people is interest in the so-called Gentile mission (see discussion below). Similarly, Q lacks any indication— such as we find in the Gospel of Mark and the *Gospel of Thomas, inter alia*—of the dismissal of purity considerations, dietary concerns, or Sabbath observance (the woes against the Pharisees in Q 11:39-52 lampoon the Pharisees in terms of caricatures of their behavior; they are not arguments about principles). Finally, Q lacks what I regard as the litmus test for a *claim* to ideological affiliation with the Jesus movements: the recognition of identity or commonality, explicit or implicit, with groups or individuals outside of the primary group. Q does single out various "outsider" individuals for comparison with themselves, for controversy and for polemic; none of these recognized interlocutors, however, are Jesus people. The main victims of Q's invidious comparisons, those who should have heeded Q's message but have failed to, are "this generation" (see esp. Q 7:31-35; 11:14-52). Among those are the Pharisees (11:39-44), scribes or lawyers (*grammateus/nomikos* [11:52]), the residents of Chorazin, Bethsaida, and Capernaum (10:13-15), the residents of Jerusalem (13:34-35), those who claim descent from Abraham (3:8), and "Israel" (7:9). What is striking here is not that a document purporting to record events from Jesus' lifetime refers to a variety of Jewish locations, persons, and institutions—these kinds of references are dictated by the setting and occur in all four canonical

Gospels, without being hailed as evidence that these texts have a Jewish audience in mind, or that they do not have a "Christian" audience in mind. (Note, however, that Q's hermeneutic operates differently than that of the narrative Gospels; see further below). The importance of these references, rather, rests with what they fail to do—address the virtues and failings of other groups who follow or adhere to Jesus in a way distinct from that of Q itself. The message of Jesus is assumed throughout to have been directed at, and only at, his ethnic compatriots, his neighbors, those in whose streets he taught (Q 13:26).[12] Q is not in conversation with other groups of Jesus people and thus cannot be said to lay claim, in this oblique but telling way, to such an identity. There are, of course, many other potential indices of belonging to the Jesus movements, some of which will be present in Q, and some absent. I have attempted here to focus on those I deem to be most common, obvious, and significant.[13]

Of even more interest is the distribution of these various indices throughout Q's literary development. Of the six typical attributes of the Jesus movements present in Q, only three (interest in Jesus, belief in the God of Israel, and possibly fictive kinship language) appear in Q[1] considered alone; the remaining three (ascription of titles to Jesus; interest in the Baptist; treatment of Hebrew Bible as predictive) are added at the Q[2] level. To be rather flippant about it, Q[2] is *twice* as "Christian" as Q[1]. Q[3], while it sharpens both the singularity of Jesus and the necessity of singular worship of the God of Israel, does not add any new definitional features of the Jesus movements. Q[3] *may*, however, uniquely of the document's strata, show—albeit only implicitly—an awareness of and an engagement with other strands of the Jesus movement. That is, the desire in Q[3] to clarify sayings with antinomistic potential (i.e., Q[2] 11:42; 16:16) may stem simply from the sayings themselves, but it may also be a defensive reaction to an awareness of antinomistic Jesus people who might use such sayings to support an agenda with which the framers of Q are not in sympathy. Such a reading would be supported by Eugene Boring's suggestion that the Gospel of Matthew constitutes, in essence, a "Q[4]" (Boring 1994), since that Gospel is obviously deeply engaged in discussion with other Jesus people and is critical both of their antinomistic tendencies and even, it would seem, their inclusion of Gentiles.

Although one would expect that the passage of time would tend to increase the development, sophistication, and distinctiveness of any belief-
based group, and hence would result in a gradual and "natural" increase
of definitional features over time, the paucity of such features at Q's initial
stage remains striking. The attribution to Q^1 of three such features disguis-
es the fact that of those three, only one is really distinctive—an interest in
Jesus. Neither the use of fraternal language nor the belief in the Jewish God
sets Q apart from its Galilean context in any way. The only truly distinctive index of Q^1's "Christianity" is an interest in Jesus; it has nothing else
of a *differentiating* character in common with other Jesus people. Oddly
enough, the same is true of Q^2. Only the ascription of titles to Jesus is genuinely distinctive; an interest in the predictive dimension of scripture or in
John the Baptist does not seem to be unique to the Jesus people. The result
is a document that shows a fair number of features in common with other,
contemporary, Jesus people, but which are not necessarily distinctive of
these movements. To put this in perspective, consider the number of these
distinctive and typical traits possessed by more "central" members of the
category of Jesus people, Paul and Mark. Of the eleven features discussed
above, Paul lacks only one: an interest in John the Baptist. Mark possesses
all eleven. Of course, both the Gospel of Mark and the Pauline corpus are
significantly larger than Q and so will include more details. Nonetheless,
the picture we get of the particular "Jesus movement" behind Q is one that
is far less distinctive, less "typical," than what we encounter in either the
letters of Paul or the Gospel of Mark. Q seems to represent a *peripheral*
member of the class of "Jesus people."

Is Q Jewish?

The discussion becomes much more interesting when we turn to the question
of Q's classification as Jewish, for here we have some fairly clear evidence of
the group's own self-perception. The people responsible for Q appear to have
considered themselves ethnically Jewish at every stage of the document's development. Interestingly, however, Q became *more* ideologically Jewish over
time; that is, it appears to have developed more and more "typical features" of

Jewish religious belief at each stage of its development. At the earliest stage, it lacks a great many of these features. With each new redaction, however, the ideologically Jewish features of the document increase, so that by its third stage of development, Q belongs firmly and quite "typically" within the Jewish religious tradition. Peculiarly, then, as Q becomes more "Christian," it also becomes more Jewish.

The Ethnic Dimension

The ethnic dimension of Q's identity is fairly straightforward. The people responsible for the document identify themselves as Jews (though not using this particular term), and at no point does it appear that they cease doing so. The most revealing texts in this regard are Q 12:30 and, perhaps, Q 6:33/34. In the former text, there is a doubly attested opposition between the putative audience of Q and "the Gentiles/nations" (*ta ethnē*): "Do not be anxious, saying: What are we to eat? Or: What are we to drink? Or: What are we to wear? *For all these things the Gentiles seek.*" This wording takes it utterly for granted that Q's auditors are not merely ethnically Jewish, but that they actively subscribe to this sense of self, such that the attribution of a behavior to non-Jews ("the Gentiles/nations") is in itself sufficient to argue against that behavior. In short, we have here an acute—and simultaneously taken-for-granted—consciousness of Jewish identity. The Q people are Jews, homogeneously and unproblematically so.

Depending on how the text is reconstructed, Q 6:33/34 may reinforce this conclusion. Its structure is essentially the same as that of 12:30: behavior of a particular type is typical of outsiders and thus should not be emulated. The only question here concerns the identity of these outsiders: Are they "Gentiles" (so Matt 5:47, *ethnikoi*) or "sinners" (so Luke 6:33, 34: *hamartōloi*)? While both versions accord with the redactional interests of the gospels in which they respectively appear, the International Q Project (IQP) has preferred the Matthean wording here, though not especially emphatically (Robinson et al. 2000, 70–71; cf. Robinson 2002, 6). The analogous wording in Q 12:30 would seem to support such a reading. If so, we would have in Q 6:33/34 the rhetorical question, "If you lend to those from whom you hope to receive, what reward to you have? Do not *even the Gentiles* do the same?" As with 12:30, the point here is not anti-Gentile polemic or a defensive assertion of Jewish identity, but rather the bland assumption that those they address are *not* Gentiles.[14]

In addition, as discussed above, Q's polemic is exclusively directed at *Jews* who have failed to heed its message or have otherwise behaved in disappointing ways. The castigation of "this generation"—comprising Galilean town- and village-dwellers, Jerusalemites, Pharisees, and "Israel"—is not a retrospective or narrative characterization of those who might have ignored Jesus in the past, but rather is leveled directly at those who are thought by the people responsible for Q to reject the message (attributed to Jesus). The "contemporizing" (Kelber 1983; but cf. Kloppenborg 1987, 34–37) tendencies of a sayings collection make the references to people and places in it much more immediate than we would expect from a "historical" narrative of past events, such as we encounter in the canonical Gospels. When Q has Jesus saying "woe to you Pharisees," this is not so much a story about what Jesus once said as an articulation of what the authors/compilers of Q felt needed to be said in their own time. And there is an immediacy, an anger, running throughout Q's redaction: polemic against "Israel" for failing to heed the Q message is the motif that organizes and inspires the document's secondary redaction (see, e.g., Kloppenborg 1987, 166–70; Kloppenborg Verbin 2000, 118–22; Koester 1990, 162–64; Luedemann 2002). None of this material is offered by way of theological or narrative explanation (and scapegoating) for Jesus' death, as we find in Mark, nor is it preliminary to a mission to the Gentiles, as in Luke-Acts; instead, the polemic has the same angry immediacy and straightforward point of reference that we find in Matthew's broadsides against the Pharisees. Q, while not in conversation with any discernible groups of Jesus people, *is* in conversation with other ethnic Jews, both in general, and with respect to specific "religious" figures (Pharisees). This conversation is strained, hostile, perhaps about to break off; but it is still the only conversation that those responsible for Q seem to care about.[15] Such an orientation, then, supports an identification of the composers and transmitters of Q as ethnic Jews.

An important qualification must be offered, however, concerning the nomenclature of "Jew." The Q people do indeed present themselves and their audience as self-evidently different from "the Gentiles"; those with whom it converses include not only the residents of Galilean towns but those of Jerusalem as well; and such exemplars of specifically Judean piety as the Pharisees are under discussion. The *ethnos* with which Q appears to identify is that which we moderns—and many ancients—would designate "Jewish." Nonetheless, Q itself never uses the term "Jew," and for good reason. The Greek word normally translated as Jew, *Ioudaios*, was derived from, and in fact also meant, *Judean*. This terminology, at least in some circles in antiquity, implied that Jews were Judeans, and Judeans were Jews. Q, however, derives from and is concerned with *Galilee*, not Judea. It appeals to Jerusalem—albeit negatively—as the holy city of the biblical epic and the location of the temple, not as the locale of its main interlocutors. And when it refers to the Jewish people *in toto*, it does so with the term "Israel" (Q 7:9; see Kloppenborg Verbin 2000, 174), or "children to Abraham" (Q 3:8), terms that are inclusive of the residents of Galilee in the north and that do not prioritize the culture or lines of descent of the Judeans to the south. Thus, although we may identify the Q people as ethnic "Jews" with minimal qualification, they themselves would probably have objected to that particular label.[16]

The final question that must be addressed regarding the *ethnic* identity of the people responsible for Q concerns the possibility of their interest in, or awareness of, a "mission to the Gentiles" (a full discussion appears in Wegner 1985, 296–334). A few problematic passages in Q—all deriving from the second, redactional, layer (Q²)—appear to present certain non-Jews in a positive light. As a result, I suspect, of the tendency to homogenize the early Jesus movements, viewing each in terms of the other, and all of them, especially, in terms of the narrative of Acts, very many scholars have seen in these passages either Q's awareness of or direct participation in a "mission to the Gentiles." Obviously, such a mission would have some bearing on the identity of the Q people, both ethnic and ideological, and so must be addressed. My contention, however, is that none of these texts witnesses to anything like a "Gentile mission"; the whole notion is an imposition onto Q of an alien context and extraneous interests and beliefs.

Of the Q passages that are adduced as evidence of a "Gentile mission," the most significant and problematic are Q 13:28-29 and Q 7:9, both of which can be read as welcoming Gentiles into either the kingdom of God, or into the movement or group represented by Q. The first of these texts reads, "Many will come from east and west, and recline with Abraham and Isaac and Jacob, but you will be thrown into outer darkness, where there will be weeping and gnashing of teeth" (Q 13:28-29). John S. Kloppenborg, against Richard A. Horsley (1995b, 38), argues that the "obvious force" of this saying is that the "many" who will dine with the patriarchs are the Gentiles, while Q's (Jewish/Israelite) contemporaries will be excluded (Kloppenborg Verbin 2000, 192). Those referred to here as replacing "you" could be understood as Diaspora Jews (so Horsley 1995b, 38), but for the fact that Q shows no interest whatsoever in the Diaspora; moreover, the reference to the patriarchs suggests that an *ethnic* contrast is in mind here (Kloppenborg Verbin 2000, 192; Uro 1987, 210–11). Likewise, "many" could refer to the righteous throughout Israel's history, as opposed to "this generation," but for the fact that the contrast here concerns *location* ("east and west") rather than time period. Indeed, if we read this text as a reference to Gentiles, as those vague "many" who live "far away," its perspective meshes that much better with what we encounter in Q 12:30 and (perhaps) 6:33/34: the unproblematized assumption that the Q people are themselves Jewish and live in a Jewish environment. It must also be stressed that Q 13:28-29 is both preceded and followed by polemical material: 13:26-27 rejects those in whose streets Jesus (apparently) taught, and 13:34-35 condemns Jerusalem and its sanctuary (Uro [1987, 213] notes this juxtaposition as well). What is striking about both of these passages is that they too contain ethnic markers. The first identifies as its target those who shared Jesus' location (geographical and social: "we ate and drank with you, and you taught in our streets"), that is, his kinsmen. The second identifies as its target the temple ("O Jerusalem . . . your house is forsaken"), quintessential symbol of national identity. That the immediate context of 13:28-29, then, is so replete with both polemical and ethnic reference further strengthens the claim that the target of this saying is indeed ethnic identity, and thus that the "many" described here are indeed Gentiles, ethnic outsiders.

Tending to confirm this conclusion is the presence of at least one text in Q in which an individual who is incontrovertibly identified as a Gentile is contrasted, *favorably*, with Q's Israelite contemporaries. In Q 7:1-10, Jesus, apparently in Capernaum, encounters a centurion who begs him to heal (miraculously) one of his slaves or servants (Matt 8:6: *pais*; Luke 7:2: *doulos*). The expression of trust in Jesus offered by the centurion, and elaborated in the passage's verbal exchange (vv. 3-8), prompts Jesus to exclaim, "I have not found such trust (*pistis*) in Israel" (Q 7:9). This remark identifies the centurion as unquestionably Gentile (insofar as it assumes that he is *not* "in Israel"), and it clarifies the point of this story for the Q redactor (see also the discussion in Theissen 1991, 225–27). The account, however originally intended, has been harnessed in Q to a polemical agenda, as both the context and comparison with parallel versions make clear (see the lucid discussion in Kloppenborg 1987, 117–21). What we have here, then, is an account of how non-Israelites have offered to Jesus the kind of reception he should have received among his compatriots, but did not (Uro 1987, 221).

These two passages in particular, with their apparent pronouncement of judgment upon Israel and their positive representation of Gentiles as responding correctly to Jesus and as joining the patriarchs at the eschatological banquet have suggested to several scholars that Q claims that Gentiles have taken the place of Jews (so Uro 1987, 213–14), and thus that the Q people either are engaging in a Gentile mission (e.g., Laufen 1980, 192–94; Lührmann 1969, 58; Manson 1971[1937], 20; Uro 1987, 210–23; Zeller 1984, 96) or at least are aware of one undertaken by other Jesus people, of which they essentially approve (e.g., Jacobson 1992, 110, 256; Kloppenborg 1987, 119; Meyer 1970, 405–17; Pesch 1982, 67). Against such a hypothesis, however, is the failure of Q, discussed above, to identify in any clear way with other groups of Jesus people; that is, Q shows no awareness of or interest in precisely those groups that we know were engaged in such a mission. Nor is there anything in Q's theology that provides an explicit rationale, explanation, or mechanism for inclusion of Gentiles, such as we find in Paul.[17] Yes, Israel is criticized, and yes, certain Gentiles are praised; but no account is offered for how those whose behavior is self-evidently unacceptable in Q[1] have now become members of the Q group, nor is there an explanation for why this might have occurred. In addition, there are numerous passages in Q—some of them actually adduced as evidence by proponents of a Q mission to the Gentiles (see, e.g., Kloppenborg 1987, 119; Uro 1987, 221–22)—which suggest that Q's positive references to Gentiles are not reflections of an actual Gentile constituent in their group, nor awareness of any real "Gentile mission," but are rather *shaming* devices, rhetorical techniques for underscoring the criticism directed at Israel. In the first layer of Q (Q[1]), the (projected) auditors are encouraged to act in a certain way because to do otherwise would be to sink to the level of Gentiles (so Q 12:30; 6:33/34); by the second stratum of the document (Q²), these individuals are now compared invidiously to either epic or hypothetical instances of Gentile repentance—once again, comparison and contrast with *outsiders* are used to comment on *insider* identity.

Perhaps the clearest such usage occurs at the end of the so-called mission charge in Q 10:2-16. This short speech lays out Q's directions to those who propagate its message; but by the end of the speech (more or less corresponding to Q² additions—i.e., Q 10:12-15—to an original Q¹ speech), instruction to "missionaries" has changed to condemnation of those who reject them. The additional Q² verses read:

> I tell you, it will be more tolerable on that day [i.e., the day of judgment] for Sodom than for that city [i.e., the city that has refused to accept the Q messengers]. Woe to you, Chorazin! Woe to you Bethsaida! For if the wonders performed in you had taken place in Tyre and Sidon, they would have repented long ago, in sackcloth and ashes. Yet for Tyre and Sidon it will be more bearable at the judgment than for you. And you Capernaum, will you be exalted to heaven? You will be brought down to Hades. (Q 10:12-15)

The obvious logic is that the various Galilean towns here condemned are *so* bad that they are *worse* than notorious sinners and enemies of Israel from the epic (scriptural) tradition. This is particularly clear we consider the promise that Sodom will fare better at the judgment than the towns in question. The whole point of focusing on Sodom is precisely that it is an emblem of wickedness and an unrepentant attitude. The behavior of those who reject the Q people is compared to the exemplary corruption of Sodom—and hyperbolically is said to be worse. We should by no means imagine a Q mission to the Sodomites! And since the structure and logic of the following saying about Tyre and Sidon are similar, and are linked to the Sodom saying, it should be understood in essentially the same way. The point here is *not* that Tyre and Sidon will fare well at the judgment; rather, it is that Chorazin and Bethsaida will fare *worse* than Israel's notorious enemies.[18] Moreover, this construction offers a hypothetical, contrary-to-fact condition: *if* such miracles had been performed in even these sinks of in-iquity, their inhabitants *would have* repented. The clear implication is not only that such miracles have *not* been performed (and hence that no such "mission" has been undertaken), but in addition that it is *obvious and self-evident* that no such "mission" has taken or will take place. The Q "mission speech" indicates, then, that the Q people are not involved in a mission to the Gentiles, and indeed do not even conceive of one.

Q's version of John the Baptist's preaching has similar implications. The relevant text has John proclaiming, "do not presume to tell yourselves, 'we have Abraham as a forefather,' for I tell you that God can raise up chil-dren for Abraham out of these rocks" (Q 3:8). As many commentators have noted, this passage constitutes an overt redefinition of God's people and an attack on "ethnic privilege" (see, e.g., Kloppenborg 1987, 167; Kloppenborg Verbin 2000, 121, 136–37; Uro 1987, 221); it dismisses claims by the unre-pentant to belong to Abraham's progeny, stating that God is not bound by such claims and can make himself heirs to his promise as he sees fit. But as with the comparison to Sodom, the point is polemical, not descriptive of any real inclusion of ethnic outsiders (one is reminded of St. Francis preaching to the birds; so also Kloppenborg 1987, 104; Kloppenborg Verbin 2000, 192–93). We should no more imagine a Q mission to the rocks than a Q mission to the Sodomites. In both cases, Q's Israelite contemporaries are threatened with replacement in obviously ridiculous terms; the point here is polemical: that *anything*—Sodomites, Tyrians, rocks—would please God more than this wicked generation (so also Kloppenborg Verbin 2000, 203). While Q is deeply invested in polemic against its Israelite contem-poraries, the shaming rhetoric (Kloppenborg Verbin 2000, 192) it uses to suggest their replacement in God's favor is only effective on the premise that a Gentile mission is not in the works, is inconceivable. Q imagines making Jews out of stones more readily than it imagines a non-Jewish field of "mission." A great many of the "positive" references to Gentiles in our text are to notorious Gentile evildoers—Sodom, Nineveh (Q 11:32), Tyre, Sidon—and so the presumption evident in Q[1] that Gentiles are *negative* examples is maintained in Q[2], but now redeployed to suggest the perfidi-ous depravity of "this generation." Such an assumption of Gentile wicked-ness is absent in a few passages suggestive of Gentile "inclusion." But these passages still have polemic as their primary focus, and they still avoid any hint of a real "Gentile mission," instead referring to individual and unsolicited acts of Gentile piety (Q 7:1-10; 11:31), or God's eschatological gathering of the just (Q 14:16-24), again, with the intent of shaming those Jews who have not responded to Q's mission. There is thus really nothing to suggest, and much to weigh against, any notion of Q's openness to non-Jews, or its awareness of any such movement among other Jesus people (so also Allison 1997, 52–53; Tuckett 1996a, 393–404).[19]

The Ideological Dimension

Moving to the issue of Q's *ideological* classification as Jewish, because of space restrictions and the massive scope of religious Judaism in the first century, it is not practical to attempt a more or less complete survey of the *possible* indices of such an identity (including an extensive consideration of those that are *not* present), as was attempted for Q's "Christian" character. Instead, I will simply indicate the ways in which Q shows commitment to various "Jewish" norms at the three different stages of its development. The basic pattern is one of *increasing* commitment to the religious ideology of Judaism and its standard markers.

There is little question that the people responsible for the earliest Q material (Q[1]) see themselves as committed to Israelite religion. They are monotheists who worship the Jewish God, who is described as a universal "Father" (so Q[1] 6:36; 11:2, 13; 12:30),[20] and whose providential care is emphasized. Ethical exhortation is offered by appeal to this God (e.g., Q[1] 6:36-38; 12:22-31); prayer to this God is exhorted (e.g., Q[1] 11:2-13); the "kingdom" here proclaimed is his (e.g., Q[1] 6:20; 10:9, 11; 11:2; 12:31). Thus, even at its earliest stage, Q is "religiously" Jewish, and heavily focused on what we might refer to—albeit rather anachronistically—as "theological" concerns, and those within the ideological framework of Judaism or, better, Israelite religion more broadly.

Yet at the same time, Q[1] is as notable for what it lacks of the typical markers of "Judaism" as for what it contains. At this early stage of the document, the arguments to adopt a certain attitude or behavior are supported by naturalistic rationales, appeals to logic, nature, ordinary behavior, and what is "self-evidently" true of God. Entirely absent are the *particularities* of Judean religion:

an interest in Torah, the Jerusalem temple, the narrative epic found in the Hebrew Bible, priesthood, prophetic oracles, purity or diet, or the Sabbath. The
sole apparent exception to Q¹'s failure to refer to scripture is in Q 12:27, where
it is asserted that "not even Solomon in all his glory was arrayed like one of
these [lilies]." But in fact no particular scriptural text is appealed to here, nor
any particular aspect of the Israelite epic; instead, a king of legendary wealth
is contrasted with the beauty of nature. The passage is thus something of the
exception that proves the rule. Q¹ situates itself within Israel's history, as this
passage demonstrates, but at the same time fails to make use of the canonical
narrative of that history, and in any case subordinates its heroes to the glories
of the natural world. Likewise, the so-called mission speech refers to meals,
but in a way that makes it clear that dietary laws are not at issue: it commands
that whatever house may welcome you, "at that house remain, eating and
drinking whatever they provide, for the worker is worthy of his reward . . . and
whatever town you enter and they take you in, eat what is set before you" (Q
10:7-8). Either the purveyors of Q¹ do not adhere rigorously to dietary laws, or
they take it for granted that those who show them hospitality will serve them
appropriate food. In neither case are dietary norms *problematized* in any way;
the text here is not exhorting obedience or disobedience to such regulations,
but is focusing instead on the gracious receipt of hospitality, wholly without
reference to purity issues. The overall "religious" situation for the first stage of
Q is nicely summarized by Kloppenborg Verbin (2000, 199):

> What is absent from Q[1]'s repertoire of arguments is as telling as what
> is present. The basis of an argumentative appeal is not the priesthood,
> or the Temple, or purity distinctions, or the Torah (or writings). This is
> surprising, since at a number of points Q might have invoked the Torah
> or examples of Israel's epic history in support of its arguments . . . Q¹ is full
> of confidence in divine providence, in God's loving surveillance, and the
> possibility of transformed human relationships; but there is no indication
> whatsoever that this is mediated by Torah or the Temple or the priestly
> hierarchy, or that it is based on oracular disclosures or commands.

By the second stage of Q's development, however, the situation has
changed markedly. All of those features of "Judaism" present in the first

stratum are of course present in the second,[21] but now many of the distinctive and familiar indices of Judean religion that were absent from Q[1] appear as well. They may appear negatively, but they are now in view. The Jerusalem temple is referred to in Q[(2)] 13:34-35 as the putative house of God (albeit now forsaken), and Jerusalem itself is now an object of scrutiny, whose status as a locale of murder and rejection of the prophets in this passage must be due more to its preeminent symbolic status for Jewish identity than to its having actually been approached by the Q people themselves. Likewise, the scriptural epic of Israel's history is now mined for texts and images to support Q[2]'s contentions. The figure of the prophet is ubiquitous in Q[2] (e.g., Q 6:23; 7:26; 10:24; 11:47, 49; 13:34; 16:16); quotations from or allusions to the prophetic texts appear (e.g., Q 7:22, 27; 13:35); and one of the main redactional titles attributed to Jesus, "the Coming One" (*ho erchomenos* [Q 3:16; 7:19; 13:35]) seems to have been constructed on the basis of Psalm 117:26 LXX ("Blessed is the one who comes [*ho erchomenos*] in the name of the Lord"). Q[2] contains allusions or references to specific biblical stories, including now one about Solomon (Q 11:31), as well as about Jonah and the Ninevites (Q 11:32), the destruction of Sodom (Q 10:12), Noah and the flood (Q 17:26-27), the murder of Abel (Q 11:51), as well as several allusions to the story of Lot scattered throughout the document (so Kloppenborg Verbin 2000, 118–21). While this stratum of Q still does not show interest in such matters as circumcision, dietary laws, or Sabbath observance, nor include controversy stories on such matters, it does directly address purity (Q 11:39, 41), tithing (11:42), and behavior in synagogues (11:43). In all of these cases, the topics addressed are raised as part of a verbal assault on the Pharisees. Similarly, the Torah and its interpretation and application are discussed in the polemical context of criticism of legal experts (Luke: *nomikoi*; Matthew: *grammateis*), who, like the Pharisees, are condemned (Q 11:46, 52). In none of these instances, notably, is any positive practice enjoined on these points: Q[2] is content to attack Pharisaic behavior; it does not propose alternative approaches to purity, or tithing practice, or synagogue behavior. Nor does it provide or suggest an alternative approach to legal exegesis. The document thus engages several specific markers of Jewish identity, but does so more, it appears, in the interest of contesting its opponents' self-understanding than in developing its own.

Nonetheless, even this rather negative engagement with such issues places Q^2 more in the mainstream of Jewish ideological identity than its Q^1 predecessor, if only because it is directly interested in defining a specific and normative definition of who is "in" and who is "out" of "proper" Judaism. And of course, Q^2 does appeal to some Jewish identity-markers in a positive way, particularly scriptural ones: the image of the prophets, their writings, and the epic tradition in general.

Q^3 goes even further. Here, finally, we encounter a nomistic sensibility, not simply an interest in scripture but a specific interest in scripture as law. This interest appears to be definitional for Q^3: the latest additions to the document "correct" potential antinomistic "misreadings" of Q^2 materials. Thus to $Q^{(2)}$ 11:42—"woe to you Pharisees, for you tithe mint and dill and cumin, and neglect justice and mercy and faithfulness"—is added "these you should have done, without neglecting the others," presumably to guard against the implication that tithing itself is being criticized. And to $Q^{(2)}$ 16:16—"the law and the prophets were until John"—is added "it is easier for heaven and earth to pass away than for one iota or one serif of the law to fall," presumably to avoid the conclusion that the law has been superseded since John (interestingly, no corresponding defense is offered for the prophets). The bulk of Q^3, however, is made up of the temptation narrative (Q 4:1-13), and here too the law is viewed as a norm for behavior. In this story, the devil asks Jesus to perform a variety of actions, all of which Jesus refuses to do on the basis of quotations from Deuteronomy. The resultant picture of Jesus—clearly intended here to authorize his (following) teaching and his standing as a sage (Kloppenborg 1987, 258–62)—is of one who is not simply obedient to Torah, but is an exegete and interpreter of Torah's demands. Jesus is able to vanquish the devil not by his personal authority or by divine intervention but by his rigorous and correct adherence to the law of Moses. The effect is to establish a nomistic ethos for Jesus and thus to suggest that all of the teaching to follow conforms to that ethos. Q^3 enhances, elevates, and retrenches the authority and standing of Jesus as God's son, as teacher, and as one who defeats the devil; but it does so by showing his conformity to Torah and by implying that *all* of his teaching reflects, elaborates, or at least respects the Jewish law.

The picture that emerges from these considerations is one in which the Q people become progressively more and more "Jewish"; that is, they increasingly situate and describe themselves deliberately in terms of the distinctive markers of Jewish religiosity. One way to think about this is in terms of an increasing self-consciousness of belonging to a particular ideological current. A "religious" interest in monotheism, God as Father, divine providence, prayer, and living according to expectations generated by the "kingdom of God" are essentially taken for granted at the Q^1 level. But because this original program is ignored, the people responsible for Q become more and more defensive and polemical, reflecting on their own identity and that of their hoped-for interlocutors as a way to account for their failures. This shift prioritizes the question of the identity both of the Q people and of "this generation," and so calls for the invocation of markers of cultural and ideological identity. Such a context helps account for the seemingly ironic fact that it is the same layer of Q (i.e., Q^2) that raises the question of Israelite replacement by Gentiles that also for the first time specifically invokes explicit markers of Jewish identity. In fact, there is no irony here at all, since both motifs derive from the effort to redefine who is a proper Jew or Israelite (see especially Kloppenborg Verbin 2000, 203). What *is* rather odd is that by the end of Q's independent literary development (Q^3), the selective invocation (e.g., prophets, scripture) and repudiation (e.g., tithing, purity) of Jewish identity markers to support the claims of Q's purveyors (heirs to the prophets) and undermine those of its competitors (e.g., Pharisees) have given way to what appears to be an acceptance and a defense of a nomistic piety shared by those competitors. In invoking and engaging the symbols of Jewish religious identity to support its *marginal* position, Q has drifted further and further from that marginality, and more and more into the mainstream.

Another way to think about this progression is in terms of an increasing engagement with specifically *Judean* forms of religiosity. There is little in Q^1 that alludes to or reflects Judean norms in particular. By the time we get to Q^2, however, Judean practices are under discussion, albeit critically. As Kloppenborg Verbin (2000, 256–57) describes it:

Q nowhere challenges circumcision (unlike Paul) or Sabbath observance (unlike Mark) and appears to assume as self-evident the distinction between Jews and Gentiles (6:33; 12:30). Given these features,
it is likely that the Q people, as other Galileans, took for granted the
principal distinguishing marks of Israelite identity—circumcision,
some form of Sabbath observance, and probably certain dietary observances. The critical points in Q's rhetoric are precisely those that
we have suggested were controverted in the Galilean population as a
whole: purity distinctions (11:39-41), tithing (11:42), and the role of
Jerusalem and the Temple in the social and religious economy of the
north (11:49-51; 13:34-35). If the woes in Q 11:39-52 are correctly
understood as burlesque, they represent a form of resistance to the
pressures (probably via the periodic presence of Pharisees) to extend
Judean forms of Temple-oriented practices to the Galilee.

But again, by the time we get to Q^3, things have changed. Now Q emerges
as defensive of the purity and tithing regulations it had earlier mocked; as
nomistic; and as taking for granted the import and value of the Jerusalem
temple (Q 4:9-12). Engagement in a particularly Judean discursive framework and symbol system has brought with it capitulation to the norms of
that discourse.

THE GROUP AND ITS AGENDA: CONCLUSION

What we encounter in Q is a window into the history of a peculiar group
of Jewish Jesus people. These people begin with a sociocultural program attributed to Jesus and grounded both in very generalized Israelite religious
sensibilities and in the assumption of ethnic homogeneity, but with little
explicit reference to shared markers of Jewish identity, nor especially with
much distinctively "Christian" content (Q^1). The program in mind is essentially a social program, an effort to reconfigure village relations in "naturalistic" and "transparent" terms, using appeals to Jesus and to the kingdom of
God to support this social vision (Arnal 2001, 168–203). As this program

is ignored or rejected, however, those responsible for it withdraw into a defensive posture that borders on sectarianism (Q^2). At this stage, more of the typical features of other Jesus people crop up, but so also does explicit discussion of Jewish identity, and with such discussion an invocation of more of the hallmarks of Jewish identity, harnessed to controversy about the proper way to be a Jew. Thus do alienation from their own ideological mainstream and polemic with their ethnic counterparts draw Q *more* into explicit discussion of Jewish identity at the time of its secondary redaction, whereas the taken-for-granted character of such identity at an earlier stage ignores many of these same markers, markers that are in fact not especially relevant to their agenda or attractive to its purveyors. In connection with their effort to redefine "insider" identity, the Q people at this stage quite naturally invoke "outsiders"—the Gentiles—who now serve to underscore the perfidy of Q^2's opponents, rather than, as in Q^1, to establish the limits of acceptable behavior. Because of Q^2's defensive stance, moreover, it engages in an inflation of Jesus' authority as a self-authorizing move, which in turn means that, at the same moment as Q develops more of the hallmarks of Jewish "religious" identity, it *also* develops more of the distinctive hallmarks of the Jesus movements as well. Q becomes "more Christian" *as* it becomes "more Jewish." Finally, at the last stage of the document's compositional history (Q^3), the polemical engagement with the discourse of Jewish identity has transformed into what appears to be an outright capitulation to the norms of that discourse; symbols deployed in support of a marginal identity in Q^2 have become in Q^3 definitive of a more "mainstream" self-positioning. If Eugene Boring is correct that the Gospel of Matthew constitutes a still later stage in the literary production of the group responsible for Q (Boring 1994)—and he does make a very good case—then we can see in Matthew a further development of the trajectory already evinced in the movement from Q^1 to Q^3 toward increasing self-consciousness of both "Jewish" and "Christian" identity, and a positioning more in terms of the mainstream of *both* ideological traditions.

These conclusions have important implications for our understanding of the ancient Jesus movements and their relationship to Judaism. On the one hand, Q witnesses to a group of ethnic Jews who find in Jesus an authoritative spokesperson. The interest in Jesus and his "kingdom of God" in no way attenuates or even calls into question the self-evident ethnic identity of the group responsible for the document and in fact provides the channel through which it expresses its commitment to at least Israelite religiosity. It is only as these taken-for-granted ideological commitments and ethnic allegiances are *called into question*—challenged by the failure of the Q people's contemporaries to take their program seriously—that Q begins to define an identity for itself more rigorously and explicitly, and with reference to precisely those discursive markers that have import for those they wish to condemn. And yet, in using these markers to define more clearly an ethos recognizable by their contemporaries, the Q people also end up making their own identity more distinctive, more recognizably distant from and *other than* that of the people they hope to censure; more and more "Christian," that is, as they appeal more and more to signifiers of "Jewish" belonging. The final traceable stages of the Q group attest to this paradox: Q³, which tries to back away from "Christian" ideas and reinforce "Jewish" ones, nevertheless inflates Jesus' authority in the process and may even engage, apparently for the first time in the Q group's history, in implicit discussions with other Jesus people. In the Gospel of Matthew, perhaps yet another product of the group responsible for Q, these contradictory tendencies are taken to an extreme with the incorporation and concomitant revision of the literary product of a completely different (and certainly antinomistic) group of Jesus people (i.e., the Gospel of Mark), and with the odd identification of Matthew's brand of "Christianity" with Pharisaic Judaism "done right."

If this outline of events has any validity, we will need to rethink entirely what we mean by and how we understand "Jewish Christianity" or "Christian Judaism" in antiquity. Certainly Q's trajectory toward increasingly explicit self-placement within the symbolic matrix of "Jewish" ideology conforms to the broader tendency of the term (and thus the concept?) "Jew" to shift, from the first century B.C.E. onward, to a designation more behavioral or ideological than geographic or strictly ethnic (see S. G. Wilson 2004). But there are more significant historical implications than this. While Q is but a single document, representative of only a single perspective, it nonetheless calls seriously into question the usual understanding of the "relationship" between "Judaism" and "Christianity" as mutually exclusive and distinct religious traditions. Such an understanding is predicated on—or itself proposes!—a historical picture in which the original Jesus movements were thoroughly and identifiably Jewish in both ethnic composition and ideological orientation. But as the Jesus movement developed, internal theological pressures (e.g., increasingly high christology, a christocentric orientation that made Jewish salvific media irrelevant) or fortuitous historical accidents (e.g., the disappearance of the "Jerusalem church," the destruction of the temple, the proliferation of Gentile churches), rendered them less and less Jewish in all respects, and, as a result, more and more distinctively Christian. Yet Q witnesses to processes that are the inverse of this scenario in practically every respect. Q is, on the one hand, the product of ethnic Jews (or "Israelites") at every stage of its development, never shifting to a "mixed" or exclusively Gentile constituency. We thus find in Q no evidence for a progressive interest in the inclusion of non-Jews. On the other hand, Q fits itself increasingly over time into the ideological matrix of Jewish religiosity; and it does so, moreover, at the same time as, and indeed as part and parcel of, a pointed critique of that same symbolic world and a drift toward increasing (but still limited) immersion in the distinctive discourses of the nascent Jesus movements. Q thus provides no evidence for a progressive withdrawal from the discursive universe of Judaism, nor for any coordination between an increasingly "Christian" identity and a repudiation of "Judaism." Quite the reverse. The more Q commits itself to the differentiating indices of the Jesus people, the more it evinces the typicalities of the normative hallmarks of its Jewish contemporaries (and vice versa). Against the usual interpretation of the "rise of Christianity," then, Q's odd history suggests instead that the Jesus people became more discursively and ideologically "Jewish" over time; that "Christian" self-definition was in fact an act of Jewish sectarian identity formation, not the birth pangs of a new religion.

SUGGESTED READINGS

Allison, Dale C. 1997. *The Jesus Tradition in Q*. Harrisburg, Pa.: Trinity Press International.

Arnal, William E. 2004. "Why Q Failed: From Ideological Project to Group Formation." Pages 67–87 in *Ancient Myths and Modern Theories of Christian Origins*. Society of Biblical Literature Symposium Series 28. Edited by Ron Cameron and Merrill Miller. Atlanta: Society of Biblical Literature.

Horsley, Richard A. 1995b. "Social Conflict in the Synoptic Sayings Source Q." Pages 37–52 in *Conflict and Invention: Literary, Rhetorical, and Social Studies on the Sayings Gospel Q.* Edited by John S. Kloppenborg. Valley Forge, Pa.: Trinity Press International.

Kloppenborg Verbin, John S. 2000 *Excavating Q: The History and Setting of the Sayings Gospel.* Minneapolis: Fortress Press.

Koester, Helmut. 1990. *Ancient Christian Gospels: Their History and Development.* Philadelphia: Trinity Press International.

Mack, Burton L. 1993. *The Lost Gospel: The Book of Q and Christian Origins.* San Francisco: HarperSanFrancisco.

Robinson, James M. 1971. "LOGOI SOPHON: On the Gattung of Q." Pages 71–113 in James M. Robinson and Helmut Koester, *Trajectories Through Early Christianity.* Philadelphia: Fortress Press.

———. 2000. "History of Q Research." Pages xix–lxxi in *The Critical Edition of Q.* Edited by James M. Robinson, Paul Hoffmann, and John S. Kloppenborg. Hermeneia Supplements. Minneapolis: Fortress Press; Leuven: Peeters.

Seeley, David. 1992. "Jesus' Death in Q." *New Testament Studies* 38:222–34.

Smith, Jonathan Z. 1988 [1982]. "Fences and Neighbors: Some Contours of Early Judaism." Pages 1–18 in *Imagining Religion: From Babylon to Jonestown.* Jonathan Z. Smith. Chicago and London: University of Chicago Press.

Theissen, Gerd. 1978. *The First Followers of Jesus: A Sociological Analysis of the Earliest Christians.* Translated by John Bowden. London: SCM Press.

Tuckett, Christopher M. 1996a. *Q and the History of Early Christianity.* Edinburgh: T & T Clark; Peabody, Mass.: Hendrikson.

Vaage, Leif E. 1994. *Galilean Upstarts: Jesus' First Followers According to Q.* Valley Forge, Pa.: Trinity Press International.

6. Matthew's Gospel: Jewish Christianity, Christian Judaism, or Neither?

Warren Carter

This chapter will engage three interrelated questions. First, is Matthew's Gospel to be classified as belonging to Jewish Christianity or Christian Judaism? Second, what does such a classification signify about the Gospel? And finally, assuming that answers to those questions can be formulated, is the classification an adequate description or categorization of Matthew's Gospel? In answering these questions, we will consider what the descriptors "Jewish Christianity" and "Christian Judaism" signify and identify the challenges and issues involved in assigning Matthew to either of these categories (section 1). Then we will outline the arguments of advocates for each position (sections 2 and 3), identify four main areas of contention between the two positions (section 4), assess their arguments (section 5), and finally engage the question as to whether these terms are adequate ways to categorize Matthew's Gospel (section 6).

I will suggest that Matthew's interaction with the rest of first-century Judaism is more aptly named Christian Judaism than Jewish Christianity, but that neither term is especially adequate for the Gospel. In particular, neither label adequately embraces the Gospel's engagement with its late-first-century world, particularly its negotiation of the Roman imperial world. That is, the labels highlight one dimension of Matthew's interaction with its cultural context (late-first-century Judaism), but regrettably mask other dimensions such as its interaction with the Roman imperial world.

1. DEFINITIONS AND ISSUES

Neither Matthew nor other first-century writers use the terms "Jewish Christianity" and "Christian Judaism." The prominence of the terms in contemporary studies of the history of the early "Christian" movement derives from the nineteenth-century German scholar F. C. Baur (1963 [1831]). Baur understood the development of early Christianity in terms of a conflict between two factions. One faction was Jewish Christianity associated with Peter, James, and Jerusalem, which upheld commitment to Jesus and observance of the practices prescribed by the Torah. The other faction was Gentile Christianity associated with Paul, which required commitment to Jesus but not observance of Torah.

Subsequent discussion of Baur's scheme has identified numerous difficulties, particularly the validity of the terms that he employed and the challenge of defining them (Klijn 1973–74; J. E. Taylor 1990). As strange as it might sound to twenty-first-century persons, both "Christian" and "Jew" are difficult terms to define in the first century (Kimelman, 1999). In this period of great diversity and change, "Judaism" and "Christianity" were not monolithic nor readily distinctive entities. For instance, those that we freely refer to in the first century as Christians infrequently use that term for themselves ("Christian" appears in New Testament writings only in Acts 11:26; 26:28; 1 Pet 4:16). Nor do the early "Christian" writings speak with one voice, and there is no uniformity of "Christian" practice. With regard to Torah observance, for example, some followers of Jesus required themselves and Gentile converts to observe all the Torah (Galatians 2; Acts 15); others required observance only of food purity laws (Gal 2:12; Acts 15:20), while still others required observance of Torah interpreted in terms of love, including the Decalogue (Rom 13:8-10).[1]

Similarly there has been much debate as to who was a Jew and how one might define Judaism (Schiffmann 1985; Cohen 1989). Some take a "primordialist" approach to ethnicity (Brett 1996; Denzey 2002), focusing on fixed or essentialist features (biological descent; kinship; shared territory; customs such as language, dress, religion). But primordialist approaches tend to be too generalizing to be useful in contexts of diversity and transition. "Circumstantialist" or "constructivist" approaches more usefully focus on boundaries or criteria for membership (genealogy, circumcision, etc.), most notably the ways that groups construct, maintain, modify, and transgress boundaries, thereby defining themselves through distinctions from others (that are often perceived to be inferior). First-century Judaism/s, marked by diversity and conflicts, attest/s significant interaction between various centers and numerous efforts to draw boundaries. Scholars have sought to identify these contested areas and centers; E. P. Sanders, for example, imagines a temple-centered "common Judaism,"[2] while others speak of a "complex Judaism" combining internal community stability with continual pragmatic compromises in negotiating foreign rule (Hengel and Deines 1995, 53). More common is to define Judaism by focusing on engagement with various overlapping clusters of boundary markers, whether twofold (birth from a Jewish mother or conversion—the latter involving circumcision [J. J. Collins 1985], as well as immersion, acceptance of Torah, and offering of sacrifice [Schiffmann 1985, 9-39, 51]), threefold (worldview, way of life, social group [Neusner 2001]), fourfold (monotheism, election, covenant/Torah, land/temple [Dunn 1991, 18-36]) or eightfold (ethnicity, scripture, monotheism, circumcision, Sabbath observance, dietary laws, purity laws, festivals [Casey 1991, 12–13]).

David Sim (1998, 275–82) illustrates the non-uniform and disputed nature of terms such as "Judaism" and "Christianity" in his discussion of Ignatius. A bishop of Antioch around the turn of the second century, Ignatius wrote seven letters some twenty or so years after Matthew's Gospel and refers to opponents who clearly do not share his views. Sim notes the contrast that Ignatius draws between "Judaism" and "Christianity" in his letter to the Magnesians (*Magn.* 8:1; 10:2). Sim argues that Ignatius defines "Judaism" as referring to a Jewish way of life that observed the Torah and distinguished Jews from Gentiles (e.g., Sabbath observance in *Magn.* 9). By contrast, Ignatius uses "Christianity" to refer to "the Gentile version of the gospel." It denoted a "non-Jewish religious phenomenon" that was law-free, having rejected the old ways of Judaism (*Magn.* 10:2). But although the matter was clear for Ignatius, it was not so for those Ignatius opposed. Sim recognizes that Ignatius is arguing against opponents who do not support such a distinction. These opponents think that one can follow Jesus and observe Torah. It is because of these competing claims that Ignatius tries to impose his view.

Not surprisingly, if the meaning of neither "Christian" nor "Jew" is clear-cut in the late first century, scholars have had considerable difficulty trying to distinguish an entity called "Jewish Christianity." Three types of definitions have been proposed, and none is without difficulty (Paget 1999, 735–42; Horrell 2000, 137–38).[3] One approach has employed an ethnic definition. Jewish Christianity comprises Jews who became Christians. But this definition is far too broad for the diversity of practice and thought evident among Jesus groups (e.g., James and Paul). A second approach takes a doctrinal view in trying to identify distinctive theological affirmations and/or a type of thought (Schoeps 1949; Daniélou 1964).[4] But such attempts have not been successful in recognizing a diversity of theological positions within "Jewish Christianity," nor in identifying affirmations peculiar to Jewish followers of Jesus. For instance, Daniélou holds that apocalyptic thinking and claims that Jesus was the Messiah were especially important in this respect; but these are also known among groups that include Gentiles (Rom 9:5; Luke 2:11, 26). A third approach that enjoys some current support focuses more on the observance of practices derived from the Torah (J. E. Taylor 1990, 327) combined with some christological element, usually recognition of Jesus as Messiah (Mimouni 1992, 184; Paget 1999, 740–42; Horrell 2000, 137–38). While this approach highlights practices and incorporates christology, its difficulty is that various Jesus groups observed Torah in different ways and to different degrees, raising the question as to whether the term "Christian Judiasm" would be more appropriate. Nevertheless, this third approach seems to highlight the key question for distinguishing "Christian Judaism" and Jewish Christianity." It is a matter of emphasis and centers in the interaction between Torah and Jesus. How much and what kind of Torah observance is necessary to constitute Christian Judaism? (S. G. Wilson 1995, 143; Paget 1999, 735–42; Casey 1991, 12–13). How much Jewishness needs to be evident? How much "Christianity" or claims about Jesus' dominating role are needed to indicate a move outside Judaism to Christianity?

Such difficulties and imprecision of definition have caused some to question the very usefulness of the term "Jewish Christianity." Raymond E. Brown (1983), for example, argues that for New Testament times, including of course Matthew, the label "Jewish Christianity" should be abandoned in favor of recognizing four types of "Jewish/Gentile Christianity" based on degrees of Torah observance including that required for Gentile converts.[5] Type 1 required circumcision and full observance; type 2 required some purity observance but not circumcision; type 3 required neither circumcision nor purity observance; and type 4 added to type 3 the irrelevance of the temple. Brown located Matthew in type 2. This approach helpfully recognizes the presence of Jews and Gentile converts, the importance of Torah, and diversity through degrees of observance. But it begs the question as to whether the term "Christianity" is the appropriate descriptor, since Brown's label "Jewish/Gentile Christianity" assumes an entity identified as Christianity. It might be suggested that in the diversity and transitions of first-century Judaisms, Brown's terms more aptly describe different expressions of Judaism practiced by followers of Jesus. If so, the label "Christian Judaism" would be more appropriate. Even here, however, we return to the problem noted above of the difficulty of adequately defining both "Christian" and "Judaism."

At stake in this question of definition as to whether Matthew should be classified as "Jewish Christianity" (a Jewish form of Christianity) or "Christian Judaism" (a Christian form of Judaism) are, as I have indicated above, matters of emphasis, of continuity and newness, of context and distinctive religious communities and traditions. Is Matthew more Jewish or more Christian? No one on either side of the debate would dispute Matthew's indebtedness to and use of Jewish traditions, nor the Gospel's advocacy of lived allegiance to Jesus. But as we shall see in more detail in section 2, some answer the question How much Jewishness? by emphasizing Matthew's continuity with the thought and practices of Judaism, though also recognizing the importance of commitment to Jesus. They see Matthew's Jesus and community primarily as authoritative reformers of Judaism—as "more Jewish," and thus an example of Christian Judaism. But as we shall see in section 3, others reverse the emphasis, seeing more Christianity than Judaism in Matthew. They answer the question How much Jewishness? by arguing that Matthew's degree of Christianity is much greater than the degree of Jewishness. While not denying some continuity with Judaism, they emphasize that commitment to Jesus has introduced something so new that it transforms the thought and practices of Judaism. Advocates of this position see Matthew's Jesus as the founder of a separate and new religion. They see Matthew as more Christian, describing it as an example of Jewish Christianity. Throughout both sections, and explicitly in sections 4 and 5, I will consider the adequacy and appropriateness of these terms for Matthew's Gospel.

2. CHRISTIAN JUDAISM

A. J. Saldarini (1994), along with other contemporary scholars (Overman 1990; Sim 1996; 1998), supports the first of these options. Saldarini has argued that Matthew's Gospel addresses a "Christian-Jewish community" and presents a Christian form of Judaism. I will summarize Saldarini's approach as generally representative of those who argue for such a position. Particularly important to his analysis are the following points.

- Saldarini employs sociological categories of deviance, sects, and kinship to locate Matthew's group, committed to Jesus, within Judaism as a group that seeks to reform Jewish society through its commitment to Jesus, its practices, conflict, and conversions.
- Saldarini emphasizes the diversity of first-century Judaism, into whose "intellectual, religious and symbolic world" Matthew's Jesus readily fits (1994, 9). Like other deviant and sectarian groups such as Essenes, revolutionists, and apocalyptic and baptist groups, Matthew's group engages this world with polemic and advocacy of its own vision for Israel's life. It does so having "been engaged in a lengthy conflict with Jewish authorities and [having] recently withdrawn from or been expelled from the Jewish assembly" (1994, 3, 112, 121).
- Saldarini defines the target of Jesus' harsh attacks in Matthew as the leaders of the Jewish community who mislead the people with their self-serving societal vision. Matthew's Jesus does not attack and condemn all Israel. His harsh words in chapter 23, for example, do originate not from someone outside the Jewish community but from someone actively engaged in internal Jewish politics.
- Saldarini argues that Matthew's protracted discussions of Jewish laws and practices do not supersede Jewish law with a new Christian law

but belong within the boundaries of late-first-century Jewish debate about the interpretation and practice of Torah. Saldarini (1994, 124) concludes, "The topics discussed, the positions affirmed and rejected, the sectarian apologetic and polemical stances, the competition for power and recognition, the maintenance of boundaries, and the creation of a world view and group identity are all similar to the agendas of numerous Jewish works found among the Dead Sea Scrolls, the apocalyptic writings, the pseudepigrapha, Josephus, and early layers of the Mishnah." Matthew's Jesus is the authoritative teacher within the Jewish community, not the founder of a new religious movement.

- Saldarini maintains that Matthew's presentation of Jesus as Messiah and Son of God is formulated within first-century Jewish understandings. Jesus' close relationship with God, participation in Israel's traditions (Abraham, David, Moses, prophets, wisdom), and doing of God's will in enacting God's reign or kingdom provide traditional Jewish warrants for Jesus' role as the divinely sent leader and authorized agent and revealer of God's intervention in Israel. Claims about Jesus as the one through whom God is active in his teaching and healing are analogous to various claims in contemporary Jewish literature.

- According to Saldarini, Matthew maintains Israel's place among the nations. The Gospel, that is, does not present the "nations" as a replacement for Israel as God's people; it only opens Israel's boundaries to believing and Torah-observant Gentiles.

- Nor does Matthew's Gospel suggest that God has replaced Israel with a separate Christian community that has clearly defined boundaries and uncontested legitimacy as the revolutionary (re)interpretation of Jewish traditions. Rather, Matthew's community has a living relationship with other groups within Judaism, including disputes over boundaries and legitimacy, as well as a reformist and conversionist mission among Jews and Gentiles. Matthew's references to "Israel," "people," and "crowds," imply God's continuing purposes for Israel.

In short, Saldarini locates Matthew within the diversity of first-century Judaism. He emphasizes that within this diversity there were debates about boundaries, identity, and legitimate interpretations of Israel's traditions and symbols, in which Matthew's Jesus participates. Matthew's Gospel is at home within the symbolic universe of first-century Judaism, negotiating the cluster of boundary markers—law (5:17-48), temple (12:6; 21:1-11), monotheism (22:37-40), way of life (chs. 5–7), social group 16:16-19), Sabbath observance (12:1-14), food purity (15:1-20) etc.—identified above as constitutive of first-century Judaism.

Furthermore, Saldarini emphasizes that in its attacks on Israel's leaders, debates over the practices of Torah, and christological claims, Matthew's Gospel does not declare the replacement of Israel by a separate and new religion of Christianity. Rather, Matthew continues mission to Israel, seeking to reform and convert according to the teaching of Jesus, who is the divinely sent emissary and authorized teacher of God's will. For Saldarini, Matthew's emphasis is on continuity with God's previous dealings with Israel. Jesus' special status and role do not separate him or his followers from Judaism but provide the basis for their mission to Israel. This mission is also open to Gentiles who believe in Jesus and commit to obey Torah (including circumcision). Matthew does not replace or supersede Israel and does not seek to establish a new religion.

3. JEWISH CHRISTIANITY

Taking a quite different approach are those, like D. A. Hagner, who see Matthew's Gospel advocating not a Christian form of Judaism but a Jewish form of Christianity (Hagner 1993–95; 2003; 2004; Stanton 1992a; 1992b). In contrast to Christian Judaism (which Hagner [2003, 196] defines as "Jews who have come to faith in Jesus as Messiah and who continue in their living as faithful Jews, participating in the synagogue and the sacrificial cult of the temple,[6] and marked above all by faithful obedience to the Torah"), Hagner defines Jewish Christianity as comprising "Jews who have come to faith in Jesus as the divine κύριος [kyrios; Lord], who affirm their faith as the fulfillment of the scriptures, whose experience involves a degree of newness that transcends the synagogue and temple, and who believe that by following the teaching of Jesus, their Messiah-Teacher, they fulfill the righteousness of the

Torah" (Hagner 2003, 196). I will summarize Hagner's approach as generally representative of those who argue for such a position. [7]

While acknowledging Matthew's use of Jewish traditions, Hagner consistently emphasizes the Gospel's boundary-breaking newness: "there is a radical newness in the Gospel of Matthew that continually moves beyond the bounds of Judaism and requires the conclusion that Matthew's community be described as a form of Christianity." And "Matthew decidedly reflects a Christianity rather than a Judaism." Matthew's community "treasured a perspective that was dramatically new compared to anything previously known in Judaism" (2003, 194, 197).

Hagner frames Matthew's newness in the larger context of "the parting of the ways," the separation of Christian groups from Judaism. While this parting involved a gradual transition and occurred in different ways in different places, the differences between Christian groups and Judaism became "increasingly apparent and unavoidable" by Matthew's time (2003, 197). Hagner thinks that Matthew's group has departed from the synagogue. While it sees itself as the completion of—or the "true"—Judaism, other groups see it as apostate. Rejecting Saldarini's language of Matthew as a "sect" within Judaism, Hagner follows Petri Luomanen in identifying Matthew's group sociologically as a cult whose new ideas comprise a new group; it is a "religious innovation" (Hagner 2003, 197–98; Luomanen 2002).

Hagner turns to the content of the Gospel, especially the relationship between christology and Torah, to support his claim of "radical newness" that places Matthew's community "beyond the bounds of Judaism." From 9:16-17 and 13:52, he notes Matthew's emphasis on "new things" that surpass the old. Hagner (2003, 201) asserts that various "new things" in Matthew's Gospel are problematic for Judaism, including:

- the eschatological announcement that the Messiah and kingdom have come, bringing fulfillment while the judgment of the wicked awaits the consummation of God's purposes;
- the belief that the Messiah is a unique manifestation of God;
- the claim that the Messiah must die a death of a criminal as one cursed, making possible forgiveness of sins;
- obedience to God centered on Jesus, not the law;

- the notion that participation in God's new kingdom involves suffering;
- a new community, the *ekklēsia*, as the center of God's salvific activity;
- the inclusion of Gentiles within this new community.

Most problematic for Judaism is Matthew's "high Christology" (Hagner 2003, 201–6). Matthew presents Jesus as definitive interpreter of the law (5:17 to "fulfill" means "to bring to intended meaning" [Hagner 2003, 202]), the one who teaches with authority (23:8-10; 7:28; 13:54; 22:33).

Jesus' interpretation represents a significant change in thinking and has "a new and radical character." The law remains important "only as taken up in the teaching of Jesus." Whereas Torah occupies a central place in Judaism, Jesus is now the center in Matthew. The call is to obey Jesus, not Torah (18:20; 24:35; 28:20). Jesus is the unique Son of God, Emmanuel. He is the divine Son of Man who will judge nations, the divinely authorized revealer who shares God's authority (11:27; 28:18) and who, as the unique representative of God, mediates between God and humanity (10:32). Indeed, "more than a representative of God, . . . he is God" (Hagner 2003, 205). The Gospel's radical stance on other matters such as Israel's election, ethnicity, the land, and temple means that "Matthew's community is more a Christianity than a Judaism" (Hagner 2003, 206).[8]

Hagner's analysis highlights key aspects of the argument for understanding Matthew as an example of Jewish Christianity. At the center are christology and Hagner's claim that Matthew's Jesus is not just a representative of God, but that he is God. This identity gives Jesus the authority to teach definitively God's will. In reinterpreting the law, Matthew's Jesus introduces something new and radical, displacing Torah from its central role and subsuming it under Jesus' teaching and person.

4. Areas of Contention

Before noting four significant areas of contention between the two perspectives, one point of common ground should be noted. Both Saldarini (1994, 3, 112, 121) and Hagner (2003, 197–98) agree that Matthew's community has probably separated from a synagogue or assembly in a time of conflict. While both scholars recognize some physical separation, neither builds an argument for his perspective on the event of separation itself. Unlike Luomanen (2002, 107 n. 3), neither deems physical separation itself to be a factor in determining whether Matthew belongs to Christian Judaism or Jewish Christianity.

We can, however, identify four significant factors that are in contention between the two perspectives.

Sect versus Cult

Although neither derives significance from the act of separation itself, both draw quite different conclusions about the nature of the Matthean community *after* it has separated from the synagogue or assembly. In an extensive discussion, Saldarini employs models from sociology and anthropology concerned with group formation and sectarian identity to argue that Matthew's group, in contrast to and in conflict with other Jewish groups, is a "deviant" group.[9] In contemporary sociology, "deviance" highlights relationships and tensions between groups within a society when a majority group tries to impose normative practices and values and another group decides not to conform, instead embracing alternative values. Deviant groups are "social movements that wish to cause or prevent change in a system of beliefs, values, symbols, and practices concerned with providing supernaturally based general compensators" (Saldarini 1994, 109; Stark and Bainbridge, 1985, 23). That is, "deviance" is about struggles for identity, boundary drawing, societal structures, and values within a society. Saldarini (1994, 113–16) also uses Bryan Wilson's typology of sects (1973) based on "responses to the world" to classify this deviant group's positive goals as a sect within Judaism. It is a reformist sect since it seeks to reform Jewish society according to its understanding of God's will revealed by Jesus. It is also a millenarian sect looking for the destruction of evil by divine intervention, and a conversionist sect seeking to change people and secure their allegiance to the group. Throughout, Saldarini emphasizes that Matthew's group is neither a replacement for nor separated from

Judaism, but is located within Judaism as one group among others seeking to reform and shape its life and future.

Hagner also appeals to sociological theory, though it plays much less of a role in his analysis. He cites Luomanen (2002) who, like Saldarini, employs aspects of Rodney Stark and William Bainbridge's work. But Luomanen contends that Wilson's definition of sects, which emphasizes "responses to the world," is inappropriate for Saldarini's analysis of Matthew. Luomanen argues that Wilson's sect taxonomy posits a reasonably coherent parent group from which the sect deviates and to which it can relate in different ways. This emphasis on a coherent parent group, he points out, is at odds with Saldarini's emphasis on the diversity of Judaism. First-century Judaism lacks the very homogeneity that the sect model requires. Luomanen finds Stark and Bainbridge's description of a "cult" more useful. In a context of tensions, sects come into being by schism, whereas cults come into being when "new religious ideas gain social acceptance" (Luomanen 2002, 128). The new ideas attested by Matthew concern "Jesus' position as Kyrios" and "a liberal interpretation of the law" (2002, 129).[10]

The Role of First-Century Judaism

Hagner briefly recognizes the contribution of recent studies that have highlighted the diversity and debates within first-century and post-70 Judaism, but this recognition plays relatively little part in his analysis. Saldarini, however, gives this dimension much greater emphasis as the context in which Matthew is to be situated. He begins his discussion with an overview of the diversity and struggles over defining boundaries, the exercise of power, and constituting identity, including the diverse interaction between Jesus groups and other Jewish groups. This material lays the foundation for Saldarini's subsequent discussions of the role of Israel in Matthew's Gospel (1994, ch. 2), of the Gospel's attack on the Jewish leaders (ch. 3), of relationships with Gentiles (ch. 4), of the nature of Matthew's group (ch. 5), of the Gospel's interpretation of Torah (ch. 6), and of Jesus' identity as God's emissary (ch. 7). Saldarini argues throughout that Matthew's engagement with these issues falls within the diverse perspectives and boundaries of first-century Judaism, and that Matthew's Gospel does not, therefore, constitute a new religion.

The Role of Torah

Both positions understand Matthew to present Jesus as the definitive interpreter of Torah in a context of disputes over its interpretation and practice. But they disagree significantly over the impact of this interpretation. Saldarini argues that Matthew's interpretation "shows the contours of his reform program for Judaism, a program which sought to neutralize the powerful and ultimately successful program of the early rabbis." All the topics that Matthew engages (Sabbath, purity and dietary laws, tithes and taxes, divorce, oaths and vows, circumcision), the positions he advocates, and his general emphasis on doing good, love, justice, and faithfulness (12:7, 12; 23:23) "fit into the agenda of first-century Judaism . . . within the range of accepted discussion and similar to those [positions] taken by other groups" (Saldarini 1994, 126).

But while Saldarini sees Matthew's Jesus within these boundaries, Hagner sees Matthew's Jesus breaking out of them. This is because Jesus' authority now takes center stage, displacing the law. "[I]t is not the law in itself that is Matthew's concern, but only the law *as mediated through the teaching of Jesus*. . . . [T]he law remains significant for these Jewish Christians but only as it is taken up in the teaching of Jesus" (2003, 202–3; Hagner's emphasis). Jesus and his words (18:20; 24:35; 28:20) take center stage.

One significant disagreement over a matter of Torah should be noted. Matthew's Gospel is silent on circumcision and on whether Gentile converts should be circumcised. Saldarini (1994, 156–60) interprets the silence by arguing that the Gospel probably assumes such circumcision as its normal practice for Jewish members and Gentile converts. If it didn't, the Gospel would have defended this non-practice in its debates about other issues of Torah practice. This requirement of circumcision clearly locates Matthew within first-century Judaism. But Saldarini also argues that even if Matthew's group did not observe circumcision or require it for Gentile converts, it would not mean that Matthew's deviant group was outside Judaism, since observance of circumcision and other practices varied. Hagner (2003, 196–97) gives less attention to this question, though he does point to the omission of any reference to circumcision in the (Gentile-inclusive) mission command of 28:20 as a likely indicator that circumcision was not required for Gentile converts. He does not explicitly indicate whether circumcision was necessary for Jewish members of Matthew's community.[11]

Christology

Basic to the disagreement over Torah is the Gospel's christology. While both Hagner and Saldarini see Jesus as integral to Matthew's Gospel, they disagree over the implications of Matthew's presentation. For Hagner (2003, 204), "Jesus is an exalted figure in Matthew far beyond any others who have been sent from God in the history of Israel." With Jesus taking the place of Torah, Matthew's community no longer remains within Judaism. Saldarini (1994, 165–93), though, does not see Matthew's Jesus as "far beyond" others sent from God. As God's emissary or Messiah, Matthew's Jesus does what other faithful and just sons of God do. As teacher and healer, he reveals and enacts God's will, as do other divinely commissioned mediators and messengers. While Matthew combines various traditions (Moses, wisdom, prophets) to present Jesus as the divinely authorized figure, he does not claim anything that does not "fit within the broad parameters of Judaism as it actually existed."

5. Evaluation

Both sides are vulnerable to some critique. In sum, Saldarini's "Christian Jewish" approach is vulnerable to the criticism that it overstates the observance of Torah and understates the Gospel's christological claims. Similarly, Hagner's "Jewish Christianity" approach is vulnerable to the criticism that it overstates the Gospel's "newness" (especially christologically) and understates its fit within the diversity of first-century Judaism. We will take these critiques in turn.

Matthew as Christian Judaism

Douglas R. A. Hare offers five critiques of Saldarini's position (Hare 2000; Riches 2000, 202-28). His points are of varying strength.

First, Hare warns against arguments from silence and urges respect for the Gospel's silence. He cautions that little can be concluded about circumcision except that we do not know. In addition, he questions the assumption that the invective of chapter 23 reflects current controversy between Matthew's community and Pharisaic Judaism.

Second, Hare is not convinced by Saldarini's discussion of the Matthew group's self-identification in 16:18 and 18:17 as *ekklēsia*. Saldarini (1994, 116–20) argues that this is not a technical term for a distinctive and separate Christian (non-Jewish) community; it denotes, rather, an assembly in relation to Israel but differentiated from opposing groups. Hare thinks Saldarini overlooks Matthew's likely knowledge of the use of the term in Paul's circles to denote largely Gentile communities. Matthew's use of the term suggests a self-understanding for Matthew's community that aligns it with an emerging Christian movement rather than identifying it as a group within Judaism. But against Hare, the exhortations to Gentile mission in Matthew's Gospel do not suggest a predominantly Gentile community, and it can by no means be assumed that Paul advocates a separate Christian movement.

Third, Hare notes that only a very limited number of verses can be employed to sustain the claim that all members of Matthew's group, including Gentiles, strictly observed Torah. These references can be interpreted in other ways so that they by no means sustain the requirement of the literal observance of all of the law by all members of Matthew's community. Matthew 5:19, for instance, encourages Torah observance without making it necessary either for participation in the eschatological consummation ("will be called least in the kingdom," not excluded) or membership in the church. When Matt 23:2-3 says "the scribes and the Pharisees sit on Moses' seat; so practice and observe whatever they tell you," this cannot be interpreted to mean obedience to the law. It is probably best understood as referring to the public reading of scripture, which Jesus authoritatively interprets (so 5:17-48), since 23:16-20 forbids obedience to the teaching of the scribes and Pharisees, while the reference in 23:23-24 to the "weightier matters" of justice, mercy, and faithfulness seem to subordinate tithing. The law as interpreted by Jesus is to be obeyed. Matthew 24:20 does not forbid travel on the Sabbath, but recognizes that it is not a favorable time.

Hare concludes that Matthew does not advocate comprehensive observance of the law, which suggests that Torah observance may have been considerably more flexible, especially for Gentile converts, than Saldarini allows. This line of arguing, though, overlooks Saldarini's discussion of specific scenes that uphold a range of practices and behaviors (Sabbath, food purity, tithing etc.) based on Torah. Nor does the Gospel provide exceptive clauses for Gentiles. In addition, the story of the tax coin in the fish's mouth should be noted (17:24-27). It exhorts payment of the tax that Rome levied on Jews after Rome had subjugated Judea in 70. Paying this tax indicates that Matthew's community belongs to the wider Jewish community (Carter 1999; 2001, 130–44).

Fourth, Hare points out, on the basis of investigations into the development of christology, that Saldarini overlooks the Gospel's support for the worship of Jesus in three instances (14:33; 28:9, 17) even while it upholds exclusive worship of God (4:10).[12] The point is substantial but its applicability to Matthew is dubious. Hare seems to assume that the three texts he cites regarding "worship" either reflect the practice of Matthew's community or (implicitly) exhort their imitation. But the Gospel gives no such instruction to worship Jesus and it is not clear that the three instances exhort worship. The verb translated "worship" can denote acts of homage or expressions of allegiance in recognition of superior authority (as the term frequently signifies in the political realm; Carter 2000a, 76, 111, 199) rather than reflect or encourage cultic activity.

Hare points out, finally, that the Gospel is pessimistic about a successful mission to Israel (ch. 10), dissociates itself from unbelieving Jews (28:15), and associates itself with believing Gentiles (24:14; 28:19). But of course the Gospel also identifies and affirms Jews who believe in Jesus.

The heart of Hare's critique of Saldarini, as with Hagner's, is christological. They agree that Torah as interpreted by Jesus is the norm for Matthew's group. Hare, though, finds the Gospel's christology, notably its replacement of Torah with Jesus "as the key to right relationship with the God of Israel," to be a decisive point against Saldarini's thesis of Christian Judaism. As we have seen in sections 2 and 4 above, Saldarini argues that Matthew presents Jesus as God's emissary or Messiah, who faithfully enacts God's will within the broad parameters of Judaism.

Matthew as Jewish Christianity

While Saldarini is perhaps vulnerable (to his critics) for overstating the role of Torah and understating the impact of christology, Hagner's thesis of Matthew as a Jewish Christian text is vulnerable for overstating the Gospel's "newness" (especially christologically) and understating the Gospel's fit within the diversity of first-century Judaism.

Hagner's highest claim about Jesus is that Jesus does not represent God but is the "one who *is* God with us." But this reading of Matt 1:23 is unlikely (Davies and Allison 1988, 217–18; Dunn 1991, 213–15). Nowhere does Matthew call Jesus God. The Gospel's citation of Isa 7:14, moreover, rules against Hagner's reading, since the citation specifically evokes the circumstances of Isaiah 7 involving King Ahaz, and the likely birth of a child from the royal line as a sign of God's faithfulness in a time of national threat. That is, the evoking of Isaiah 7 points to a human and kingly figure who will be, in circumstances of imperial threat, an agent of God's purposes, like Jesus (Carter 2000b; 2001, 93–107). On the other hand, consistent with Saldarini's general point that the Gospel works within established categories of Judaism is the observation that God has been "with" God's people previously (Num 23:21; Deut 2:7), particularly for the establishment of God's just and liberating purposes (Isa 43:5; Ezek 34:30; Zech 8:23).

Also undermining Hagner's claim of a high christology is Saldarini's demonstration that the expression "son of God" does not burst the boundaries of Judaism but is in fact well at home in first-century Judaism. The term denotes agents of God's purposes, those who faithfully enact God's will. It does not yet carry the ontological categories used in later centuries to describe the Father–Son relationship (and to be fair Hagner does not claim that it does). Saldarini (1994, 172–77, 193) rightly observes that "Matthew did not claim for Jesus divinity in the way that Greek theologians two centuries later did." Rather Jesus is God's emissary and agent, commissioned to manifest God's saving purposes and reign.

Hagner's claim that Jesus' teaching displaces Torah is also overstated. While Hagner (2003, 203) recognizes the importance of Torah for Matthew, his claim that the Gospel presents a shift to Jesus as the center where "it is finally the words of Jesus, not Torah, that are of ultimate authority," suggests in effect something of a relegation or subordination of Torah. But it is not accurate to describe Matthew's center only in terms of Jesus without also explicitly including Torah when Jesus' interpretation of Torah constitutes his teaching.

Christopher Rowland (1999, 785–90) underlines this point by arguing that it is a mistake to see authoritative revealer figures in Jewish apocalyptic traditions (with which Matthew's Jesus has affinity [e.g., 11:25-30]) as either opposed to or subordinating Torah and the tradition of authoritative writings. Rather they are deeply indebted to it and draw on it as interpreters and revealers of the divine purposes. *1 Enoch*, for example, upholds the law as part of the people's history with God (*1 En.* 93:6) while its scenes of judgment on the "kings and mighty ones" and "mighty landowners" (*1 En.* 46–48; 53) and its numerous woes on powerful and rich oppressors are heavily indebted to the denunciations of the prophetic traditions (*1 En.* 94–100; Rowland 1999, 783).[13] Rowland (1999, 789) argues that revealer figures interpret scripture as well as receive direct revelations as purveyors of "higher wisdom through revelation." Matthew 5 demonstrates this unity, with its explicit interpretation of scripture in the six units that constitute 5:21-48, along with its declarations or revelations of the divine will, announced, for example, as blessings in 5:3-12. The beatitudes frequently draw on the scriptural tradition but formulate it afresh with the authority of Jesus commissioned to declare God's saving presence and reign (1:21-23; 4:17; Carter 2000a, 128–57). Jesus' words that will never pass away (24:35) and that are to be taught to his followers (28:19-20) derive from, cohere with, and interpret Torah and the traditions, as is typical of various Jewish revealer figures.

Klyne Snodgrass (1996) also resists the exclusive christological reading offered by Hagner in arguing rightly that Matthew's center comprises "Christ and Torah." "How," he wonders, "have law and scripture become set over against Jesus and Christology? Such an antithesis is foreign to

Matthew's theology. The law is not removed by Christology. Rather, the word of God and the Son of God cohere and function together like hand and glove" (1996, 126). Snodgrass argues that Matthew presents Jesus as the one who interprets the law "by a special hermeneutical key so as to reveal the divine intention of the law" (1996, 105). This hermeneutical key to the law (and to the prophets also, as Snodgrass emphasizes [1996, 106–11]) is love or mercy. This key is not something foreign to or imposed on the tradition but derives from it. In 22:37-40 Matthew's Jesus sums up the law and the prophets by requiring love for God and neighbor, citing Deut 6:5 and Lev 19:18. Twice Matthew cites Hos 6:6 to show mercy to be at the heart of the tradition (9:13; 12:7) and 23:23 identifies justice, mercy, and faithfulness as the weightier matters of the law. Such emphases in Jesus' teaching are not foreign to the Law and the Prophets but derive from them. Snodgrass rightly argues that their use as a hermeneutical key does not set Jesus over against Torah but produces teaching that is "an explanation of what the law and prophets really are" (Snodgrass 1996, 113). Nor is Jesus' formulation unique in Judaism. Philo understands the Decalogue as a summary of the law (*Decal.* 20, 154) and love for God and humans as a summary of both (*Decal.* 108-10; *Spec. Laws* 2.63). Snodgrass's claim that "Christ and Torah" more accurately represents Matthew's center seems convincing. Hagner of course disagrees, commenting that "it is fairer to Matthew's perspective to say that Christ is the center of Matthew, and that the Torah is *in effect* preserved only through Christ's teaching" (2003, 203 n. 38).

The other Matthean assertions of newness that Hagner claims "are, mildly put, problematic for Judaism" are similarly open to critique, partly because Hagner overstates Matthew's claims to newness or uniqueness, and partly because he minimizes Jewish contexts. Space does not permit a comprehensive discussion of each item but the following initial points can be noted, which indicate that Matthew's claims are not significant problems for Judaism.[14]

- How problematic is Matthew's declaration that the Messiah and the kingdom had come without the judgment of the wicked? (Hagner 2003, 201). Given diverse scenarios of the establishment of God's purposes in early Judaism, Matthew's emphasis on the present yet future completion of God's reign (which included future judgment [25:31-46]), and Jesus' declarations of judgment (ch. 23), the problem does not seem insurmountable. The new age did not materialize as some expected, but this is not so unfamiliar. Jewish traditions offer various examples of the nonmaterialization of the expected promised age, or what might be called partial or incipient demonstrations of God's reign through an anointed figure. In various idealized scenarios, the king, for example, appears as agent of God's reign operative in and through the king's reign, including judgment on the wicked (e.g., Psalm 72). Events such as the return from Babylonian exile, facilitated by the Messiah Cyrus the Persian (Isa 44:28—45:1), exhibited God's reign at least in part (Isa 52:7). Qumran knows a tension (similar to Matthew's) between the present and the future, the now and the not yet. Along with expectations that the Messiah will transform the world, there is also evidence that for some the coming of the messiahs is not expected to impact human existence significantly (so *Messianic Rule* [1QSa]; Nickelsburg 1992, 586–87; J. J. Collins 1997, 79–81). John J. Collins (1997, 82–90) notes that when the expected end of the age in *Damascus Document* 20:14 forty years after the death of the Teacher did not happen, there were no major consequences or loss of eschatological expectation.

- Matthew's claims of the Messiah's manifestation of God's purposes are not unique to Matthew. Messianic traditions were diverse (de Jonge 1992; Charlesworth 1992; J. J. Collins 1995). Other texts that deal with messiahs imply some unique role in and manifestation of God's purposes. But the descriptions of expected messiahs[15] and Josephus's depictions of the various figures who evoked prophetic (*Ant.* 20.97–99 [Theudas]) or kingly (*Ant.* 17.273-77 [Simon]; 17.284 [Athronges]; *J.W.* 7.153–55 [Simon bar Giora]) paradigms in undertaking actions that would reenact previous displays of God's will in delivering the people (Horsley and Hanson 1985; Horsley 1992; J. J. Collins 1995, 195–214) bear no hint that they have somehow burst the boundaries of Judaism. What is more, they and/or their followers routinely suffer the same fate at Roman hands that Matthew's Jesus suffers. The death of a messianic figure is not unique; *4 Ezra* 7:29, in fact, explicitly names the death of the messiah before the new age is inaugurated.

- Matthew's Jesus identifies suffering as an inevitable aspect of participating in God's reign until its completion (5:10-12; 10:16-39; 24:6-28). But this was not a new element. To participate in God's soon-to-be-victorious purposes was understood in diverse Jewish traditions to involve various forms of suffering for God's people and the wicked, whether already present (*4 Ezra* 5:2-3) or still future (*1 En.* 100:1-4; *2 Baruch* 25–29; Allison 1985, 5–25).

- The claim that Matthew's community, the *ekklēsia* (Matt 16:16-19), is central to God's salvific activity does not pose challenges for Judaism. Various communities made similar claims. Qumran understood itself in salvation history to be the righteous remnant to whom the right interpretation of the law was given and among whom the Messiah/s will appear (Nickelsburg 1992, 586–87). Moreover, Matthew's attacks on the leaders of the post-70 scribal-Pharisaic movement indicate that they had a similar understanding. In 15:13 Jesus declares that these "blind guides" have not been planted by God and will experience judgment. In the three parables of 21:28—22:14, they are eliminated from participation in God's purposes, and in chapter 23 they are the object of Jesus' curses. Such condemnations make little sense without a context of communal competition over claims about central roles in God's salvific activity and over diverse visions of what this salvific activity looks like.

- Matthew's vision of the involvement of Gentiles in the community of Jesus' disciples and in God's eschatological purposes (Carter 2004)[16] similarly falls within a wide spectrum of Jewish negotiations of the Gentile world (Barclay 1996). Pentateuchal (Gen 12:1-3 [Abraham]; Kuschel 1995, 29–49), prophetic (Isa 25:6-10) and psalmic (72:8, 11, 17) traditions recognize Gentile inclusion in God's blessing. Daniel's kings Nebuchadnezzar and Darius acknowledge God's sovereignty (Dan 2:47; 3:28—4:27; 6:25-28). The *Psalms of Solomon* include in God's purposes Gentiles who acknowledge the Davidic messiah's rule (17:29-34). *1 Enoch* sees

righteous, law-observant Gentiles included in God's eschatological purposes (83–90). *2 Baruch*, frequently hostile to the nations,
acknowledges proselytes (41:4-6) and anticipates that some of the
nations (those who have not oppressed Israel) will be spared at
the Messiah's appearing (*2 Baruch* 72). *4 Ezra* laments in vain for
the nations (7:62-74). In terms of social interaction, Donald B.
Binder (1999, 380–87) notes a tradition of "pious Gentiles," including those who sacrificed in the temple (see Josephus, *J.W.*
2.411–16), "literary evidence for the attraction of Gentiles to Jewish laws and traditions," and the presence of Gentile proselytes and
God-fearers in synagogue communities, including in Antioch,
a likely provenance for Matthew's Gospel (Josephus, *J.W.* 7.45).
Philo claims that everywhere "thousands" of synagogues "stand
open" every Sabbath (*Spec. Laws* 2.62–63), and Josephus imagines
that everywhere Gentiles imitate Jews in observing Sabbath, fasting, and food laws, and practicing unanimity, charity, hard work,
and endurance (*Ag. Ap.* 2.282–86). Shaye J. D. Cohen (1989, 26)
elaborates seven levels of Gentile involvement with Jewish communities ranging from admiration of aspects to Judaism to joining
a Jewish community and conversion to Judaism involving (variously) exclusive acknowledgment of Israel's God, observance of
practices of the law, and integration into the Jewish community
(see Jdt 14:10).

Such observations flesh out and support Saldarini's claim that Matthew
operates within the broad parameters of first-century Judaism.

Finally, among the conclusions that Hagner draws from his emphasis
on the Gospel's putative newness is that Matthew was probably "regarded as [an apostate from Judaism] by the Jews" (2003, 208). The
use of the unqualified term "the Jews" indicates little recognition of the
diversity of late-first-century Judaism. Hagner does not specify which
Jews might have regarded Matthew as apostate, nor does he define what
he means by the term. It is, though, fair to conclude from the article's
content as well as from the preposition "from" in the expression "apostate from Judaism" that Hagner has in view renouncing or abandoning

one's commitment to a community and the practices that constitute a particular way of life—in this instance, Judaism. Lawrence H. Schiffman (1985, 41) offers a somewhat similar definition: "an apostate is one whose *actions* are not consonant with the standards of behavior set by his religious community."

Hagner might have some support for this claim that (all? some?) "Jews" so regarded Matthew if the Gospel portrayed characters identifying Jesus and/or his followers with this term, but it does not.[17] Nor can it be established that the social separation of Matthew's group from a synagogue was a formal expulsion which might indicate that Matthew's group had violated a local group's established "norms of belief or conduct" even if not general Jewish norms (Horbury 1985, 13). But the Gospel does not specify either cause or means. Moreover, studies of apostasy from Judaism around the first century tend not to support Hagner's claim. Barclay's discussion (1995; 1998) of a range of Jewish texts finds that declarations of apostasy vary considerably and there is no standard definition of where and how the boundary is crossed. If any generalization is possible, Barclay argues, apostates are guilty of two breeches: idolatry and abandonment of the food laws. Matthew does not endorse the former and, however 15:1-20 is read, the omission of Mark 7:19 ("Thus Jesus declared all foods pure"), the redefinition of handwashing as a human tradition (15:2-9), and the focus on moral-social purity (15:10-20), indicate that he does not rescind purity requirements either. But even if the Gospel did, does apostasy mean that a person is now outside the Jewish community, as Hagner implies? Schiffmann (1985, 41–51) argues from Tannaitic material that it does not. "Jewish status could never be canceled, even for the most heinous offenses against Jewish law and doctrine."

From these observations, it seems that Hagner overemphasizes the christological uniqueness and newness of the Gospel while underplaying the diversity of first-century Judaism. The above factors suggest, though, that attention to the diversity of first-century Judaism, as evident in Saldarini's discussion, provides a context in which Matthew's Gospel belongs. It does not make claims that are outside the range and boundaries of first-century Judaism.

6. CONCLUSION

From the factors considered above, Saldarini's description of Matthew as an example of Christian Judaism centered in Jesus' role as the definitive interpreter of the Law and the Prophets seems more appropriate than Hagner's overstated emphasis on the Gospel's newness and christological displacement of Torah that constitutes a form of Jewish Christianity.

Yet several factors suggest that neither term is ultimately satisfactory. I will mention just two.

First, as I observed at the outset of this chapter, both formulations attempt to employ combinations of terms ("Christianity/Christian," "Judaism/Jewish") whose meanings in the first century are imprecise, whose formulation in the singular and often opposite each other misleadingly suggests well-defined and monolithic entities, and whose use, especially in the case of "Christianity," may well be anachronistic. Both formulations—Christian Judaism and Jewish Christianity—seem to assume the two entities "Judaism" and "Christianity" and seek to determine whether Matthew is more Jewish or more Christian. In taking this approach, both formulations fail to recognize the Gospel's role in larger historical processes where change and development rather than fixed and static entities are to the fore. It may be more accurate to think of Matthew in terms of a larger historical panorama, somewhere in between, neither this nor that, with a liminal identity and location.

The question with which this chapter has been engaged has dominated much scholarly discussion of Matthew's gospel for a long time. But its familiarity to scholars from their socialization into the scholarly guild and its tempting but apparently insoluble nature have blinded scholars to other facets of the Gospel's negotiation of its multifaceted world. Matthew's world is not contained by a synagogue though frequently that is the only horizon that contemporary interpreters engage. Interaction with first-century Judaism (whatever its particular forms) is not the only negotiation that is undertaken by the Gospel and its late-first-century audience. A huge part of Matthew's world, almost completely neglected by scholarship, comprises Roman imperialism. The Gospel's plot concerns the crucifixion—a distinctly Roman form of execution—of its main character, and the

Gospel's late-first-century audience encounters Roman imperial power on a daily basis. This does not mean that engagement with first-century Judaisms is irrelevant, but it does recognize that they are also negotiating Roman power freshly asserted in the destruction of Jerusalem in 70 CE. Recent work on Matthew's Gospel has only just begun to attend to how the Gospel engages Roman power and to assess where this interaction belongs on the spectrum of the numerous ways that other Jewish and non-Jewish peoples negotiated Roman power (Carter 2000a, 2001, 2003a, 2003b, 2004; Riches and Sim 2005).

Suggested Readings

Carter, Warren. 2001. *Matthew and Empire: Initial Explorations.* Harrisburg, Pa.: Trinity Press International.

Hagner, Donald. 2003. "Matthew: Apostate, Reformer, Revolutionary." *New Testament Studies* 49:193–209.

———. 2004. "Matthew: Christian Judaism or Jewish Christianity?" Pages 263–82 in *The Face of New Testament Studies: A Survey of Recent Research.* Edited by S. McKnight and G. Osborne. Grand Rapids: Baker Academic.

Horrell, David. 2000. "Early Jewish Christianity." Pages 136–67 in vol. 1 of *The Early Christian World.* Edited by Philip Esler. London and New York: Routledge.

Saldarini, Anthony J. 1994. *Matthew's Christian-Jewish Community.* Chicago Studies in the History of Judaism. Chicago and London: University of Chicago Press.

Sim, David. 1998. *The Gospel of Matthew and Christian Judaism: The History and Social Setting of the Matthean Community.* Studies of the New Testament and Its World. Edinburgh: T & T Clark.

7. THE JOHANNINE COMMUNITY AS JEWISH CHRISTIANS? SOME PROBLEMS IN CURRENT SCHOLARLY CONSENSUS

Raimo Hakola

It has been quite common in recent studies to include the community be-hind the Fourth Gospel among various forms of first-century Jewish Chris-tianity. It has become all the more evident that even John's distinctive ideas about Jesus come from various Jewish traditions. Though scholars have not denied that many features in John suggest a break with those tenets most often regarded as distinctive to Jewish identity, they rationalize these features by placing John in the context of a conflict with rabbinic Judaism that explains the distancing of the Johannine Christians from the basics of Jewishness. But if the evidence for such a conflict is meager, as I claim, the definition of the Johannine group as a Jewish-Christian group becomes problematic. Rather than seeing in John's portrayal of the Jews and Jewish-ness a response to the violent policy of John's opponents, I take this por-trayal to suggest that the Johannine Christians themselves saw their faith in Jesus not only in continuity with earlier Jewish tradition but also in con-trast with that tradition. John's ambivalent attitude toward Jewishness and some fierce attacks against characters who seem to represent some types of Jewish Christians indicate that it may be misleading to label the Johannine Christians as Jewish Christians, even though there is no way of denying that the roots of these Christians were firmly on Jewish ground.

JOHN'S JEWISHNESS IN THE PAST AND PRESENT

For the mainstream of scholarship at the end of the nineteenth and at the beginning of the twentieth century, John's portrayal of the Jews and Judaism showed how far the fourth evangelist and his audience had drifted away from the Jewish roots of Christianity. Such Johannine peculiarities as the generalizing use of the expression "the Jews," Logos christology, determinism, and dualism were understood to be characteristics of the Hellenistic environment in which John wrote; the word "Hellenistic" was used to describe a wide variety of phenomena whose lowest common denominator was that they were regarded as non-Jewish in one sense or another. Specific Jewish or Jewish-Christian concerns were more often than not seen as only a minor part of the specific background from which the timeless message of the Gospel emerged. For one leading force in nineteenth-century scholarship, F. C. Baur, John reflected a time when earlier conflicts between Hellenistic Christians and Jewish Christians were left behind and the separation of Christianity from Judaism was complete.[1] According to Rudolf Bultmann, a principal voice in twentieth-century German scholarship, the Jews in John represent the unbelieving world as seen from the point of view of Christian faith. Bultmann elevated Jesus' conflict with the Jews above occasional historical circumstances and saw it as an expression of humanity confronted by God's revelation.[2] C. H. Dodd's *Interpretation of the Fourth Gospel* (1953), the single most important English-language study of John in the twentieth century, has been described as "the full flowering of the emphasis on Hellenism in New Testament study" (Davies 1999, 188).

Though scholars like Adolf Schlatter (1930[1903]) and Hugo Odeberg (1968[1929]) had made attempts to interpret John in a Jewish context, their contributions did not change the general course of scholarship. This change came only after the discovery of a set of manuscripts which proved that previous definitions of what is Jewish and what is not had been misleading. The discovery of the Dead Sea Scrolls in the late 1940s changed previous ways of understanding Judaism and Christianity. The scrolls demonstrated that there was not just one way of being a Jew, but that Judaism was divided into many different groups having individual beliefs of their own. The scrolls also contained many beliefs that had formerly been regarded as alien to Judaism and characteristic of Hellenistic or Gnostic thinking. For example, scholars soon found some obvious points in common with John's dualism and the dualism evident in the Community Rule (Hakola 2005a, 198–210). These observations were part of an ongoing and thorough reversal in the search for the context of early Christianity. Early Christianity was increasingly placed in the context of diverse first-century Judaism, and early Christians were essentially seen as Jews among other Jews. The pendulum of study also swung "from regarding the Fourth Gospel as the most Hellenistic of the gospels to assessing it as the most Jewish" (Meeks 1975, 163).

As a result of this change in the course of scholarship, it has become common to describe all first-century Christianity, not just some individual writings and schools, as Jewish Christianity (Dunn 1991, 234). The Johannine community is also now regularly included among other Jewish-Christian groups, even though scholars have not been able to shut their eyes to the features that somehow reflect an outsider's position in relation to Jewishness in John. Jesus' enemies are mainly called simply "the Jews," the Jewishness of different festivals and customs is underlined (e.g., 2:6; 4:9; 5:1; 6:4), and the Johannine Jesus refers to the law as "your law" (8:17; 10:34; cf. 7:19, 22; 15:25) or to Abraham as "your father" (8:56). Furthermore, the conflict between Jesus and his Jewish enemies is more consistent and hostile than in the Synoptics. While in earlier scholarship these kinds of features were taken to show that John stems from a non-Jewish environment, in recent decades, scholars have ascribed these features to a specific Jewish-Christian group whose attitudes to Jewishness were shaped by their own history in a radical way.

Since the publication of J. L Martyn's book *History and Theology in the Fourth Gospel* (2003[1968]), it has been almost axiomatic among Johannine scholars to think that John reflects a bitter and violent conflict between the Johannine group and its opponents identified as representatives of the post-70 emergent rabbinic Judaism.[3] The point of departure for Martyn is John 9, which he presents as a drama reflective of the history of the Johannine community. Martyn proposes that the Gospel of John should be read as a two-level drama that tells not only of Jesus' life but also about the contemporary situation of the Johannine Christians. Martyn connects the passages that tell of the exclusion from the synagogue (9:22; 12:42; 16:2) to the *Birkat ha-Minim*, a Jewish prayer against heretics, and maintains that this prayer played a crucial role in the process that led to the separation of the Johannine Christians from their fellow Jews.

Martyn gives a precise meaning and place for the terms "Christian Jews" and "Jewish Christians" in his history of the Johannine community. According to Martyn (2003, 70), an inner-synagogue group of Christian Jews became a separate community of Jewish Christians when they were forced out of the synagogue. Not all Johannine scholars have followed Martyn in the use of this terminological distinction, and some details in his reconstruction have been largely abandoned.[4] The general outline of Martyn's model, however, is still widely applied in discussions concerning John's position relative to Jews and Jewishness.[5] Attempts to place the Johannine community among other Jewish and early Christian groups are all dependent on the question of the role of the alleged conflict between the Johannine group and an emerging Jewish leadership class.

The current scholarly consensus based on Martyn's model has been called into question in recent years. Adele Reinhartz has challenged the historical presuppositions behind the two-level reading strategy. Following some earlier critics who disputed Martyn's references to certain rabbinic passages, Reinhartz notes that this strategy cannot be supported by external evidence (1998, 115–18; 2001a, 37–40). Reinhartz also points out that the two-level reading is one-sidedly based on John 9, while there are other models for interaction between Jesus' followers and the Jews in John. If read as a reflection of the social reality behind the Gospel, John 11 speaks of ongoing and peaceful communication between Johannine Christians and other Jews (1998, 121–30; 2001a, 40–48). According to Reinhartz,

> [John] reflects the complex social situation of the Johannine community but not the specific historical circumstances that gave rise to that situation. The largely negative portrayal of the Jews and Judaism within the Gospel must therefore be grounded not in a specific experience but in the ongoing process of self-definition and the rhetoric that accompanies it. (1998, 137)

Drawing on recent rabbinic studies, I have suggested elsewhere that it is not just some minor details in Martyn's model that are misleading, but that the whole scenario needs to be reconsidered (Hakola 2005a, 16–22, and 41–86). The early rabbinic movement has been repeatedly described in recent studies as a relatively powerless group concerned with issues of purity. This view emerges from the study of the earliest layers of Mishnaic laws as well as from the study of legal case stories connected to rabbis of different eras.[6] Early rabbis were not representative of Judaism at the time, nor were they in any position to enforce their views on a deviant minority like the early Christians. References to the *minim*, a term covering different groups that rabbis regarded as heretical, are far too miscellaneous and scattered to be used as evidence for a large-scale harassment of dissidents by rabbis. On the basis of rabbinic evidence, it is simply misleading to suppose that the rabbis were the instigators of any kind of systematic oppression of the minim in general, or early Christians in particular (Cohen 1984, 50; Setzer 1994, 161; Goodman 1996, 506).

The lack of evidence for a synagogue-organized persecution of early Christians should make us careful not to underplay the significance of Johannine theological and religious development as a factor in the estrangement of the Johannine group from Judaism. One of the basic presuppositions of the consensus of opinion is that the separation from the Jewish community took place against the will of the Johannine Christians, who were completely observant and kept Jewish law. It is emphasized that the Johannine Christians did not reject the synagogue "voluntarily nor for theological reasons. They did not assert that the faith of the Fathers no longer agreed with the teaching of the revealer and that an alternative religious practice would have to be established" (Zumstein 2001, 469–70; cf. von Wahlde 2001, 443). The eventual rupture between originally observant Christian Jews and other Jews is ascribed, on the whole, to the policy of John's alleged opponents. It is also supposed that the social rupture between a religious establishment and an oppressed minority explains why Jesus' attitude to some basics of Jewish identity is ambivalent in John. But is the external pressure enough to explain the change of the Johannine Christians from inner-synagogue, observant Christian Jews to Jewish Christians who defined themselves anew in opposition not only to their opponents, but also to many central Jewish tenets?

JOHN AND CENTRAL TENETS OF JEWISHNESS

It is not only continuity but also contrast that characterize Jesus' relationship with such representative figures of Jewish tradition as Moses and Abraham. In John 6, Jesus, as the true bread of life, is contrasted with the manna given by Moses (Hakola 2005a, 158-70). After the Galilean crowd has referred to the manna miracle experienced by the wilderness generation, Jesus corrects the understanding of the crowd: "Very truly I tell you, it was not Moses who gave you the bread from heaven, but it is my Father who gives you the true bread from heaven" (6:32).[7] The change in verb tenses is significant, for it shows that the manna was given in the past whereas Jesus' Father gives the true bread in the present time. The use of the adjective "true" emphasizes the contrast between these two gifts: the use of this word in John implies a difference between what is real and what is not real (cf. 1:9; 4:23; 15:1). The manna is not the true bread from heaven, but is connected to perishable food that does not lead to eternal life (v. 27). This becomes even clearer when Jesus later says that the fathers who ate the manna died whereas those who eat the true bread that descends from heaven will not die (vv. 49-51, 58). Jesus alone is capable of producing life, whereas the manna of Moses is associated with death. It is denied that the manna of the past has any relevance for salvation and life in the Johannine sense, and the wilderness generation is excluded from the salvation and life manifested only in Jesus (Luz 1981, 127; Theobald 1997, 362; for a different interpretation, see Zumstein 2004, 123–39). Jesus' revelation is presented not as a natural continuation of the past but as a superior alternative to the past traditions. The same contrast between life and death is evident also in John 8, where the dead Abraham is compared with Jesus, who gives life to his followers (Theobald 2004, 172–82; Hakola 2005a, 187–97). While Moses and Abraham have positive functions in John as Jesus' witnesses, Jesus' superiority over these figures is also made clear.

It is most probable that the clash with the basics of Jewish identity had implications for the religious practice of the Johannine community. The story in John 5:1-18 is told in such a way that it is no surprise to the readers that Jesus broke the Sabbath (Hakola 2005a, 113–30). Jesus' liberal attitude to the Sabbath is taken for granted and developed into a christological argument, which shows that the writer is not interested in details connected to a literal observance of the Sabbath. As John Ashton (1991, 139) notes, "for him the Sabbath healing is just a stepping-stone to the affirmation of Jesus' divinity." It is not very likely that the Johannine Christians would have continued to keep the Sabbath themselves while accepting without further ado that their Lord habitually broke it or even abrogated it, as is stated by the narrator in 5:18. Those scholars who want to argue that John does not present Jesus breaking the law here tend to theologize the Sabbath and overlook questions concerning its observance in practice. For example, Dorothy A. Lee (1994, 112) says that "on the literal level" Jesus' sign in John 5:1-18 "signifies that Jesus has broken the Law; on a symbolic level it means that Jesus is engaged in doing the *ergon* [i.e., work] of God. That he should break the Law is, in Johannine terms, absurd." Severino Pancaro (1975, 30) says that Jesus' attitude toward the Sabbath is paradoxical because "as the Son of God, Jesus does not violate the Sabbath, he abolishes it." John 5:17 shows "that, although the Sabbath is abolished, the law is fulfilled, not violated." Pancaro also notes that John "avoids having even the Pharisees say that Jesus violates or abrogates the Law; what he (apparently) violates and abrogates is the Sabbath" (522).

The above explanations spiritualize the Sabbath in a way that was foreign to most Jews. It is not likely that Jews not sharing John's convictions on Jesus would have understood how one can fulfill the purpose of the law by acting deliberately against one of its principal commandments. The argument made for Jesus' Sabbath transgression is circular because it is based on the acceptance of Jesus as God's agent on earth. Only those who accept this can take Jesus' Sabbath action as a sign of his close relationship to God, whereas others are bound to see this action as a transgression. This suggests that the whole argumentation is meant to reinforce the faith of the believers in Jesus and not to convince those who falsely blame Jesus for transgressing the Sabbath.[8] In John 5:17, Jesus' well-known habit of breaking the Sabbath is connected to a Jewish view that God does not rest on the Sabbath. Jesus' liberal attitude toward the Sabbath regulations is taken as a demonstration of his heavenly origin. Jesus' liberal stance on the Sabbath is no longer a disputed matter, but the narrator takes this stance for granted when making his basic christological claim.

When the Johannine Jesus later returns to his healing on the Sabbath in John 7:19-24, he does not attempt to show that what he did on the Sabbath was not against the law; the reference to circumcision on the Sabbath rather indicates, for him, that even the Jews do not keep the law in all instances (Hakola 2005a, 130–42). Jesus refers to circumcision on the Sabbath because circumcision gives a precedent for how the Sabbath can be broken in certain cases. Jesus here accuses the Jews of acting in an inconsistent way: they regard his work on the Sabbath as a transgression of the law although they do not regard circumcision on the Sabbath as such (Loader 2005, 144). They apply to their own action different standards than to his action, which means that their judgment is not correct (7:24).

Jesus sees here a discrepancy between two central obligations of the law, circumcision on the eighth day and the Sabbath, and uses this discrepancy to undermine his opponents' appeal to the law. This implies that neither of these principal matters of Jewishness was of practical importance for the Johannine group (thus also Loader 2005, 153). It is unlikely that people for whom circumcision was a crucial part of their Jewishness would have referred to the contradiction between circumcision and the Sabbath laws in this way.

Does pressure from the outside or even persecution explain this kind of attitude to the basics of Jewish identity? Is this attitude the result of a development which meant that the Christian Jews who originally belonged—and always wanted to belong—to the shared synagogue community were expelled by their fellow Jews? Comparative evidence suggests that this conclusion is by no means self-evident.

During recent decades the Johannine community has repeatedly been compared to the Qumran community. Scholars have not only found resemblance in the world outlook of these communities but have also suggested that the relationship to the surrounding world is expressed in similar terms in John and in some writings of the Qumran community. The dualistic distinction between light and darkness and the division of the world into the spheres of God and the devil characterize both John and the Community Rule and some other Dead Sea Scrolls.[9] Many scholars have taken this as an expression of a similar social position of these groups, which saw themselves as God's representatives in a world dominated by evil.[10] We do not know the exact historical experiences that led to the emergence of these worldviews, but it is safe to assume that both the Qumran community and the Johannine group felt marginalized from their surrounding society and threatened by the hostile world. However, these groups took a very different stance toward central Jewish symbols (Destro and Pesce 2001, 201–27; Hakola 2005a, 221–25).

In the case of the Qumran community, the social alienation from other Jews led to a more intense clinging to the principal pillars of common Jewish identity. For example, even though the relationship of the Qumran group to the Jerusalem temple was endangered or even broken, temple traditions continued to attract the members of the sect in a variety of ways. It can be said that the loss of the connection to the Jerusalem temple increased its symbolic significance for them. In a similar way, the Damascus Document shows that social isolation from their fellow Jews led the sectarians not toward laxity in regard to Sabbath laws but to a more intensified observance. Thus it seems that the pressure experienced from the outside did not always lead to an ambivalent attitude to the basic components of Jewish identity, as is the case in John. This suggests that such external factors as social antagonism or even persecution do not provide a sufficient rationale for John's portrayal of the Jews and Jewishness, all the more so because the evidence for such antagonism is meager.

If we claim that John's standpoint on Jewishness is shaped exclusively by the policy of his opponents, we must presume a hierarchical picture of first-century Judaism, where the practice of religion is in the hands of religious experts who define the boundaries of what is acceptable and what is not. During recent decades, however, it has become more and more clear that "there was not one ruling, all-powerful group in Early Judaism; many groups claimed to possess the normative interpretation of the Torah" (Charlesworth 1990, 37). Even though such things as the Sabbath and circumcision created a common bond between different Jewish groups, their observance was not controlled by any leading body. Adherence to the Torah and the keeping of individual commandments or the veneration of Moses, Abraham, and other patriarchs were not characteristics of an authoritative religious body alone, but were widespread among different Jewish groups. The example of the Qumran community shows that antagonism and ostracism could lead to the denunciation of one's opponents, but not necessarily to the criticism or even rejection of principal Jewish symbols evident in John. For example, it is difficult to understand why exclusion from the synagogue would have led to laxity in regard to the literal observance of the Sabbath and circumcision, and caused the Johannine writer to refer even to common Jewish festivals and customs as an outsider by emphasizing their Jewishness. John Ashton, with many others, regards Jesus' conflict with the Jews in John as another Jewish family dispute, but even he admits (1991, 155 n. 55) that "the Gospel's heavy-sounding insistence on the Jewishness of Jewish feasts and customs" indicates "the (increasing) disaffection of the Johannine group from the official religion of the central Jewish party. Even Greek converts, surely, would hardly need reminding that the Passover was a 'feast of the Jews.'" Nevertheless, this explanation very much presupposes a Judaism where essentials of Jewish religion were defined by an official ruling party. However, if authority was not centralized for decades or even centuries after the destruction of the Jerusalem temple in 70 CE, then it is better to see in John's portrayal of the Jews and Jewishness a more prolonged process of drifting away from what both different Jewish groups and outsiders regarded as distinctive to Jewishness than the result of the conflict with some official Jewish body.

The above conclusion fits well what we know of the general development of the relations between Jews and early Christians in the first century. We are told that such early Christian groups as the Hellenists (Acts 6–8) were harassed by their fellow Jews, but early evidence also indicates that not all those who believed Jesus to be the Messiah were being persecuted alike. For example, it seems that the Hellenists in the early church especially faced opposition because of their criticism of the temple and perhaps because of their liberal attitude to circumcision.[11] This should engender caution in explaining the separation of the Johannine community solely in terms of christological developments within the community. Given the diversity of messianic beliefs among different Jewish groups, it is not likely that faith in Jesus as the Messiah alone was a sufficient reason for the breach between the Johannine Christians and other Jews. Faith in Jesus as the Messiah may have played an important role in the process of separation, however, if it led to the abandonment of some basic Jewish religious practices. The growing sense of isolation may have led to more extreme

claims concerning Jesus' heavenly origin, but it is not necessarily the christological formulations that originally caught the eye of other Jews in John's
environment. Rather than being a cause of exclusion, "high" christology
may have been the result of increasing alienation that further fermented an
already ongoing process.

This conclusion has implications for the way we classify the Johannine
community in relation to other early Christian communities. As noted
above, recent developments in the field of New Testament scholarship have
led many scholars to describe all forms of early Christianity in the first
century as some sort of Jewish Christianity. This has been a necessary corrective to the earlier scholars, many of whom believed that New Testament
writings including John were filled with Hellenistic ideas foreign to the
Jewish mind. Studies done during recent decades have made it clear how
various aspects of John's theology are firmly rooted in diverse Jewish traditions. Even the most distinctively Johannine theological innovation, the
presentation of Jesus as God's Logos and Son, who descends from heaven
to the darkness of this world, is no longer regarded as a characteristic of
the non-Jewish setting of the Johannine community.[12] Thus Daniel Boyarin
(2001, 281) can confidently conclude that such early Christian groups as
the Johannine Christians did not

> distinguish themselves from non-Christian Jews theologically, but
> only in their association of various Jewish theologoumena and my
> thologoumena with this particular Jew, Jesus of Nazareth. The charac
> teristic move that constructs what will become orthodox Christianity
> is, I think, the combination of obviously Jewish Messianic soteriology
> with equally Jewish Logos theology in the figure of Jesus.

If we think in terms of John's background, the Gospel and the community
behind it can be described as *Jewish*-Christian insofar as the theological ideas
of the Gospel come from diverse Jewish traditions. In this sense, John clearly
originates from the multiform Judaism of the first century. This description
is problematic, however, if we take into consideration John's ambivalent attitude to the basics of Jewishness. Neither its outsider's position toward the
law and individual commandments nor its contrast between Jesus and the

founding fathers of Jewish tradition can be explained away by referring to the allegedly traumatic history of the community. These features are not products of the forcible and unwilling marginalization of a group of Christian Jews but characteristics of a group of early believers in Jesus who assessed various aspects of Jewishness exclusively in the light of their faith in Jesus. These believers defined themselves anew, not only in continuity with but also in opposition to basic matters of Jewishness. The drive for new identity was not the final outcome of pressure from external forces but the prime mover in the process of self-definition.

The moving away from what most Jewish groups—and outsiders as well—regarded as essential for Jewish identity makes the outlook of the Johannine community very different from those groups that have traditionally been taken as representing Jewish Christianity. A combination of faith in Jesus and the observance of such basic Jewish religious obligations as the Sabbath, circumcision, and/or dietary laws has often been regarded as one of the main characteristics of all the different Jewish-Christian groups. This is true both in the case of the group that gathered around James, the brother of Jesus, in the early church in Jerusalem, and in the case of later Jewish-Christian groups that, according to the scattered references in the writings of the church fathers, continued to flourish well into the fourth and even into the fifth century.[13] It may oversimplify the diverse nature of early Christianity if we use the same term for these groups and the Johannine Christians, whose way of interpreting their faith in Jesus led them on a collision course with basic matters of Jewish identity. The classification of the Johannine group as one of the varieties of Jewish Christians is all the more problematic because there is evidence in the Gospel itself of polemic against groups or individuals sharing qualities usually connected with Jewish Christians.

BELIEVING JEWS IN JOHN

According to many scholars, Jewish Christians (or, to use Martyn's terminology, Christian Jews) are referred to in John 8:30-31, where the Johannine narrator says that many Jews believed in Jesus (Dodd 1968, 43–45;

Schnackenburg 1971, 259–60; Martyn 1978, 109-15; Brown 1979, 77; Dozeman 1980, 343; Bondi 1997, 490; Theobald 2004, 175–77; Dunderberg 2006, 194).[14] In the course of the dialogue in 8:31-59, even the believing Jews are counted among those who try to kill Jesus. Jesus here bunches the believing Jews together with other Jews in such a way that they lose their distinctive characteristics. Jesus' harshest words in the Gospel "You are from your father the devil" (v. 44) are addressed not to those who have been openly hostile to him right from the beginning, but to those Jews who are said to believe in him. How can we explain this harsh condemnation of these Jewish believers?

According to the two-level reading strategy, the persecution of the Johannine Christians explains Jesus' denunciation of the believing Jews. Martyn takes the believing Jews in John 8:30-31 to be Christian Jews who tried secretly to maintain a dual allegiance after the Jewish authorities had decided that one must be either a disciple of Moses or a disciple of Jesus. For the Johannine Christians, "these former colleagues of theirs turned out to be horribly instrumental in the martyrdom of some of the Johannine evangelists, presumably by functioning as informers intent on preserving monotheism (vv. 37, 40, 44, 59)" (Martyn 1978, 114). This explanation presumes the scenario of persecution that I have criticized above. There is nothing in Jesus' words here that would suggest that the Jews in question take part only indirectly in the killing of Jesus. Furthermore, the Johannine narrator does not hint in any way that the believing Jews try to hide their faith in Jesus. Scholars have also found references in John 12:42-43 and in the story of Nicodemus who comes to Jesus by night in 3:1-21 to Christian Jews who tried to remain in the synagogue while secretly believing in Jesus (e.g., Rensberger 1989, 37–51). We must not automatically accept, however, that these passages provide an unbiased account of the disposition of those believers whom John opposes. In 12:42, it is said that even some of the authorities feared to confess their faith in Jesus, "for they loved human glory more than the glory that comes from God." The charge that someone is a lover of glory was a conventional rhetorical insult both in Hellenistic polemic and in Jewish and Christian traditions.[15] The claim that believing Jews feared to confess their faith may simply be a part of the attempt by the Johannine writer to denigrate the faith of those who believed in Jesus in a way he regarded as deplorable.

Jesus' words "If you continue in my word, you are truly my disciples, and you will know the truth, and the truth will make you free" are both a challenge to continue in his word and a promise of truth and freedom to the believing Jews (8:31-32). The Jews in question answer by appealing to Abraham: "We are descendants of Abraham, and have never been slaves to anyone" (v. 33). It is tempting to see in this appeal a connection to certain passages in Paul's letters which suggest that Paul's Jewish-Christian opponents may have appealed to Abraham in a similar way.[16] It may be impossible, however, to describe the convictions of John's believing Jews in greater detail. From John's point of view, the appeal to Abraham is another variation on how different characters appeal to the founding fathers or to the basic institutions of Israel for opposing what Jesus has done or said (cf. 4:12; 5:39, 45; 6:31; 9:29-30). Thus, the believing Jews do not seem to have any particular beliefs here that would be characteristic of them only, but are lumped together with other Jews. Perhaps all we can say of them is that, from John's point of view, their refusal to accept the freedom Jesus offers shows that belonging to Abraham matters to them more than becoming disciples of Jesus (Neyrey 1987, 520–21).

The Johannine Jesus refutes his opponents' appeal to Abraham in two ways. In 8:37-40, he says that the Jews are not doing what Abraham did and not doing what they should do as Abraham's children, while in 8:52-59 Jesus makes it clear that he himself is the standard by which even Abraham should be measured. Abraham has a role to play in salvation history, but his position as simply a witness is "vastly reduced in relationship to that of Jesus" (Bondi 1997, 492–93). From John's point of view, Abraham's "story is finished; he has come and gone. 'The Jews' are only able to call upon the memory of his story" (Moloney 1996, 113; in a similar vein, Theobald 2004, 182).

What Jesus says of Abraham is close to what he has earlier said of Moses. Both Abraham and Moses are portrayed as witnesses of Jesus, but the Johannine Jesus also makes it clear that they both lack what he himself has. The contrast between Jesus and Abraham very much resembles the contrast between Jesus and Moses as presented in John 6. It is thus interesting that here too a group of believers appears that is not willing to follow John in setting Jesus in opposition to the founding fathers of the Jews.

The narrator relates that, after Jesus' bread of life speech, many of his disciples were offended by his bold words and thus "turned back and no longer went about with him" (John 6:66). This is often taken as an indication of a later schism inside the Johannine group, a schism not dissimilar from that referred to in the Johannine epistles. The disciples who withdraw from Jesus' company are taken to represent Jewish Christians who did not share John's view of the Eucharist put forward in 6:52-59 (Brown 1979, 74; de Boer 1996, 63–67 and 250). However, the contrast between Moses' manna and Jesus' revelation characterizes the whole narrative dialogue in John 6:25-59. Therefore, it may be that these disciples were offended by the content of the entire speech, not just by its final section possibly dealing with the Eucharist (6:52-59). Still, in his final words of the speech, Jesus emphasizes the contrast between his bread and the manna eaten by the wilderness generation (6:58). The narrator says that some of Jesus' disciples murmured at his words (6:61), which connects these disciples to the Jews who have earlier murmured at Jesus (6:41) and to the wilderness generation, who showed their lack of belief by murmuring (Exod 16:2). The disciples who turn back may stand for those who did not see any contradiction between Moses and Jesus, and so did not follow the evangelist and his circle away from the Jewish community. The reason for the separation of these Jewish Christians from the Johannine Christians may not have been fear at all, but the desire to hold to basic matters of Jewish identity that had been abandoned by the Johannine Christians. In John 8:31-59, the Johannine writer maintains that there was no real difference between these Jewish Christians and those who had been responsible for Jesus' death, and in this way undermines their position.

Considering the criticism against Moses' manna in John 6:25-39, it is interesting that discipleship of Jesus is presented as incompatible with discipleship of Moses in John 9:27-29. The Pharisees seize the ironic suggestion of the once-blind man, "Do you also want to become his disciples?" and revile him by saying, "You are his disciple, but we are disciples of Moses." This discussion is often taken as an expression of the self-understanding of the Jewish religious leaders at the time the Gospel was written. It is said that these leaders considered themselves the disciples of Moses and understood this as excluding the possibility that one can be a disciple of Jesus at the same time (most recently de Boer 2001, 272–73; Menken 2001, 456–57). There is not much evidence, however, that Jewish identity was formulated by any Jewish group in terms of discipleship to Moses. Given the crucial role of Moses and his law among different Jewish groups, it is actually amazing that there is only one exact terminological parallel that scholars have been able to trace in the bulk of Jewish literature to the expression "the disciples of Moses."[17] This lack of terminological parallels may not be accidental; it may suggest that the passage in John does not reflect the self-expression of the real-world Jewish legal experts at the time the Gospel was written. As John 6 makes clear, John regarded the belief that Moses and his gift could bring life as antithetical to faith in Jesus, who alone can give life to those who receive him. It is likely that this contrast reflects a real-life breaking away from the Jewish community. Although the Johannine Christians had moved away from a Jewish identity based on the observance of the Mosaic law, they also understood themselves in continuity with Jewish tradition by claiming that they have Moses on their side (John 5:45-47). The Johannine Christians came to terms with this discrepancy by attributing the choice between Jesus and Moses to those who represent the hostile parent body of the believers in the Gospel.

The above interpretation could explain why the believing Jews are condemned so harshly in John 8:31-59. The Johannine writer sees the believing Jews as an example that shows that it is impossible to continue to practice traditional Judaism and to be a believer in Jesus at the same time. John's references to these Jews are stylized and brief and so we do not know exactly what kind of group they formed, or what their detailed practices or convictions were. Given the crucial symbolic role that James, the brother of Jesus, enjoyed among different Jewish-Christian communities, it is possible to see, in the hostile picture of Jesus' brothers in John 7:1-10, a further allusion to the influence of Jewish Christians in John's surroundings.[18] This allusion, however, does not say much more about the specifics of the Jewish Christians that the Johannine writer has in mind.

There may be good reasons not to reconstruct a clearly defined group of Christian Jews or Jewish Christians inside or outside the synagogue on the basis of John's vague references. The persecution scenario is based on the assumption that Jewish synagogue communities had strict boundaries that were defined by a strong leadership class. But there is evidence that Jewish synagogue communities were not so clearly defined but open to their surroundings in many different ways. For example, Shaye Cohen (1999b, 140–74) has shown that even the Gentiles could interact with Jewish communities in a variety of ways—from admiring some aspects of the faith of the Jews to full conversion. The evidence for different types of "sympathizers" and full converts shows that the boundary between Jews and Gentiles was crossable.[19] It is fully possible that the boundary between the Jews who came to believe in Jesus and other Jews still also remained open and fluid at the end of the first century. I have suggested above that there was not one ruling class among the Jews even after the destruction of the temple; the Jews' responses to Jesus' followers were not backed by any authorities, and it may be that these responses were not so completely negative as is suggested by early Christian polemics against the Jews.[20] There is no reason to doubt that it was possible for Jews who came to believe in Jesus to interact with synagogue communities and their members in different ways. Some who believed in Jesus may have become alienated from their fellow Jews to the extent that they felt expelled from the synagogue. Some other believers may have continued to interact with other Jews and found the practice of basic matters of Jewishness still attractive, which prompted their fierce denunciation by John (see Kimelman 1981, 234–35; Reinhartz 1998, 136–37). John connected even these believers with the devil, creating in the process an imaginary universe where the sons of light and the sons of darkness are much more clearly distinct from each other than they ever were in real life.

Conclusion

This discussion has suggested why it may be problematic to include the Johannine community among Jewish-Christian communities. This inclusion is problematic because of John's ambivalent attitude to basic markers of Jewishness and because of John's harsh condemnation of the Jews who believed in Jesus. While the Johannine community could be defined as a

Jewish-Christian group if we accept an ethnic or an ideological definition of Jewish Christianity, the Johannine community does not fit into a praxis-based definition of Jewish Christianity. I concur with James Carleton Paget that the praxis-based definition of Jewish Christianity is the most satisfactory, even though it is not without problems.[21] As Paget rightly notes, "in the ancient world Jewishness was often associated with certain practices, and it was the adoption of these practices, in particular circumcision, which was seen to make a non-Jew Jewish" (1999, 740).

While I resist the classification of the Johannine community as a Jewish-Christian community, I do not in any way deny that John originates from a Jewish world; some passing references in such passages as John 10:16 ("I have other sheep that do not belong to this fold") or 11:51-52 ("Jesus was about to die for the nation, and not for the nation only, but to gather into one the dispersed children of God") may suggest that the Johannine writer was not unaware of discussions connected to the presence of Gentiles in early Christian communities, but otherwise John presupposes a predominantly Jewish setting. It is not really decisive, however, that the ethnic and the cultural background of the Johannine community was most certainly Jewish because "Jews who became Christians represented a variety of opinions, not least in relation to their attitude to their Jewish heritage. . . . To accept a purely ethnic definition of Jewish Christianity is not really to define anything meaningful at all " (Paget 1999, 733–34).

Paget has also noted (1999, 736–39) problems in ideological definitions that define as Jewish Christianity those types of Christian thought that are expressed in forms borrowed from diverse Jewish traditions. According to these definitions, it is clear that the Johannine Christians, who reformulated many traditions they shared with various Jewish groups, could be counted among Jewish Christians. But as Paget notes, the use of Jewish traditions in a text is not contradictory to anti-Jewish tendencies, which makes purely ideological definitions of Jewish Christianity problematic. To describe the Johannine community as a Jewish-Christian community on the basis of Jewish materials used in the Gospel is to overlook the fact that this material is, more often than not, used to underscore faith in Jesus as a superior alternative to Jewish beliefs and practices. This shows how originally Jewish elements may well have contributed to the emergence of an identity that was not founded on basic matters of Jewishness but was, at least at some points, created in conscious opposition to them.

John's alienation from the basics of Jewishness and some passing but virulent attacks against Christian believers who did not see any contradiction between faith in Jesus and the observance of Jewish practices suggest that John should not be placed on a Jewish-Christian trajectory of early Christianity. It may not be accidental that John had no impact on those Jewish-Christian groups that flourished in the first Christian centuries.[22] Some remarks by the church fathers suggest that these groups used either a Gospel somehow akin to the Gospel of Matthew or a Gospel harmony based on the Synoptics—but not on John.[23]

Finally, labeling the Johannine community a Jewish Christian group is problematic in the light of John's unspecified way of using the term "the Jews" to designate Jesus' opponents. In most cases, this term is laden with mistrust and hostility. There have been attempts to define this term as referring only to some particular Jewish group, be it Judeans or the Jewish authorities, but these attempts are not convincing (Hakola 2005a, 10–16, 225–31). The indiscriminate use of the term shows that, even in those instances where "the Jews" could be understood as a specific group of Jewish leaders or Judeans, the conflict between these groups and Jesus is raised to a new and more general level (see Culpepper 1996, 114). As Adele Reinhartz says, the various ways of using the term in John tend "to blur the fine distinctions and nuances and to generalize the meaning to its broadest possible referent, that is, the Jews as a nation defined by a set of religious beliefs, cultic and liturgical practices, and a sense of peoplehood" (2001b, 348).[24] This general, negative use of the term suggests that the Johannine writer was well aware of his drift away from Jewishness. John and his community no longer understood themselves in terms of Jewish identity and, consequently, chose to refer to other Jews using a word covering the widest possible referent; they thus acknowledged that those things that were common to different Jewish groups were no longer theirs. Whatever discussions and controversies originally followed this separation from Jewish ethos, John understood them all as imitating the original rejection of Jesus by his contemporaries. For him, the reasons for Jesus' rejection are ultimately and solely rooted in the world's hatred, which means that "the Jews" become identical with the unbelieving and hostile world that has hated Jesus and his followers "without a cause" (John 15:25). This hatred gained its full momentum when Jesus was illegally put to death by "the Jews," which for the author illustrates that there is no reason other than the wickedness of the world for the suffering of the innocent righteous.[25] Therefore, it is unlikely that the Johannine community would have themselves welcomed a designation derived from a term that was for them ominous and suspicious, an icon of the world's hatred.

SUGGESTED READINGS

Bieringer, Reimund, and Didier Pollefeyt. 2004. "Open to Both Ways . . . ? Johannine Perspectives on Judaism in the Light of Jewish-Christian Dialogue." Pages 11–32 in *Israel und seine Heilstraditionen im Johannesevangelium: Festgabe für Johannes Beutler SJ zum 70. Geburtstag*. Edited by M. Labahn, K. Scholtissek and A. Strotmann. Paderborn: Ferdinand Schöningh.

Bieringer, Reimund, Didier Pollefeyt, and Frederique Vandecasteele-Vanneuville, eds. 2001. *Anti-Judaism and the Fourth Gospel*. Louisville, Ky.: Westminster John Knox.

Boyarin, Daniel. 2001. "The Gospel of the *Memra*: Jewish Binitarianism and the Prologue to John." *Harvard Theological Review* 94:243–84.

Brown, Raymond E. 1979. *The Community of the Beloved Disciple: The Life, Loves, and Hates of an Individual Church in New Testament Times*. London: Geoffrey Chapman; New York: Paulist.

Hakola, Raimo. 2005a. *Identity Matters: John, the Jews and Jewishness*. Novum Testamentum Supplements 118. Leiden: Brill.

Loader, William R. G. 2005. "Jesus and the Law in John." Pages 135–54 in *Theology and Christology in the Fourth Gospel: Essays by the Members of the SNTS Johannine Writings Seminar*. Edited by G. van Belle, J. G. van der Watt, and P Maritz. Bibliotheca ephemeridum theologicarum lovaniensium 184. Leuven: Leuven University Press.

Martyn, J. Louis. 2003 [1968]. *History and Theology in the Fourth Gospel*. 3rd ed. New Testament Library. Louisville, Ky.: Westminster John Knox.

Meeks, Wayne A. 1975. "'Am I a Jew?'—Johannine Christianity and Judaism." Pages 163–86 in *Christianity, Judaism and Greco-Roman Cults: Studies for Morton Smith at Sixty. Part One*. Edited by Jacob Neusner. Studies in Judaism in Late Antiquity 12. Leiden: Brill.

Pancaro, Severino. 1975. *The Law in the Fourth Gospel: The Torah and the Gospel, Moses and Jesus, Judaism and Christianity according to John*. Novum Testamentum Supplements 42. Leiden: Brill.

Reinhartz, Adele. 1998. "The Johannine Community and Its Jewish Neighbors: A Reappraisal." Pages 111–38 in *"What Is John?"* Vol. 2, *Literary and Social Readings of the Fourth Gospel*. Edited by Fernando F. Segovia. Society of Biblical Literature Symposium Series 7. Atlanta: Scholars Press.

———. 2001a. *Befriending the Beloved Disciple: A Jewish Reading of the Gospel of John*. New York: Continuum.

Rensberger, David. 1989. *Overcoming the World: Politics and Community in the Gospel of John*. London: SPCK.

Wahlde, Urban C. von. 2000. "'The Jews' in the Gospel of John: Fifteen Years of Research (1983–1998)." *Ephemerides theologicae lovanienses* 76:30–55.

8. The Religious Context
of the Letter of James
Patrick J. Hartin

Biblical scholarship has tended to vacillate between three different approaches to the Letter of James.[1] These approaches reflect different positions regarding the relationship between the Letter of James and what is termed the Jewish and Gentile worlds:

- Those who see the Letter of James as a document that arose within the world of Second Temple Israelite religious thought. It was later "baptized" through the insertion of a few references to Jesus Christ (Spitta 1896; Massebieau 1895). This group of scholars would classify the Letter of James as being originally what has been termed a "Jewish" document.
- Those who see this writing as a late document emerging from the world of the early followers of Jesus (see Dibelius 1975, 20–21). This view stresses its roots within the world of the followers of Jesus, who are established as a clear group outside of the world of Israelite religious thought and practice. This group of scholars would classify the Letter of James as being originally what is termed a "Gentile Christian" document.
- Those who see the Letter of James as emerging from the world of Second Temple Israelite thought and culture while at the same time demonstrating connections to the world of the followers of Jesus (see Johnson 1995, 118–21). This group of scholars would classify the Letter of James as being originally what has been termed a "Jewish Christian" document.

The present study endorses the third perspective indicated above, name-ly, that the Letter of James is a "Jewish Christian" document. The writer of this letter clearly sees himself as part of Second Temple Israelite religious thought and traditions while at the same time being a follower of Jesus. The writer did not see a contradiction between these two groups. Rather, he viewed the thought and belief of Jesus of Nazareth as still rooted in the thought world of Israel. Elsewhere I have argued that James (of Jerusalem) is clearly the true heir to Jesus of Nazareth (see Hartin 2004). My clas-sification of the Letter of James in this way is supported by its religious thought, its self-understanding, and its identity. I shall demonstrate this in the study that follows. Through a detailed examination of the letter's reli-gious thought and worldview, it will emerge that the letter is clearly situ-ated within the thought context of the traditions of Second Temple Israel while at the same time endorsing the traditions of Jesus of Nazareth.

While most studies employ designations such as "Jewish" and "Chris-tian," or "Judaism" and "Christianity" in referring to the Letter of James, I shall avoid using these terms because I believe such designations are anach-ronistic. These terms carry with them meanings that are not appropriate for that early period in the development of Christianity. The word "Juda-ism" would imply that a unified understanding of Israel's religion existed at the beginning of the first century C.E. This unity in thought came only much later, fostered by the compilations of the Mishnah and the Talmud. On the other hand, terms such as "Judaisms" also fail to capture the reality of the situation. It was not as though the people of Israel were interpret-ing their faith in totally opposing ways. Rather, they were laying stress on different aspects of their faith. The same can be said about the world of "Christianity." The communities behind the New Testament documents showed that they interpreted in divergent ways their understanding of Je-sus' message and their response to that message. No unified understanding of Christ's message and its implications for the life of the believers had yet been produced. It was, however, a matter of differences in nuance rather than in essence. Only toward the end of the second century C.E. did hostil-ity arise between groups that had developed opposing systems of thought, each laying claim to the title "Christianity," for example, the Docetists and the Gnostics.

Instead of using the terms "Judaism" and "Christianity," I shall speak of the religious views of *the members of the house of Israel* and *the followers of Jesus* as do those who follow the methodology of the social-scientific study of the world of the New Testament (e.g., Malina and Rohrbaugh 2003, 427). I shall attempt to show how the Letter of James relates to both of these groups and where we can situate it in relation to them.

I put the emergence of the Letter of James in the latter half of the seventh decade of the first century C.E., just prior to the destruction of the city of Jerusalem in 70 C.E. (see Hartin, 2003, 16–25).

One of the strongest arguments that has been put forward against dating the composition of the Letter of James prior to the destruction of the city of Jerusalem and the Temple in 70 CE as well as against its belonging to the world of the Second Temple house of Israel is the excellent quality of the Greek of this letter (see the discussion in Hartin, 2003, 22–24). For example, about 8 percent of all the words (73 out of a total of 570 words) in the Letter of James are not found elsewhere in the New Testament. The letter is clearly not a translation from an Aramaic original, which has led some scholars to conclude that someone like James, who was born in Palestine, could never have composed it in Greek. As Martin Dibelius (1975, 17) argued: "Nor does the language of our text point to an author who spent his life as a Jew in Palestine."

This conclusion has been challenged by many scholars who have demonstrated the great influence that Hellenistic culture and the Greek language had on the world of Palestine. This has been supported by studies coming chiefly from the world of archaeology (see Meyers 1986, 4–19) These studies have shown how extensive the knowledge and use of Greek were in Galilee. One should also remember the picture of that first community in Jerusalem painted in the Acts of the Apostles. The description showed the first major conflict within the fold of the followers of Jesus between Hebrew-speaking and Greek-speaking believers. This dispute led to the appointment of a group of seven to care for the Greek-speaking believers in Jerusalem (see Acts 6:1-7). Against this background there is no reason to argue that the Letter of James could not have been composed in Jerusalem.

Further, it is not my contention, nor the contention of most scholars, that James, "the brother of the Lord" physically wrote this letter.[2] That he was the source behind this letter, acting as its authority figure, is evident. In line with the concept of authorship in the world of that time, the letter is attributed to James by one of his followers with the intention of handing on the traditions and teaching of James to communities outside Palestine who were united with the community in Jerusalem in their bonds with the house of Israel.

I would envisage the community of James as existing like the other groups of Second Temple Israel such as the Pharisees and Sadducees prior to the destruction of Jerusalem in 70 CE. After the destruction of the temple it would be the Pharisees and the followers of Jesus who would struggle fiercely against each other for the claim to represent the true heart of Israel's traditions. I do not see the Letter of James being composed in this period of ever-escalating conflict in the years after 70 CE, for there is no strong polemic against another group within the house of Israel. At the same time, the Letter of James shows no concern for the world of the Gentiles—it presumes a community of followers of Jesus that had not accepted large numbers of Gentiles and for whom an outreach to the Gentile world was not an issue.

Just as there were different groups within the world of Second Temple Israel, so too among the followers of Jesus there were also different groups holding a centrality of belief in Jesus of Nazareth as the Messiah. They differed from each other regarding their interpretations and relationships with the house of Israel as well as with the world of the Gentiles. One can envisage each group of the followers of Jesus being situated on a continuum demonstrating its closeness or separation from the house of Israel. Along such a continuum, I would place the community to whom James writes as being the closest of all the New Testament traditions to the house of Israel.

THE LETTER OF JAMES AND ISRAEL'S HERITAGE

James's thought cannot be explained apart from this context within the religious thought and traditions of Second Temple Israel. Further, this study will show that James continues to speak to a community that does not see itself as separated from the house of Israel. The members of this community are still within that orbit.

Eschatological Hope
of the Twelve-Tribe Kingdom

Of fundamental importance to any study of the Letter of James is taking seriously the context in which the letter situates itself, namely, that of the eschatological hope of Second Temple Israelite thought. James opens his letter with the address: "To the twelve tribes in the Dispersion" (1:1). The word "Dispersion" translates the Greek term *diaspora,* which literally means "scattering" (see Hartin 2003, 50). With the article, *hē diaspora* captures either the Israelite understanding of *those places outside the land of Israel* where the Israelites were scattered (see Deut 30:4; Neh 1:9; Jdt 5:19), or *those Israelites* who were actually scattered outside of the land of Israel. The Letter of James takes up this literal understanding of the Diaspora, whereby the writer addresses those areas outside Israel where people of the house of Israel are living. James is thus addressing his letter to "the twelve tribes" who are living in areas outside the land of Israel.[3]

In its original meaning, the phrase "the twelve tribes" refers to the people of Israel as a whole, namely, the people descended from the patriarchs, Abraham, Isaac, Jacob, and his twelve sons. These twelve sons became the forefathers of the twelve tribes on whom the people of Israel depended for their identity. For example, "Moses . . . built an altar at the foot of the mountain, and set up twelve pillars, corresponding to the twelve tribes of Israel" (Exod 24:4). When James addressed his letter to "the twelve tribes," he was doing so against the background of the eschatological hope of the house of Israel. "The twelve tribes" expressed the belief that God was about to fulfill his eschatological promise in sending God's Messiah to establish God's kingdom (see Hartin 1996, 490–92; 1999, 70–71; 2004, 50–55; Jackson-McCabe 2003; 1996, 510–15). This hope rested on the foundational belief that the tribes were God's chosen people, heirs to the promises God had made to Abraham, with whom God had established "an everlasting covenant" (see Gen 17:1-8). The covenantal promises of a land and posterity were passed on from Abraham through Isaac to Jacob. From Jacob's twelve sons the people of Israel trace their origins as the twelve tribes of Israel. At the conclusion of Jacob's blessing of his sons just before his death, the biblical writer notes: "All these are the twelve tribes of Israel, and this is what their father said to them when he blessed them, blessing each one of them with a suitable blessing" (Gen 49:28).

The central promise made to David by the prophet Nathan rekindled belief in the perpetuity of God's promises to the twelve tribes. At the same time a new dimension was added to this promise. Not only did the promise made to Abraham incorporate a line of descendants who lived in God's covenant, but it also included the perpetual continuation of David's kingdom. The fulfillment of the promise would be through the lineage of David. As Nathan says to David: "Your house and your kingdom shall be made sure forever before me; your throne shall be established forever" (2 Sam 7:16). Not only does the identity of the people of Israel consist in being God's children from Abraham living in a covenant relationship, but this covenant relationship now incorporates the promise of the perpetual endurance of the Davidic kingdom.

The belief in the endurance of the Davidic kingdom as the future fulfill-ment of the promises made through Abraham and the twelve tribes was severely put to the test when the northern kingdom of Israel and the south-ern kingdoms of Judah were destroyed. As a result of the Assyrian invasion and destruction of the northern kingdom in 721 B.C.E., and the Babylonian conquest and destruction of the southern kingdom a century later in 589 B.C.E., not only was the nation destroyed, but most of the inhabitants, es-pecially the leading people, were carried off into captivity. The Diaspora was born. The hope was generated and began to grow in intensity that someday in the future God would intervene to reconstitute God's twelve-tribe kingdom. This hope in a reconstituted twelve-tribe kingdom was re-inforced through the preaching and teaching of many of the prophets. For example, the prophet Ezekiel envisaged the reconstitution of the nation of Israel through the future redistribution of the land among the twelve tribes: "So you shall divide this land among you according to the tribes of Israel" (Ezek 47:21; see also ch. 48; 37:15-28).

This hope in the reconstitution of Israel's twelve-tribe kingdom endured through subsequent centuries. The Israelite people continued to live under the dominion and rule of foreign powers, and their continual oppression gave urgency to the survival of their eschatological hope. Especially under Roman rule (from 63 B.C.E. onwards), this longing gained more and more attention, as can be seen from writings circulating at that time. Thus, for example, the *Psalms of Solomon* (middle of the first century B.C.E) present the eschatological hope that Israel's kingdom will eventually be reestablished:

> *See, Lord, and raise up for them their king,*
> *the son of David, to rule over your servant Israel*
> *in the time known to you, O God.*
> *Undergird him with the strength to destroy the unrighteous rulers,*
> *to purge Jerusalem from gentiles*
> *who trample her to destruction. . . .*
> *He will gather a holy people*
> *whom he will lead in righteousness;*
> *and he will judge the tribes of the people*
> *that have been made holy by the Lord their God.*
> *He will not tolerate unrighteousness (even) to pause among them,*
> *and any person who knows wickedness shall not live with them.*
> *For he shall know them*
> *that they are all children of their God.*
> *He will distribute them upon the land*
> *according to their tribes;*
>   *the alien and the foreigner will no longer live near them.*
> (17:21-28; trans. Wright 1985, 667)

This same hope in the restoration of the twelve-tribe kingdom lies behind the traditions of Matthew's Gospel. Matthew's Jesus proclaims the fulfillment of those eschatological hopes in the reconstitution of Israel's twelve-tribe kingdom. Two passages in Jesus' proclamation support this understanding. In the first instance, Jesus directs the ministry of his disciples solely toward "the lost sheep of the house of Israel" (Matt 10:5-6). Jesus tells his disciples not to go to the Gentiles, and he envisages their role as gathering together the house of Israel that has been scattered. Like a shepherd who seeks out those sheep that have been scattered, so Jesus' disciples are to bring together the scattered people of Israel. Jesus also envisages his own ministry as directed toward the same "lost sheep of the house of Israel" (Matt 15:24).

The task of bringing together the people of Israel begins in Jesus' own ministry and continues through the activity of his followers and perseveres until the end of time. The eschatological hope in the reconstitution of Israel's twelve-tribe kingdom will be fulfilled only at the end-times, as is seen in Jesus' promise to his followers in the Q saying: "Truly I tell you, at the renewal of all things when the Son of Man is seated on the throne of his glory, you who have followed me will also sit on twelve thrones, judging the twelve tribes of Israel" (Matt 19:28; Luke 22:29-30).

This hope in the reconstitution of the twelve-tribe kingdom extends throughout the whole religious tradition of the house of Israel. The ministry of Jesus and that of his followers lie within this same tradition and provide the context for James's use of the term "to the twelve tribes in the Dispersion." Just as Jesus directed his ministry to the "lost sheep of the house of Israel," so James addresses his letter to those members of the house of Israel who had been scattered throughout the nations. More than this, James sees his task as continuing that of Jesus, namely, bringing together, reconstituting Israel's twelve-tribe kingdom. James presents his community as constituting "the first fruits of his [God's] creatures" (1:18). This indicates that the recipients of James's letter are those from the house of Israel who have embraced Jesus' message. James's community constitutes the beginning of those eschatological hopes in the reconstitution of that twelve-tribe kingdom. James's community lies firmly within the house of Israel and its traditions, while at the same time being a beacon that points to the fulfillment of God's eschatological promises.

The Torah

James discusses the law in three passages, 1:25; 2:8-12; and 4:11-12.

- 1:25: "But those who look into the perfect law, the law of liberty, and persevere, being not hearers who forget but doers who act—they will be blessed in their doing."
- 2:8-12: "You do well if you really fulfill the royal law according to the scripture, 'You shall love your neighbor as yourself.' . . . So speak and so act as those who are to be judged by the law of liberty."

- 4:11-12: "Do not speak evil against one another, brothers and sisters. Whoever speaks evil against another or judges another, speaks evil against the law and judges the law; but if you judge the law, you are not a doer of the law but a judge. There is one lawgiver and judge who is able to save and to destroy. So who, then, are you to judge your neighbor?"

These passages identify the law by means of a number of phrases: "the law of freedom," "the perfect law," "the royal law." An examination of these descriptions helps to explain James's concept of the law, as well as to identify the letter's religious background. By examining those literary traditions that give expression to James's religious milieu, one can see that the concept of law expressed in this letter is clearly at home within the world of Second Temple Israelite religious thought.[4]

Nowhere does James define what he means when he refers to the "law." Scholars are divided on the meaning of James's reference to the law. For example, Peter Davids (1982, 99–100) sees the law as referring to the new law that the Messiah has come to perfect: "One must agree with Davies that James sees Jesus' reinterpretation of the law as a new law" (citing Jas 2:8 and Davies 1989, 402-405). On the other hand, I have been convinced by the insightful arguments of Robert Wall (1997, 83–98) who sees James's reference to the law as referring to the biblical Torah. Wall supports his perspective by an analysis of other passages in the New Testament where "[t]hree narratives about James . . . anticipate the idea of law found in [the Letter of] James" (1997, 84). From these passages in the Acts of the Apostles (15:13-21; 21:15-26) and the Letter to the Galatians (2:11-18) it emerges that James is arguing that those who wish to remain as members of the covenant people and be recipients of God's future blessings need to observe the Torah (see Wall 1997, 86). As the biblical Torah, the law is an expression of God's covenant relationship with God's people. The Torah becomes the way in which they can carry out God's will and show their identity as God's covenant people. I shall refer to the law in James as *the Torah* to emphasize the understanding of the Torah as God's will and to avoid the connotations that the term "law" carries in English. It is noteworthy as well that nowhere does the Letter of James make reference to any specific ritual or cultic laws. It is specifically the moral aspects of the biblical Torah that the letter has in mind.

The Torah must be viewed against the background of the concept of purity rules that define the boundary markers for the society, which Jews, together with all the peoples of the Mediterranean world, considered essential for the proper ordering of society. By establishing and maintaining right relationships between God, the community, and the individual, these boundary markers were the means by which a correctly ordered society functioned. Malina (1993, 74) emphasizes that the true aim of purity rules is to establish and foster access to God:

> If purity rules are to facilitate access to God, and if the God to whom one wants access has human welfare as the main priority in the divine will for the chosen people, it follows that proper interpretation of purity rules must derive from giving primary consideration to relationships with one's fellows. This is what righteousness is about. For righteousness means proper interpersonal relationships with all those in one's society between God and covenanted human beings and between human beings and their fellow beings.

The language of purity is central to the Letter of James. The starting point is undoubtedly the letter's very definition of religion: "Religion that is pure and undefiled before God, the Father, is this: to care for orphans and widows in their distress, and to keep oneself unstained by the world" (1:27). James's concept of religion envisages a duality of space: that area to which his community belongs and that area outside his community. In other words, the space where his community exists is sacred, while the space outside the community is profane. James identifies the space outside the community as "the world," and the task of those who belong to the community is to keep themselves apart from the world ("unstained by the world").[5] The space of James and his community is "pure and undefiled before God," while the space outside is defiled.

This duality between the space of access to God and the space of the world runs throughout the whole letter. In Jas 4:4 the writer issues his central call to decide between "friendship with the world" and "friendship with God." It is James's way of expressing the duality between the sacred and the profane, between his community, with access to God, and the world outside, which rejects that access. This same duality is expressed in James's contrasts between the two types of wisdom: "the wisdom from above" and the wisdom that is "earthly" (3:13-18). In defining the "wisdom from above," James says that it is "first pure" (3:17). In other words, the wisdom from above communicates access to God. As Malina says:

> Their purpose [i.e. purity rules] is not to lop off ever greater portions
> of God's people from access to God, symboled by the clean and the sa-
> cred of the purity rules. . . . Rather, they are to facilitate access to God.
> The purity rules are to make this access easier, not close it off. Another
> way to say this is: "The sabbath was made for human beings, not hu-
> man beings for the sabbath" (Mark 2:27). (1993, 173)

The function of the Torah is to define what the purity rules are and what the community must do in order to preserve their sacred space and to remain separate from the profane world. Faithfulness to the purity rules and to the Torah ensures that the individual, the community, and God all remain in right relationships. As James challenges his hearers/readers, "Draw near to God, and he will draw near to you. Cleanse your hands, you sinners, and purify your hearts, you double-minded. . . . Humble yourselves before the Lord, and he will exalt you" (Jas 4:8-10).

The Torah and its purity rules define the boundary markers for the society. They set down the way in which the community can remain in right relationship with God and with one another as the community of God's chosen people. The Torah exercises a socializing function for the members of James's community. This is what Peter L. Berger and Thomas Luckmann (1966, 120) have called the process of "socialization which may be defined as the comprehensive and consistent induction of an individual into the objective world of a society or a sector of it."[6] By calling his community to adhere to the biblical Torah, James is reminding them of what it means for them to be part of God's covenant people, "the twelve tribes in the Dispersion" (1:1). By abiding by the Torah, the believer carries out God's will and lives with access to God. Abiding by the Torah is essential for all who belong to James's community.

James's small parable of the mirror (1:23-25) challenges those who look into the mirror of the Torah not to go away and forget what they have seen, but to put the Torah into practice. James focuses on the dimension of social responsibility in his definition of religion: "Religion that is pure and undefiled before God, the Father, is this: to care for orphans and widows in their distress . . ." (1:27). Johnson (1982, 391–401) has argued convincingly that the origin of James's treatment of the law lies in a "halachic midrash" on Lev 19:12-18. Noteworthy in these verses from Leviticus is the reference made to the "love of neighbor" (Lev 19:18) as well as to the social responsibility of the community to the poor (Lev 19:15). Both aspects are central to James's discussion of the Torah in Jas 2:8 (love of neighbor) and 2:1-7 (concern for the poor).

The importance James gives to the Torah in his letter is further supported by the studies of Gerald Sheppard (1980, 110–19) on wisdom literature and its relationship to the Torah. He has demonstrated that the wisdom writings used the Torah to support their own arguments. They wished to merge the traditions related to the Torah with their own reflections on their faith that had developed from their own world and worldview. The Letter of James in general has long been defined by some scholars as belonging to the genre of wisdom literature.[7] James operates in ways analogous to the wisdom tradition of the house of Israel in that he communicates wisdom instruction to his community by drawing on his reflections of the Torah and its importance within the framework of his community.

Not only is there a connection between wisdom literature and the Torah, but Eckhard J. Schnabel (1985) in his work *Law and Wisdom from Ben Sira to Paul* also notes a tendency to identify these two concepts. He shows that the Book of Sirach was the first to identify the law and wisdom (1985, 344). In his exhaustive study he has also demonstrated how the law and wisdom are identified in almost every tradition subsequent to the Book of Sirach.[8] The Torah and wisdom come together in their ethical concern and teaching: together they promote a way of life through adherence to the biblical Torah. As Schnabel says, "The Jewish writings of the first century AD equally place the ethical dimension into the centre of their concern. The Author of Fourth Maccabees argued that true [philosophy] consists in a pious life obeying the Jewish law" (1985, 345).

Not only is the Letter of James a wisdom writing that employs the Torah in its ethical admonitions, but it also identifies wisdom and the Torah. This can be seen from the use the letter makes of the adjective *teleios* ("perfect").

James 1:4-5 uses the word *teleios* twice to show that perfect wisdom comes from God, and 1:25 describes the Torah as *nomos teleios* ("the perfect Torah"). James 3:17 speaks of the wisdom that comes down from above. In this way James shows that he is in line with the traditions of the house of Israel and owes his understanding of the Torah and wisdom to his heritage and roots within the world of Israel.[9]

Besides identifying the Torah as the "perfect Torah," two other descriptions of the Torah are given in the Letter of James: "the Torah of freedom" and "the royal Torah."

The Torah of Freedom

The Letter of James defines the Torah further by referring to it on two occasions as the Torah of freedom (1:25 and 2:12). An examination of the literary background of this identification of the Torah with freedom shows once again James's indebtedness to his background within the traditions of the house of Israel.

For example, 4 Maccabees connects the notion of royalty and liberty with the law: "To the intellect he gave the Law, and if a man lives his life by the Law he shall reign over a kingdom that is temperate and just and good and brave" (4 Macc 2:23). Later, 4 Macc 14:2 says: "O reason, more kingly than kings, more free than freemen!" (Anderson 1985, 2:547, 559).[10]

This concept, "the law of freedom" is found also in Stoic writings and philosophy.[11] For example, the Stoics presented the idea that freedom comes from obeying the law of nature. They argued that only the wise person is truly free (e.g., Seneca, *On the Blessed Life* 15.7). Fabris (1977, 33) sums up their views well:

> For the Stoic authors only the wise person is truly free because he submits to the universal law. In fact true wisdom consists in recognizing and submitting to the universal law, *logos tēs physeōs*, and obedience to such law necessarily brings with it interior freedom.

It is not necessary, however, to resort to Stoic philosophy to account for the origin and meaning of this expression in the Letter of James.[12] It is far more likely that James uses a phrase that is part of the common language of the world and that the writer was using it very differently from the way the Stoics interpreted it. A good example that shows James's distance from the Stoic perspective is provided by the saying "only the wise person is rich" (see Epictetus *Diatr.* 1.30). This phrase emanates from the Stoic concept of riches as a philosophical category that expresses the privilege of the wise, as do other categories such as liberty, royalty, autonomy. For James, however, poverty and riches are used in a totally different context. They have a religious connotation: one may be poor according to the world but rich in faith. The use of James's concept of "the law of freedom" is not derived from any philosophical background, but is rather connected to the biblical context of the reversal of values whereby poverty and riches are viewed in a religious framework of a relationship to faith in God. This shows again that James is more at home in the world of the traditions of the house of Israel than in any other context.

For James, then, "the perfect law, the law of liberty" gives expression to his understanding that the Torah furnishes the means of socialization for the community. This is clearly different from the Stoic concept of law, in which law is universal and knows no boundaries since it is possessed by all people through their human nature (see Hartin 2003, 113). For James, the Torah, on the other hand, provides moral and social guidelines for the community on how their behavior should identify them as members of this particular community, created as God's firstfruits. Thus, the Torah liberates them from the world, which is considered evil and destructive to God's new society. The Torah is perfect and frees the community to achieve its identity and true relationship with God and one another.

James demonstrates an attitude to the Torah that is distinctly different from that of Paul as well. For Paul, belief in Christ actually frees one from the Torah (Rom 6:15-23; 7:6-12; Gal 2:4; 4:21-31; 5:1, 13). Central to Paul's theology is the thesis of the opposition between two ways of life. One way is centered on faith in Jesus; the other is centered on observance of the Torah. Paul's main concern is to oppose those who attribute any *salvific function* to the law; James's concern lies with *the social function* of the law. James is not entering the conflict in which Paul is involved. He shows that he is heir to traditions in early Christianity that still preserve a very positive understanding to the Torah. The same positive approach to the Torah is evident in the Sermon on the Mount (Matt 5:17-20). Both James and the Jesus of the Sermon on the Mount portray the Torah as providing the social fabric of norms that enable those who belong to that new society to remain in relationship with one another and with God. In effect, James is saying to his community: "This is who we are as a community and the Torah frees us to maintain this relationship with one another and with God."

The Royal Torah (James 2:8)

James 2:8-13 provides a further description of the Torah as "the royal law": "You do well if you really fulfill the royal law" (2:8). The term "law" and the verb *teleō* ("to fulfill, to bring to an end") forge a connection with the view of the law that is found in Jas 1:25. The law referred to here must be interpreted consistently, as it has been previously, as referring to the biblical Torah. The whole law is intended and is not to be restricted to just one command or instruction, otherwise the Greek word *entolē* (meaning injunction or commandment) would have been used (see Davids 1982, 114).

The significance of the expression "the royal law" emerges in the context of the entire passage (Jas 2:1-13). The royal (*basilikon*) law must refer back to 2:5, where James uses similar vocabulary to speak about a kingdom: "Has not God chosen the poor in the world to be rich in faith and to be heirs of the kingdom (*basileias*) that he has promised to those who love him?" The Torah is aptly described as the "royal law," for it gives social identification to the members of the kingdom. The Torah is the means of socialization for the group of believers whom James has described in 2:5 as members of the "kingdom."

Here, the Letter of James reflects the theological horizons of the wisdom traditions with their view that the fulfillment of the Torah is the path to perfection. The book of Wisdom develops this consistently:

> The beginning of wisdom is the most sincere desire for instruction, and concern for instruction is love of her, and love of her is the keeping of her laws, and giving heed to her laws is assurance of immortality, and immortality brings one near to God; so the desire for wisdom leads to a kingdom. (Wis 6:17-20)

Love of wisdom is demonstrated by keeping wisdom's laws, which lead to a relationship with God. This relationship brings immortality as well as the inheritance of a kingdom. This is similar to James's concept of fulfilling the "royal law" (2:8). By carrying out the Torah, the expression of God's will for God's covenant people, one inherits a kingdom and enters into a relationship with God.

James also reflects here those traditions of the house of Israel that reach back to the foundation of the Israelite covenant of Sinai. The reference to the kingdom is what Malina (2000, 24) would call "a high context statement," since James does not explain exactly what he understands by this term—he presumes that his hearers/readers have a clear understanding of this "kingdom." In establishing the Sinai covenant, the people of Israel are created as God's kingdom: "Indeed, the whole earth is mine, but you shall be for me a priestly kingdom and a holy nation" (Exod 19:5-6).

James 2:8 goes on to argue that this royal law is encapsulated in the command of love: "You shall love your neighbor as yourself" which is a direct quotation from the Septuagint text of Lev 19:18c. Luke Timothy Johnson (1982) has drawn attention to the influence that Leviticus 19 plays on the thought of the Letter of James.[13] This insight is extremely important, for it shows once again James's dependence on the traditions of the heritage of the house of Israel.

When James says, "if you really fulfill the royal law according to the scripture, 'You shall love your neighbor as yourself'" (2:8), the phrase "according to the scripture" is to be understood as referring to the scriptural context of Leviticus 19, where the law of love is enunciated. In other words, James says that the law of love must be carried out in the way in which it is illustrated in this context. Not only does he have the text of Leviticus in mind, but he wants to stress the context in which this law of love of neighbor occurs. As was indicated previously, Lev 19:15-18 shows concern for the poor and their treatment in just and impartial ways: "You shall not render an unjust judgment; you shall not be partial to the poor or defer to the great: with justice you shall judge your neighbor" (Lev 19:15).

The Function of the Torah in the Letter of James

This examination of the use and meaning of the concept of "law" in the Letter of James shows how it fits into the milieu of the literary traditions and heritage of Judaism. In particular, a study of the literary background of the concepts of law of freedom, the perfect law, the royal law, identifies the context of the letter as belonging to the world of the Second Temple traditions of the house of Israel.

James does not simply base himself on one particular text (except perhaps in his use of Lev 19:12-18, as Johnson [1982] has argued). Instead, James is heir to a particular religious heritage or tradition that is reflected in a common usage of language and thought exemplified most characteristically in the rich literary background of the concept of Torah. This study endeavors to illustrate that James is breathing the same rich religious heritage.

The Torah functions for James's community as a way to maintain the common moral and social boundaries that separate them from the wider world. At the same time the Torah orients them with a specific social concern for the poor in their midst.

James's community differs from the wider society in which it is situated; in fact, the wider society appears as a threat. Part of the socialization process of the Letter of James is to instruct and train the community to meet this threat from the world. They are to keep themselves "unstained by the world" (1:27). While the community is willing to welcome whoever comes into their midst, its openness does not mean that boundaries do not exist. The community clearly distinguishes itself from the world. The moral exhortations enable the community to see that its values are distinct from the values of the wider world. Nevertheless, James's community does not retreat from the world in the way that the Qumran community did. James never imagines that his community should set up institutions that would separate them from the wider society. As Johnson observes:

> First, there is absolutely no indication in James that Christians are to observe ritual separation from other people or from any class of objects which are regarded as "impure." Nor does James ever suggest that Christians flee the customary social structures and seek or establish alternative life styles. On the contrary, as we shall see, he envisages Christians taking full part in the affairs of the world: commerce, landowning, judging, owning and distributing possessions, having houses for hospitality.[14] (1985, 172)

While living in the world, the community is to be conscious that what drives and motivates them is not the values of the world but the values that come from their faith, from the Torah.

The Theological Vision of the Letter of James

Martin Dibelius's assessment of the Letter of James influenced scholarship on the letter throughout much of the twentieth century. He argued that it was impossible to construct a theological vision from the letter since it was composed of a collection of largely independent and loose sayings: "(T)he admonitions of [James] do not apply to a single audience and a single set of circumstances; *it is not possible to construct a single frame into which they will all fit*" (1975, 11, 47–48).

It is true that it is not possible to arrive at a systematic and comprehensive understanding of James's faith in the same way that we can for Paul from his numerous writings. Nevertheless, from what the letter does say it is possible to deduce some understanding of James's theological perspective. There is far more of a connection among the sayings than Dibelius acknowledged. In this consideration I wish simply to draw attention to James's concepts of faith and of God with the intention of showing how much the letter is at home in the world of Second Temple Israelite theological belief and vision.

Faith

The Letter of James is concerned with outlining how faith is to be lived, rather than with expressing concretely what the content of that faith is. As R. C. H. Lenski (1938, 538) observed: "This entire epistle deals with *Christian faith*, and shows how this faith should be genuine, true, active, living, fruitful."

Faith is another of the letter's high-context statements that presume an understanding among its first century C.E. hearers/readers that we, as twenty-first-century readers, lack. Nowhere does the letter define what is understood by the concept *faith*. Nevertheless, by carefully examining the Letter of James one is able to give some specific description to James's understanding of faith. For James the importance of faith emerges from the number of times he uses the noun *pistis* ("faith") (some sixteen times: 1:3, 6; 2:1, 5, 14[2x], 17, 18[3x], 20, 22[2x], 24, 26; 5:15) and the verb *pisteuein* ("to believe") (some three times: 2:19[2x], 23). True faith demonstrates a total trust and confidence in God. This is seen in 1:3, where James argues that "the testing of your faith produces endurance." As Andrew Chester (1994, 25) states, "'faith' in 1.3 denotes complete trust in God and absolute commitment to him, which survives the ultimate eschatological testing and is shown to be true precisely by this." The poor are those who demonstrate a firm trust in God, and for this reason they are proclaimed to be those who will be "heirs of the kingdom" (Jas 2:5). They, too, will endure into the eschatological age because of their firm trust in God.

Another dimension of James's letter is its *communitarian characteristic*: James has in mind the faith of the community rather than simply the faith of the individual. Certainly the faith of the individual is implied and referred to, but it must always be seen as subsisting through a community of faith. Trust in God in the context of a community requires that this faith be demonstrated in action. In describing the scene where a poor person is discriminated against on entering the community, James comments: "Has not God chosen the poor in the world to be rich in faith and to be heirs of the kingdom that he has promised to those who love him? But you have dishonored the poor" (2:5-6).

For James, what is important is *how faith functions*, rather than defining what the content of faith is. Faith functions as a demonstration of trust in God. Total trust and confidence in God lead one to act in the manner in which God acts, by showing a special concern for the poor.

God

James again shows what social scientists refer to as a "high-context compression" in that he shares a specific understanding of God with his first-century C.E. hearers/readers that does not need him to explain it in any way. We as readers from a different worldview and context can strive to fill in the gaps only in a very tenuous way.

The most striking aspect of the religious thought of the Letter of James is that it concentrates on God; it is above all *theocentric*. Its focus is not on Jesus Christ, to whom the letter refers specifically by name only twice (1:1;

2:1).[15] James's understanding of God is clearly understandable only in the context of the Israelite understanding of and belief in God. As in the Hebrew Bible, the foundational understanding of God is *monotheistic*. James makes allusions to the profession of faith in God made by the house of Israel from the beginning of their nation: "Hear, O Israel: The LORD is our God, the LORD alone" (Deut 6:4-5). By contrasting the faith of the believer with the faith of demons, James shows that there is one thing they hold in common: belief that God is one: "You believe that God is one; you do well. Even the demons believe—and shudder" (Jas 2:19). This belief in one God demands total and exclusive trust in God. This image of God lies behind the duality that runs throughout the letter: the challenge to shun friendship with the world for friendship with God (4:4). It also accounts for the criticism of the "double-minded man" (*anēr dipsychos*) in Jas 1:8. By vacillating, one shows a lack of trust in the one God.

James gives a good insight into his understanding of God that conforms closely to the essential idea of Israel's concept of God. In James, God is conceived of as the creator of the world, as well as the creator of humanity. God is "the Father of lights" (Jas 1:17), the creator of the heavenly bodies. This clearly conforms to the Israelite understanding of the creation of the world as demonstrated in the Book of Genesis ("And God said, 'Let there be light'; and there was light. And God saw that the light was good; and God separated the light from the darkness" [1:3-4]). For James every human person is created in "the likeness of God" (Jas 3:9), just as in the creation story in Genesis human beings are created in God's likeness: "Then God said, 'Let us make humankind in our image, according to our likeness'" (1:26). Probably the most common title James uses for God is "Lord" (*kyrios*) (six times: see 1:7; 4:10, 15; 5:4, 10, 11), which corresponds to the Hebrew *Adonai*, the usual designation for God in the Hebrew Bible. Another common term for God in James is "Father" (three times: see 1:17, 27; 3:9). The origin of the typically Christian understanding of God as Father lies clearly once again in the world of Israel, where God was identified as the Father of the nation (Exod 4:22; Deut 14:1; 32:6; Hos 11:1; Jer 3:4, 19; 31:9). James also defines God as the only "lawgiver and judge" (Jas 4:12). This thought corresponds to the emphasis in the first five books of the Torah on God as the one who gave the law to his people: "Moses came and told the people all the words of the LORD and all the ordinances and all the people answered with one voice" (Exod 24:3). James further defines God as "compassionate and merciful" (Jas 5:11), which conforms to the basic Israelite concept of mercy and loving-kindness (*hesed we'emet*), which was the foundation for the whole covenant relationship between God and human beings. Finally, in James all good gifts, especially the gift of wisdom, come from God (see Jas 1:5; 3:17). The same concept is found in the context of the world of Israelite thought: "For the LORD gives wisdom; from his mouth come knowledge and understanding" (Prov 2:6; see also Job 28).

For James, God is also the champion of the poor and the oppressed. "Has not God chosen the poor in the world to be rich in faith and to be heirs of the kingdom?" (2:5). Once again this image of God being on the side of the poor is central to the Israelite concept of the poor: "Because the poor are despoiled, because the needy groan, I will now rise up,' says the LORD; I will place them in the safety for which they long'" (Ps 12:5). James also shows the characteristic Israelite belief that at the end of time God will vindicate the poor, the oppressed, and the marginalized of society by judging and punishing the rich (5:1-6; "you have fattened your hearts in a day of slaughter" [5:5]).

A final implication that can be deduced from this letter is that James endorses the imitation of God. As human beings, we are created in God's likeness (3:9). This likeness implies that we should act like God. Since God is the one who champions the poor, it means that in like manner James's hearers/readers should also demonstrate concern for others, especially the poor (1:27; 5:19-20). The origin of James's understanding of this need to act in imitation of God lies once again in the fundamental call of the covenant and the Holiness Code as expressed in the Book of Leviticus: "Speak to all the congregation of the people of Israel and say to them: You shall be holy, for I the Lord your God am holy" (Lev 19:2). This same call to imitate God is reflected in Jesus' teaching in the Sermon on the Mount: "Be perfect, therefore, as your heavenly Father is perfect" (Matt 5:48). Luke renders this as: "Be merciful, just as your Father is merciful" (Luke 6:36).

The notion that God is the one whom the reader must imitate sets James apart from the rest of the New Testament writings, in which Jesus Christ is the one whom the Christian is called to imitate. "Come to me, all you that are weary and are carrying heavy burdens, and I will give you rest. Take my yoke upon you, and learn from me; for I am gentle and humble in heart, and you will find rest for your souls. For my yoke is easy and my burden is light" (Matt 11:28-30). Once again James shows his closeness to the vision and thought of the Hebrew scriptures in his understanding of God and the believer's relationship with God.

THE LETTER OF JAMES AND THE TEACHING AND MINISTRY OF JESUS

The above examination illustrates that James's theological vision lies within the very heart and center of Second Temple Israelite religious thought and belief. The essential vision of Israelite belief is clearly reflected in this letter. This is why certain scholars were able to claim that James was originally a "Jewish" document that was later "Christianized." From the confession of Israelite faith in a God who is one, to an endorsement of the prophetic vision of God as a champion of the poor, James clearly breathes the very air of Israelite thought and belief.

Despite its roots in these traditions and this religious thought world, the Letter of James also demonstrates another dimension. It shows clear connections to the heritage and teachings of Jesus of Nazareth.

Direct References to Jesus Christ in the Letter of James

One of the most striking features of the Letter of James, looking at it from its context in the New Testament, is that it says very little about Jesus directly. As was indicated above, the Letter of James adopts a *theological* rather than a *christological* approach (see Johnson 1995, 164).

- Only two direct references are made to Jesus in the letter (Jas 1:1and 2:1). In the opening verse James identifies himself in the biblical sense as a servant both of God and of Jesus: "James, a servant of God and of the Lord Jesus Christ." James shows here the custom, common in the early writings of the New Testament, of using the title Lord (*kyrios*) in reference to Jesus particularly in liturgical contexts: "Come, Lord Jesus! (Rev 22:20) and "Our Lord, come!" (1 Cor 16:22). The title Lord (*kyrios*) in the Hebrew writings was always used to refer to God. The New Testament shows a process whereby Jesus is in an indirect way slowly acknowledged as God.

- The most interesting reference to Jesus occurs in 2:1: "My brothers and sisters, do you with your acts of favoritism really believe in our glorious Lord Jesus Christ?" This verse is ambiguous owing to its stream of genitives. Literally it would read: "the faith of our Lord Jesus Christ, the glory" (*tēn pistin tou kyriou hēmōn 'Iēsou Christou tēs doxēs*). Generally, interpreters have understood the genitive "of our Lord Jesus Christ" to be an objective genitive whereby it would be interpreted as the believer's "faith in the Lord Jesus Christ" (see Mayor 1954 [1913], 79; Ropes 1978 [1916], 187). However, in line with interpretations of similar expressions in the letters of Paul, I have argued recently that it would be more appropriate to understand it as a subjective genitive whereby what is held up for emulation is the faith of Jesus himself in God the Father (see Hartin 2003, 129–30; Hays 1983, 170–74; Wall 1997, 109–10).

- The Letter of James refers to Jesus indirectly on a few occasions through the use of the word "Lord," which is used eleven times. In six of these occurrences it clearly refers to God the Father (1:7; 4:10, 15; 5:4; 10, 11). In the other five instances it refers to Jesus (1:1; 2:1; 5:7, 14, 15).

The Jesus who emerges from the references in the letter is the risen glorious Jesus Christ rather than the Jesus of history. As the servant "of the Lord Jesus Christ" (1:1), James demonstrates that he is carrying out the will of the risen Jesus. His relationship to Jesus is celebrated in those worship experiences where Jesus is acknowledged as Lord by using a title that is used of God in the Hebrew scriptures. The faith of Jesus that believers are called to emulate is the faith of the one who now is "the Lord of glory."

Once again the Jesus referred to is the risen Jesus whom the Father has raised to share his glory. Finally, the risen glorious Christ is again referred to in those references that look toward the end of time, when the Lord will return (5:7). This is the same risen glorious Jesus in whose name the sick are anointed (5:14) and in whose glory they are promised to share (5:15).

The surprising fact that there are so few direct references to Jesus in the letter is offset by the indirect connections to the person of Jesus that can be seen through the use of the Jesus' sayings as well as through conformity with the vision, teaching, and message of Jesus. All this indicates that for James, Jesus' importance lies in a focus not on his person but rather on his message. This is supported as well by the attention given to the imitation of God rather than the imitation of Jesus. In the development of early Christianity, the shift from a stress on the message to a reflection on the nature of the messenger developed slowly. The Letter of James again points to a context in the early development of Christianity, when the emphasis was on the message that Jesus came to preach rather on Jesus as messenger.

James's Use of the Jesus Sayings Tradition

Scholars have often noted similarities between the Letter of James and the sayings traditions of Jesus. I have examined this issue on many previous occasions (see Hartin 1991, 141–72; 2003, 81–88). Here I should simply like to make a few observations that are relevant to this specific topic. As with the letters of Paul, James does not quote verbatim any saying of Jesus. He never openly refers to any of Jesus' teachings. However, there are many instances in which it appears that James is alluding to the teaching or the sayings of Jesus. In examining connections between the text of James and the traditions of the Jesus sayings, the central issue is to identify what actually constitutes an allusion. Peter Davids (1982, 68) has given, in my opinion, the clearest explanation of the concept of an allusion: as "a paraphrastic use of phrases or ideas from a logion, with the probable intent of reminding the reader of it."

In recent studies on the concept of textuality in the classical and New Testament worlds, Vernon Robbins (1991) has made some interesting findings. He has shown that in the rhetorical education of the ancient world, the aim was not simply to memorize a text or to copy the text verbatim, but rather to use the text as an exemplar and to rewrite or to perform the text anew.[16] This helps one to understand more clearly the way in which James uses both the Hebrew scriptures and the sayings traditions of Jesus.

Throughout the Letter of James one notes a number of allusions to the Hebrew Bible by which James uses the text in his own way to support his argument and vision. A good illustration of this is Jas 1:9-11, which says that "the rich will disappear like a flower in the field." Behind these verses of James lies the text of Isa 40:7-8, which says that the flower will fade but "the word of our God will stand forever." Although James does not quote this text verbatim, it clearly lies behind the force of his argument.

I contend that James operates in a similar way with regard to the teaching of Jesus as it is expressed in the sayings traditions that handed on his message. See, for example, James's statement in 2:1-7: "Has not God chosen the poor in the world to be rich in faith and to be heirs of the kingdom that he has promised to those who love him?" (2:5). Behind James's argument here about the avoidance of discrimination against the poor, lies Jesus' saying in the Sermon on the Mount: "Blessed are the poor in spirit, for theirs is the kingdom of heaven" (Matt 5:3). What James does is to perform the text of Jesus' saying in his own way by using it in the context of his own teaching regarding the avoidance of discrimination against the poor.

In this way, James not only bases his instructions on the teaching and authority of the Hebrew scriptures, but he also grounds himself on the message and teaching of Jesus of Nazareth.

James and the Vision, Teaching, and Message of Jesus

The movement that Jesus began in Second Temple Israel was what can be termed "a restoration movement" (Hartin 2003, 85). The picture of Jesus that emerges from the Gospel of Matthew is of someone who did not set out to establish a new religion; rather he worked within the confines of the religious traditions and heritage of the Israel of his day. He was intent on

challenging and reforming the religious life of the house of Israel by re-
newing it and bringing it to a clearer understanding of the demands of the
Torah as the will of God. "Do not think that I have come to abolish the law
or the prophets; I have come not to abolish but to fulfill" (Matt 5:17). As
noted previously, Matthew presents the mission of Jesus as confined originally to the house of Israel. In answer to the Canaanite woman's request for
him to heal her daughter, Jesus replies: "I was sent only to the lost sheep of
the house of Israel" (Matt 15:24).

As we have seen, James is interested in the message of Jesus rather than
in his person as such. James demonstrates exactly the same vision that the
Jesus of Matthew's Gospel demonstrates. His address to his hearers/readers
as the "twelve tribes in the Dispersion" captures the same intent as Matthew's Jesus. James saw his community as the beginnings ("the firstfruits"
[1:17]) of this twelve-tribe kingdom that Jesus set out to restore. "In both
the preaching of Jesus and the letter of James, God is at work reconstituting
the people of Israel as the 'twelve-tribe kingdom'" (Hartin 2003, 85).

Characteristic of Jesus' teaching in all the Gospels is his outreach to the
poor and the marginalized of society. His concern for the poor is in line
with the tradition of the prophets and their proclamation that God was
the one who championed the cause of the poor. When James takes up the
cause of the poor and challenges his hearers/readers to avoid every form
of discrimination against them, he is not just following the traditions of
the prophets; he is also continuing Jesus' vision. Just as Jesus' message was
countercultural, so too is James's. In his community James envisages equal-
ity among all, where the rich are brought low and the poor raised up (1:9-
11). The same is true of the message of Jesus, who proclaims: "All who
exalt themselves will be humbled, and all who humble themselves will be
exalted" (Matt 23:12; see also Luke 14:11; 18:14).

Most scholars will acknowledge that the Letter of James reflects Jesus'
ethical teaching (see Laws 1980, 14; Penner 1996, 254). However, not only
does James remain true to Jesus' ethical teaching; he also reflects many
other dimensions of Jesus' ministry in his wisdom instructions. As David
Rhoads (1998, 485) notes: "Other elements of Jesus' teaching that may be
reflected in the wisdom of James include: healing, forgiveness, rescuing
sinners, prohibiting oaths, a commitment to the poor, the encouragement

that those who ask will receive, and the affirmation that God gives good gifts." Without doubt James shows that he is continuing Jesus' mission and teaching. There is nothing in the Letter of James that does not conform to the vision, teaching, and mission of Jesus.

CONCLUSION

My study of the Letter of James demonstrates that this writing lies fully within the world of the house of Israel as well as within the world of the followers of Jesus Christ. It is almost like the confession that Christians make in Jesus Christ as being fully divine and fully human. It is not *either one or the other,* it is *both . . . and.*

On the one hand, as this study has consistently argued, the traditional world of the Letter of James is clearly that of Second Temple Israel. Its theological vision is at home in that world, as is its stress on the centrality of the Torah as the guiding force for carrying out God's will in the lives of believers. The eschatological hope in the reconstitution of God's twelve-tribe kingdom is another dimension that unites the Letter of James with the thought of Second Temple Israel. The thought world of Second Temple Israel was no monolithic entity. Certain features did unite all the members of the house of Israel, such as a belief in one God; that they were God's chosen people; that God had communicated the Torah to give direction to their lives—to name but a few. However, differing interpretations of these very basic common beliefs gave rise to different groups within the confines of the house of Israel, such as the Pharisees, the Sadducees and the Essenes.

On the other hand, the community to whom the Letter of James was written also acknowledged the importance of Jesus and faith in him. They acknowledged Jesus as the Messiah ("Christ" in 1:1 and 2:1). His message, stressing a commitment to the poor and outcasts, gave inspiration for their way of life. Finally, Jesus' sayings lay behind James's instructions, which he delivered in an authoritative manner as he did with the Hebrew scriptures. The community to whom the Letter of James was written was a community still at home within the world of the house of Israel, while at the same time accepting the vision of Jesus of Nazareth and his interpretation of Israel's traditions as the authentic interpretation.

Because the community to whom James wrote was a community that possessed its own teachers (3:1) and elders (5:14), as well as a commitment to faith "in our glorious Lord Jesus Christ," this community was clearly distinguished from other groups within the world of the house of Israel. James's instructions are designed to give identity to his group and to foster the socialization of his group. Nevertheless, James's context still remains that of a group or community of believers for whom the Torah remains vital for their faith and life.

SUGGESTED READINGS

Chester, Andrew, and Ralph P. Martin. 1994. *The Theology of the Letters of James, Peter, and Jude.* New Testament Theology. Cambridge: Cambridge University Press.

Hartin, Patrick J. 2003. *James.* Sacra Pagina 14. Collegeville, Minn.: Liturgical.

Hays, Richard B. 1983. *The Faith of Jesus Christ: An Investigation of the Narrative Substructure of Galatians 3:1–4:11.* Society of Biblical Literature Dissertation Series 56. Chico, Calif.: Scholars Press.

Johnson, Luke Timothy. 1982. "The Use of Leviticus 19 in the Letter of James." *Journal of Biblical Literature* 101:391–401.

Malina, Bruce J. 1993. *The New Testament World: Insights from Cultural Anthropology.* Rev. ed.. Louisville, Ky.: Westminster John Knox.

McKnight, Scot. 1999. "A Parting within the Way: Jesus and James on Israel and Purity." Pages 83–129 in *James the Just and Christian Origins.* Edited by Bruce Chilton and Craig A. Evans. Leiden: Brill.

Rhoads, David. 1998. "The Letter of James: Friend of God." *Currents in Theology and Mission* 25:473–86.

Robbins, Vernon K. 1991. "Writing as a Rhetorical Act in Plutarch and the Gospels." Pages 142–68 in *Persuasive Artistry: Studies in New Testament Rhetoric in Honor of George A. Kennedy*. Edited by Duane F. Watson. Sheffield: JSOT Press.

Verseput, Donald, J. 1997. "Reworking the Puzzle of Faith and Deeds in James 2:14-26." *New Testament Studies* 43:97–115.

Wall, Robert W. 1997. *Community of the Wise: The Letter of James*. New Testament in Context. Valley Forge, Pa.: Trinity Press International.

9. John's Jewish (Christian?) Apocalypse

John W. Marshall

For two centuries, the category "Jewish Christianity" has been operative in the interpretation of John's Apocalypse. Through this time it has served the dual function of acknowledging the ways in which the Book of Revelation is Jewish and at the same time positioning it as non-Jewish, as superseding Judaism, and as standing in a median position within an evolutionary scheme that leads from Judaism to Christianity. Interpreters from F. C. Baur (1792–1860) through R. H. Charles (1855–1931) and David Aune (1939–) have described the author as a Jewish Christian standing between a primitive Judaism and a mature Christianity. The present essay is written from a position of principled disagreement with such a reading. It seeks to examine the history of scholarship that has used the category "Jewish Christian" to understand the Apocalypse, and to justify the classification of the Apocalypse simply as Jewish.

The Book of Revelation is an apocalyptic treatise written in the last half of the first century in Asia Minor by an otherwise unknown figure named John (Rev 1:1 4, 9; 22:8). John Collins, leading a Society of Biblical Literature project on apocalyptic literature, has defined the apocalyptic genre as "a genre of revelatory literature with a narrative framework, in which a revelation is mediated by an other-worldly being to a human recipient, disclosing a transcendent reality which is both temporal, insofar as it envisages eschatological salvation, and spatial insofar as it involves another, supernatural world" (Collins 1979, 9). Though the generic identity of Revelation is complex and formed by multiple subgenres such as lament, hymn, letter, dialogue, mythological narrative, scriptural allusion, etc., apocalypse has served interpreters well as a macro-genre for understanding the text as a whole.

234 JEWISH CHRISTIANITY RECONSIDERED

John describes himself being on the island of Patmos and receiving a series of visual and auditory revelations given by the "one like a son of man" (Rev 1:13) and by a series of angelic figures that function as revealers (Rev 1:1; 10:9; 17:7; 19:9; 21:9; 22:6; 22:8; 22:16). John receives and passes on communications between the revealing spirits and the angelic guardians of human congregations (chs. 2 and 3), sees the action of the heavenly throne room, and learns of the problem of who can bring on the eschatological resolution of history and the redemption of God's people from the earth (chs. 4–5). What follows is a two-part recapitulation of the destruction of the "great city" (chs. 6–11 and 12–17). After the judgment of the great city, figured as the whore "with whom the kings of the earth have committed fornication" (chs. 17–18, quoting 17:2), the text concludes with a visionary account of the vindication of the holy city, the new or renewed Jerusalem, and John's exit from the vision (chs. 19–22).[1]

Dating the Apocalypse is a complex matter, and the majority of modern interpreters place it at the end of the first century. A significant alternative proposal understands Revelation to have been composed in close chronological relation to the reign of Nero and the events of the Judean war. Dating the Apocalypse also stands in a circular relationship to ways in which an interpreter understands its religious provenance: dating it earlier makes it more difficult to argue for a Christianity distinct from Judaism, especially when the enterprise of taxonomy is understood as a task of social history rather than the history of theologoumena. Conversely, dating Revelation later also provides data that suggest that a distinction of Christianity from Judaism—again, conceived social-historically—is not a given even at a later date. It must, however, be said that my analysis here takes place with an understanding of Revelation having been composed around 69 or 70 CE, before news of the fall of Jerusalem reached John in the province of Asia.[2]

The first portion of this essay tracks the use of the term "Jewish Christian" in scholarship on the Apocalypse. In some cases, it is a general description of the work or the author; in other cases, a description of hypothetical sources underlying the finished Book of Revelation. With the exception of the deeply problematic work of the Tübingen School, "Jewish Christianity" is an inconsistent, undertheorized, unilluminating, and ultimately detrimental category in the interpretation of the Apocalypse.

Beyond this, in many cases it facilitates an insidious combination of anti-Semitism and Christian supersessionism. The second portion of the essay argues for the application of the categorization "Jewish" to the Apocalypse. By abstaining from the category "Christian" and working with the understanding of the Apocalypse as Jewish, I argue that we can achieve a more comprehensive understanding of the religious milieu of the text and avoid several traditional problems in its interpretation.

DESCRIBING THE APOCALYPSE AS "JEWISH CHRISTIAN"

According to R. H. Charles, the premier commentator on the Apocalypse in the early twentieth century, "John the Seer, to whom we owe the Apocalypse, was a Jewish Christian" (Charles 1920, 1:xxi). According to Rudolf Bultmann, the dominant scholar of early Christianity in the middle of the twentieth century, "the Christianity of Revelation has to be termed a weakly Christianized Judaism" (Bultmann 1955, 175). According to David Aune, the preeminent commentator at the close of the twentieth century, John "moved from the role of Jewish apocalypticist to Christian prophet," passing through a stage in which he functioned "as a Jewish-Christian prophet" (see Aune 1983, 212; Aune 1997, 1:cxxii, cxxi). In each of these cases, an essentially developmental schema of the movement of Christianity through time governs the use of the concept of Jewish Christianity.[3]

This developmental schema deploys Judaism as a groundable entity that can provide a foundation for an otherwise undocumentable (in the case of the Apocalypse) transition from Judaism to Christianity. There can be no mistake that John's Apocalypse knows of no such entity as "Christianity," describes no break with Judaism, undertakes no polemic against it, does not conceive of the world in a three-part taxonomy of Christians/Jews/pagans, and does not consider itself to be a hybrid of Judaism and Christianity. On the other hand, John's language, name, literary universe, social habitus, political loyalties, cosmological vision, and even his messianism all stand squarely within Second Temple Judaism. The category "Jewish Christianity" performs the dual function of masking the untenability of "Christian" while simultaneously acknowledging the appropriateness of the category "Jewish." The combination of the two enforces a subordination: either the Judaism of "Jewish Christianity" positions Christianity as that which supersedes Judaism (see Charles), or the Judaism of "Jewish Christianity" functions to subordinate the Apocalypse within the canon of Christianity (see Bultmann).

F. C. Baur, Hegelian Historiography, and Jewish Christianity

The understanding of the Apocalypse of John as Jewish Christian starts with F. C. Baur and the Tübingen School in the mid-nineteenth century. Under the influence of a Hegelian metanarrative of history, Baur imagined the character of early Christianity to be generated by a binary conflict of Pauline/Hellenistic Christianity and Petrine/Jewish Christianity.[4] Baur's understanding of the Apocalypse of John is only tangentially presented in his *Church History of the First Three Centuries* (Eng. trans. 1878 [1863]), but takes the following line: working with the understanding that the John who wrote the Apocalypse is John the apostle of Jesus, Baur sees the Apocalypse as standing in direct opposition to a Paulinism that offered some flexibility with regard to the eating of food offered to idols. Without going so far as to name the Apocalypse as "Jewish Christian," Baur (1878, 85, cf. 155 [1863, 81 cf. 148]) suggests that it takes up the issues that in the eyes of "Jewish Christians" are "the distinctive mark of that lax Pauline Christianity which was on such good terms with heathenism." It is clear from Baur's subsequent expositions of the anti-Pauline impetus of the Apocalypse of John and his focus on the "Judaistic character of the Apocalypse" (1878, 85 [1863, 81]) that Baur regards it as an instance of the Jewish Christian movement.

Baur contrasts the Pauline movement strongly with the Apocalypse. The former is characterized by freedom, liberal dispositions, enlightenment, and universalism (1878, 85, 86 [1863, 81, 82]), and the latter is a "Judaistic reaction" (1878, 86 [1863, 81]), driven by strictness and "Jewish particularism" (1878, 87 [1863, 83]). These contrasts show clearly his valuation of the Apocalypse and Jewish Christianity. When he comes to the Gospel of John, Baur's Hegelian metanarrative structure turns the crank of history and portrays the

Gospel writer as one who seizes the venerable name of the apostle John and "spiritualises" (1878, 154 [1863, 147]) the (by implication, carnal) Judaistic doctrines of the Apocalypse in symbiosis with the universalistic Pauline transcendence of nationalistic Judaism. Thus, Baur sees Jesus' words on the cross in John, *tetelestai*, "it is finished" (John 19:30), as referring to Judaism itself. At this point it is worth quoting Baur (1878, 157 [1863, 150]) substantially:

> What we have to recognize in the moment of the death of Jesus is the turning-point between the two religious economies, the passage from the Jewish consciousness of the Old Testament to the Christian consciousness of the New. The old is run out and has reached its end: the new has come into existence. With his last word on the cross he who was sent by the Father has finally discharged all claims which Judaism and the Old Testament had a right to make upon him as the promised Messiah, and placed himself in a completely free relation to them. Judaism and the Old Testament now belong to a period that has run its course.

It is crucial to see the deeply theological work done by Baur's historical categories of Pauline and Jewish Christianity. These are fundamentally developmental categories that enable Baur to read the evidentiary archive as a witness to a Hegelian movement of the world-historical spirit from Judaism and from Hellenistic thought to Christianity as the synthesizing entity containing the new world-historical spirit. The category "Jewish Christianity" is not, for Baur, an acknowledgment of the specific ethnic heritage of a particular believer; Paul is not a Jewish Christian. Jewish Christianity, in its formative appearance as a category of historical analysis in general and of the Apocalypse in particular, is a value-laden and subordinate category in an effectively racist schema of Christian development (Kelley 2002, xvi, 254).

The aftermath of Baur is immense. Friedrich Engels, depending also on Bruno Bauer (another Hegelian scholar of, among other things, early Christianity), adopts the Gentile Christian vs. Jewish Christian binary.[5] In characterizing the Apocalypse specifically, Engels (1957b, 181 [1882, 304]) sees it as firmly planted in favor of the Jewish Christian party. The schema that governs Engels's understanding—inherited from F. C. Baur, Bruno Bauer, and

Franz Ferdinand Benary—is completely developmental and, on the basis of a dismissal of the authenticity of the Pauline letters, posits the Apocalypse as the "crudest" and "most primitive" form of Christianity to which there is direct literary witness (Engels 1957a [1882], 185, 189). Engels considers early Christians to have been a sect of Judaism (1882; 1894-95, 461; 1957a, 185) and the Apocalypse to be their only literary remains. The directness of Engels's writing makes clear the developmental and anti-Semitic metanarrative that drove much German scholarship in the wake of Hegel.

The formulations of F. C. Baur reverberate both through scholarship on Revelation and through the theorization of Jewish Christianity in the twentieth century. The developmental character of Baur's theorization of Jewish Christianity allows it to stand as a repository of negative value even when the formalized Hegelianism of Baur has no place in an exegete's work. After Baur, Bauer, and Engels, the role of the category "Jewish Christianity" in the interpretation of the Apocalypse splits into two streams: (1) discussion of a single author or dominant editor of the Apocalypse and (2) discussion of sources and events lying behind the composition of the Apocalypse as we have it.[6]

Partitioning the Apocalypse

In the late nineteenth century, especially in German criticism, there was a massive movement to describe the Apocalypse as a compilation of sources. This tendency carried over into the world of English-speaking scholarship in the work of R. H. Charles, who tamed the impulse to a small extent, through the work of Josephine Massyngberde Ford and the massive commentary of David Aune. Chronicling the proposals is a dizzying endeavor,[7] but it remains important to note the problems that drove scholars to their source-critical proposals and the role the category "Jewish Christianity" played in these proposals. In addition to the exemplary success of source criticism in the Synoptic Problem, source criticism of Revelation was driven by the combination of clear understandings of the elements of Revelation that were evidently Jewish, and difficulties in integrating these elements into a picture of orthodox Christianity. In 2001, I put the problem this way:

> As the source critics faced the Apocalypse with all its challenges . . .
> they juggled two variables: (1) textual integrity and (2) the herme-
> neutic framework that accompanied their conception of Christianity
> and its application to the Apocalypse of John. They squarely faced the
> incompatibility of these variables and chose to hold onto the latter.
> Textual integrity was the ball they dropped, but the text of the Apoca-
> lypse of John seemed to shatter along different lines each time a new
> critic dropped it. (2001, 155)

Critics like Daniel Völter (1882; 1886; 1893; 1911 [1904]), who was a
significant driver of source criticism of the Apocalypse, employed the hypothesis of Jewish Christian sources underlying Revelation in order to explain the landscape of the text. Völter's work went through five editions and
changed each time, but his final proposal distinguishes an original core by
John (perhaps John Mark) in the mid 60s of the Common Era, an update
by the same author near the end of Nero's reign, and an interpolation by
the "Jewish Christian" heretic Cerinthus.[8] Readers can refer to Völter's own
work for detailed justifications of these hypotheses, but it is sufficient to
note that Völter casts onto Cerinthus some of the problems that plague
interpreters who attempt to find an orthodox christology in Revelation,
namely, the priority of Michael in defeating Satan's forces (Rev 12:7-2), the
lack of status differentiation between the Lamb and Moses (Rev 15:3), and
the subordination of the "one like a son of man" to the announcing angel
(Rev 14:14-19). In Völter's analysis, the hypothesis of a sub-Christian and
heretical Jewish Christianity "explains" these features.[9]

Völter's primary adversary was Eduard Vischer, a student of Adolf von Harnack. Vischer proposed a discrete Jewish source and a Christian redaction.[10]
Harnack's discussion of the possible relation of "Jewish Christianity" and Revelation depends on Vischer, who, according to Harnack, demonstrated that
Revelation was not Jewish Christian but rather a Christian document that incorporated otherwise unattested Jewish sources (Harnack 1961 [1896], 1:100–
101). That is to say, for Harnack Revelation remains properly supersessionist,
having incorporated the value of Judaism without being contaminated by it.

Beyond the competing theories of Vischer and Völter, a panoply of theories have envisioned the Apocalypse as composed of parts that were either

Jewish or Christian.[11] Working with the category "Jewish Christianity," Karl Erbes (1891; cf. Barton 1898, 780) sees the Apocalypse as composed in three stages by Jewish Christian authors, while Charles Bruston (1888; cf. Barton 1898, 779) proposes a Jewish Christian author writing before the Judean war whose work was redacted twice: once by a Christian under Domitian, and subsequently by a Jewish Christian in the early second century. In each case, the interpreter pulls away from an author he calls "Christian" those elements of the text that are difficult to integrate into the interpreter's picture of Christian doctrine and lays them instead at the door of a hypothetical Jewish Christian.[12]

By the time R. H. Charles published his magnum opus, the International Critical Commentary on Revelation (1920), source-critical theories of the composition or compilation of the Apocalypse had been under discussion for a generation. But more so than many of his predecessors and contemporaries, Charles attempted to elaborate the character of the contributors. In opposition to the "author," of whom he thinks quite highly, Charles posits an editor/disciple of the original author, to whom Charles assigns—one might say, on whom he blames—the arrangement of Revelation 20–22 as well as several other minor elements of the text. The role this hypothetical editor figure plays in Charles's reconstruction of the genesis of the Apocalypse is crystallized in Charles's summary:

> He [the editor] was apparently a Jew of the dispersion, a better Grecian than his master, but otherwise a person profoundly stupid and ignorant; a narrow fanatic and a celibate, not quite loyal to his trust as editor; an arch-heretic, though, owing to his stupidity, probably an unconscious one. (1920, 1:xviii, with sentiments elaborated in 1:lv).

This editor figure functions as the alter ego of Charles's idealized author, and he is never directly dignified with the label "Christian." Charles's bifurcation of the authorship of the Apocalypse into two parties, a praiseworthy author and a blameworthy editor, performs a function complementary to the integrative role that the term "Jewish Christianity" purports to undertake. To clarify: on the one hand, programmatically naming the author as "Jewish Christian" enables Charles to integrate Christianity into his analytical apparatus and provides a narrative that draws positively on the heritage of Judaism; on the other hand, bifurcating the authorship into a "great Christian prophet" and a "shallow-brained fanatic" Jewish editor (1920, 1:lv, xviii) allows Charles to leave behind negative characteristics that he wants to associate with a Jewish editor—especially an insufficiently elevated and consistent christology. His theory of authorship forms the antidote to the contamination that "Jewish Christianity" had implied since Baur.

While Charles posits small-scale Jewish Christian sources in addition to his larger hypothesis of genius author and stupid editor, he represents in the main a retreat from the baroque character of earlier source hypotheses. Together with a similar movement in German criticism (e.g., Bousset 1906; though cf. Bousset 1899, col. 194), the bulk of twentieth-century scholarship took Revelation basically as a whole, with perhaps Jewish sources integrated in places like 11:1-9 and 7:1-8. The only major breaks from this pattern were the work of Marie-Emile Boismard (1952, 161–81), who posited serial Johannine authorship with the late addition of chapters 1–3, and Josephine Massyngberde Ford (1975, 379–80), who, quite idiosyncratically, proposed that John the Baptist himself was the author of the bulk of Revelation 4–11; that a disciple of John who had some knowledge of Jesus was responsible for chapters 12–22 (with a complex array of specific interpolations in chapters 20–22); and that a Jewish Christian redactor writing for a Jewish Christian community after 70 CE added Revelation 1–3 and a few specific alterations to the main text. Ford's thesis has not won followers, but it represents a serious attempt to deal with the lack of fit between the Apocalypse and her vision of Christian literature. Ford boldly opted for clarity in her attempt to deal with the lack of fit; more commonly, scholars have opted for the undefined category of "Jewish Christianity" to address the challenges presented by Revelation.

Theorizing Jewish Christianity after Baur

If Jewish Christianity was a category overdetermined by a Hegelian metanarrative in the treatment of F. C. Baur and his heirs, in its move to the mainstream[13] of English-speaking academia it became a deeply confused and prejudicial category that neither drove historical-critical analysis nor underpinned a philosophical reading of history.

R. H. Charles, who took the lead in English-speaking commentary on Revelation, opened his work in this way: "John the Seer, to whom we owe the Apocalypse, was a Jewish Christian who had in all probability spent the greater part of his life in Galilee before he emigrated to Asia Minor."[14] Over the course of analysis, Charles describes the author of the Apocalypse as a "Jew" ("The author . . . was a Palestinian Jew" [1920, 1:xliv]), as a "Christian" ("This great Christian prophet whose work fitly closes the canon . . ." [1:lv]), and as a "Jewish Christian" (1:xxi, 57). The three terms are never defined, and Charles's deployment of them seems to be related to his desire to praise the author of the Apocalypse theologically (i.e., as a Christian) or to locate him historically (i.e., as a Jew or Jewish Christian). Charles never defines his use of the term Jewish Christianity, but several elements are obviously constitutive of the category for him: geography, language, natal religion, ethnicity, and theology.[15] Of these, theology (and ethics as a subset thereof) is the only justifiable way that John can be categorized as "Christian," and Charles's varying uses of "Jew," "Jewish Christian," and "Christian" depend on the type of analysis he is undertaking. Charles deploys the traditional Christian figuration of Judaism as national, ethnic, particular, and focused on the letter of the law—the carnal in contrast to the spiritual. In tandem with this vision, Charles characterizes Christianity as universal, ethical, and spiritual. It is this trope of Christian anti-Judaism, this clichéd contrast, that holds together the otherwise unstable categories.

After Charles, the category "Jewish Christian" rarely finds programmatic definition in the interpretation of the Apocalypse. Instead, several dimensions of the category rise to prominence inasmuch as they are useful to the scholar on an ad hoc basis: relation to the heritage and especially the writings of Judaism; geographic or ethnic origin; theological deviance from an imagined orthodoxy; and social-historical setting. The painful irony should not be lost, however, that "Jewish Christianity" is used to distinguish forms of devotion to Jesus that differ from the form attributed to that follower of Jesus—namely, Paul—who most loudly proclaims his Judaism and speaks most highly of Judaism.[16] From this point of view, it is a self-indicting category. Viewed with an eye to the deeply contradictory uses to which "Jewish Christianity" is put, it is an utterly protean category.

The intensity with which the literature of the Hebrew Bible and Second Temple Judaism saturates the consciousness of John is apparent to all scholarly readers. Charles (1920, 1:lxv–lxxxiv) and Moyise (1995) offer overviews of the scholarly debates on whether John knew and used such literature in Greek or in Hebrew, and the specific noncanonical literature that was available to him. Many interpreters mention this immersion in the literature of Judaism in their discussions of the identity of John. Many, like Frederick J. Murphy (1998, xiii, 27–30), see such a literary and narrative immersion as constitutive for the categorization of John as "Jewish Christian." Only Robert K. MacKenzie (1997, 24–28, 60–74) has vigorously denied that John's literary environment suggests a heritage in Judaism, suggesting that a Gentile appropriation of scripture was sufficient and that John's usage of Jewish pseudepigraphical texts is not distinctively Jewish.

Many scholars use the term "Jewish Christian" to identify John with no immediate goal other than to locate his geographic and ethnic origin; in English this trend begins with Moses Stuart (1845, 230, cf. 221) and crops up repeatedly throughout the twentieth century (e.g., Hemer 1986, 8). The name John itself is often, and with justification, taken to indicate a heritage in Judaism. MacKenzie (1997, 7–9), however, argues that this is a Gentile Christian's investment in Judaism. The broadly persuasive arguments that the Apocalypse was composed in western Asia Minor necessitate a theory of dispersion or emigration, and usually the Judean war or the crisis under Caligula is brought in to supply a rationale.

The peculiar character of John's Greek is an industry in itself, and again Charles (1920, 1:cxvii–clix) and Aune (1997, 1:clx–ccxi), together with Stanley E. Porter (1989, 582) and Allen D. Callahan (1995, 453), review the literature thoroughly. Language functions in the deployment of the category "Jewish Christian" as an indicator of ethnic and geographic origin. The strong position in favor of a Jewish origin is apparent in Charles's formulation (1920, 1:xxi) that "while he [John] wrote in Greek he thought in Hebrew." Again, MacKenzie (1997, 78–165) has mounted vigorous arguments against any suggestion that John's mother tongue was Hebrew or Aramaic and against any inference from the character of his language that he was a Jewish Christian.

"Jewish Christianity" is frequently used with another sense that accompanies its geographical/ethnic/linguistic function: it often designates a theology or pattern of commitment that stands in variation to "orthodoxy." Customary issues are christology and the practice of boundary-marking Jewish observance. David Flusser's comment (1969, 144) on the christology of Revelation is an example:

> The book of Revelation . . . contains a very developed Christology. Its author was himself a Hebrew-thinking Jewish Christian. Christology is not a product of Hellenistic Christianity. It seems that it was developed in Jewish Christian circles, different from those in which the Synoptic tradition was formed.

Flusser integrates into this comment the issues of language and ethnicity but focuses on theology. He also adopts a Hellenistic/Jewish binary that overschematizes the variety of participants in the movement devoted to Jesus and underplays the diversity of Judaism. Nevertheless, "Jewish Christianity" allows him to allude to the Apocalypse's deep differences from later dominant patterns of thinking about Jesus. The subordination of the Son of Man is only the most startling example when viewed from a position of orthodox Christianity.[17]

Jürgen Roloff also describes John as a Jewish Christian, but he pulls his theology toward later Christian normativity. According to Roloff (1993, 48), "although a Jewish-Christian himself as regards his origins, John shares this perspective of gentile Christians [i.e., supersessionism]"; John thinks that "Judaism, which rejected faith in Christ, no longer belongs to the people of God." Roloff cannot or will not give up a picture of John's thinking as consistent with normative Christian understandings of Judaism. For him the category "Jewish Christian" does not indicate that John's theology is anything but normatively Christian.

The social-historical payoff of the category "Jewish Christian" comes in the notoriously fractious attempts of scholars to find a plausible context of persecution exterior to the Apocalypse that can be matched to the focus on persecution within the Apocalypse, especially in the messages to angels of the seven assemblies in Revelation 2–3. The possibility of persecution plays a large role in the interpretation of the Apocalypse. Some scholars attempt to use accounts of local persecution in Rome to justify the reaction of John in Asia Minor, and others shift the focus to perceived rather than actual persecution (Gager 1975; Stuart 1845, 222; A. Y. Collins 1984a, 30) or deny the actuality of persecution altogether (Thompson 1990). It also a frequent tactic to suggest that Roman reactions to the activities of Diaspora Jews in the aftermath of the Judean war created a frying pan and fire dilemma in which followers of Jesus, especially Jewish ones, had to choose between liability to observances of imperial cult (or persecution as a consequence for nonobservance) and exemption from observance of the imperial cult through an affiliation with Judaism that would entail either abandonment of devotion to Jesus or persecution by synagogue authorities for that devotion. Colin Hemer (1986, 10) sees in such circumstances "a new occasion of disunion between Jewish and gentile Christians." So also Elisabeth Schüssler Fiorenza (1991, 54, cf. 123) suggests that John is a "Jewish Christian" with a failing ability to claim his identity as a Jew: "The situation of Christians in Asia Minor was aggravated because Jewish Christians like John were less and less able to claim their political privileges and identity as Jews." While the logic of positing a conflict between Jewish and non-Jewish devotees of Jesus may appear sound, such a conflict has no direct echo in the text of the Apocalypse.

The variety of manners in which Jewish Christianity is conceived and deployed in the last hundred years of analysis of Revelation completely lacks theoretical definition. While Baur's Hegelianism is out of fashion, an undisciplined eclecticism has replaced it. In a fascinating reversal of Baur, MacKenzie (1997, 3, 42) can argue that Paul is a Jewish Christian and John is not. In truth, the use of the category "Jewish Christian" has not advanced beyond Moses Stuart's long-forgotten and offhand use of the phrase in 1845, the earliest I found in English.

At the turn of the third millennium, Frederick Murphy and Ben Witherington, in complementary and contradictory ways, exemplify this lack of progress. Murphy (1998, 1) declares in the first page of the preface to his commentary that John was a Jewish Christian, and that one of the most important motivations of the commentary is to participate in a renewed and positive scholarly interest in "the Jewishness of earliest Christianity." The concept "Jewish Christian," however, never receives theorization, definition, or substantial deployment in his commentary. John is simply a Christian once Murphy's commentary is under way. Ten pages of discussion of the author and the social situation never mention Jewish Christianity (1998, 33–42). Witherington, on the other hand, makes no initial nod to the category Jewish Christianity in his extensive discussion of the author; reading Witherington on the topic leaves no impression that "Jewish Christian" is an important or productive way to understand John. But throughout the body of his commentary, Witherington repeatedly repairs to the category "Jewish Christian" in explaining puzzling moves in John's text. Twice, in fact, Witherington (2003, 42, 157) writes the same sentence: "it is understandable how an exiled Jewish Christian prophet after AD 70 might see himself as being in the same position as Ezekiel." Some source criticism is in order. Drawing on his habits—or more likely his notes—carelessly, Witherington has not noticed his repetition or his deployment of a category that has had no place in his general description of John and yet appears repeatedly in his analysis (2003, 31, 33, 42, 134, 157, 185, 220, 232). What for Murphy was a theoretical commitment with few discernible implications functions for Witherington as a stopgap with no disciplined theorization. This range of affairs, including the absence of both disciplined theorization and consistent usage, is the current state of "Jewish Christianity" in the study of the Apocalypse.

Reading the Apocalypse as Jewish

Over the course of the last two centuries the term "Jewish Christian" has been more of a symptom of critical insight than a generator of it. Baur recognized diversity and conflict among the devotees of Jesus. Völter and the other source critics recognized the inadequacy of "Christianity" to a historical interpretation of the Apocalypse. Charles and those of us who labor in his aftermath recognize the importance of Judaism to the development of devotion to Jesus (often oversystemized as "Christianity"). But "Jewish Christianity" has usually served to prevent those insights from reaching full fruition. It has served as a repository for recognizing difference—even difference as stark as that proposed by

Ford. It has acknowledged the Judaism of the Apocalypse while taming that insight and subordinating it to Christian supersessionism.

It is my contention that the Apocalypse of John ought to be understood as a Jewish document.[18] It gives strong evidence of its cultural and religious position within Judaism and no counterevidence of being "Christian" in a sense that would justify such a classification within a polyadic understanding of religion—that is, a view of religion that understands it to be composed of a broad range of phenomena rather than simply or preeminently belief (see below). The mediating category "Jewish Christianity" is not an appropriate historical description of the Apocalypse because of its evident apologetic role in Christian supersessionist theological attempts to understand Judaism. Reading the Apocalypse as Jewish proceeds from an understanding of the inapplicability of the term "Christian" and depends on showing the benefits of reading it as Jewish.

The Term "Christian"

Obviously the Apocalypse does not categorize itself as Christian: the term does not appear. In fact, there is no evidence that it existed in 70 CE or even by 96 C.E.[19] The narrative of Acts 11:26 concerns the first half of the first century, as does the account of Paul's self-description in Acts 26:28, but these accounts themselves are later, almost certainly later than the Apocalypse. Paul himself never uses the term. Moreover, even in Acts, the term never rises to a dominant description of a religious group, still less one that looks like the community in which the Apocalypse arose. Tellingly, and in stark contrast to the Apocalypse, the term arises in documents that often represent distinctly pro-Roman dispositions.[20] The other early occurrences of the term for Christian (*christianos* in Greek and *christianus* in Latin) occur in the *Didache*, Ignatius of Antioch, 1 Peter, Pliny's ninety-sixth letter, Suetonius's *Lives* of Nero and Claudius, and Tacitus's *Annals*. The occurrence of *christianos* in Josephus (*Ant.* 18.3.3 §64) is almost surely an interpolation.

All of this is to say that there is nothing indigenous about the term "Christian" at the end of the first century or in the social setting of John's

Apocalypse.[21] As a result of this lack of any self-categorization as Christian, it is up to the interpreter to apply or refrain from applying the term to the Apocalypse, to justify that action methodologically, and to follow it through with rigor. In this endeavor, approach is nearly everything. When the Apocalypse is approached from within a Christian framework—or from a framework that takes as given later Christianity's strategies of self-definition and textual ownership—John's revelation may well appear to be Christian. That is to say, it may share theologoumena that Christians see as self-definitional. This harvesting of theologoumena from a text is a thoroughly religious strategy of classification, and the identification of Jesus as Christ in Rev 1:1 is only the beginning. The same basic procedure allowed Justin Martyr to claim that Socrates and Heraclitus were Christians (*1 Apol.* 46), and Eusebius to claim the same regarding Abraham and Adam (*Hist. eccl.* 1.4.6). As these examples show, however, insider categorization is not necessarily compatible with historical-critical and polythetic taxonomy.

Schemes of classification that rely on a single differentiating characteristic—that is, monothetic schemes—are insufficient to create a taxonomy of religion because, as a phenomenon, religion is composed of so many relevant elements (see Smith 1982, 1–18). Religion is a polyadic[22] phenomenon and demands a polythetic scheme of classification. Jonathan Z. Smith's illustration makes this clearer: even though circumcision was in many cases treated by Jews as the hallmark of Judaism, it is not sufficient to the task of distinguishing Jews from non-Jews in the ancient world. Beyond the obvious, though often overlooked, problem of distinguishing Jewish from Gentile women that such a strategy entails, it is also well-known that circumcision was practiced by non-Jews in the ancient world and that it was possible to recognize uncircumcised men as Jews (Smith 1988, 12, citing 1 Macc 1:15; 2:46-47 and *Jub.* 15:33-34).

What then would an appropriate, polythetic scheme of classification look like? I have elsewhere (Marshall 2001, 51) suggested that

> [t]he presence or absence of a single figure, belief, text, or practice cannot be regarded as a decisive criterion for identifying a religious group. Rather, what is at issue is whether a constellation of religious practices shares a significant cluster of traits that distinguish them from other religions.[23]

In the case of the Apocalypse of John, the result of such a strategy of classification is, on one hand, the retreat of beliefs and theologoumena from a dominant position in the classificatory endeavor and, on the other, a broader consideration of potential differentiating factors, for example, ethnic mappings, calendrical practices, food practices, circumcision, mythological/narrative heritage, social boundaries and solidarities, and ritual practices. Obviously information about all of these elements of religion is not available in direct and detailed form for the author and audience of the Apocalypse; but there is no indication in what is available that any of these represent differentiators from Judaism.

Reading Revelation as Jewish

Calendrical and Ritual Practice

The calendrical and ritual practices of John's community are not directly available from the Book of Revelation but are often inferred from the narrative contained in it. While Adela Yarbro Collins (1984b, 1278) has suggested that John's religiosity "probably involved the rejection of traditional observance of the Sabbath," the prominence of the number seven, the pattern of rest after six events, and so forth, show how John's understanding of the structure of the cosmos grew from his Jewish calendrical sense.

Arguments that John draws his depiction of heavenly worship from Judaism's temple cult and from forms of worship current in synagogues, on the other hand, are widely made. John promises that those who heed his message will dwell in the temple of God (Rev 2:11; 7:15). At the culmination of the first cycle of destruction of the great city, God's servants are rewarded in 11:19 with a vision of the heavenly temple and the ark of the covenant (no "new covenant" is in view). Similarly, the second cycle of Rome's destruction is announced from and proceeds out of the heavenly temple (Rev 15:5-8). The vision of God's victory culminates in an extension of the temple to the whole renewed Jerusalem, where God dwells with his people (Himmelfarb 1997, 89–104). Obviously temple cult was not what John's community practiced in western Asia Minor, but they idealized the temple as the center of their historical/cosmo-logical mythology.

John's Apocalypse does not offer halakic discussions of topics such as the particulars of dietary practice, the necessity of circumcision, or the broader observation of Torah that was important to the self-defini-tion of Second Temple Judaism. The tendency of interpreters has been either to avoid such social questions or to fill in the blanks with an im-age drawn from their picture of normative Christianity. R. H. Charles (1913, 35) zeroes in on the term *nomos* and writes that "the Apocalypse exhibits a decidedly anti-legalistic character. The Law is not once men-tioned in the New Testament Apocalypse." Although Charles is correct about the occurrence of the term, his extrapolation to an "anti-legalistic character" is nothing short of blindered. Twice John makes it absolutely clear that the people he envisions as ideal "keep the commandments of God" (Rev 12:17 and 14:12). Very rarely have commentators had anything substantial to say on these declarations, preferring instead to concentrate exegetical labor on ideas such as the faith or witness of Christ. This focus on items of theological interest occludes the valuable witness to the practice of John's religion. John's text offers no reason to suggest that keeping the commandments meant anything of a differ-ent order from what the phrase would have meant for other first-cen-tury Jews. Attempts like David Aune's (1996, 280–81; 1997, 2:709–13) to suggest that John refers only to moral rather than ritual command-ments is without foundation (see E. P. Sanders 1977, 112; 1994 [1992], 194–95). John's concern with purity, seen most clearly in the declara-tion of Rev 21:27 that "nothing unclean shall enter" the holy city,[24] tes-tifies to his investment in the practice of Judaism. The repeated motif of the washed and ritually pure robes of the saints also picks up this concern (Rev 7:4; 15:6; 19:8, 14; 22:14). On the other hand, Babylon is the haunt of the unclean spirits (Rev 18:2). John's clear and repeated declaration that his idealized community keeps the commandments of God, especially seen in relation to his repeated valuing of purity in his community and his attribution of impurity to his antagonists, suggests that there is no reason to imagine John's religiously motivated practice as different from Judaism.[25]

Mythological Heritage

There has never been doubt about the extent of John's debt to the Hebrew Bible. The specific contours of John's interaction with the literature of Second Temple Judaism that did not become canonical is less clear. Since John's practice is to inhabit a mythological world as a prophet rather than to refer to writings through citation formulae, discerning allusions to other texts is a matter of judgment and argument. Charles (1920), Aune (1997), Fekkes (1994) and Ruiz (1989) all make strong cases for the richness of John's involvement with the literature of Second Temple Judaism, of which the Hebrew Bible must be considered a portion. While there are important interactions with Greco-Roman and ancient Near Eastern mythological themes (Boll 1914, 151; Chevalier 1997; Malina 1995; Marshall 2005; A. Y. Collins 1981, 377–403; 1984b, 1221–87), such interaction is part of being Jewish in the Greco-Roman world rather than contrary to it. John's imaginative world is clearly Jewish in both the textual and mythological narrative resources he uses to portray it and in the particular future he imagines in a renewed Jerusalem, where temple is all in all.

Ethnic and Political Identity

The ethnic mapping that informs John's Apocalypse is clearly the unity of Jews vs. the multiplicity of Gentiles. The contrast is clearest in the visions of the 144,000 drawn from the twelve tribes of Israel set in contrast to the "great multitude which no man could number, from every nation, from all tribes and peoples and tongues" (Rev 7:1-10). This binary mapping is repeated in Rev 14:1-6 and the multiplicity of Gentiles is a recurring trope (Rev 10:11; 11:9; 17:15). The problem posed by the ethnic map implied in Rev 7:1-10 and 14:1-6 was a key factor in driving the source critics of the nineteenth century through their rococo proposals. Their insight was salutory; their solutions less so.

In Revelation 2–3, John slanders a group as "those who say they are Jews but are not, but are a synagogue of Satan" (Rev 2:9). While he mentions only slander by such a group in Rev 2:9 and in the message to the assembly at Philadelphia (Rev 3:7-13), and makes promises of their submission to the protagonist community, John does not specify the precise conflict in a way that clarifies the historical situation. It is necessary, however, to understand what John does and does not say. He *does* treat the term "Jew" as one that belongs to him. He does *not* portray the dividing line between the group he favors and the group he opposes as the line between Jews and Christians. Most importantly—and contrary to the best efforts of biblical commentators—he does not make beliefs concerning the divinity or the messianic status of Jesus the issue that divides him from his opponents; no argument over christology is in view. What we learn from John's slander of these two groups is that he is completely invested in the traditional Jewish abstention from idol worship and that he considers "Jew" a designation that belongs to him and his community. The line that he draws in 2:9 is not a line between Jews and Christians, and, according to John, the people he slanders are not Jews.[26]

John, in other words, is committed to Judaism through and through. He makes no clear criticism of Judaism or of other Jews as such. His rhetorical work is directed to helping his Jewish community live in relation to the Greco-Roman world, but unsullied by it. He gives no indication of self-consciously intending to represent a sect of Judaism rather than the whole.[27] Unlike Paul, who positions himself as a Jew living outside Judaism for the sake of Gentiles (Gaston 1987; Gager 2000), John's primary axis of solidarity is with Judaism. His program addresses the means by which Jews in the Diaspora ought to remain faithful during the trying circumstance of the Judean war—by separating themselves from the nations and the work of the nations, which implies subordination to the satanic power of Rome. At the same time, John stands within Judaism in imagining a massive influx of Gentiles.[28] Unlike the Gospels of Matthew, Mark, and John, the Apocalypse has no anxiety over its position within Judaism or obvious animus against other groups of Jews. It is not striving to claim its place in Judaism against other sects or social institutions. Unlike the Gospel of Luke and Acts, John's Apocalypse does not stand outside Judaism, naming Christianity as a distinct entity and picturing it as laying claim to the legitimacy and antiquity of Judaism while at the same time superseding it. While John's Judaism is certainly atypical in its focus on Jesus as the Lamb of God who will initiate the eschaton, vindicate God's people, and draw in an innumerable number of Gentiles, his rhetorical position does not limit him to solidarity only with those who share the peculiarities of his theology.

Chapter 11 of Revelation provides an instructive example of these solidarities. The first two verses describe the combination of peril and protection that John envisions for "the holy city." By "the holy city" John consistently indicates Jerusalem—in this case on earth, but also through what he envisions as its heavenly counterpart. Revelation 11:3-13 narrates the destruction visited on "the great city," by which John consistently refers to Rome/Babylon. The great city that John describes elsewhere as having "dominion over the kings of the earth" is in Rev 11:8 portrayed as the city "allegorically called Sodom and Egypt, where their Lord was crucified." This allusion to the crucifixion almost always leads interpreters to understand Jerusalem rather than Rome; but coupled with the "allegorical" (or more literally "spiritual") sense in which Rev 11:8 identifies the city as Sodom and Egypt, the reference to the crucifixion does not yield to any literal interpretation. No city literally is Sodom and Egypt. Understanding the great city of Rev 11:8 in a manner consistent with all of John's other very clear identifications of the great city as Babylon and Rome leads to a different, if uncommon, conclusion: Rev 11:8 describes Rome as the spiritual (not literal) locus of the crucifixion. Far from calling for the destruction of the earthly center of Judaism, Jerusalem, John's Apocalypse stands alone among the extant writings of those devoted to Jesus in the first century in his stark blaming of Rome for the crucifixion.

In the midst of the Judean war, John wrote in Asia Minor with one eye on the turmoil of Rome—a year of four emperors, civil war, and a crisis so great and so potentially fatal that a Roman historian described it as looking like the empire's end (Tacitus *Hist.* 1.11)—and another on Judaism's stalled revolt in Judea, where the countryside had been ravaged and Jerusalem was surrounded by the most powerful army in the world. John wrote in solidarity with Jerusalem and in conflict with Rome. He argued strenuously that his community ought to keep itself pure from the idolatry of Rome, and hope in the eventual and decisive replacement of Rome's empire with God's empire, and in Rome's punitive and utter destruction. To the extent that he wrote with the sectarian impulse (Duff 2000, xiii, 189; Frankfurter 2001, 403–25) seen in the conflict with the figures he describes variously as the Nicolaitans, Balaam, and Jezebel, John wrote in order to ensure the purity of Judaism as he understood it. The line that separates his community from those he opposes in no way corresponds to a division between Christians and Jews. John's solidarities and social boundaries are those of a Diaspora Jew facing the problem of the Judean war.

Summary

Focusing on questions beyond insider theological issues—for example, Does John see Jesus as the Christ?—treats the Apocalypse as data in the study of religion rather than in the practice of theology. Moreover, attending to the social, ritual, practical, and ethical dimensions of religion in addition to the mythological makes it possible to understand historically several textual complexes in the Book of Revelation that have often been enigmatic for interpreters. In reading the vignettes of 144,000 drawn from the tribes of Judaism or standing on Mount Zion (Rev 7:1-10 and 14:1-6), interpreters have striven in vain to make John's two-part taxonomy into a three-part one that includes Christians. In reading John's conflict with "those who say they are Jews but are not" (Rev 2:9; 3:9), commentators have consistently reversed John's description and made the objects of his anger into Jews. Allusions to those differentiae that are crucial to a disciplined taxonomy of religion—namely, what people actually practice and believe they should practice—have been nearly ignored in favor of discussions of Christian theological topics (i.e., the witness of Jesus and faith of Jesus in Rev 12:17 and 14:12 rather than the practical commandments of God). And one of the most fundamental structures of the work—the conflict of the great city and those loyal to it with the holy city and those loyal to it—has been violated in traditional readings of Revelation 11. One of the key benefits of understanding the Apocalypse as Jewish is that it avoids these sorts of problems, problems that are largely created by the category Christianity. When the Apocalypse of John is read as a Jewish document, the Jews can be Jews, keeping the commandments means keeping the commandments, those drawn from Israel are from Israel, and the holy city Jerusalem remains distinct from the great city Rome (Marshall 2001, 3).

Conclusion

Adela Yarbro Collins (1984b, 1278) has portrayed John as "alienated from the Judaism of his time to a significant degree," and described a general "conflict with Jews" as a fundamental element of the rhetorical program of the Apocalypse (1984a, 84). As can be seen from the discussions of the exigence of the Apocalypse by Hemer (1986, 10) and Schüssler Fiorenza (1991, 54, cf. 123), the category "Jewish Christian" facilitates this misunderstanding. Overwhelmingly, the category serves to distance the value of Revelation from anything that the analyst does not want to adopt from Judaism. Without denying the potential value of "Jewish Christianity"as an analytical apparatus in general, it does much more harm than good in the case of the Apocalypse. John's deep investment in Judaism—understood narratively, ritually, socially, theologically, culturally, and historically—needs to be understood through the category that makes sense of it: the book is Jewish.

Suggested Reading

Aune, David E. 1997–1998. *Revelation*. 2 vols. Word Biblical Commentary 52A–B. Dallas: Word Books.

Barton, George A. 1898. "The Apocalypse and Recent Criticism." *American Journal of Theology* 2:776–801.

Baur, Ferdinand Christian. 1878 [1863]. *The Church History of the First Three Centuries*. 3rd ed. Translated by Allan Menzies. 2 vols. London: Williams and Norgate. Translation of *Kirchengeschichte der drei ersten Jahrhunderte*. Tübingen: L. F. Fues, 1863.

Charles, R. H. 1920. *A Critical and Exegetical Commentary on The Revelation of St. John*. International Critical Commentary 44. New York: Scribner.

Collins, Adela Yarbro. 1984a. *Crisis and Catharsis: The Power of the Apocalypse*. Philadelphia: Westminster.

Engels, Friedrich. 1957a. "The Book of Revelation." Pages 183–89 in *Marx and Engels on Religion*. Moscow: Progress.

————.1957b. "Bruno Bauer and Early Christianity." Pages 173–82 in *Marx and Engels on Religion*. Moscow: Progress.

Frankfurter, David. 2001. "Jews or Not? Reconstructing the 'Other' in Rev 2:9 and 3:9." *Harvard Theological Review* 94:403–25.

Gager, John G. 1975. *Kingdom and Community: Ths Social World of Early Christianity*. Prentice-Hall Studies in Religion. Englewood Cliffs, N.J.: Prentice-Hall.

Kelley, Sean. 2002. *Racializing Jesus: Race, Ideology, and the Formation of Modern Biblical Scholarship*. London and New York: Routledge.

Marshall, John W. 2001. *Parables of War: Reading John's Jewish Apocalypse*. Waterloo, Ont.: Wilfrid Laurier University Press.

Witherington, Ben. 2003. *Revelation*. New York: Cambridge University Press.

10. The Holy Vine of David Made Known to the Gentiles through God's Servant Jesus: "Christian Judaism" in the *Didache*

Jonathan A. Draper

It is ironic that one of the most Jewish of early Christian writings is actually addressed to the Gentiles, both formally and in content (Tomson 2005, 133). The longer title of the *Didache* designates it as "The Teaching of the Lord through the Twelve Apostles to the Gentiles." Whether this is original, as I would argue (Draper 2000a, 121–22), or not (Niederwimmer 1998, 56–57), it clearly captures the orientation of the work. It provides teaching and instructions designed to prepare Gentiles for admission to baptism and the eucharistic meal of a community of Christian Jews. In presenting this catechesis, the text provides a rare glimpse of the community life and worship in an early Christian community striving to be faithful to the Torah. It is thus hardly surprising that its closest literary connections inside the Christian canon are to Matthew's Gospel. It seems to have emerged either from the same community at a different stage in its development or from a community that shared a common tradition. Whereas Matthew is more strident in his condemnation of the Pharisees, he does not contest their control of society. He advocates that Christians should be "invisible" within the Jewish community as a whole, fasting, praying, and giving alms in secret to avoid the very real possibility of being hauled off before the Roman-sponsored authorities ("governors and kings" in Matt 10:17-23) by those who now control public assemblies and the "public square" (6:2-5) and "sit on the seat of Moses" (23:1-2) (Draper 2005a, 217–41). The *Didache*, on the other hand, still contests the right of the "hypocrites" to control society, advocating public practice of a separate calendar for fasting and different words for the thrice-daily public prayers (8:1-3). Nevertheless, in contrast to Matthew, the invective against the Pharisees is relatively restrained.

Of course, the evidence could be read in two ways. Huub van de Sandt and David Flusser (2002), for instance, argue that this is a community that has already "crossed the great divide" and turned its back on Judaism for good. I would argue that it indicates instead a community that seeks to maintain its position within the bounds of the broad and diverse Jewish Diaspora, while at the same time resisting the growing domination of the Pharisaic party. The positions adopted on issues of Torah by this community sometimes seem strange when read exclusively against the later consensus of rabbinic Judaism, but they can all be shown to relate to first-century debates within and between parties in Israel (Alon 1996; Flusser 1996; van de Sandt and Flusser 2002; Tomson 2005). For this reason, the use of the words "Judaism," "Jew," and "Jewish" in their modern sense is misleading and has its roots in an anachronistic assumption that the victorious party— the Pharisaic-rabbinic party—had a monopoly on the definition of what it meant to belong to Israel in the first century CE. It seems, in any case, that the word "Jew" was used largely by non-Israelites to describe them, characterizing them in terms of the largest and most well known Israelite region, "Judea" (much as some English speakers call people from the Netherlands "Hollanders"), whereas they themselves used the term "Israelite" in discussion among themselves (see Tomson 1986, 126, 266–89; 2000, 301–40; Draper 2000b, 347–59). Even among the rabbis, the real discussion relates to whether or not a person or a group belongs to "all Israel" (*m. Sanh.* 10), rather than whether they remain "Jewish" (see Draper 1991b).

However, use of the traditional terminology "Jew," "Jewish," and "Judaism" is to some extent unavoidable and will be used in this discussion for convenience. When the *Didache* is placed against the background of this terminology, I would describe it as "Christian Judaism." "Judaism" because its community considered itself a faithful group within "all Israel" and indeed stood in a tradition of Torah interpretation close to the Pharisaic-rabbinic party. At every point where a comparison is possible, for instance, the teaching of the *Didache* is closer to Pharisaic-rabbinic teaching than it is to the teaching of the Dead Sea Scrolls, except where the teaching is shared by all parties in Israel (Draper 1983). "Christian" because its community believed that Jesus was the Davidic messiah inaugurating the coming of God's eschatological kingdom, which could be "made known" to Gentiles as well as to Israelites, and which defined itself with regard to Jesus as "Christian" (12:4). "Jewish Christian" implies that there is an entity called "Christianity" in existence, separate from Israel, that provides the primary reference point of identity, and that ethnic Jews might belong to it like other ethnic groups while trying to maintain their cultural identity. The reality in the *Didache* community is the reverse: its primary reference point is Israel and the Torah, as these are affirmed and fulfilled in Jesus, and Gentiles may belong to this community only if they are prepared to respect the cultural world of Israel.

DATE AND PLACE OF COMPOSITION

The *Didache* appears to have incorporated a number of earlier traditions, written or oral. It can be broken down into four large sections: the Two Ways (1–6), the Liturgical Section (7–10), Various Rules relating to Communal Life (11–15) and the Apocalypse (16). This apparent symmetry, however, breaks up on closer examination, and there are underlying strands that indicate a coherent originary stratum. For instance, the section on the Two Ways presents material for catechesis prior to baptism (Draper 1997). The Eucharist appears to be for a baptismal celebration (Draper 2000a). The rules on visiting apostles and other visitors may relate to the collection and disposition of firstfruits (Draper 2005b). The Two Ways schema probably originally concluded with an Apocalypse (Bammel 1996). In other words, whatever its origin and later redaction, the material has a coherent ordering and logic, which can and should be explored in detail for its own sake (Milavec 2003). It is not simply an arbitrary collection of tradition.

However, the composite nature of the text means that some of the material may be considerably older than the final redaction of the text. For this reason it is difficult to give a date for the work as a whole. It appears to reflect a relatively undeveloped christology, to know apostles and prophets actively at work alongside bishops and deacons, to celebrate the Eucharist as part of a full meal without invoking the words of institution taken from the Last Supper. It appears to make independent use of material known to us from the written Gospels, though this is a matter of debate (see the collection of essays in van de Sandt 2005). These characteristics have led some scholars today to date the text as early as 50–70 CE (Jean-Paul Audet, Aaron Milavec, Michelle Slee), others as late as 100–110 (Rordorf and Tuilier 1998; Niederwimmer 1998). My own suggestion (Draper 1995; cf. R. A. Kraft 1965; Giet 1966) is that the text is "evolved literature," which was in continuous use as a community rule, and hence was continuously edited before being subordinated to Matthew's Gospel ("engage in all your activities as you have learned in the gospel of our Lord" [15:4]) and taken up finally into an even bigger community rule (in book 7 of the *Apostolic Constitutions*). Nevertheless, it does not reveal a literary dependence on Matthew's Gospel and should not be dated later than 100 CE.

The place of origin is as uncertain as the date of composition and for the same reasons—that the only evidence is internal to the text itself. Its close links with Matthew's Gospel seem to require that it originated from the same region and milieu. Many also see the description of wandering apostles and prophets as pointing to Syria. The discussion of the "yoke of the Lord" and food laws in 6:2-3 seems to indicate that it emerged at a time of conflict over the extent of obedience to the Torah required of the Gentile converts to the community, and its solution seems to relate in some way to the situation depicted in Acts 15. For these reasons Antioch seems a not inappropriate suggestion for the context of a community struggling to remain faithful to the Torah while opening itself to Gentile converts (Draper 2003; Slee 2003).

The Yoke of the Lord
and the Admisson of the Gentiles

In many ways, the instructions in *Did.* 6:1-3 represent a crux for the interpretation of the text as representative of Christian Judaism (Draper 2003):

> Take care that no one lead you astray from the path of this teaching, since that one teaches you apart from God. For if you can bear the entire yoke of the Lord, you will be perfect; but if you cannot, do as much as you can. And concerning food, bear what you can. But especially keep from food sacrificed to idols; for this is a ministry to dead gods.[1]

Many scholars (e.g., Niederwimmer 1998, 35–41; Rordorf and Tuilier 1998) have seen 6:1 as the original conclusion to the Jewish Two Ways, and 6:2-3 as provided by the Christian editor in order to join the Two Ways to the liturgical section. The question of "perfection" then relates to the "paradoxical demands" of the teaching of Jesus found in 1:3b-6 and in the Sermon on the Mount/Plain in the Synoptic tradition (Rordorf and Tuilier 1998, 32–33, though they believe that the section was originally [non-Christian] "Jewish"). Yet this depends first of all on the very modern and erroneous feeling that the teaching of Jesus is "paradoxical," cannot be fulfilled, and hence creates a crisis for the conscience (which can be resolved only by an acceptance of the good news that salvation is through grace alone appropriated by faith; see Stendahl 1986). Second, it depends on the interpretation of "perfection" as an ethical category rather than a code word for living according to the Torah. In the *Manual of Discipline*, for instance, walking in the Way of Light is the same as "walking perfectly" (*halak betamim* [1QS 1:8; 8:20; 9:6, 8, 19; cf. 1QSb 1:2; CD 1:21; 7:5]). In my opinion, the idea of an instruction that says to new Gentile convert, "The teaching of Jesus we have presented to you is an intolerable burden, so you only have to keep as much of it as you can," would be absurd. On the other hand, a requirement to become a full, Torah-observant proselyte would indeed present the Gentile converts with a major obstacle to joining the community. Certainly, the phraseology relates to the saying of Jesus found in Matt 11:28-30, but not by way of literary dependence, since Matthew's sense is the opposite: "Take my yoke on your shoulders, it's easy to carry!"

Instead, as Stuiber (1961), Flusser (1996) and Deutsch (1987) have shown, "taking on oneself the yoke of the Lord" is a technical term for obedient observance of the Torah in both the *Didache* and Matthew. So R. Nehunya b. Ha-Kanah (Tannaite of the first or second generation) states, "He that takes upon himself the yoke of the law, from him shall be taken the yoke of the kingdom and the yoke of worldly care" (*m. 'Abot* 3:5; cf. 6:2; *b. B. Metsi'a* 85b; *t. Sotah* 14:4; *2 Bar.* 41:3). The problem dealt with in the *Didache* relates to its nature as catechesis for Gentiles joining a Christian Jewish community. Can Gentiles become members of the eschatological community? If so, does membership require that Gentiles become circumcised and take upon themselves the full requirements of the Torah? If not, how can they share worship and table fellowship? We know from Paul and from Acts that this was the burning issue for the first generation of those who saw Jesus as the Messiah of Israel.

Even *Did.* 6:1 indicates the existence of controversy between the community and those who "would lead you astray." The connection "for" seems to supply the substance of what is at issue. The Two Ways section is understood as instruction in the ethical aspects of the Torah, and the division in the Christian community relates to the Gentiles and the Torah. The *Didache* accepts the admission of Gentiles to the community without requiring that they be circumcised and become full proselytes. It does require, however, that they keep the halakot set out in the Two Ways (the "universal laws"), and that they abstain "*strictly*" from food offered to idols, as the absolute minimum for fellowship. In addition, they should strive to keep as much of the Torah and the food laws (*kashrut*) as they are able to, while "being perfect" is postponed to the eschatological time of the Lord's coming on the clouds (16:2). This solution to the problem of the admission of the Gentiles is close to what is accepted at the Council of Jerusalem described in Acts 15—the "universal laws" and the prohibition of food offered to idols (15:20, 29)—even though Luke is an apologist for Paul and sees the "yoke" of Torah as a burden that "neither our fathers nor we have been able to bear" (15:10). The opponents of the community, such as Paul, argue that Gentiles must under no circumstances keep the Torah, because it has been set aside by the eschatological new covenant, which has already been inaugurated by the Messiah. Hence, the Torah is a "yoke of slavery" (Gal 5:1) or the "yoke of necessity," which has been set aside by the "new yoke of our Lord Jesus Christ" (*Barn.* 2:6; cf. Justin, *Dial.* 53:1; *Didascalia* 52.17–35). Paul also regards the prohibition of food offered to idols as merely a temporary concession to the "weak," which does not have to be observed in the marketplace or the home, except for tactical reasons when the Christian is informed that it has been offered to idols (1 Cor 10:25-30).

The short instructions in *Did.* 6:1-3 seem to me to provide the clue to the nature of the quarrel between the Christian Jewish communities and the Pauline communities. The former see the agreement of the Council of Jerusalem (whether it happened as Luke describes it or not) as requiring Gentiles only to take a first step of minimum observance, while encouraging the progressive adoption of the Torah, which could—and perhaps should—ideally result eventually in circumcision and full membership in Israel. The latter see the agreement as a maximum observance necessary to placate the conscience of the "weak" and facilitate table fellowship, which should not under any circumstances lead to circumcision and Torah observance. This echoes a long-standing debate in Israelite tradition about whether it was possible and/or desirable for a Gentile to become a Jew, that is, whether God's blessing came only through Israel or whether a righteous Gentile may inherit God's blessing as a Gentile.

The Two Ways

The Jewish character of the Two Ways instruction, with which the *Didache* begins, was quickly noted after the discovery of the text in 1883. For instance, Charles Taylor (1886) produced a commentary based on parallels with the Talmud and argued that this Two Ways section was based on a Jewish source. Alfred Seeberg (1903; 1906) and Günter Klein (1909) argued that this underlying Jewish source represented Jewish propaganda or catechesis aimed at Gentile Godfearers attached to the synagogues of the Diaspora, which had been taken up and used by the early Jewish Christian church for baptismal catechesis. What gives this plausibility is that the material is clearly intended for such use in the *Didache*, which begins the instructions concerning baptism with the words, "Having said all these things in advance, baptize . . ." (7:1). In addition, a version of the Two Ways found in the *Didache*, without the material taken from the Jesus tradition in 1:3b-6, circulated independently in a Latin translation as *Doctrina apostolorum*.

However, the Christian Jewish nature of the text was challenged by a number of scholars who saw the text as a late (and possibly Montanist) fictional composition based on literary sources inside and outside of the New Testament (Robinson 1920; Muilenburg 1929; Connolly 1932). They pointed to the existence of a Two Ways teaching in the *Epistle of Barnabas* 18–29 that was remarkably close to that found in the *Didache* also and argued for this letter as the source of the material, which was widespread in early Christian tradition. This would mean that the *Didache* would have little value as evidence for Christian Judaism or for Christian origins in general. The discovery of the Dead Sea Scrolls, however, proved that the instructions on the Two Ways has its roots in Second Temple Judaism. The Two Ways material in the *Didache* and other early Christian writings clearly parallel the description found in the *Manual of Discipline* (1QS 3:13–4:26; see Audet 1996) of the Way of Light and the Way of Darkness, presided over by the Spirit of Truth and the Spirit of Falsehood respectively. On the other hand, a close comparison of the text of the Two Ways in the *Didache* with the more dualistic Dead Sea Scrolls corpus shows that the *Didache* material is closer in its ethos to the ethical form of the tradition found in the rabbinic *Derekh Eretz* (and the *Testament of the Twelve Patriarchs*), especially *Did.* 3:1-6 (Draper 1983, 65–76; van de Sandt 1992). This is not because the ethical form is later, as supposed by M. J. Suggs (1972, 60–74), but because it reflects the "covenantal" language of the Deuteronomic tradition prior to the kind of influence of Iranian dualism found in the Scrolls (and analyzed by Erhard Kamlah [1964]). Both forms existed side by side in Jewish and Christian texts of the Second Temple period, as Rordorf correctly notes (1996). The recent extensive study by Huub van de Sandt and the late David Flusser (2002) has argued for a Hasidic substratum that was edited by both Qumran sectarians and early Christians, though I would argue that the mediation of the tradition may be through oral rather than literary relations (see Horsley and Draper 1999; Kelber 2004). In any case, the Two Ways material clearly has a catechetical function in the *Manual of Discipline*, related to the initiation of new members of the community. The basic Two Ways framework is edited to reflect the particular values and beliefs of the Essenes. It seems likely that the origin of the *Derekh Eretz* also lies in catechesis. Thus, the emergence of this material in an early Christian Jewish catechesis for Gentiles, designed to introduce new members to the basic ethical and legal worldview of the community, is understandable. The earliest Christian Jewish communities followed a well-beaten track used by various Jewish groups to initiate new members, but gave it a particular stamp aimed at Gentiles (Draper 2003, 106–23).

The "first instruction" of the Way of Life includes the double command to love God and one's neighbor as oneself, which is presented in the Synoptic tradition as the command of Jesus summarizing the Torah (Matt 19:19; 22:39; Mark 12:31; Luke 10:25-28). The *Didache* offers a different and shorter version, independent of the Gospel tradition, and seems to confirm that this was understood as a summary of the law in Jewish tradition prior to Jesus' use of it (as Luke's account also suggests). The *Didache* contains the words not found in the Synoptics, "You shall love the God *who made you*," which relates to the understanding that the Two Ways are constituted by God at the creation of the world (cf. 1QS 3:17-19: "He has created man to govern the world, and has appointed for him two spirits in which to walk until the time of His visitation: the spirits of truth and falsehood"). Certainly the command to love one's neighbor as oneself, derived from Lev 19:18, is widely used in the rabbinic tradition as a summary of the law (K. Berger 1972; Nissen 1974). Moreover, like *Targum Jonathan* to Lev 19:18, the Two Ways teaching couples the command to love one's neighbor with the negative form of the golden rule (Matt 7:12 uses the positive form), which is also seen as a summary of the Torah (Dihle 1962). It is significant that Rabbi Hillel is also reported as giving a Gentile the golden rule as a summary of the Torah (which could be recited while standing on one leg!) at the beginning of catechesis ("Go and learn"; *b. Shab.* 31a). In other words, the Christian Judaism reflected in the *Didache* again draws on common Jewish tradition to formulate its response to the new circumstances of the community, faced by the desire of Gentiles to join.

If the Jesus tradition found in 1:3b–2:1 is seen as a later addition to the Two Ways source, then the summary of the Torah in the double love command and the golden rule is followed by lists of vices based largely on an expansion of the second half of the Decalogue. Gedaliah Alon (1996, 166), for instance, argues that this material is "based, in the main, on *Torat hamidot*, which devolved from Scripture and which permeates the Tannaitic *Mishna*." The Two Ways set out the fundamental laws of human behavior, which, according to Jewish understanding, applied to Gentiles as much as to Jews. These fundamental laws are often derived from God's command to Adam (e.g., *b. Sanh.* 56b) or to Noah (e.g., *Jub.* 7:20; *Gen. Rab.* 34:8; *b. Sanh.* 59b) prior to his covenant with Abraham (Draper 1983, 68–72; van de Sandt and Flusser 2002, 162–72). The early sources vary in the number of such laws, but the earliest list seems to consist of five prohibitions: against bloodshed, sexual impurity, idolatry, blasphemy, and robbery (the order in the *Didache* is influenced by the Decalogue, but see *Sifra Lev.* 18:4; *b. Yoma* 67b, cited by van de Sandt and Flusser 2002, 166). Among these halakic instructions of the Two Ways, Alon (1996, 172–78) finds parallels in rabbinic halakah on abortion (*Did.* 2:2; e.g., *b. Sanh.* 57b), on magic (*Did.* 3:4; e.g., *m. Sanh.* 10:1), on slavery (*Did.* 3:1, e.g., *b. Yebam.* 47b; *Mekilta of Rabbi Ishmael* 7). Louis Finkelstein (1930) has argued plausibly that these laws developed during the Maccabean period, when the temple state had jurisdiction over large numbers of Gentiles. However, they may also reflect the need of Jews living in the Diaspora for ground rules to govern their relations with their neighbors. In the *Didache* the ethical rules of the second half of the Ten Commandments are directed toward Gentile practices often attacked by Jewish writers (e.g., Philo of Alexandria), such as contraception, abortion, abandoning babies, sexual immorality, pederasty, homosexuality, magic, potions, divination, incantations, astrology, and, above all, idolatry. All of these things are characteristics of the Way of Death. To this material drawn from the Decalogue, the *Didache* subsequently added material associated with the teaching of Jesus and makes it the "first interpretation" of the double love command (1:3a), while the earlier material is retained as the "second interpretation" (2:1).

Didache 3:1-6 presents a tightly constructed fivefold block of material in 3:1-6, which may have come from an independent source, since it is not found in other Christian sources for the Two Ways. It finds close parallels in *Derekh Eretz Zuta*. The block is introduced with the instruction, "My child flee from all evil and everything like it" (3:1; cf. *Derekh Eretz Zuta* 2:7; *Avot de Rabbi Nathan* 2:2). Each prohibition then follows the formula with minor variations: "My child do not do/ be . . . or . . . or . . . . For from all these are born acts of . . . ." This kind of teaching is often characterized as "setting a fence around the Torah," the avoidance of minor transgressions or even innocent behavior that may lead on to breaches of major commandments (van de Sandt and Flusser 2002, 165–79). It is this kind of affirmation of the Torah, ensuring the fulfillment of the major precepts by avoiding minor infringements, that also lies behind the "greater righteousness" of the Antitheses of Matt 5:17-48, rather than a rejection of the Torah in favor of the gospel (Draper 1999; van de Sandt and Flusser 2002, 193-237).

HALAKOT ON FASTING AND PRAYER

The material in *Didache* 8, concerning fasting and prayer, is loosely linked to its context by the instructions on baptismal fasting. In addition, the inclusion of the Lord's Prayer links this section with the baptismal section, since the Lord's Prayer forms part of the *missa fidelium* (including the Eucharist), which was early distinguished from the *missa catechumenorum* (including the readings from scripture and the sermon) in the liturgical practice of the church (e.g., by Origen; see Srawley 1949, 42–43). Since the unbaptized were excluded from the *missa fidelium*, this would imply that the recitation of the Lord's Prayer was reserved for the baptized (see Manson 1955-56; Jeremias 1967). However, it is clearly an addition to the underlying schema of the text, occasioned by new exigencies in the community, since it does not begin with the formula *peri de* (6:3; 7:1; 9:1, 3; see Draper 1996, 223–43), and refers to "the gospel," a designation that is found elsewhere only in the latest stratum of the *Didache* (11:3; 15:3, 4; see also Garrow 2004, 129–41). It seems that, whereas the Two Ways material is largely directed toward differentiating the new converts from the Gentile culture from which they come, this material seeks to differentiate the converts from a rival faction within Judaism, namely, the "hypocrites." Nevertheless, the addition must have been made at an early date, since it still seems to predate the Gospel of Matthew. The term "hypocrites" is not "a general reference to (pious) Jews" (as argued by van de Sandt and Flusser 2002, 292; cf. Harnack 1884, 4-25; Audet 1958, 367–68; Niederwimmer 1998, 132), any more than it is in Matthew's Gospel, where the term occurs thirteen times and is explicitly linked with the "scribes and Pharisees" (23:13). This is a dispute within "Judaism," between different parties contending for control of the public space.

Peter Tomson (2005, 137–41) has rightly pointed to the halakic nature of the instructions, which dovetail with what we know of the disputes within "all Israel" in the first century CE. Mondays and Thursdays were the days maintained by the Pharisaic party as the days for fasting because these were market days when people gathered together in the towns and villages, "on which also the Torah was read out and court sessions held, occasions which facilitated the prayer gatherings connected with fasting" (2005, 135–36). This calendar was, however, opposed by the Sadducees and the Essenes, who argued on the basis of a 364-day solar calendar for the limitation of religious festivals, and hence special fasting and prayer days, to Sunday, Wednesday, and Friday to avoid prejudicing the sanctity of the Sabbath (Jaubert 1957; cf. van de Sandt and Flusser 2002, 293; Tomson 2005, 136–37). It seems likely, then, that the choice of days reflects not so much a special "Christian" emphasis as a resistance to the Pharisaic assumption of power over the broader Jewish community that matches the opposition of other Jewish parties contending for control. In any case, it serves to mark the community of the *Didache* off from the Pharisees but to locate the community specifically *within* the broader social context of "Judaism" (Draper 1996, 233–35).

In the same way, the instruction to pray the Lord's Prayer three times a day reflects a widespread tradition in Israel (Dan 6:11; *m. Ber.* 4:1; see Tomson 2005, 138–39). Rabbinic debate relates to the wording of the threefold prayer, with the party of Rabban Gamaliel seeking to enforce the use of the *Shemoneh 'Esreh* for the thrice daily prayer by everyone, against R. Eliezer, who opposed any fixed prayer for these times, and against R. Akiba and R. Joshua who allowed a shorter summary of these eighteen *berakot* (*m. Ber.* 4:3-4). Here the *Didache* is aligned with other parties in Israel that observe a thrice-daily prayer: the *Didache* presents a short "summary prayer" for use in its community against the long and rigid *Shemoneh 'Esreh* imposed by Rabban Gamaliel but opposed even by members of the Pharisaic party. Tomson suggests that the Lord's Prayer used here may not be particularly unique to Jesus and his followers, but may reflect a more widespread usage (Tomson 2005, 139). Again, even though the use of this prayer reflects and furthers the opposition between the community and the Pharisaic party, it does not show that the *Didache* community has "broken with Judaism," since it is not essentially a Christian innovation (even if it has its origin in the teaching of the historical Jesus, as argued by Luz 1989, 367–89) but a reaction to the growing influence and power of the rabbis found in other Jewish groups also (Draper 1996, 235–38).

RITUAL PURIFICATION OF GENTILE CONVERTS

At first sight, the baptismal instructions in *Didache* 7 are startlingly different from what might be expected. There is no reference to baptism of repentance for the forgiveness of sins, which underpins baptism in Mark and "Q" (Mark 1:4; Q 3:2-4, 7-9). In fact there is no mention of sins at all in the context of baptism. Nor is there reference to baptism into the death and resurrection of Christ as the basis for Christian initiation, which characterizes Paul's teaching (Rom 6:1-11). *Didache* specifies only four things: instruction in the Two Ways prior to baptism (including the rules on the "yoke of the Lord," *kashrut* and *'aboda zarah* in 6:1-3); prebaptismal fasting of the one baptizing and the one being baptized; the recital of the Name of the Trinity or of "the Lord" over the baptized person, and the use of ritually pure "living" or running water. The bulk of the instruction concerns what kinds of water can be used.

Yet this is what could be expected in a Jewish community admitting Gentiles into its fellowship. The concern is fundamentally with ritual purity; it is halakah rather than doctrine that is at issue (see Tomson 2005, 131–35). Hence the grade of water used is of fundamental significance, and the rules mirror those found in the Mishnaic tract *m.Mikwa'ot*: the best water is running water, which should be used when it is available. If none is available, then a large quantity of cold water will do. If there is no cold water, then a sufficient quantity of hot water will do (probably natural heat is referred to here). If there is no water at all, except drawn water, then a minimum of three logs of pure water must be poured over the head so that there is no connection between the source of the water and the impurity (*m. Mik.* 2:2; *t. Mik.* 3:13; *b. Ber.* 22a). The uncleanness of a Gentile that derives from idolatry is very literally understood, and the removal of that uncleanness is also very literally understood. The same reasoning underlies the instructions for one or two days of fasting, since the purpose is to ensure that food eaten in the state of idolatry is purged, with the one baptizing present during this period to ensure that nothing is eaten. Both of these aspects are reflected in the romance of *Joseph and Asenath*, in which the Gentile heroine fasts for seven days so that her mouth becomes "estranged from the table of idols" (xi), and she washes in "living water" at the instruction of an angel (xiv).

Baptism "in the name of the Father, Son, and Holy Spirit," which parallels Matt 28:19, brings the Gentile into the sphere of God's presence, power, and authority. It is likely that this trinitarian reference is a later redaction of the earlier formula of baptism "in the Name of the Lord," which is found in *Did.* 9:5, to bring it into line with the later trinitarian formula. It is possible that the same process underlies the Matthean reference to trinitarian baptism, since Eusebius knows of a text of Matthew without it (Coneybeare 1901; Lohmeyer 1951; Green 1968; Kosmala 1965; Flusser 1966; Vööbus 1968). At least, one must acknowledge that there is no other evidence in the *Didache* for a high christology such as would be required by the trinitarian formula. The reference to the "name of the Lord" is open to debate, if the trinitarian formula is late. Aaron Milavec (2003, 663–66) argues that "Lord" in the *Didache always* refers to "the Lord God" and not to Jesus as "Lord." The Name in the Lord's Prayer (8:2) is the Name of the Father. So also the reference to the indwelling of the Name in the prayers after the eucharistic meal (10:2). Baptism "in the Name of the Lord" is thus likely to have the same reference, particularly if Jesus is seen as bearing the Name of the Lord and mediating it in baptism.

CHRISTIAN *BERAKOT* OVER THE BREAD AND WINE

The instructions on baptism make no mention of the death of Jesus but concentrate on the ritual purity of the water and so, by implication, on the ritual purification of the initiated person. In the same way, the instructions on the Eucharist contain no reference to the words of institution, the Last Supper, or Jesus' sacrificial death on the cross. Instead, the meal symbolizes and effects the incorporation of the Gentiles into Israel, which requires the ritual purity of the participant. No one is to share in the meal without having been baptized "in the Name of the Lord." "For also the Lord has said about this, 'Do not give what is holy to the dogs'" (9:1). "If anyone is holy, let him come; if anyone is not, let him repent. Maranatha! Amen" (10:6). The background of this is not the saying of Jesus found in Matt 7:6, but rather the question of *tohorot*, the holiness of what is offered in the temple extended to what is eaten in the community. The Septuagint of Lev 22:10 prohibits the foreigner from eating *tohorot* with very similar words. This reservation is practiced among the Pharisees with regard to the *'am ha'arets* and among the Essenes with regard to nonmembers (e.g., *m. Tem.* 6:5, 1QS 3:4-6; see van de Sandt and Flusser 2002; Seidensticker 1959). For instance, in the later tractate on the admission of proselytes, *Gerim*, there is a similar worry about the purity of food in the community (1:9; 3:2). Those who join the Qumran community are not permitted to touch *tohorot* until they have completed one year of probation and "gone into the water," and may not touch the drink of the community until they have completed a second year (1QS 6:13-23). In the instructions on the weekly Eucharist of the community, likewise, the *Didache* insists on confession of transgressions before the Eucharist "in order that your sacrifice may be pure" (14:1).

The eucharistic meal of this community is a full meal, since it involves "having enough to eat" (10:1). The eucharistic prayers follow what is known about the Jewish *berakot* in the first century CE, which, however, is rather limited. Care should be taken in using later rabbinic rules, such as *m. Berakot* and the *Birkat Ha-Mazon* in analyzing these prayers (Draper 2000a; Rordorf 1997, 239–41; *contra* Talley 1976; Riggs 1984). There is no evidence that there were rules that were enforced as early as the first century CE., when the *Didache* reached its final form. The formulation of the rabbinic tradition probably began only after Yavneh toward the turn of the century (Bradshaw 1997, 4; Zahavy 1990, 14–16; 1991, 42—68) or even as late as the fourth century (Reiff 1991, 110). Nevertheless, the later developments reflect the earlier oral tradition, and they show marked similarities (as was observed early in the study of the *Didache;* see, e.g., C. Taylor 1886; Turner 1912; Klein 1909).

A blessing over the cup of wine begins the meal, followed by a blessing over the broken bread. The full meal is followed by a further set of blessings, probably over a further cup of wine (as in the oldest form of Luke 22:17-20; see Metzger 1971, 173–77). The *berakot* over the cup and the bread are formulaic and undeveloped, as is the *berakah* after the meal: "We give you thanks, our Father, for . . . which you made known to us through Jesus your child. To you be glory for ever" (9:2, 3). These simple prayers before and after the meal are then given a poetic expansion in the manner that later came to be known as *piyyutim*, which are also concluded with the seal (with minor variations), "For yours is the power and the glory for ever" (9:4, 10:5). This seems likely to reflect very closely the form of a communal meal in first-century Judaism. The early Coptic text of these eucharistic prayers (10:8) includes a *berakah* over incense or perfume, which may also reflect the practice at extended meals or *symposia*, where further edification or discussion took place.

The content of these Christian Jewish *berakot* is highly significant for an understanding of the community's self-awareness, cryptic as they are. The blessing over the cup thanks God for "the holy vine of David, your servant/child, which you made known to us through Jesus your servant/child" (9:2). This Davidic christology is repeated in the final acclamation of the prayers, "Hosanna to the house of David" (10:6 in the Coptic text, which I consider to be the earliest form; "to the God of David" in the Jerusalem text; "to the son of David" in the *Apostolic Constitutions*). The vine of David is a reference to the covenant people of Israel of which David is king (as in Ps 80:8-16), as well as to David's own royal house that is restored by Jesus (the "shoot of David" in such prophetic texts as Jer 33:15; Isa 11:1). A similar prayer for the restoration of the "shoot of David" is found in the fifteenth benediction of the *Shemoneh 'Esreh* and it is reflected in the exegesis of Qumran (4QFlor 1:11; 1QH 6:15-16). In other words, the Gentile Christians who are the addressees of the text are associated with Israel in some way, which stops short of full incorporation, since they do not become the vine but come to know it. This, in my opinion, relates to the admission of Gentiles to community meals without requiring full conversion to Judaism and circumcision; that is, they do not have to "be perfect" and "take upon themselves the full yoke of the Lord" (6:2). This relates to and contrasts with the wording found in

John 15:1-11, where members of the community are understood as forming the branches of the vine, organically connected to Jesus as the vine of David (and so may reflect John's "inner Jewish" orientation; see Draper 2000b).

The *berakah* over the broken bread thanks God for "life and knowledge" made known to the Gentile converts through their instruction in the "way of life," and also through their baptism into the community. The poem that follows prays for the gathering up of the church "from the ends of the earth into your kingdom" in 9:4 and similarly in "from the four winds into your kingdom which you have prepared for it" in 10:5, so that the Davidic christology finds an echo in the language of the community gathered into the eschatological kingdom of Israel. This does not seem to me to represent any kind of supersessionism, by which the Gentiles replace the Jews in the covenant people, as argued by van de Sandt and Flusser (2002, 325–29), since the Gentiles are not the "vine of David," but only come into association with it, 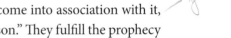 "come to know it through Jesus God's servant/son." They fulfill the prophecy that Gentiles will associate themselves with Israel in the eschatological age.

The Apocalypse

The eschatology of the *Didache* also presents many features characteristic of Christian Judaism. Ernst Bammel (1996) has rightly observed that the eschatological conclusion to the *Didache* (16:1-3) is linked to the Two Ways material in 1–6: "Be watchful for your life. Do not let your lamps be extinguished or your robes be loosed; but be prepared. . . . For the entire time of your faith will be of no use to you if you are not found perfect at the final moment." He found evidence that the Two Ways catechetical schema already possessed such an eschatological conclusion in Jewish examples such as Pseudo-Phocylides; *Sibylline Oracles* 2.149-54; the *Testament of Asher* 6:4-6; and the *Damascus Document* 20:22-34 (the end of the Cairo Recension). Bammel finds a similar eschatological conclusion added to the Mishnaic tractate *Berakhot* in the Tosefta and the Jerusalem Talmud, which then emerges also in *b. Menah.* 43b. This confirms the hypothesis already advanced by Seeberg (1903), Klein (1909) and Daube (1956, 118ff., 135ff.)

that Jewish proselyte catechesis originally ended with such an eschatological warning.

The material in the *Didache* finds echoes in Q. Luke 12:35-38 has the opening injunction in a positive form, "Let your belts be fastened and your lamps burning." Matthew 24:42-44 has "Watch therefore, for you do not know on what day your Lord is coming." However, the negative form found in the *Didache* seems to reflect a more Jewish tone, and the combination of the two sayings makes the original Passover imagery more distinct. The picture is of people at the Passover meal waiting in a vigil through the night, ready for the Lord to bring their deliverance. Similar use of Passover imagery with an eschatological edge is found in the saying of R. Jeremiah (*y. Kil.* IX, 32b, 9; XII,35a, 9), "Clothe me in a white robe with a border, clothe me in my socks, put sandals on my feet and my staff in my hands, and set me aside, so that I shall be prepared when the Messiah comes." What is more unexpected is the instruction to "gather together frequently, seeking what is appropriate for your souls" in the face of the coming judgment (16:2).

This ethical eschatological warning in 16:1-2 is developed by the addition of further characteristic apocalyptic material that envisages a time of trial and crisis before the end (see 1QS 10:17; 11:13), when the betrayers and persecutors will come from inside the community ("the sheep will be turned into wolves, and love into hatred" [16:3]). It seems that this division in the community may revolve around the Torah, since the "betrayal" is characterized by an increase in "lawlessness" (*anomia*), which could refer to wickedness in general, but could also refer to breaches of the Torah (Draper 1996, 340–63). A similar sense of evil emerging from inside the community is conveyed by the description of the "world-deceiver" manifested "as a son of God" and performing "signs and wonders" to lead the world astray (16:4). Whether this reflects an actual schism or not is unclear; but Elaine Pagels's study, *The Origin of Satan* (1995), shows that Satan is typically not the unknown but the "intimate enemy." In any case, the time of crisis will be a time of testing that demands endurance, a process of burning that tests and purifies (16:5). This is a widespread eschatological theme derived from the prophets (e.g., Isa 66:15-16; Mal 3:2-4; 4:1; *4 Ezra* 5:8; *Sib. Or. .* 4:159; 1QH 6:17-19; 3:29-32; 1 Cor 3:13).

Only those who hold fast to the faith represented in the Way of Life
(16:1-2) will be saved "by the curse itself." This enigmatic expression
has widely been taken to refer to Jesus, since "itself" could be rendered
"himself" (see Gal 3:13; so Harnack 1884, 62-63; Rordorf and Tuilier
1998, 197-98 n. 6; Wengst 1984, 99 n. 137). The problem is that Jesus has
not yet been mentioned and is not the logical referent here. Moreover,
there is no evidence that Jesus is understood as Savior in the *Didache*
community, which reflects only an eschatologically oriented Davidic
christology. Another possibility is that the reference is to the "fire of
testing" as the agent of salvation (Draper 1983, 317; Milavec 1995). On
the other hand, it is possible that the curse is referred to the Torah as the
source of salvation despite the heavy burden of bearing it. This is the way
the "yoke" of the Torah is described to proselyte converts before baptism
in *Gerim*, for instance: "Why do you want to become a proselyte? Do
you not see that this people are debased, oppressed and degraded more
than all other people. . . ." Paul also refers to the Torah as a curse, "all
who rely on observing the law are under a curse" (Gal 3:10), and the
logic of his argument is that this curse of the Torah was taken by Jesus
on himself on believers' behalf. If, as I have suggested (1996, 340–63),
the community of the *Didache* is in bitter contention with Paul, then
this counterargument would make sense: "It is the curse [of the Torah]
which saves." Echoes of this debate can be heard in Justin Martyr, who
tries to maintain a compromise position in his *Dialogue with Trypho* 57.
He argues that a Gentile Christian who is circumcised and lives as a full
Jew will be saved "if he does not strive in every way to persuade other
men,—I mean those Gentiles who have been circumcised from error by
Christ, to observe the same things as himself, telling them that they will
not be saved unless they do so." A final possibility, which could indeed
be combined in some way with the previous suggestion, relates to the
cursing of the *minim* promulgated by Rabban Gamaliel after Yavneh in
the Pharisaic/rabbinic communities with which the *Didache* contend-
ed—that is, the cursing of those Christian Jews who tried to remain in
the synagogue for the purpose of forcing them out. Justin speaks in the
same chapter of those Jews "who have anathematized and do anathema-
tize this very Christ in the synagogues, and everything by which they

might obtain salvation and escape the vengeance of fire" (Roberts and Donaldson 1986-89, 1:218). His reference combines the concept of the purifying fire with the concept of the curse that saves. If this is taken to be the background of the saying in the Didache, then it would reassure Christian Jews that it is this very curse pronounced on them and their Christ by the "hypocrites" which saves them from destruction in the "fire of testing."

The apocalypse concludes with a series of three signs that precede the coming of the Lord "on the clouds of the sky." Here, for the first time, the *Didache* shows its understanding that the decisive event in God's eschatological plan has taken place with the coming of Jesus as Messiah and will be fulfilled with the return of the Lord. It is particularly interesting here that these signs appear to reflect the tradition of holy war in Israel, which was taken up and developed by the prophets (Draper 1993, 1-21). First the tribal totem (usually a pole and a crosspiece with a figure attached, for example, a snake or an eagle) is set up on a mountain or a high place. Then the trumpet is blown, and finally the people of Israel are gathered in to be mustered for war (e.g., Jer 51:27; Isa 18:3; 49:22). In *Didache* the totem or sign spread out in the sky is followed by the sound of the trumpet and finally by the ingathering of eschatological Israel (16:6). It seems likely that the crucifixion (pole, crosspiece, and a human figure) has been understood in terms of the sign or totem inaugurating war. Matthew 24:30 weaves this pattern into material he draws from Mark 13, while *Didache* shows no evidence of any knowledge of Markan material—a sign of its independence from the Synoptic Gospels (Kloppenborg 1979, 54-67; cf. Draper 1996, 72-91). The resurrection of the dead to join the Lord on the clouds inaugurates the final judgment of humankind, in which the righteous departed join the ingathering of Israel into the eschatological kingdom (cf. 9:4; 10:5). At this point the text breaks off, either because the last page of a scroll is lost, or because the contents were objectionable to a transcriber; but it is possible that material on the final judgment of each according to works once followed, as in the equivalent passages in Matt 25:31-46, the *Apostolic Constitutions*, and *Barnabas* (16:8).

A final interesting aspect of the apocalypse is its insistence that only the righteous will share in the resurrection of the dead (16:7), so that judgment would be only of the living. As a proof text for the resurrection of the righteous, the *Didache* cites Zechariah 14:5. This text is used in a number of rabbinic writings to justify the resurrection of the martyrs of Israel (*b. Pes.* 50a; *Midrash Rabbah: Ruth* 5; *Midrash Rabbah: Ecclesiastes* 5). It also lies behind Paul's teaching in 1 Thess 3:13; 2 Thess 1:3-10; and several passages in the Synoptic Gospels, where "saints" is used interchangeably with "angels" (Matt 25:31; Mark 8:35-38; and parr.). It seems likely, therefore, that this text was used widely by Jewish writers to argue for the resurrection of the martyrs in the eschatological age and that the *Didache* represents a very early form of the tradition (Draper 1997, 155–79). Moreover, there is a connection between the ethical Two Ways tradition and resurrection in the Dead Sea Scrolls (1QS 3:13—4:26). Nickelsburg (1972, 144–68) suggests that this way of thinking must be dated back at least to the second century BCE. It suggests that the *Didache* understands the resurrection of Jesus, as "the son/servant of God" in the line of David (9:2, 3; 10:2; taking up the tradition of the "suffering servant of Isaiah") also from the perspective of the vindication of the righteous martyrs in Israel. That is why the Lord comes on the clouds, accompanied by the saints, to judge and condemn the wicked, and to join the righteous in establishing the kingdom "on earth as it is in heaven" (8:2). This is a trace of early Christian Jewish tradition and not a later interpolation as argued by Garrow (2004, 43-44, following Niederwimmer 1998, 225 n. 27).

APOSTLES, PROPHETS, TEACHERS, AND FIRSTFRUITS

The final form of the text of the *Didache* seems to reflect a community in transition with regard to its leadership, with a "charismatic" leadership of prophets and teachers in competition with the local twofold leadership of bishops and deacons (15:1-2). The bishops and deacons are likely to be relatively wealthy patrons of the community, who host worship and eucharistic meals in their homes. The key requirement for bishops and deacons is that they be "gentle men who are not fond of money" (15:1). The grievance between them and the prophets and teachers is that these "charismatics" are receiving the "honor" that is due to them as patrons. The *Didache* resolves the issue by reenforcing their claim to honor "along with the prophets and teachers" (15:2; see Draper 1995).

Significantly, apostles do not form part of this competing leadership since they are not a part of the local leadership but arrive from outside the community for brief visits. On the one hand, they must be welcomed "as the Lord himself," reflecting the Jewish tradition that "a man's apostle/representative is as himself" (e.g., *m. Ber.* 5:5; *b. Ned.* 72b; *b. Qidd.* 41b). This is a particular application of the general principle for visitors to the community, "Everyone who comes in the name of the Lord should be welcomed" (12:1). On the other hand, neither the apostle nor for that matter the visitor is allowed to stay more than one or two days: if he or she stays three, he or she is a "false prophet" (11:5).[2] This is not because apostles were "wandering charismatics" with a permanently itinerant ministry, but because the apostle is always en route somewhere other than the community unless he or she arrives with letters from the sending community providing credentials and stating the nature of the business (Horsley and Draper 1999, 29–45). He or she would normally be unknown personally to the community, so that the letters would be crucial to prevent the exploitation of the community's resources by frauds. An attempt to stay for more than an overnight stop, or two nights if they arrive on the eve of the Sabbath and so cannot travel on without breaking the law, would show that they are not really on a mission elsewhere.

Reception of the apostle would imply that the community accepts the authority or good standing of the sending community. A good example of the dynamics involved is provided by the letter of the Elder to Gaius in 3 John. The letter authenticates Demetrius as the Elder's apostle and requires Gaius to provide hospitality in the face of the refusal of Diotrephes to accept him. In the same way, the representatives of Jerusalem who seek to enforce Torah observance in Paul's communities come with letters of authority (2 Cor 3:1) and should therefore be accepted "as the Lord," that is, as "apostles of Christ" (2 Cor 11:13). Paul rejects them as "false apostles," since his "letters" of authorization are provided by the community itself "written not with ink but with the Spirit of the living God" (2 Cor 3:3). Paul's polemic against the institution of "apostles" confirms the schema found in the *Didache*. He himself uses the same system of "authorization by letter" of people sent by the community to carry the offering to Jerusalem (where his letter would accompany their letter in 1 Cor 16:3). Such hospitality toward traveling co-religionists was essential in the first-century Mediterranean world (MacMullen 1974, 83-85), particularly in a community manifesting the kind of concern with food offered to idols and ritual purity shown in *Did.* 6:3; 7:2-3; 9:5. It supported the widespread and growing network of relations between early Christian communities across the Mediterranean.

In the final form of the text, apostles are coupled with prophets (11:3, 7-11) who seem to come from outside the community and seem also to be intent on settling in its midst. In my opinion, these instructions are a later interpolation into the instructions on apostles and disrupt the underlying pattern. If the original instructions were given "through the twelve apostles to the Gentiles," then it is likely that the community would be under some obligation to send contributions back to Jerusalem in the fashion of Paul's "collection." This is the reason for the existence of a block of material on the collection of firstfruits in *Didache* 13, which would have followed instructions on apostles. The general principle relating to apostles is extended to visitors in general and to prophets and teachers as well: "The worker is worthy of his or her hire" (13:2-3), which is known also in Matt 10:10 and Luke 10:7 (cf. 1 Tim 5:18), where it clearly applies to the right of apostles. It extends the rights of a threshing ox in Deut 25:4 to the rights of laborers in the field (see Tomson 1990, 126–28). Those who are engaged full-time in the work of the community are entitled to support, while the principle for others is, "Let them work and let them eat" (12:3).

The means by which the community organized the support they owed to Jerusalem, which would be taken there by the apostles, was the system of firstfruits. I have argued elsewhere that this represents Christian Jewish halakah (Draper 2005b; cf. del Verme 1993, 113–39). In the Torah firstfruits (*bikkurim*) were not payable by Gentiles nor by Jews outside of *'erets Yisrael* (*m. Bik.* 1:10 in the name of R. Jose the Galilean; Philo *De Somniis* 2.75). However, it seems that Diaspora Jews did consider themselves under the obligation to pay tithes (*ma'aserot*), temple tax (*shekalim*), and perhaps firstlings (*bekorot*), which were collected in the synagogue and sent to Jerusalem. Philo loosely referred to these as "firstfruits" (*De Legatione ad Gaium* 156–57), even though he knows that firstfruits proper are not paid by Jews outside Palestine (*De Somniis* 2.75). Since firstfruits proper were not required of Diaspora Jews, they might be paid voluntarily, particularly since firstfruits were widely offered to the gods in the Gentile world. Thus, the *Didache* could require them of all members of the Christian community, Jew and Gentile, without jeopardizing what was already formally owed by Jews in the Diaspora to maintain their good standing in the community and was paid through the formal representatives of the Jewish community (*ma'aserot, shekalim,* and *bekorot*). Christian Gentiles would pay to the Christian community the firstfruits they used to pay to the gods (see the tractate *Gerim* 1.3). Christian Jews, on the other hand, who "bore the whole yoke of the Lord" as observant Jews living "according to the commandment" (13:5, 6), would have paid their social obligations (*ma'aserot, shekalim,* and *bekorot*) to the synagogue as well as their firstfruits proper (*bikkurim*) to the church.

In Israel, perishable firstfruits from locations far from Jerusalem were normally consumed by local priests, while nonperishable firstfruits and the *produce* of the firstfruits (*hallah* and *hullin*) were taken up to Jerusalem at one of the major festivals. In the *Didache,* I would argue that the original motivation for the collection of firstfruits was to send what was nonperishable to support the apostles in Jerusalem, while the perishable would be used to support the poor (13:4) and those engaged full-time in the work of the community (traveling apostles initially, and later resident prophets and teachers [*Did.* 13:1-2]), who could perhaps have been regarded as the equivalent of the local priests in Israel. When the prophets gain ascendancy in the community of the *Didache* (seen already in 10:7), and when the Jerusalem community has been destroyed by the war of 68–70 CE, they come to be regarded as the equivalent of "high priests," so that the firstfruits stayed in the community and were no longer sent to Jerusalem.

CONCLUSION

The *Didache* provides evidence for the life and thought of an early Christian Jewish community and its interpretation and practice of Torah in Christian halakah, which has been preserved in its present form by accident.

The document was copied by a twelfth-century scribe with a number of other early Christian writings, many of which would otherwise be lost to us. It had been brought into line with later Christian thought and incorporated into the seventh book of the *Apostolic Constitutions*. Here it has been stripped of much of what is distinctive to Christian Judaism, such as the connection between "bearing the whole yoke of the Lord" and "perfection"; keeping *kashrut* and refraining strictly from food offered to idols; the ritual purity of baptismal water and the eucharistic meal; the relationship between the "vine of David" and the Gentiles; and the resurrection of the righteous only to return with the Lord on the clouds to join the righteous living in the eschatological kingdom. It has usually been regarded as a pseudepigraphical work, making the claim to apostolic authorship to bolster its authority. However, if dependence on the Gospel of Matthew is ruled out, as many modern scholars now believe, then its core should be dated early. Milavec (2003, vii–xxxvii) has suggested on the basis of a narrative reading of the text that it should be dated between 50 and 70 CE. Another study by Michelle Slee (2003) of the quarrel about the issue of table fellowship in the early Christian movement, reflected in Paul, Acts, Matthew, and *Didache*, likewise puts the latter in Antioch at the heart of the struggle in the mid-first century and earlier than Matthew. The earlier the date for this text is pushed, the more likely it is that it was associated from the beginning with, or even originated from, the twelve apostles in Jerusalem, as its title states. Most recently Alan Garrow (2004) has argued, on the basis of careful redaction-critical analysis, that Matthew is dependent on the *Didache* and that he regards it as containing the teaching of Jesus, since he already knew it as "The Teaching of the Lord through the Twelve Apostles to the Gentiles." This is why he can put sections of it on the lips of Jesus (Garrow 2004, 163).

It has been a slow process, which began with the discovery of the Dead Sea Scrolls and the recognition that the Two Ways tradition in the *Didache* did not derive from the *Epistle of Barnabas* (Audet 1996 [orig. 1952]), but the re-evaluation of the place of this enigmatic text in the history of Christian origins is now in full swing. What is clear is that it presents primary material for the study of the first adaptation of the followers of Jesus to the world of Diaspora Judaism and to the Gentiles who wished to associate themselves with the one they proclaimed as the "son/servant" of God in the line of David. They found a way to admit Gentiles into the knowledge of the "vine of David" without requiring that they submit to circumcision, and to admit them to table fellowship without requiring that they observe *kashrut*. However, they maintained that full observance of the Torah was necessary to be "perfect," even if the submission of the Gentiles to the law could be postponed until the eschatological age, when the Lord would come on the clouds to establish his kingdom on earth for the righteous departed together with the righteous living.

Suggested Readings

Del Verme, Marcello. 2004. *Didache and Judaism: Jewish Roots of an Ancient Christian-Jewish Work*. New York and London: T & T Clark International.

Draper, Jonathan A. 1996. *The Didache in Modern Research*. Arbeiten zur Geschichte des antiken Judentums und des Urchristentums 37. Leiden: Brill.

Garrow, Alan John Philip. 2004. *The Gospel of Matthew's Dependence on the* Didache. Journal for the Study of the New Testament Supplements Series 254. London and New York: T & T Clark International.

Harnack, Adolf von. 1884. *Die Lehre der zwölf Apostel nebst Untersuchungen zur ältesten Geschichte der Kirchenverfassung und des Kirchenrechts*. Texte und Untersuchungen zur Geschichte der altchristlichen Literatur 2.1-2. Leipzig: Hinrichs.

Jefford, Clayton N. 1989. *The Sayings of Jesus in the Teaching of the Twelve Apostles*. Vigiliae christianae Supplements 11. Leiden: Brill.

———. 1995. *The Didache in Context: Essays on Its Text, History and Transmission*. Leiden: Brill.

Milavec, Aaron. 2003. *The Didache: Faith, Hope, and Life of the Earliest Christian Communities, 50–70*. New York and Mahwah, N.J.: Newman.

Niederwimmer, Kurt. 1998. *The Didache: A Commentary*. Hermeneia. Minneapolis: Fortress Press.

Robinson, Joseph Armitage. 1920. *Barnabas, Hermas and the Didache: Being the Donnellan Lectures Delivered before the University of Dublin in 1920*. London. SPCK.

Rordorf, Willy, and Andre Tuilier. 1998. *La Doctrine des Douze Apôtres (Didache)*. 2nd ed. Sources chrétiennes 248. Paris: Les Editions du Cerf.

Van de Sandt, Huub, ed. 2005. *Matthew and the Didache*. Assen: Royal van Gorcum; Philadelphia: Fortress Press.

Van de Sandt, Huub, and David Flusser. 2002. *The Didache: Its Jewish Sources and Its Place in Early Judaism and Christianity*. Assen: Royal van Gorcum; Minneapolis: Fortress Press.

11. THE PSEUDO-CLEMENTINES

F. Stanley Jones

Around 220 CE, a Jewish Christian composed a historical novel about the beginnings of Christianity. S/he likely lived in the valley of the Orontes River, which flows to Antioch. Much of what the author was seeing and hearing about as Christianity did not accord with the Christian tradition that s/he knew. S/he desired to rectify this situation. In an ingenious way, the author produced the first truly Christian novel, one that could stand alongside the popular pagan novels of the time and one that, in fact, later had an enormous impact on Western literature via the medieval Faust legends.

The title chosen for this novel about the first months and years after the crucifixion was *The Circuits of Peter* (*Periodoi Petrou*). The novel began with a letter of Peter to James, the brother of the Lord and the bishop of Jerusalem. Following an account of James's reaction to the appeal that the records of Peter's discourses be safeguarded, the author added another letter to James, this time in the name of Clement. Clement writes that Peter has been martyred in Rome and that he is fulfilling Peter's last request to send James a brief account of Clement's life and travels with Peter, which is what then follows. Clement reminds James that he has already sent books of Peter's discourses to him while he was traveling with Peter.

This involved opening to *The Circuits of Peter* was apparently modeled on another popular novel of the day entitled *The Wonders beyond Thule*, which similarly began its account of a fantastic voyage with a complex of letters and documents and played throughout with layers of the tale (one story repeatedly within another). Just as complicated is the actual historical fate of *The Circuits of Peter*—a fate shared with many other ancient Christian apocrypha. *The Circuits of Peter* was independently reworked by two early-fourth-century writers. Only their redactions survive. These redactions are commonly called the *Homilies* (H) and the *Recognitions* (R), though their original titles seem to have been *Clementia* and *Recognition of the Roman Clement*. Two Greek manuscripts of the *Homilies* still exist, while the *Recognitions* is known largely only through ancient translations into Syriac and Latin from the mid-fourth and early fifth centuries.[1]

The Jewish Christian author of *The Circuits of Peter* apparently recognized a gap in the narrative of the *Acts of Peter*: There was room for an account of Peter's activity between his time in Palestine and his later stay in Rome. *The Circuits of Peter* creatively fills this gap. The choice of Clement as a central figure for his/her novel was a bold move. S/he wished to claim Clement, the bishop of Rome following Peter, as a witness for his/her own brand of Christianity.

At the time of *The Circuits*, the Roman empire was ruled by the Severan dynasty (193-235 CE), which itself was closely connected with Syria. Severus had married into an influential family from Emesa in Syria. Members of this family were effecting a new religious openness at the imperial level, and the ruling emperor at the time of the composition of *The Circuits of Peter*, Marcus Aurelius Antoninus, established the gods of Emesa (especially Elagabal, after whom the emperor was widely named) in central positions of the Roman pantheon. Historical accounts of the times indicate that the regional pride of this part of Syria was on the rise. Interestingly, Hippolytus provides details about an Alcibiades, a Syrian Jewish Christian from Apamaea, who came to Rome about this time on a mission with the Jewish Christian *Book of Elchasai*. *The Circuits of Peter* can thus be understood as yet a further expression of West Syrian regional pride. Of concern here is the nature of *The Circuits of Peter*: Is it Jewish Christian?

"Jewish Christian" is a modern term introduced by historians to group together several ancient varieties of Christianity that remained closer to the Jewish heritage of Christianity than did the evolving Great Church. Justin Martyr and the following heresiologists know of sociologically identifiable groups of believers in Christ who are distinguishable, above all, by practices that set them apart from the evolving Great Church and that bring them into closer proximity with Judaisms of the day. Examples of such practices are observance of the Sabbath, circumcision, observance of commands regarding sexual purity, attendance at a synagogue, observance of the Jewish calendar, and direction of prayer toward Jerusalem. The simple terms "Jewish Christian" and "Jewish Christianity" have been employed in English regularly in this way since at least the early eighteenth century and will be preferred in this essay. This choice of terminology does, however, presuppose the recent debates about nomenclature for Jewish Christianity (Jones 1995, 164 n. 21). It builds on the proposals by Marcel Simon (1996 [1986], 237–38; 1965, 1–11) and Georg Strecker (1988, 311).

These last critical studies have properly set aside as an unhistorical abstraction Jean Daniélou's ideological definition of "Jewish-Christian" as "Christian thought expressing itself in forms borrowed from Judaism" (1964, 9, originally in italics). In an article in 1976, Bruce Malina similarly wanted to distinguish the historical groups spoken of above from Daniélou's broad "Jewish Christianity," but instead of abandoning Daniélou's definition, he kept it as a term for the Great Church and proposed the introduction of the term "Christian Judaism" for the sociologically identifiable groups. While Malina's distinction is correct, his new terminology has proven a source for confusion. Thus, in recent work some scholars are varying between the terms Jewish Christianity and Christian Judaism as if one were addressing whether the preponderance of the group described was Christian or Jewish (e.g., Saldarini 1994). This is not the way in which Malina introduced the term "Christian Judaism." Furthermore, this type of weighing does not seem fully appropriate for the study of the historical phenomenon. Various aspects of Jewish Christian groups will reflect various degrees of religious influence. Who can decide how much weight should be given to each aspect when computing a grand total? It has also been properly pointed out that ancient Jewish Christianity was not a monolithic phenomenon (nor were Gentile Christianity or Judaism); this specific subdivision of the subject does little to match or account for the varieties of Jewish Christianity that are known. Similarly inadequate for historical purposes is the distinction between "Ebionites" and "Nazoraeans" that eventually crystallized in the heresiological tradition, not least because its employment for the early period is anachronistic.

For these reasons, this essay sticks with the traditional term "Jewish Christianity," though one further qualification is in order. Particularly given the decision to accept the Old Testament as scripture of the Great

Church, it was always possible for Great Church Christians to adopt more distinctively Jewish practices (and it still is). Such "judaizers," however, seem to be generally distinguishable from traditional Jewish Christians, who genetically derive from the earliest followers of Jesus.[2]

THE JEWISH CHRISTIANITY OF *THE CIRCUITS OF PETER*

The author of *The Circuits of Peter* speaks of believers in Jesus, whom s/he associates with the Gentiles, and of believers in Moses, whom s/he associates with the Hebrews. The author aligns him/herself with neither of these groups. Instead, s/he suggests that the true worshiper of God is one who believes both of these teachers. This self-definition in a middle category, between Gentile Christians and Hebrews, makes it quite possible that the author is a Jewish Christian. (The texts and references that stand behind these statements and the following ones will be presented and discussed below.)

Further evidence of the author's Jewish Christianity is found in the remarks s/he makes about the "law of God" and "purity," which must be observed in addition to belief in Jesus. Here the author is attempting to correct Gentile believers of his/her day: Peter asserts that a number of regulations, which the author him/herself affirms to have come from the Jewish tradition, must be observed by the worshiper of God. Among these regulations, avoidance of intercourse with a menstruating woman is most clearly affirmed as the "law of God." This practice of menstrual separation is widely attested in the Jewish tradition, of course, but it is also known to the author of the nearly contemporary *Didascalia* as observed by those "who have been converted from the People."[3] Menstrual separation would thus accord with an understanding of the author as a Jewish Christian.

The author of *The Circuits of Peter* also states that "we" do not share a common table with unbelieving Gentiles. This attitude is unusual in early Christianity and again points in a Jewish Christian direction. The author's belief is that food offered to idols, blood, carrion, or suffocated animals all constitute the "table of demons" and that participants at such meals are impure and must be avoided.

The author's awareness of the Jewish origin of his/her attitude toward purity is expressed in his/her unusual exegesis of Jesus' saying regarding inward and outward purity (Matt 23:25-26). The author seems to be aware that some Gentile Christians use this saying to reject Jewish rules regarding purity. In any event, the author explicitly states that Jesus did not criticize all the Pharisees and scribes but only certain ones of them. The context of this argument is a justification of the need to wash the body with water. While which types of baths the author has in mind is not fully apparent, prescriptions for bathing are similarly found among assuredly Jewish Christian groups such as the Elchasaites.

With respect to the Christian elements in the author's thought, matters seem to come to a head in the statement that baptism "under the thrice-blessed invocation" is absolutely necessary for salvation beyond, however that peculiar formula is to be interpreted. Even though the author thinks that good works are also expected, not even the most righteous person ever to live can be saved without baptism.

These views of *The Circuits of Peter* must be distinguished from a number of statements made by the author of the *Homilies*. The Homilist can affirm, in contrast, that God accepts whoever believes either Moses or Jesus, as long as that person does not hate the one s/he has not recognized. Indeed, God himself hid Jesus from the Hebrews, so they are not condemned for their ignorance. Nor is the Homilist even completely insistent on the acceptance of one of these teachers, since s/he can affirm that Clement's mother, a pagan, would have been saved if she had died in her attempt to preserve her chastity.

The Homilist also alters the story of Clement to have him instructed in Judaism already during his early life in Rome before his encounter with the Christian proclamation. S/he makes statements that would imply that Clement's conversion under Peter is actually a conversion to Judaism. Finally, the Homilist speaks of a current command for Christians to honor "the chair of Moses."

It is not completely clear how these elements in the *Homilies* are to be understood historically. On the one hand, it is likely that the Homilist lived in a community mixed with Christians, Jews, and pagans. S/he urges respect for all who act righteously and implies that they will be saved. In the Homilist's mind, Christianity (when compared with paganism) is closely allied with Judaism. All hate between the two is condemned. Christians are further exhorted to show particular respect for Jewish religious leaders and to listen to what they say, even if they are considered sinners. On the other hand, the Homilist proves him/herself elsewhere to be a flamboyant writer. S/he introduces several ancient superstars into the story (the notoriously anti-Jewish Apion and the stellar astrologer Anoubion); s/he involves them in a set of farces and ruses; and s/he ascribes to Peter himself not only a readiness to lie or dissimulate but also several outrageous doctrines such as the view that the Old Testament is shot through with spurious passages. All in all, it seems best not to focus on the Homilist in the current discussion of Jewish Christianity in the *Pseudo-Clementines*.

The Texts

Some passages from *The Circuits of Peter* that underlie the above remarks may now be reviewed. Texts will be presented in reverse order, moving back through the presentation toward the beginning. Those ideas and phrases that are found in both the *Homilies* and the *Recognitions* are the ones that can be assuredly ascribed to the underlying *Circuits of Peter*. Though *The Circuits of Peter* has not survived intact, the many extended verbatim parallels between the *Homilies* and the *Recognitions* make *The Circuits* virtually available.

The following passage illustrates the necessity of baptism for salvation according to *The Circuits*:

Recognitions 7.38.3-4	Homilies 13.13.2
Now to such a degree, he [Peter] said, is chastity pleasing to God that even to those who are in error it confers some grace in the present life. For future blessedness is reserved only for those who observe chastity and justice through the grace of baptism.	Now to such a degree, he [Peter] said, are the matters of chastity pleasing to God that even to those in error He imparts on account of it a little grace in the present life. For salvation beyond is assigned only to those who have been baptized on account of hope in Him and who chastely deal in righteousness.

The differences between the two versions here are minor and seem largely attributable to the fact that this passage of the *Recognitions* has been preserved not in the original Greek but only in the ancient Latin translation (i.e., the translator rephrased slightly). In this text, Peter is explaining why Clement's mother survived a shipwreck, despite having been born under a horoscope that indicated that she would die at sea (R 9.32.5-6 par. H 14.6.3; see Jones 2001). The variance of the author of the *Homilies* from the emphatic position on baptism enunciated in *The Circuits* is found in H 13.20.2, where Peter says to Clement's mother, "Take heart, woman! While many have suffered many evils on account of adultery, you suffered on account of chastity, and therefore you did not die. But even if you had died, you would have a saved soul." *The Circuits*, in contrast, affirms that not even the most righteous person ever to live can be saved without baptism (R 6.8.5 par. H 11.25.2; cf. H 13.21.2).

Regulations for purity are presented in the following:

Recognitions 4.36.4	Homilies 7.8.1
Now the things that pollute both the body and the soul are these: to participate in the table of the demons, that is, to eat food sacrificed to idols or blood or carrion that has suffocated and if anything is something that has been offered to demons.	The service established by Him is this: . . . not to partake of the table of demons, I mean, of things offered to idols, of carrion, of suffocated animals, of animals killed by beasts, of blood.

The Circuits seems to reflect here (see also H 7.4.2; 8.19.1, 23.2) a living independent transmission of the commands generally referred to as the Apostolic Decree, which is found also in Acts 15:20, 29, 21:25. Scholarship has not always appreciated, however, that Gentile Christians also widely observed such regulations in the ancient and Byzantine church (Böckenhoff 1903; Six 1912). Much more remarkable is the point that the baptized are not allowed to eat with the unbaptized, which is repeatedly made throughout the course of the novel (R 1.19.5 par. H 1.22.5; R 7.29.3-5 par. H 13.4.3-5; R 7.36.4 par. H 13.11.4; cf. R 2.71). Here is an example:

Recognitions 7.29.3	Homilies 13.4.3
But we also observe that: Not to have a common table with gentiles unless they should believe and, when truth has been received, should be baptized and consecrated through the trine invocation of the blessed name, and then we eat with them.	In addition to these things, we do not live indiscriminately and do not partake of the table of gentiles, just as we are not able to eat with them since they live impurely. Yet whenever we persuade them to consider and do the matters of the truth, being baptized in a certain thrice blessed invocation, then we eat with them.

The slightly unusual baptismal formula "under the thrice blessed invocation" is regularly found in *The Circuits* (see also R 4.32.2 par. H 9.19.4; R 6.9.3 par. H 11.26.3). Regardless of how this formula is to be interpreted exactly, the following passage indicates that the author understood his/her observances, particularly washing the body and avoidance of sex with a menstruating woman, as derived from the Mosaic tradition:

Recognitions 6.10-11	Homilies 11.28-29
(R 6.10.5) There is, indeed, a distinctive observance of our religion that is not so much imposed on humans as properly desired for the sake of purity by everyone who worships God: the care of purity, I say, of which there are many sorts, but first of all that everyone should observe not to be joined in intercourse with a menstruating woman. For the law of God considers this accursed. (6) Even if the law had not mentioned these things, would we like beetles freely wallow in dung? We ought to have something more	(H 11.28.1) Yet it is necessary to introduce at some time to these things something that is not held in common to humans but is rather distinctive of the service of God. I mean keeping pure: Not to have intercourse with one's own wife when she is in menstruation, for the law of God commands this. (2) But why? Even if keeping pure were not established for the service of God, would you, like beetles, wallow pleasantly? Thus, as humans, who have something more than unreasonable animals have

than animals have, since we are rational humans and are fit for heavenly sentiments, for whom the greatest efforts should be to protect the conscience of the heart from all filth. (R 6.11.1) But it is good and contributes to purity even to wash the body with water. But I say it is good not as if it is the principal means by which the mind is purified, but rather because this by which the body is purified is a consequence of that good. (2) For so even our teacher thus criticized certain of the Pharisees and scribes—who seem to be better than the rest and are separate from the multitude—calling them hypocrites because they were purifying only the things that were seen by humans but the hearts, which only God sees, they were leaving polluted and filthy. (3) To certain of them, therefore, not to all, he said, "Woe to you scribes and Pharisees, hypocrites, because you clean what is outside on the cup and the plate, but inside they are full of filth."

(to be rational), cleanse the heart of evils with heavenly reason, but wash the body with a bath! (3) For keeping pure is truly good, not as if purity of the body precedes the cleansing of the heart but because what is clean follows the good. (4) For even our teacher immediately rebuked some of the Pharisees and scribes among us—those who are separate and, as scribes, know the laws better than others—because they were purifying only the things seen by humans but were neglecting the pure things of the heart seen only by God. (H 11.29.1) Therefore, he used this famous saying truly for the hypocrites among them and not for all, for he said to listen to some of them because they were entrusted with the chair of Moses. (2) Yet to the hypocrites he said, "Woe to you, scribes and Pharisees, hypocrites, because you cleanse the exterior of the cup and the plate, but inside it is full of filth."

The author here affirms the legitimacy of the (apparently living Jewish) tradition. S/he is denying that the tradition is inherently "hypocritical." His/her objection to these people (scribes and Pharisees), whom s/he elsewhere classifies among the Hebrews, is rather that they have "hidden" the key of the kingdom of heaven, namely, knowledge, that they received from Moses (R 1.54.7, 2.30.1, 46.3 Syriac, H 3.18.2-3, 18.15.7-16.2). The Homilist takes a different slant on this material and states that Christians "are commanded to honor the chair of Moses" while adding "even if those seated are considered sinners" (H 3.70.2).

Finally, there is the fascinating text in which *The Circuits* distinguishes itself both from Gentile believers in Jesus and from Hebrew believers in Moses. Here the author is defining him/herself as standing between these groups, and thus as a Jewish Christian. This text is virtually unique in this regard and supplies an invaluable basis in reality, though a neglected one, for what scholars often speculate about when they speak of Jewish Christians as somehow located between Judaism and Christianity. Since the two versions of the text diverge, the common wording (what can assuredly be ascribed to *The Circuits*) will be italicized in order that the original intention of the text might be seen.

Recognitions 4.5	*Homilies* 8.5-7
(R 4.5.1) For thus it was also given to *the Hebrews* from the beginning to love *Moses* and to *believe* his word. Hence it is also written, "The people believed God and his servant Moses." (2) What therefore was of special gift *from God* toward the nation of *the Hebrews* we now see to have been given also to *those who are called* to the faith *from the nations.* (3) But the means of *works* is entrusted to the power and will of *each one*, and this is unique for them. But *to have a desire toward a teacher of truth is a gift from* the heavenly father. (4) But *salvation* is in this: that you do the will of the one for whom you have conceived love and desire through the grace of *God*, lest that word of his should be said to you which he spoke: "But *why do you*	(H 8.5.1) For *the Hebrews* who believe *Moses* and do not observe the things spoken through him are not being saved unless they observe the things spoken to them, (2) because even their *believing* Moses has occurred not of their will, but *of God*, who said to Moses, "Behold I am coming to you in the column of a cloud in order that the people might hear me speaking to you and might believe you forever." (3) Since then *belief in teachers of truth has come from God* to both *the Hebrews* and *those called from the nations*, while good *deeds* have been left for *each one* to do by his *individual judgment*, the reward is justly given to those who do well. (4) For there would not have been a need for the coming of either Moses

say to me '*Lord, Lord*' *and do not do what I say?*"

(5) Therefore, it is of the distinctive gift granted by God to *the Hebrews* that they should believe *Moses*, but to the nations, that they should love *Jesus*.

For the *Lord* also indicated this where he *said, "I praise you, Father*, Lord *of heaven and earth, because you have hidden these things from the wise* and prudent *and have revealed them* to children." (6) By this it is declared, at any rate, that the people of the *Hebrews*, educated out of the Law, did *not recognize him*, but the people of the gentiles recognized Jesus and venerate him, because of which it will also be saved, not only recognizing him but also doing his will. (7) But the *one who is from the gentiles* and has it from God to love Jesus should have it of his *own undertaking* to believe also *Moses*. (8) And again the Hebrew who has it from God to believe *Moses* should have it of his own undertaking to believe in Jesus, so that each of them, having in themselves something of divine gift and something of their own industry

or Jesus if they had desired of themselves to understand what is reasonable. Nor does *salvation* occur through belief in teachers and calling them lords. (H 8.6.1) For this reason, Jesus is hidden from *the Hebrews* who have taken *Moses* as a teacher, but Moses is hidden from those who have believed *Jesus*. (2) For since there is one teaching through both, God accepts the one who has believed one of these. (3) But believing a teacher occurs for the sake of doing the things spoken by God. (4) Since this is so, our *Lord* himself *says, "I praise you, Father of heaven and of earth, because you have hidden these things from the wise* presbyters *and you have revealed them* to nursing babes." (5) Thus, God himself hid the teacher from those who already knew what to do, but revealed [him] to those who did not know what to do. (H 8.7.1) Therefore, because of the one who hid, neither are *Hebrews* condemned for their ignorance of Jesus, if doing the things of Moses they do not hate the one they have *not recognized*, (2) nor again are the *ones from the nations* condemned who, because of the revealer, have not recognized *Moses*, if they too do the things spoken through *Jesus* and do not hate the one they have not recognized. (3) And some will not profit from calling teachers lords but not doing the

| might be perfect from *both*. | things of servants. (4) For this reason, our Jesus said to someone who often called him lord but did nothing of the things he had commanded, "*Why do you say, 'Lord, Lord,' and do not do what I say?*" For saying will not profit anything, but rather doing. (5) Thus, in every respect there is need for good works, but if someone should be deemed worthy to recognize *both* as of one teaching proclaimed by them, this man has been deemed *rich* |
| (9) For our Lord spoke of such a *rich* man who brings forth from his treasures *new things* and *old*. | in God, having understood *old* things to be new in time and *new things* to be old. |

Several distinctive views of the Homilist immediately catch the eye and must be separated out: Salvation comes from works, quite apart from belief in any teacher (this implies that even a pagan can be saved, just as the Homilist asserted of Clement's mother in H 13.20.2). Indeed, if humans had simply wanted to be reasonable, there would not have been a need for either of the teachers (H 8.5.4; see also H 3.31.2, 32.1). Furthermore, Hebrews are not condemned, because God himself hid Jesus from them since they already knew what to do (H 8.6.5). H 18.17.1 repeats that God did not hide from them the way of life that leads to the kingdom. The remarks about not hating the other teacher seem to indicate that the Homilist wishes to dispel all hate between the two communities.

Once the typical slant of the Homilist is isolated, the original intention of this passage emerges. *The Circuits* states that belief in one of the teachers is a gift of God and that the believer should make the effort, alongside deeds, to believe the other teacher too. For salvation, each person should have something of divine gift and something of his/her own industry. *The Circuits* is consciously forging the Jewish Christian path between the two known options, which s/he declares insufficient. *The Circuits of Peter* is thus apparently a surviving witness to ancient Jewish Christianity. It promotes distinctively Jewish practices (menstrual separation, avoidance of meals with nonbelievers), and it explicitly depicts the true Christian as occupying a position between Gentile believers and Hebrews.

Jewish Christian Sources of *The Circuits of Peter*

Above it was suggested that ancient Jewish Christians are distinguishable from "judaizers" not least because of their genetic relationship to the earliest followers of Jesus. Another way of verifying the Jewish Christian identity of the author of *The Circuits of Peter* is thus to investigate her/his relationships with earlier Jewish Christians. In particular, it seems relevant to ask if the author employed Jewish Christian sources in his/her composition. The following will briefly discuss two readily identifiable Jewish Christian sources that the author of *The Circuits of Peter* employed in his/her novel: the *Book of Elchasai* and an anti-Pauline counter–Acts of the Apostles. Of concern here are especially the traits in these works that would allow their identification as Jewish Christian.

The Book of Elchasai

There is broad agreement among scholars that the introductory Pseudo-Clementine "document" called the *Contestation* (the account of James's reaction to the appeal that the records of Peter's discourses be safeguarded) is dependent on the *Book of Elchasai*. Both contain, for example, a distinctive oath that invokes strikingly similar "witnesses" (heaven, earth, water, and air with mention also of bread and salt):

Epiphanius, *Panarion 19.1.6*	Pseudo-Clementine *Contestation 2.1, 4.3*
[Elchasai] appointed salt, water, earth, bread, ether, and wind as an oath for them unto service.	(2.1) Now let him say, "May I have as witnesses heaven, earth, water, in which everything is contained, and in

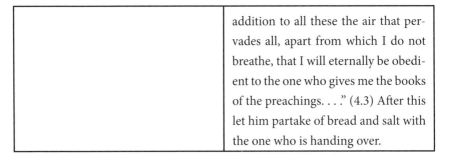

	addition to all these the air that pervades all, apart from which I do not breathe, that I will eternally be obedient to the one who gives me the books of the preachings. . . ." (4.3) After this let him partake of bread and salt with the one who is handing over.

Scholars have long debated the degree to which the *Pseudo-Clementines* have been influenced by the *Book of Elchasai*, with some having gone so far as to call the author of *The Circuits* an Elchasaite (Hort 1901, 131). There is no need to attempt a resolution of all the issues here. It is sufficient to repeat, as indicated above, that *The Circuits* apparently opened with three "documents," the second of which was the *Contestation*, and that the *Contestation* shows clear indications of dependency on the *Book of Elchasai*. What do we know of the *Book of Elchasai* and in what respects is it seen to be Jewish Christian?[4]

Predictions of eschatological turmoil in the *Book of Elchasai* refer to Trajan's war with Parthia and allow the *Book of Elchasai* to be dated rather precisely to 116–117 CE. Though the *Book of Elchasai* is preserved only through fragments cited by church fathers, there is good documentation for the description of an appearance of a ninety-six-mile-high Son of God, evidently also called Christ, with a similarly sized female, who is said to be the Holy Spirit. This description would seem to assure the Christian nature of the *Book of Elchasai*, though a few scholars have maintained that the *Book of Elchasai* was originally purely Jewish.[5] There are two practices prescribed by the *Book of Elchasai* that most readily qualify it as Jewish (and thus Jewish Christian). First, the *Book of Elchasai* instructs that when one prays, one should pray in the direction of Jerusalem:

> For he [Elchasai] hinders praying toward the east, saying one should not turn in this manner but rather should face Jerusalem from all regions; some should turn to Jerusalem from the east toward the west, others should turn to it from the west to the east, others from the north toward the south and from the south toward the north so that

from all sides the countenance is facing Jerusalem. (Epiphanius, *Panarion* 19.3.5)

This traditional Jewish practice sets the *Book of Elchasai* off from Gentile Christianity in which prayer toward the east had quickly established itself.[6]

Second, the *Book of Elchasai* prescribes observance of the Sabbath, another well-known Jewish practice that was abandoned by the Gentile Christians:

> There are wicked stars of impiety. This has now been said to us, pious ones and disciples. Be on guard against the authority of the days of their rule; do not undertake the commencement of works in their days; and do not baptize man or woman in the days of their authority, whensoever the moon traverses one of them and conjoins with them. (3) Guard the day itself until it goes out away from them, and then baptize and engage in every commencement of your works. Now honor furthermore the day of the Sabbath, for it is one of those days. (4) But guard against commencing also on the third day of the week, for when three years of the Emperor Trajan are again completed—from the time when he subjected some of the (areas) of the Parthian's authority—when three years have been completed, the war will flame up between the angels of impiety of the north. All the kingdoms of impiety will be disturbed because of this. (Hippolytus, *Refutatio* 9.16.2-4)[7]

Observance of the Sabbath is urged here on the basis of astrology: Mars and Saturn, the "stars" of Tuesday and Saturday, were universally known in antiquity as malefics.

An early-third-century promoter of the *Book of Elchasai* reportedly said that "believers ought to be circumcised and live according to the law" (Hippolytus, *Refutatio* 9.14.1). It is not certain that such a statement was in the *Book of Elchasai*, but a comment in the Pseudo-Clementine *Contestation* 1.1 that a teacher should be "a faithful circumcised person" might be a further instance of dependence on the *Book of Elchasai*. Another possible continuity in this Jewish Christian tradition might be vegetarianism (Epiphanius, *Panarion* 19.3.6; Pseudo-Clementine R 7.6.4 par. H 12.6.4). Such continuities can be used to verify the Jewish Christian nature of ancient texts and movements, even if the practices themselves are not specifically Jewish. In any event, the date of the *Book of Elchasai* is significant in the current context because it allows the Jewish Christian tradition of the *Pseudo-Clementines* to be traced back at least a century before the composition of *The Circuits of Peter*.

An Anti-Pauline Counter–Acts of the Apostles

The next source of *The Circuits of Peter* to be discussed, an anti-Pauline counter–Acts of the Apostles, also contains such elements of Jewish Christian continuity with the *Book of Elchasai*. In particular, one finds in both the rejection of sacrifices and the condoning of dissimulation, or denial with the lips though not in the heart. This anti-Pauline counter–Acts of the Apostles is readily distinguishable from the rest of *The Circuits* by its differing narrative framework and its use of Acts.[8] As it is found in R 1.27-71, this text is a review of sacred history from creation to the seventh year after the crucifixion. In the seventh year after Jesus' death, the apostles are assembled in Jerusalem and hold a debate with the unbelieving Jews on the topic of whether Jesus is the Christ. Eventually, James the brother of Jesus persuades all the people and the high priest to be baptized. The baptism of the entire Jewish nation is disrupted by a certain unnamed person who enters the temple, causes a commotion, and eventually throws James down from the top of the stairs to his death. When this unnamed person later receives a commission from the high priest to go with letters to Damascus in order to persecute the believers, his identity as Paul is clarified, and the parodying of Luke's Acts of the Apostles is also apparent. Here are the highlights:

Recognitions 1.69.8–70.2, 6-8, 71.3-4 (Syriac)	*Recognitions* 1.69.8–70.2, 6-8, 71.3-4 (Latin)
In seven full days he [James] persuaded all the people together with the high priest so that they should	He [James] persuaded the whole people and the chief priest during seven succeeding days to hasten immediately

immediately make haste to proceed to baptism. (1.70.1) Then a certain person who was the enemy entered the temple near the altar with a few others, while he cried out and said, (2) "What are you doing, O people, the children of Israel? How have you been carried off so quickly by wretched men who have strayed after a magician?" . . .

(6) When he had said those things, he rose first, seized a firebrand from the altar, and began to smite with it. (7) Then, when the rest of the priests saw him, they also followed his example. (8) In the great flight that thus ensued, some fell upon others and others were smitten. There were not a few who died so that much blood poured forth from those who had been killed. Now the enemy threw James from the top of the stairs. Since he fell and was as if dead, he did not smite him a second time. . . .

(1.71.3) The enemy, before the priests, promised Caiaphas the high priest that he would massacre all those who believe in Jesus. (4) He departed for Damascus to go as one carrying letters from them so that when he went there, the nonbelievers might help him and might destroy those who believe. He wanted to go there first because he thought that Peter had gone there.

to acquire baptism. (1.70.1) When the matter had reached the point that they should come and be baptized, a certain hostile person entered the temple with only a few others and began to shout and say, (2) "What are you doing, O men, Israelites? Why are you so easily duped? Why are you led headlong by the most miserable persons who have been deceived by a magician?" . . .

(6) When he had said these things, he grabbed a brand from the altar and first initiated the massacre. (7) When the others saw him, they, too, were carried away with similar madness. (8) There was a clamor of all, of the smiting as well as of the smitten. Very much blood was shed. A confused flight ensued. When in the meantime that hostile person had made his way to James, he pushed him from the highest flight of stairs. Since he believed him to be dead, he made no effort to mishandle him further. . . .

(1.71.3) That hostile person had received a commission from Caiaphas the high priest to persecute all who believed in Jesus (4) and to go to Damascus with his letters so that even there, when he had gained the help of the nonbelievers, he might bring destruction on the believers; but he was hastening particularly to Damascus because he believed that Peter had fled there.

The final words here ("the high priest," "letters," "departure for Damascus") disclose the dependence of this text on Acts 9:1-2; 22:4-5; 26:10-12 as well as the identification of James's opponent as Paul. While this passage asserts that James survived the fall, it is likely that the original source described James's death at the hands of Paul (the denial of a second strike is the telltale sign of alteration that allowed *The Circuits* to preserve James for its novelistic framework).

The anti-Pauline stance of this material is often considered sure evidence of its Jewish Christian origin. The search for distinctive Jewish Christian observances here, nevertheless, is somewhat problematic. The author contents him/herself with a global assertion by Peter that the only difference between "us who believe in Jesus" and the "nonbelievers among our people" is whether Jesus is the prophet (the eternal Christ) foretold by Moses (R 1.43.1-2). This author does, however, display an ethnic awareness—already surfacing in the reference to "our people"—that clearly points in a Jewish Christian direction. According to the source, Abraham was shown a specific number to be filled with believers. Since some of the people became unbelievers, it was necessary for Gentiles to be called to complete the number shown to Abraham—a situation that the author terms "confusion" (R 1.42.1). Alongside this ethnic Jewish awareness (see also R 1.32.1: "our race, the Hebrews"), the author upholds an attachment to the land of Judea that is exceptional in early Christian writings and that seems Jewish Christian. According to this source, the believers do have to flee Jerusalem after the mayhem caused by that certain violent person, but they never depart from the land. Instead, it is predicted that they will be preserved in a place in the land when the war comes to destroy the temple, put an end to sacrifices, and drive the unbelievers from the land (R 1.37.2, 39.3). The author apparently connects this thought with the hope for an earthly "kingdom of heaven," centered in Jerusalem (without a temple) where the "poor" will be filled with food and drink. Combined with the description of certain believers who secretly remain among the unbelieving Jews (R 1.65.2, 66.4), all these elements point in a Jewish Christian direction.

The anti-Pauline source of R 1.27-71 dates from the end of the second century.[9] Its concern with the land and with Jerusalem might well indicate that it derives from this region. Again in this case, one can trace the Jewish Christian tradition even further back on the basis of the use of other Jewish

Christian writings. In particular, the source apparently employed the *Gospel of the Ebionites* in its statements that the Pharisees were baptized by John (Epiphanius, *Panarion* 30.13.4; R 1.54.6-7) and that destruction will come because of continued sacrifices (Epiphanius, *Panarion* 30.16.5; R 1.37.2-4, 39.3, 64.1-2).[10]

Summary

This essay has brought together the evidence that most directly establishes the Pseudo-Clementine *Circuits of Peter* to be Jewish Christian: *The Circuits* explicitly stakes out a position between Gentile believers in Jesus and Hebrew believers in Moses and asserts that the worshiper of God should both be baptized and observe regulations for purity that are found in the Jewish tradition. The clarity of this evidence for the Jewish Christian nature of *The Circuits* allows *The Circuits* to serve as something of an anchor or landmark for the definition and study of the broader historical entity "ancient Jewish Christianity."

Furthermore, this essay has briefly described two Jewish Christian sources employed by *The Circuits*, namely, the *Book of Elchasai* and an anti-Pauline counter–Acts of the Apostles. *The Circuits* is thus seen to have arisen out of a larger historically identifiable Jewish Christian context—in continuity with this Jewish Christian tradition and in continuation of it. Now that the Jewish Christian nature of *The Circuits* has been established, this fascinating novel awaits further exploration as a gold mine for Syrian Jewish Christianity in the early third century.

Suggested Readings

Frankenberg, Wilhelm. 1937. *Die syrischen Clementinen mit griechischem Paralleltext: Eine Vorarbeit zu dem literargeschichtlichen Problem der Sammlung.* Texte und Untersuchungen zur Geschichte der altchristlichen Literatur 48.3. Leipzig: J. C. Hinrichs.

Hort, Fenton John Anthony. 1901. *Notes Introductory to the Study of the Clementine Recognitions: A Course of Lectures*. London: Macmillan.

Jones, F. Stanley. 1993. "The Pseudo-Clementines: A History of Research." Pages 195–262 in *Literature of the Early Church*. Vol. 2 of *Studies in Early Christianity: A Collection of Scholarly Essays*. Edited by Everett Ferguson. New York and London: Garland. Originally published in *The Second Century* 2 (1982): 1–33, 63–96.

———. 1995. *An Ancient Jewish Christian Source on the History of Christianity: Pseudo-Clementine "Recognitions" 1.27–71*. Society of Biblical Literature Texts and Translations 37, Christian Apocrypha Series 2. Atlanta: Scholars Press.

———. 1997. "An Ancient Jewish Christian Rejoinder to Luke's Acts of the Apostles: Pseudo-Clementine *Recognitions* 1.27–71." Pages 223–45 in *The Apocryphal Acts of the Apostles in Intertextual Perspectives*. Edited by Robert F. Stoops, Jr. Semeia 80. Atlanta: Scholars Press.

———. 2001. "Eros and Astrology in the *Periodoi Petrou*: The Sense of the Pseudo-Clementine Novel." *Apocrypha: Revue internationale des littératures apocryphes* 12:53–78.

———. 2004. "The *Book of Elchasai* in Its Relevance for Manichaean Institutions with a Supplement: The *Book of Elchasai* Reconstructed and Translated." *ARAM* 16:179–215.

Rehm, Bernhard, ed. 1992. *Die Pseudoklementinen I: Homilien*. Edited by Georg Strecker. 3rd rev. ed. Die griechischen christlichen Schriftsteller der ersten Jahrhunderte 42. Berlin: Akademie.

———, ed. 1994. *Die Pseudoklementinen II: Rekognitionen in Rufins Übersetzung*. Edited by Georg Strecker. 2nd rev. ed. Die griechischen christlichen Schriftsteller der ersten Jahrhunderte 51. Berlin: Akademie.

Smith, Thomas, Peter Peterson, and James Donaldson, trans. 1978 [1886]. "Pseudo-Clementine Literature." Pages 67–346 in *The Twelve Patriarchs, Excerpts and Epistles, the Clementina, Apocrypha, Decretals, Memoirs of Edessa and Syriac Documents, Remains of the First Ages*. Vol. 8 of *The Ante-Nicene Fathers: Translations of the Writings of the Fathers down to AD 325*. Edited by Alexander Roberts and James Donaldson; American reprint revised by A. Cleveland Coxe. 10 vols. Repr., Grand Rapids: Eerdmans.

NOTES

Introduction

1. One might also note here Bellarmino Bagatti's *The Church from the Circumcision: History and Archaeology of the Judaeo-Christians*, which was translated from its original Italian (1962) in 1971 and reprinted in 1984. This book, however, is primarily a survey of material remains supposedly from early Jewish Christians, intended particularly for students of archaeology (1984, 2). The book has in any event been sharply criticized, so that one recent author could state flatly, "No such archaeological evidence appears to exist" (Paget 1999, 732).

2. The most recent sustained treatment is Simon Mimouni, *Le Judéo-christianisme ancien: Essais historiques* (1998).

3. In a manner reminiscent of Hort's distinction between "Judaic" and "Judaistic Christianity," Schoeps (1969, 9) acknowledges that the term "Jewish Christianity" might also be used in a more general sense to denote Christians who, "proud of their [Jewish] origin, formed separate groups within the churches and sometimes, perhaps, even established congregations alongside the Gentile Christian churches," but were nonetheless part of the "Great Church"; see in this respect his description of the author of James as "a Great-Church Jewish Christian" (1949, 343: "*ein großkirchlicher Judenchrist*"). As a rule, however, Schoeps uses the term more narrowly with reference to a sectarian "party" that was in basic conflict with the "Great Church"; see esp. 1949, 7; 1969, 9–10.

4. Even here, however, the matter is not clear-cut. The Jerusalem community has an ambiguous relationship to Jewish Christianity in the work of Adolf von Harnack, and the same is true of the Ebionites in the work of Daniélou. See further on these scholars Chapter One.

Chapter One

1. The usefulness of categories is of course relative to some purpose. In a scholarly context, the stated purpose is generally said to be primarily descriptive or analytical. Nonetheless, one must also reckon with usefulness relative to some ideological or theological purpose in scholarship as well. For a very illuminating example, see Bruce Lincoln, *Theorizing Myth: Narrative, Ideology, and Scholarship* (1999).

2. I have argued at length elsewhere (Jackson-McCabe 2001) that this is the case with the Letter of James. One could arguably raise the same issue with regard to E. P. Sanders's (1976)

attempt to clarify the religion of Philo in terms of the "covenantal nomism" that he takes to be definitive of all early Judaism.

3. The category made its way into the center of the historical imagination of Christian origins in the wake of F. C. Baur, on whom see below. Use of the category itself, however, goes back at least to the 1600s (Myllykoski 2005a).

4. Approaches to Jewish Christianity have themselves been subject to differing categorizations; compare, for example, the alternative typologies found in Daniélou 1964, 7–9; Mimouni 1992, 182–83; Paget 1999. For a more historically organized treatment, see Luedemann 1989, 1–32; also Klijn 1973–74.

5. Whether the fourteen years mentioned in Gal 2:1 includes or is in addition to the three years of 1:18 is not entirely clear; see H. D. Betz 1979, 83–84 and Martyn 1997, 181–82.

6. Note, for example, that nothing is said about the status of the Gentile mission prior to Paul's active participation in it. Was it already underway before he became involved? And if so, what relationship did any of the others involved in it (e.g., Barnabas?) have with the Jerusalem apostles? It is noteworthy that Luke-Acts, which has a different rhetorical agenda, creates a quite different impression of the situation. Note in any case that Paul's subsequent account of the conflict in Antioch, which assumes a mixed gathering of Jews and Gentiles, suggests that the separation of the two missionary spheres should not be overblown.

7. See, in addition to the canonical works 1–2 Peter, the *Epistula Petri* included in the Pseudo-Clementines, the *Gospel of Peter,* and the *Apocalypse of Peter*; and in addition to the canonical Gospel, letters, and Apocalypse ascribed to John, the *Apocryphon of John.*

8. For accessible accounts of the sources and their problems, with varying estimations of their historicity, see Pritz 1988, 122–27; Luedemann 1989, 200–213; and S. G. Wilson 1995, 145–48.

9. The competitive nature of such genealogies in early Christianity is illustrated well by the early orthodox creation of a fictitious personality called "Ebion" as the founder of the Ebionites (e.g., Strecker 1996, 280–82)—a transparently rhetorical effort to locate the origin of the group somewhere other than in the original Jerusalem community.

10. The classic instance would be the apostle Paul. While himself clearly of Jewish descent (e.g., Phil 3:4-6; 2 Cor 11:22), the form of religion Paul championed has frequently been understood as the precise opposite of Jewish Christianity. So, e.g., Joan E. Taylor (1990, 315): "Paul was therefore not a Jewish-Christian even though a Christian Jew." On the other hand, Gentiles are sometimes included, as by Munck, under Jewish Christianity depending on the character of their religion; see Daniélou 1964, 9; but contrast, e.g., S. G. Wilson 1995, 143–68.

11. For a general treatment of Baur's work, particularly as it pertains to the New Testament, see Baird 1992, 258–69. Only some of Baur's German writings are available in

English translation. The account that follows is based on his *Church History of the First Three Centuries* (Eng. trans. 1878); see also *Paul the Apostle of Jesus Christ* (Eng. trans. 1873–75; repr. 2003).

12. Representatives of the Tübingen School differed among themselves in the detailed work of sifting the data. For Baur's own sorting of the evidence, see 1878, 1:44–183, and esp. 99. For a brief account of the Tübingen School, see Baird 1992, 269–78; further Harris 1990.

13. Harnack can indeed refer to what is frequently called "the Great Church" or "mainstream" Christianity as "anti-Jewish Christendom" (1961 [1896], 1:290). Cf. his *What Is Christianity?* (1986 [1957]), where, explaining his famous statement, "It was Paul who delivered the Christian religion from Judaism" (176), Harnack characterizes Paul's formulation of "the inner and essential features" of Jesus' message as having "transformed [the Gospel] into the universal religion, and laid the ground for the Great Church" (180), while simultaneously "portend[ing] the downfall of the religion of Israel" (179).

14. See Harnack 1961 [1896], 1:287–317. Here Harnack says little more regarding first-century Jewish Christianity than that "Jewish Christians formed the majority in Palestine, and perhaps also in some neighboring provinces" (1:290) before moving on to his primary interest: the extent to which it was a factor "in the development of Christianity to Catholicism." He does not in this context explicitly spell out the relation of Peter and the Jerusalem community more generally to this Jewish Christianity.

15. Cf. the analogous (if more overtly theological) formulation offered subsequently by Hort (1894, 5) between "Judaic" and "Judaistic Christianity." Unlike "Judaic Christianity," the latter "ascribes *perpetuity* to the Jewish law . . . thus confounding the conditions Providentially imposed for a time on the people of God when it was only a single nation, the people inhabiting Palestine,—confounding these Providential conditions with God's government of his people after its national limits were broken down and it had become universal."

16. Ritschl 1857, 107, 120. Note that "Judaic" is used in distinction from "Old Testament" (*alttestamentlich*) influence; thus the thoroughly apocalyptic book of Revelation, for example, is said to be the most *judaistisch* book of the New Testament (20), while the Letter of James is not *judaistisch* at all, but *alttestamentlich* (115). Note in this connection that *judaistisch* has a negative connotation for Ritschl, inasmuch as *Judaismus* in general, from the time of Ezra on, is characterized in terms of "epigonism," that is, as a second-rate imitation of "the classical time of the Old Testament religion" (115).

17. It is important to recognize nonetheless that, as a rule, Schoeps (1949, 7–8) explicitly reserves the term "Jewish Christian" (*judenchristlich*) for what he considers the "extremist"

form, also called Judaists and Ebionites, that stood outside the "Great Church." This narrow usage, however, seems to be at least in part a function of his limited interest in that particular group. He is in any case not entirely strict about it, as is clear from his discussion of the Letter of James: it is, he says (1949, 343), "a late Jewish Christian [*judenchristliche*] writing, however in no way an Ebionite one"; its author, rather, was a "Great Church Jewish Christian [*großkirchlicher Judenchrist*]." For more on his use of terms, and the reconstruction of Christian origins within which they function, see Schoeps 1969, 1, 9–10, 18–37 (cf. 1949, 7–8, 256–305).

18. It is, however, G. Dix's *Jew and Greek* (1953) that Daniélou (1964, 7 and 9 n. 14) cites as a key influence in this respect.

19. There is a strange ambiguity surrounding Daniélou's classification of the canonical literature. His criteria fairly demand that most, indeed perhaps all, the works of the New Testament be categorized as Jewish Christian, and he hints in this direction in passing, explicitly classifying Paul as such, and speaking more generally of Jewish Christian theologizing within the New Testament (1964, 1, 9). But the New Testament as a whole is left out of his otherwise extensive investigation, with no explanation offered. It is this oddity that seems to have presented the opening for Longenecker's study.

20. On one hand, one might say that this is simply because they fell outside the scope of his limited study of orthodoxy. It should be noted, however, that Daniélou's scheme, which identifies Christianity as a revealed truth, generates a fundamental ambiguity regarding the proper classification of such heterodox forms (i.e., forms that are not, or at least not fully, reflective of revealed truths). While he does speak generally of heterodox Jewish Christianity, his notion that such groups and texts are relevant to the history of archaic Christian theology only insofar as "they preserve certain elements which *they had in common with Jewish Christianity*" effectively excludes them from the category, at least as strictly formulated. Thus his marginal treatment of them: "Since the object of this volume is to present the history of archaic Christian theology [i.e., Jewish Christianity!], there is no need to give a detailed account of these [subsequent, heterodox] systems" (1964, 55; my emphasis).

21. Both continue, in fact, to use Jewish Christianity in Daniélou's sense of the term. As noted above, Malina (1976, 49) restricts it to "the historically perceived orthodox Christianity that undergirds the ideology of the emergent Great Church." According to Klijn (1973–74, 426) the proper "object of the study of Jewish Christianity is to detect the presence, the origin, the development and the disappearance of . . . Jewish influence" on Christianity. He has in mind, more specifically, "the immense Jewish influence on the Church *apart from the many ideas already adopted in the New Testament*

and taken over by ecclesiastical writers of a later date" (his emphasis). The rationale for excluding from this study those Jewish features found in works that were ultimately selected for inclusion in the New Testament—itself a fourth-century product—is no more obvious here than it is in the case of Daniélou's work.

22. To make matters more confusing, Harnack also occasionally employs the term "Christian Judaism," but apparently with two quite different senses. On one hand, it can be used interchangeably with "Jewish Christianity" (1961 [1896], 307–8). Elsewhere, however, he uses "Christian Judaism" to convey almost precisely the opposite notion: not a particularistic Christianity but a universalized Judaism. "Original Christianity was in appearance Christian Judaism, the creation of a universal religion on Old Testament soil" (287).

23. The designation of the Second Temple era as "early" (as opposed to "late" or "intertestamental") Judaism is itself indicative of this shift in scholarship; see further Kraft and Nickelsburg 1986, 1–30.

24. Boyarin vacillates between the use of "Judaism" and "Judaeo-Christianity" to designate an overarching category that includes all Jews and all Christians until the fourth century; see, e.g., Boyarin 2003, 76, 80; 2004, 20, 23.

25. The idea that categories are our own creations even while reflecting the external social realities they are intended to organize is nicely captured by the paradoxical formulation of Boyarin (2003, 77; see also 2004, 21): "One might say that Judaism and Christianity were invented to explain the fact that there were Jews and Christians."

26. Somewhat differently from Boyarin (see the immediately preceding note), Satlow (2005) argues that second-order categories (i.e., those that are not native to a group or text under study) should be approached "in a purely utilitarian fashion" as "definitions that we create in order to select data to compare." As such, he says, "*[t]hese categories have no independent existence; they need not indicate anything 'real'*" (293, his emphasis). Satlow thus argues forcefully that scholars need not be constrained by prior definitions of terms. "Myth," for example, "is whatever we say it is in the context of a given argument and in relation to specific sets of concrete data" (295). Nonetheless, even he does not advocate "that we abandon an attempt to find a shared technical vocabulary, only that we resist the urge to define rigidly and essentially" (295).

27. Thus Satlow's (2005, 290) characterization of Smith's notion of rectification. Note that Satlow himself, however, places much greater emphasis on redescription as the aim of comparative study.

28. The fact that Jesus is also venerated in Islam makes it clear that there must be much more to it than that—notwithstanding Quispel's (1968, 92) enigmatic and rather bizarre reflections on

the implications of the possible historical influence of Jewish Christianity on Islam: "is Islam a religion of its own? Is a new religion possible after the coming of Christ?"

29. Lincoln's identification of four broad "domains"—discourse, practice, community, and institution—as "necessary parts of anything that can properly be called 'religion'" (2003, 5–8) may provide a helpful heuristic device for envisioning the various types of features that should be accounted for in such study.

Chapter Two

1. This analogy breaks down if the people in question happen to own a spectrometer. Technically, red and orange converge at a wavelength of 622 nanometers. Unaided by such an instrument, however, one could not make this extremely fine distinction. Would that the study of religion yielded such precise answers!

2. That it was in conflict with many other contemporary expressions of that faith is certain.

3. I do not attempt in this essay to differentiate between Jerusalem and Judean Christianity more broadly. The two terms are not interchangeable, to be sure, but they do overlap extensively.

4. The extent to which Paul is ignored and Acts dismissed in many reconstructions of "early Christianity" is truly extraordinary—and a clear failure of historical method. Setting aside Paul and Acts, one can construct whatever first-century church "history" one desires. See Johnson 1996, 92–102.

5. I am referring to 1 Thessalonians, 1 and 2 Corinthians, Galatians, Philippians, Philemon, and Romans, and not to the so-called Deutero-Pauline letters, 2 Thessalonians, Colossians, Ephesians, 1 and 2 Timothy, and Titus.

6. I write this as one who is sometimes criticized for being *too* skeptical of Acts.

7. My list is based in part on E. P. Sanders's description of "normal" or "common" Judaism, "what the priests and the people agreed on" (E. P. Sanders 1992, 47). Compare Morton Smith: "Down to the fall of the Temple, the normative Judaism of Palestine is that compromise of which the three principal elements are the Pentateuch, the Temple, and the 'amme ha'arez, the ordinary Jews who were not members of any sect" (M. Smith 1960–61, 356). Note that I said "common and important," not "universal and essential," which category is finally indefensible. One can find exceptions to almost any characterization of a religion.

8. Belief in the God of Israel, for example, was a more or less universal part of earliest Christianity, so that does not distinguish Jewish Christians from Gentile Christians.

9. I have argued this case in detail; see 2002, 185–200.

10. Acts 3:19-21 links Jewish repentance with the return of Christ, a point also found in Romans 11. The parallels are explored in my article; see 2002, 185–200.

11. In particular, see Hill 1992, chapters 2 and 3.

12. It is most unlikely that the Jerusalem church ever rescinded its agreement and so required Gentiles to convert to Judaism. Among other things, such a volte-face makes inconceivable Paul's continued recognition of their authority. I do not take up this issue in the present essay, however, because the focus is on the Jerusalem church's own continued observance of the law.

13. A number of scholars have argued that Stephen distinguished sharply between the well-favored David and his rebellious son Solomon, who wrongly "built a house" for God (Acts 7:46-47). Among other things, this supposed contrast ignores the author's dependence on 2 Samuel 7 and Psalm 132, both of which concern David's explicit wish to build a *temple*. Psalm 132, quoted in Acts 7:46, itself is most probably "part of the festal liturgy of the feast of the dedication of the Jerusalem Temple." (Weiser 1962, 779). To be sure, Luke would not wish to localize all worship in the temple; his attitude is probably that expressed by Paul in the Areopagus speech: "The God who made the world and everything in it, he who is Lord of heaven and earth, does not live in shrines made by human hands" (Acts 17:24). This is a sentiment that any Jew might make in a polemic against paganism and a view with which few Jews would likely disagree (see 1 Kgs 8:27). This is somewhat similar to Luke's attitude toward the law; he regards it as inherently good but also inherently insufficient. To be sure, Luke is not arguing for a return to Jewish institutions, but neither is he arguing that these same institutions are by their nature evil. (The question of Stephen's attitude toward the temple is discussed in much greater detail in Hill 1992, 69–81.)

14. See Hill 1992, chapter 3, "Stephen and the Hellenists."

15. Hurtado's tour de force should be consulted by anyone writing in the field of Christian origins.

16. Hurtado refers primarily to Mack's *A Myth of Innocence: Mark and Christian Origins* (1988).

17. The "gnat" most strained at is nonchristological Q material. Hurtado does a commendable job of exposing the weaknesses of such arguments in his chapter "Q and Early Devotion to Jesus" (2003, 217–57).

Chapter Three

1. Marcion is a radical example of this line of interpretation from the second century.

2. For a discussion of the history of the view that opposes the particularism of Judaism and the universality of Christianity see Buell and Hodge 2004, 235–42; also Park 2003, 1–20.

3. See the more detailed critique of Baur in Sumney 1990, 15–22. Other schemes that envision only two types of early Christians have also been proposed (e.g., Walter Schmithals [1971] finds Gnostics opposed in every Pauline letter), but this approach also suffers from being too simple to account for the data of Paul's letters.

4. Paul's usual term for those in his churches is "saints." This designation shows how central the adoption of a moral life was in Paul's understanding of believing in Christ.

5. It may be important to note that this use of "Christian" in 1 Peter has outsiders in view. So it is still not the usual way Christ-believers speak of one another.

6. For use of *ethnē* by both Greeks and Romans to refer to all "others" and for further discussion of the problems with the terms "Jew," "Gentile," and "Christian," see Saldarini 1998, 124–29.

7. For arguments for this view, see Furnish 1984, 35–41, who argues that all of chapters 1–9 is a single letter. For our purposes, it does not matter whether the second request for participation for the collection is a renewal of an immediately preceding request or a request sent to other churches. One's decision about this matter does not influence decisions about the identity of the opponents at Corinth.

8. For a detailed treatment of this understanding of the opponents of 2 Corinthians, see Sumney 1990; 1999, 79–133.

9. Some now argue, however, that there were no Jews in Paul's churches. See Gaston 1987, 8, where it is asserted that Antioch is the only example of a mixed congregation in this period.

10. For a detailed argument for this understanding of the teachers at Galatia, see Sumney 1999, 134–59.

11. Research on Gentiles who were attracted to Judaism in this period indicates that Jews welcomed some kinds of association in the synagogue with Gentiles that did not include full conversion to Judaism or complete adoption of the Torah as interpreted in that community. Such "righteous Gentiles" were even included in the eschatological kingdom. See, e.g., Fredricksen 2002, 244–47, and the texts she cites.

12. Questions about whether Philippians is a single letter or composed of three letters with chapter 3 itself being a letter distinct from the rest of Philippians are inconsequential for this discussion.

13. To see a conflict between Paul's rejection of teachers who demand that Gentile Christ-believers be circumcised and his kinder words in Phil 1:15-18, as does Park (2003, 72–73) is seriously to misunderstand both those texts and the issues at hand. Philippians 1:15-18 does not address the same opponents as those Paul mentions in Philippians 3 or

the view he rejects in Galatians 1. For a detailed argument for this view of the opponents of Philippians, see Sumney 1999, 160–87.

14. These privileges included the right to assemble weekly and nonparticipation in the civic cult, whether the emperor cult or the cult of the gods of the city.

15. Fredricksen (2002, 255–56) may be correct that requiring circumcision was an innovation. Those advocating circumcision in Galatia do not seem to have thought that its theological implications were many or weighty.

16. For discussion of these opponents of Paul, see Sumney 1999, 160–87.

17. Nickelsburg (2003, 174–83) similarly argues that what distinguished early Christ-believers from non–Christ-believing sects was that christology rather than Torah was what was determinative for identity. However, he does not seem to leave enough room for as much diversity as we have found among Jewish Christ-believers when he accepts the idea that all such believers "set aside most of Mosaic Torah" (175).

18. See the outline of "Jerusalem theology" in Gaston 1984, 69–70. Though his method for arriving at this understanding of that community's theology has some faults, he arrives at a plausible view.

19. Stephen G. Wilson (1995) argues that the problem with Gentile Christians attaching themselves to the Torah in the second century was most importantly viewed as a threat to Christian identity.

20. See Eisenbaum 2003, and for a fuller version of much of this material; also Eisenbaum 2004. Her evidence includes 1 Macc 12:21 and Josephus, *Ant.* 12.226, where both Spartans and Jews are said to descend from Abraham.

21. See Holmberg 1998, 421–25 for discussion of this relating of identities. He distinguishes between the concepts "identity" and "self-definition" in a way that can be helpful in understanding the relationship Paul sees between identity as a Christ-believer and as a Jew.

Chapter Four

1. Pritz is followed by Mimouni 1998, 82–86; Blanchetière 2001, 145, 183, 238–39, 521; Bauckham 2003, 162.

2. My discussion of the Ebionites has been greatly assisted by cooperation with my friend and colleague Sakari Häkkinen (cf. Häkkinen 1999; 2005). However, my understanding of the Ebionites' relation to the Nazarenes as well as to the *Book of Elchasai* and the *Pseudo-Clementines* may not always be in harmony with Häkkinen's views.

3. For the study of the indicators of Jewish-Christian profiles, see also Luomanen 2003, 265–69. The approach was first sketched in Myllykoski and Luomanen 1999.

4. Scholars have debated whether the historical Cerinthus was a Gnostic or a Jewish-Christian teacher. Ireaneus's heresiology (*Haer.* 1.26.1) pictures him more like a Gnostic, but Epiphanius (*Pan.* 28) counts him among the conservative Jewish Christians who opposed Paul. For the discussion, see Myllykoski 2005b.

5. When Epiphanius lists the dwelling places of the Ebionites, he also remarks that there are Ebionites in Cyprus where he himself was bishop (*Pan.* 30.2.7–8; 30.18.1). The Ebionite literature he used was probably derived from them.

6. If the *Pseudo-Clementines* are compared with the earlier evidence about the Ebionites, there is nothing that would necessitate their classification as Ebionite writings. Therefore, the reason why Epiphanius connected the *Ascents of James* and the *Circuits of Peter* to the Ebionites must be that they were in use in communities that were understood to be Ebionite in Epiphanius's time.

7. See Irenaeus, *Haer.* 1.26.2; 3.11.7; Hippolytus, *Haer.* 7.34.1–2; 10.22; Origen, *Cels.* 5.65; *Hom. Gen.* 3.5; *Hom. Jer.* 19.12.2; Eusebius, *Hist. eccl.* 3.27.1–6; 6.17.

8. Epiphanius also tells a story about the apostle John meeting Ebion in a bathhouse (*Pan.* 30.24.1–6). Irenaeus had presented the same legend but with Cerinthus and John as the main characters (see Irenaeus, *Haer.* 3.3.4).

9. In this chapter, the terms "Gospel of the Ebionites," "Gospel of the Nazarenes," and "Gospel of the Hebrews" appear in quotation marks because these Gospels are scholarly reconstructions. The names do not appear in ancient sources and no manuscripts of these Jewish-Christian Gospels have survived.

10. It is possible that the claim was supported by the Ebionites' own *Acts of Apostles*.

11. The passage is attributed to the Pseudo-Clementine *Basic Writing* by Jones 2005, 321. For the *Basic Writing*, see below.

12. For a detailed analysis of this passage, see Luomanen 2006.

13. I agree with Jones (1995, 3, 118–38), however, that it is to be located more specifically in *Rec.* 1.27–44.1 and 53.4–71.6. I rely on Jones's (1995) translation of *Rec.* 1.27–71 from the Syriac in what follows.

14. Jones (1995, 122), along with several others, attributes *Rec.* 2.42.5 to the *Basic Writing*. *Rec.* 1.45.1–2, for its part, belongs to the section (*Rec.* 1.44.2–53.3) that has been inserted in *Rec.* 1.27–71. However, Jones (1995, 135) argues that this was done by the editor of the *Basic Writing*.

15. *Rec.* 1.47.1–4 was probably in the *Basic Writing*. See nn. 13 and 14 above.

16. Circumcision is not clearly documented in the parallel passages of *Rec.* and *Hom.* However, in the *Adjuration*, an introductory letter to the *Homilies*, it is stated that only the

circumcised are qualified to receive Peter's sermons, and in *Rec.* 1.33.5, circumcision is depicted in a positive light. On the basis of these references, it can be assumed that circumcision was practiced in the community of the *Basic Writing* (Jones 2005, 323).

17. As we have seen above, there are grounds for assuming that the version of *Rec.* 1.27–71 (and/or the *Basic Writing*) that was used by Epiphanius's Ebionites was even more critical of temple worship and the Prophets than the version that is now available as part of *Recognitions*. My hypothesis is that Epiphanius's Ebionites had available a version of the *Basic Writing* of the *Pseudo-Clementines*, which Epiphanius called the *Circuits of Peter,* and a separate, earlier and more critical version of *Rec.* 1.27–71, entitled the *Ascents of James*. When the *Ascents* was incorporated into the *Basic Writing* (or into the *Recognitions*), it was partly rewritten to comply better with a more positive evaluation of the Prophets and Mosaic law. Another possibility is that Epiphanius's Ebionites had chosen some of the more critical parts of the writings that were earlier produced among them and elaborated these ideas in their disputes with Epiphanius.

18. It is possible that the Ebionites also possessed such companions to the *Book of Elchasai*. If worked into the text of the book itself, these additions would make a new edition, a sort of manual for purification and repentance. Cf. Jones's thesis (1996), according to which the *Book of Elchasai* is to be classified as a primitive church order.

19. In contrast to Luttikhuizen (2005, 355–56), who denies the use of the *Book of Elchasai* among these movements.

20. For the Ebionites' interpretation of the Eucharist, see Luomanen 2005b.

21. Although the term "True Prophet" in the *Pseudo-Clementines* is more typical of the *Basic Writing* than of *Rec.* 1.27–71, there is no doubt that the Christ of *Rec.* 1.27–71 fulfills a prophetic task as the prophet announced by Moses.

22. Irenaeus's main point is to criticize the Ebionites because they do not believe that God was united with humanity in Jesus. Nevertheless, his argument carries conviction only if the Ebionites' chalice contained no wine.

23. According to Irenaeus, the Ebionites' views "with respect to the Lord are similar to those of Cerinthus and Carpocrates" (Irenaeus, *Haer.* 1.26.2). As a matter of fact, the available Latin translation of Irenaeus's *Refutation* (the original Greek is lost) reads *non similiter,* which would mean that the Ebionites' christology was *not similar* to that of Cerinthus and Carpocrates. In practice, this would suggest that the Ebionites believed in the virginal conception, did not separate Christ and Jesus, etc. However, Hippolytus's *Refutation* includes an almost verbatim parallel of this passage in Greek; it reads, without the negative, *homoiōs,* "similarly" (Hippolytus, *Haer.* 7.34.1). Because this reading

also suits the context better, it is usually considered to be the original reading derived from Irenaeus's Greek *Refutation*.

24. See Bless, Fiedler and Strack, 2004, 67–68; Wilkes 1997, 57–62, 209–10, 294–96.

25. According to Acts, Philip headed to Samaria after Stephen's execution and had success there (Acts 8:4-7). Acts also refers to Cyprus as the target of the missionary work that followed Stephen's execution (Acts 11:19-20). Furthermore, in Luke's view, the religiosity of both Samaria and Cyprus was characterized by false prophets and magicians (Acts 8:4-25; Acts 13:4-12; cf. the Ebionite's use of the *Book of Elchasai*). Thus, it is possible that some Hellenists found refuge among the Samaritans or closely related groups after the execution of Stephen. In any case, it seems clear that Epiphanius's Ebionites and *Rec.* 1.27–71 found something to build on in the traditions connected to Stephen. Stephen's "proclamation," as it is described in Acts, probably found acceptance among Hellenistic Jewish Christians who criticized the temple and sacrifices and saw Jesus mainly as a prophet predicted by Moses. See further Luomanen 2005b.

26. Not only Epiphanius's Ebionites but also modern scholars have suggested that "poor" as the self-designation might go back to the Jerusalem community. If such is the case, there is no need to restrict this term only to the "Hebrews" of the early church. Even the Hellenists of the Jerusalem community were surely bilingual enough to understand the meaning of the Hebrew word *ʾebyon*. Moreover, we know that Epiphanius's Ebionites did perceive of themselves as "Ebionites" although they spoke Greek and used Greek scriptures.

27. This section summarizes the main points of the detailed analysis of *Pan.* 29 in Luomanen 2005a. Compared to the earlier article, this section also goes further in illuminating the process from Epiphanius's point of view.

28. The term "social identity approach" is an umbrella term that nowadays refers to Henri Tajfel and John Turner's *social identity theory*, mainly developed in the 1970s in Bristol, to Turner's *self-categorization theory* developed in the mid-1980s, as well as to later adaptations of these theories. For an introduction, see Tajfel 1980; Hogg and Abrams 1988; 1999.

29. Iessaeans as the title of the first Christians is not discussed by other church fathers. In Syriac, however, Christians are called not only *natsraye*, but also *yeshuaye*, and a cognate title is to be found in Arabic as well. Therefore, it is possible that Epiphanius knew these titles from Syriac traditions and connected them to the first Christians because, being Semitic, they had a ring of authenticity.

30. For the term Nazarene in general, see Goranson 1992, 1049–50; Schaeder 1967, 874–79.

31. For Jerome's life, see Kelly 1975.

32. The present standard view of the Jewish-Christian Gospels distinguishes three different Gospels: The Greek "Gospel of the Hebrews" that was known to Alexandrian writers,

the Semitic "Gospel of the Nazarenes," and the Greek "Gospel of the Ebionites" that was quoted by Epiphanius (see Vielhauer and Strecker 1991; Klijn 1992). For the criticism of this reconstruction, see Mimouni 1998, 209–11, 215–16; Petersen 1994, 29–31, 39–41. I have dealt with the problems of the standard view in Luomanen 2003, and more extensively in Luomanen 2006 and Luomanen (forthcoming), which also presents an alternative reconstruction.

33. For the conflict between Augustine and Jerome, see Kelly 1975, 217–20, 263–72; and Hennings 1994, 274–91.

34. Different versions of the prayer are discussed by P. Schäfer (1975, 57–61), who suggests that *notsrim* were included in the prayer in localities where the "Nazarenes" had become a problem. In most cases, the "benediction" refers only to the *minim*.

35. Klijn (1972, 253–54) thinks that the Nazarenes' exposition attacks only the Jewish leaders but it is hard to find such a distinction in the texts.

36. The *Didascalia Apostolorum* is usually dated to the third century. That it was still in use in Syria in the latter half of the fourth century is clear from the fact that Epiphanius found it in the hands of the Audians, who were Syrian Christians and, in his view, heretics (*Pan.* 70.10.1–4; cf. *DA* XXI).

37. See *DA* II, IV, XIX, XXVI. For *DA*'s use of the term *deuterōsis* see Fonrobert 2001, 495–99.

38. Irenaeus's heresiology is probably based on Justin Martyr's (lost) *Syntagma* (written before 150 CE). However, most scholars think that Justin's heresiology did not mention Ebionites because Justin's other works show that he did not regard them as clearly heretical (Häkkinen 2005, 248–49). The source of Irenaeus's information about the Ebionites is thus unknown.

Chapter Five

1. While the two-source hypothesis has been the dominant scholarly position for almost 150 years, a small number of scholars advocate alternative views that eliminate any need for this hypothetical source; so, e.g., Farmer 1977; Farrer 1955; more recently Goulder 1989; Goodacre 1996. For replies, see Kloppenborg Verbin 2000, 39–41; and Tuckett 1996a, 16–31.

2. The most notable reconstruction of Q is that of the International Q Project (Robinson, Hoffmann and Kloppenborg 2000); see also Mack 1993; Robinson 2002. For the purposes of the following discussion, I will assume an original Q comprising the following texts: Q 3:7-9, 16-17; 4:1-13; 6:20-23, 27-49; 7:1-10, 18-35; 9:57-62; 10:2-16, 21-24; 11:2-4, 9-35,

39-44, 46-52; 12:2-12, 22-31, 33-34, 39-40, 42-46, 51-59; 13:18-21, 24-30, 34-35; 14:11, 16-24, 26-27, 34-35; 15:4-10; 16:13, 16-18; 17:1-4, 6, 20-21, 23-37; 19:12-13, 15-26, 28-30. My subsequent quotations of Q texts will be based on—but not necessarily identical to—the reconstructed text of Q given in Robinson 2002.

3. It must be stressed that Kloppenborg's analysis is redaction-critical and describes the literary development of Q as a document, not the oral prehistory of the units that comprise Q; nor is it based on tradition-historical speculations about which concepts are "primitive" and which are "developed." This approach is what sets Kloppenborg's work to a large degree apart from that of alternative hypotheses such as those of Siegfried Schultz (1972) or, more recently, of Dale Allison (1997), which proceed on tradition-historical assumptions, rather than strictly literary analysis.

4. For a nuanced introductory discussion of the complexities of ethnicity and its relationship to culture, see Spickard and Burroughs 2000; see also Eller 1999, esp. 47–48.

5. This essentially monothetic type of classification, with specific reference to the issue of Jewish Christianity, is undertaken effectively and intelligently by Stephen Wilson (quoting Lloyd Gaston): "what elements are the minimum necessary to justify the label? Clearly there must be 'enough relation to Torah as covenant and commandments' to justify the label 'Jew' and 'enough relation to Jesus' to justify the label 'Christian'" (S. G. Wilson 1995, 143). In spite of the elegance of this formula, the use of Torah as the single index of Judaism is too restrictive, and at the practical level, there is the difficulty of determining just how much is "enough."

6. As opposed to *biological* classification, Smith's main analogy, where such inquiry is not an option and would probably not be valid even if it were an option.

7. In fact, Smith's process assumes the validity of self-identification as the key to identifying members of a grouping, from which one then defines the (polythetic) characteristics of the group. In other words, to define Judaism in terms of a set of common (but not mandatory) characteristics of Jews requires that one know who the Jews are, so that their characteristics can be enumerated. Smith makes this initial identification by focusing on ancient Jewish graveyards; and burial in such a location is of course an implicit claim to belonging. In the case of ethnic identity, self-perception and claims to belonging are not irrelevant. In fact, this is how ethnic identity tends to be measured in modern census surveys—individuals are *asked* to indicate their ethnic identity. Ethnicity is not "race," and it is not an objective or brute fact. On the other hand, it *is* a question of (perceptions of) one's ancestry and so is not entirely voluntary. Nonetheless, the litmus test of self-identification can be applied to questions of ethnicity just as much as to questions of ideological commitments, ideals, and the like. Indeed, self-claims to particular identities will often involve, imply, or be based on a considerable overlap between *ethnos* and *ethos*.

8. As is well known, *Christianos* ("Christian") occurs only three times in the entire New Testament, and only in very late documents: Acts 11:26; 26:28; 1 Pet 4:16. *Christianismos*

("Christian-ism" = "Christianity") never occurs; apparently its earliest usage is Ignatius (*Romans* 3:3; *Magnesians* 10:1, 3a, b; Philadelphians 6:1; cf. *Martyrdom of Polycarp* 10:1). Thus, terminologically speaking, inquiring into whether Q, or Paul's letters, or Mark is a *Christian* text is indeed anachronistic. As for "Jew" (*Ioudaios*) and "Judaism" (*Ioudaïsmos*), while the terms are attested in the first century (not least among Christian sources, including Paul's two references to "Judaism" in Gal 1:13-14, the only uses of that particular term in the entire New Testament), Smith notes that in a sample of 944 Jewish funerary inscriptions from antiquity, ranging from Galilee to Egypt to Rome, only *seven* called the deceased a "Jew," and only *one* referred to "Judaism" (Smith 1988, 15). In addition, the (usually unintended) implications of such terminology are also problematic. Even when an ancient author *does* use the term "Christianity" (e.g., Ignatius) or "Judaism" (e.g., Paul), the set of beliefs that constitute that religious discourse are almost certainly *not* those that the terms call to mind for us modern readers. Thus it is unquestionable that Ignatius is a Christian; but this can hardly be taken to mean that Ignatius believed and practiced what modern Christians believe and practice.

9. John the Baptist is fairly prominent in Q (the Baptist material all derives from Q's second stage), and so some of the sayings in the document are attributed to John (Q 3:7-9, 16-17; 7:19). Many more verses, however, are devoted to *Jesus'* words *about* John than are devoted to John's own words: Q 7:22-35; 16:16. The inclusion of John's words in 3:7-9, 16-17 is actually justified in Q by their applicability to Jesus, which is explored in Q 7:18-23. John's prominence in Q, therefore, is a function not of any independent importance he has for the composers of Q but of his connections to Jesus.

10. I am not listing here simple references in Q to God as Father, such as Q 11:2, since in such texts the role of God as Father is not exclusive to Jesus and so does not in any way imply that Jesus is uniquely or distinctively the Son of God.

11. This trait once again provides an example of how polythetic classification does, and does not, work. Henotheistic reverence for the God of Israel is not a feature that is distinctive or unique to the Jesus movements or to Christianity, as it is shared with most forms of Judaism, as well as Islam. But as it *is* a feature that appears with great frequency among Christian texts and groups, it may be considered one among several of the indices of Christian identity. Moreover, it should be noted once again that this attribute is not *necessary* to classify a document, individual, or set of ideas as Christian: some Christians (e.g., Marcion) *denied* that the God of Israel was the true God and that worship should be directed to him and him alone.

12. Conversely, in the canonical Gospels (some more than others), we are presented with various *types* of people who listened to Jesus, as well as those who failed to listen to him. The

treatment of the disciples in the Gospel of Mark (see especially Weeden 1979) and the Gospel of John (see Brown 1979, 71–88) seems to reflect polemic or discussion about followers of Jesus distinct from the author's groups. Likewise, Mark 4:1-20 seems to be an extended characterization of different ways of being "Christian." In Acts of the Apostles, the author is especially inclusive, appearing to draw together into a unified institution various figures representing all kinds of different strains of Jesus people: Peter, Simon Magus, James, Paul, Apollos, and so on. By contrast, Q 6:46 is simply an exhortation to implement, rather than simply listen to, the teacher's words (see especially Kloppenborg 1987, 185–87) and should be understood to refer not to distinct "outsider" groups but to the immediate audience of Q itself. The same is true of Q 9:57.

13. I have not considered here, for instance, interest in circumcision (absent from Q). The issue of dining practices may or may not be present in Q, though it does seem to be another repeated feature of the various Jesus people. The way I have counted each index, too, is open to dispute and revision. For instance, should concern for purity regulations, dietary rules, and Sabbath observance be treated as a single point, as I have here, or as three separate points? Attempting to define and defend just what the indices for the Jesus movements are would require its own article, possibly its own book. All of this indicates, of course, the differences between the approach I have taken here, and that taken by Smith (1988). Smith is starting with a data set that he knows is "Jewish" (grave inscriptions) and using it to flesh out what the multiple definitional features of Judaism might be. I am working in the *opposite* direction, assuming that I know what the main definitional features of the Jesus movements might be (!), in order to determine whether a given data set (Q) qualifies as belonging to one of those movements. The circularity involved in either procedure is inevitable and is only really problematic if one wishes to propose radically *different* criteria for "Christian" identity.

14. The Jewish identity of the Q people is also asserted, for similar reasons, by Allison 1997, 53; Arnal 2001, 247 n. 13, 256 n. 61; Bultmann 1994[1913], 32; Horsley and Draper 1999, 95; Kloppenborg Verbin 2000, 199, 256; Tuckett 1996a, 399, 402–3, and many others. Kloppenborg (2000, 256) also notes that Q uses Aramaic words without translation or explanation ("Gehenna" in Q 12:5 and "mammon" in 16:13; both texts are *probably* from the first layer of Q). Of course the use or knowledge of Aramaic need not indicate Jewish identity.

15. The finality with which $Q^{(2)}$ asserts judgment against this generation is debated. For the view that Q's rhetoric indicates that its purveyors have abandoned all hope for Israel's repentence, see, e.g., Lührmann 1969, 47–48; and Kloppenborg 1987, 148, 167–68. For the

opposing view that Q still sees itself as involved with Israel, see, e.g., Horsley 1995b, 38; and Steck 1967, 286.

16. I say this without prejudice to the issue of cultural differences between Judea and Galilee and the differences that may have existed in religious practice. The fact that Q recognizes the people of Jersualem as among the unrepentant "generation" they castigate is an indication that *they*, at least, view both Judeans and Galileans as belonging to the same *ethnos*, whose behavior is contrasted to "the Gentiles." Note, too, that Samaritans identified themselves as "Israel," and most definitely not as *Ioudaioi* ("Judeans"/"Jews"). The Samaritans, however, associated their identity with Mount Gerizim, not Jerusalem.

17. Paul, that is, describes both how the Gentiles come to the Jesus movements (i.e., through his own elaborate missionary efforts) and provides a theological rationale for how this occurs, that is, by virtue of being "in Christ." Q addresses neither problem. A similar observation is made by Risto Uro (1987, 214): "It is true that the saying [Q 13:28-29] says nothing of the way in which Gentiles reach salvation. There is no reference to missionary efforts."

18. The sting of this saying is much diminished if we assume a positive judgment on Tyre and Sidon. Its threatening character is predicated on the assumption of an emphatically negative judgment against these cities.

19. Note, too, that all of these "positive" references to Gentiles occur in the second layer of the text, Q^2. If the Q people were, at this point (and presumably as a function of the rejection of their message, and their consequent invocation of judgment against "this generation"), engaged in a mission to the Gentiles, this would imply that their attitude toward ethnic belonging had changed radically since the composition of Q^1. Such a shift is in itself not implausible, but becomes so when we consider the tertiary and final stage of Q's development (Q^3), which assumes and/or defends the import of temple and Torah. We would thus be forced, with Koester (1990, 170–71), to imagine a pendulum-like movement from exclusion of Gentiles, to inclusion, to reassertion and defense of Jewish religious norms. This scenario is possible, but it seems much simpler to assume a consistent attitude toward Gentiles throughout.

20. At the Q^1 stage, there may also be a reference to God as "Most High" (*hypsistos*), a standard Jewish designation. This term occurs in Luke 6:35; Matthew, however, has "Father" here, and most reconstructions prefer this wording as original. It is striking that at the secondary stage of Q's redaction, references to God as "Father" have ceased to be universal; now God is father *only* of Jesus (see $Q^{[2]}$ 10:21-22).

21. This is due only in part to the retention in the secondary redaction of Q of the materials from the document's first layer; the materials added at the Q^2 stage also in themselves manifest those features of "Jewish" religiosity that appear in Q^1.

Chapter Six

1. For one (disputed) view of Matthew's Gospel as opposing Paul and his law-free gospel, see Sim 1998, 165–213.

2. Sanders (1994, 45–303) focuses on practices of common people and the beliefs underlying them (3), particularly emphasizing the temple and related activities and personnel, but also identifying law observance, the synagogue, theocentric theology, future hope, and covenantal nomism. For critique, see Hengel and Deines 1995, 53.

3. Mimouni (1992, 164) suggests four different definitions determined by observance, christology, a system of doctrines, and a system of concepts. This fourfold scheme is less satisfactory since the last two are difficult to distinguish and contain christological claims (the second category).

4. Longenecker (1970) explores Jewish Christianity within the conceptual and linguistic framework of Judaism and geographically centered in Jerusalem (3–4), emphasizing christology (25) and the conviction that Jesus is the Messiah. For critique of Daniélou's approach, see Kraft 1972.

5. Bauckham (1995, 471–75) does not share Brown's conviction that Jewish Christians were interested in converting Gentiles.

6. This element of the definition is problematic for the debate, since Saldarini (along with most Matthean scholars) clearly locates Matthew's Gospel after the destruction of the temple in 70 CE.

7. I follow Hagner 2003 throughout; see also Hagner 2004.

8. Hagner finishes his article by rightly arguing that his conclusion about the "Christian" nature of Matthew does not automatically render this reading anti-Semitic.

9. Saldarini chooses the term "group" rather than "community" because the latter suggests "separation from and independence from Judaism" (1994, 87).

10. Several observations cast doubt on the usefulness of Luomanen's analysis: (1) Setting tension and schism over against new ideas can be a false antithesis when new ideas can cause tensions. (2) Saldarini's discussion of Matthew's christology shows that it remains well within Jewish boundaries. (3) The term "liberal" does not seem an accurate description of Matthew's interpretation of the law.

11. Hagner (2003, 196–97) appeals to Brown's fourfold scheme (1983) and agrees with Brown in locating Matthew in the second division (no circumcision for Gentile converts but observance of some purity laws; Brown is not explicit on circumcision for Jewish Christians).

12. Hare tries to claim 18:20 and 28:20 as further support for worship of Jesus but neither text explicitly endorses worship. Rather they affirm Jesus' presence with disciples.

13. Matthew's contemporary, the author of *4 Ezra*, emphasizes the giving of the law but locates it in the larger history of God's dealings with the people, including David and the "current" distress of Babylonian exile (*4 Ezra* 3:1-36; 7:17-25). Similarly *2 Baruch* upholds the gift and demand of the law but in the context of previous events such as Adam's sin and the coming of prophets and holy men (48:42-47; 84:1—85:3).

14. I readily recognize that Hagner does not always elaborate these points so, to be fair, my critique may not address the exact emphasis that he has in mind.

15. For example, 1QS 9:11-12; *Pss. Sol. 17*; *1 En.* 46–48; 52:4; *2 Bar.* 29–30; 39:7—40:2; 72:2; *4 Ezra* 7:26-29; 11:1—12:3, 31-35.

16. Matthew has inclusive (ch. 2, magi; 12:18-21; 15:21-28; 28:18-20) and hostile (5:46-47; 6:7-8, 31-32; 10:17-22; 24:4-14) references. Mission to Gentiles is endorsed (28:18-20, contra Sim, 1998, 215–56), and Gentiles are included in the judgment in 25:31-46.

17. Graham N. Stanton (1992b) discusses accusations of Jesus as magician and deceiver, and the contesting of claims to the title Son of David, but does not equate any of these with apostasy.

Chapter Seven

1. For Baur's views on John, see Kümmel 1972, 137–38. For a short history of the study of John's presentation of the Jews, see Hakola 2005a, 5–10.

2. On Bultmann's great significance for Johannine studies, see Ashton 1991, 44–66.

3. The second and revised edition of the book appeared in 1979. My references are to the third edition (2003), which is a reprint of the second edition with the exception that five excursuses found in the second edition are missing. The page numbers in the third edition do not correspond to earlier editions.

4. In particular, John's alleged connection to the *Birkat ha-Minim* is highly disputed. For the reasons why this prayer should not be linked with John, see Hakola 2005a, 45–55.

5. Martyn's influence is clearly seen in most articles in a recent collection on John and anti-Judaism (Bieringer et al 2001). For example, R. Alan Culpepper (2001, 69) notes that "specific points [in Martyn's model] continue to be debated, [but] it is widely agreed that the Fourth Gospel reflects an intense and apparently violent conflict between Jews and Johannine Christians."

6. Neusner 1988, 76–121; Hezser 1997, 360–68; Cohen 1999a, 961–71. Many other rabbinic scholars (e.g., Martin Goodman, Lee I. Levine, Hayim Lapin, Günter Stemberger) have also made observations pointing in the same direction. For the full discussion with references, see Hakola 2005a, 55–65.

7. The Scripture quotations contained in this chapter, unless otherwise noted, are from the New Revised Standard Version Bible.

8. For a different view, see Asiedu-Peprah 2001, 231. Asiedu-Peprah says that the Johannine Sabbath stories would have functioned as "a means of persuasion and an appeal to the opponents of the Johannine Christians" to acknowledge the christological claims made in these stories.

9. For dualisms in John and in 1QS, see von Wahlde 2001, 418–44; Hakola 2005a, 197–210.

10. For example, Esler (1994, 70–91) has described both the Johannine community and the Qumran group as "introversionist sects."

11. For the Hellenists, see Räisänen 1992, 149–202.

12. For a different view, see Casey 1991, 23–40. Casey sees christology as the main indicator of how the Johannine Christians had drifted away from Jewishness and adapted "Gentile self-identity." For Casey (1991, 38), this Gentile self-identification is "a necessary cause of belief in the deity of Jesus, a belief which could not be held as long as the Christian community was primarily Jewish."

13. For a general introduction to these groups, see Wilson 1995, 143–59. For a detailed presentation of the evidence concerning Ebionites and Nazareans, see Petri Luomanen's chapter in this book.

14. The Johannine narrator here uses slightly different expressions in speaking of believers among the Jews. In v. 30, he says that as Jesus spoke, "many believed in him" (the verb *pisteuein* with the preposition *eis*); in v. 31, he notes that Jesus was speaking to the Jews "who had believed him" (my translation; the verb *pisteuein* with the dative). These different expressions are sometimes taken to mean that v. 30 would refer to those whose faith is deeper than the faith of those mentioned in v. 31 (e.g., Moloney 1996, 103). John Painter (1993, 385–88) has shown that both these expressions are used interchangeably for partial and authentic faith in the Gospel; so too Brown 1979, 76. There is thus no reason to think that the narrator is speaking of two different groups.

15. For Hellenistic material, see Johnson 1989, 432. For Jewish and Christian material see Hakola 2005a, 155.

16. John's believing Jews are connected to Paul's opponents by Dodd 1968, 45-46; Dozeman 1980, 346–52.

17. The term appears in *b. Yoma* 4a, but this passage does not support the view that Jewish legal authorities generally used the self-expression "the disciples of Moses" in the first century C.E. The discussion connected with the Day of Atonement explains the appearance

of the term in this passage, but this discussion is unlikely to reflect first-century practice. See Hakola 2005a, 174 n. 117.

18. Thus Brown 1979, 75–76; Dunderberg 2006, 187–98. Dunderberg compares "the beloved disciple" in John to the presentation of James as Jesus' beloved brother in Jewish-Christian traditions. Dunderberg concludes that "the Beloved Disciple could have been part of the author's debate with Jewish Christians, in whose traditions James was described as the beloved one of Jesus. If so, the author not only denigrated the brothers of Jesus and Jewish Christians, but also replaced their icon, James, with another, anonymous disciple" (p. 202).

19. Cohen 1999b, 54; see also Rajak 2001, 346–48. Rajak emphasizes the "activity on the boundaries," which speaks for the openness of Jewish Diaspora communities.

20. Claudia Setzer (1994, 167) has noted that in early Christian sources Jews are every now and then presented as fair-minded and tolerant, even though the negative portrayals of Jews are dominant. Setzer asks whether the trend to depict Jews in more positive terms "is not underrepresented in ancient literature." The favorable mentions of Jews would not have served early Christian communities, because if Jews are sensible and fair-minded, their refusal of Christianity becomes more problematic than if they are hard-hearted, vicious, and ignorant of their own scripture (p. 168).

21. For different definitions of Jewish Christianity, see Paget 1999, 733-742.

22. For an attempt to connect later traditions concerning the Nazarenes to the Johannine Christianity, see de Boer 1998, 243. It is, however, uncertain whether we can trace later traditions in rabbinic sources or in church fathers back to the first-century situation. For example, the word *notsrim*, which may in some talmudic passages refer to Christians in general or to Jewish Christians, appears only in the later Babylonian sources but not in the Palestinian ones. The passages where this term appears most likely stem from a later period, when Christianity was a notable factor in the society where these passages were formulated. See Hakola 2005a, 46–47 n. 26. It is also uncertain whether we can reconstruct a clearly defined group of Nazarenes on the basis of the references made by Epiphanius and Jerome. Petri Luomanen (2005a, 309) has shown that there is "no historically reliable evidence which would justify an assumption that, among Syriac/Aramaic-speaking Christians, there would have been a more or less organized faction with borders defined by characteristically 'Nazarene' doctrines, practices or self-understanding, distinct from other Syriac/Aramaic-speaking Christians." See also Luomanen's chapter in this volume.

23. For Jewish-Christian Gospels, see Klijn 1992, 27–43. The so-called *Gospel according to the Ebionites* shows a harmonizing tendency similar to Tatian's *Diatessaron*. But where Tatian made

extensive use of John in his Gospel harmony, these Jewish Christians composed their Gospel harmony with the help of the three Synoptic Gospels alone (p. 38). The *Gospel of the Nazarenes,* however, is usually seen to be somehow connected to the Gospel of Matthew (p. 42).

24. See also S. G. Wilson 1995, 76: "The term has shifted decisively from a local to a universal plane of meaning. *Hoi Ioudaioi* have become the Jews in general."

25. I have elsewhere suggested that the portrayal of Jesus as an innocent victim at the hands of the Jewish rulers validated the social identity of the Johannine Christians, who had abandoned basic markers of Jewish identity and marginalized themselves in relation to other Jews. See Hakola 2005b, 140–63.

Chapter Eight

1. Throughout this study I shall refer to James as the author of the letter without intending to take a position on the identity of this James. I use the name James as author here simply as an easy reference tool, since the writer names himself in this way (1:1). In a similar way the reference that is used throughout this study to "James's community" designates the recipients or the hearers/readers who receive this Letter of James, not the community from which James writes this letter.

2. The question of the authorship of this letter is one that is much discussed in scholarship, and there is no unanimity on the issue. For a discussion of the problem, see Hartin 2003, 16–25.

3. James's use of this expression is very different from the way in which 1 Pet 1:1 uses the term, "To the exiles of the Dispersion . . ." In 1 Peter the word "Dispersion" is used in a metaphorical sense; the author is addressing communities that see their true homeland as heaven. Here on earth they are living outside their true homeland, and consequently the term "Dispersion" refers in a metaphorical sense to their lives here on earth as they look forward to attaining their true homeland in heaven.

4. For more detailed discussion of this topic see Hartin 1999, 78–85 and 2003, 111–16.

5. Malina (1993, 168–69) gives an excellent graphic illustration of the spatial arrangement of the profane and the sacred.

6. See also Perdue 1990, 23–27.

7. As Wall (1997, 19) states: "In my view, wisdom is the orienting concern of this book by which all else is understood: after all, James refers to wisdom as the divine 'word of truth,' which is graciously provided to a faithful people to make sense of their trials and to guide them through those trials in order to insure their future destiny of a perfected human existence."

8. Schnabel (1985, 162–63) writes: "The identification of law and wisdom is to be found in all circles: among hasidic groups (Enoch), in the Pharisaic fellowships (Bar[?], PsSal,

4Ezr, ApcBar), and in the Alexandrian diaspora (EpArist, Sib 3, SapSal, 4Macc). The identification is upheld in the wisdom tradition (SapSal) in apologetic-philosophical treatises
(EpArist, 4Macc), in hymnic compositions (PsSal), in parenetic books (Enoch), as well as
in the apocalyptic tradition (Enoch, Sib 3, 4Ezr, ApcBar). The identification is expressed
both in Hebrew/Aramaic (Bar, Enoch, PsSal, 4Ezr, ApcBar) and in Greek (EpArist, Sib 3,
SapSal, 4Macc)."

9. Note that Ps 19:7-8 also speaks of the Torah as being perfect: "The law of the Lord
is perfect, reviving the soul." In the LXX this is Ps 18:8-9, where the Greek word used for
"perfect" is *amōmos*.

10. See also Fabris 1977, 41–42.

11. Dibelius (1975, 116–20) gives a very detailed examination of the phrase "the perfect law,
the law of liberty" (Jas 1:25) and provides many examples from the world of the Stoics to illustrate their understanding of the freedom that is brought by the law. Dibelius (1975, 116–17)
sums up their position as follows: "But insofar as the true wisdom consists in obedience to that
cosmic Reason which governs all and the neglect of which can only lead men into foolish and
destructive conflicts, the ethical preaching of Stoicism (especially popular Stoicism) indeed demands an obedience which brings with it the state of utmost inner freedom."

12. Other scholars in more recent times, however, have argued strongly for a connection
with the world of Stoic thought. See especially Matt Jackson-McCabe, *Logos and Law in the
Letter of James* (2001).

13. Johnson states: "Beginning with some clues derived from the use of Leviticus 19 in
Pseudo-Phocylides, I have shown that in addition to the direct citation from Lev 19:18b in
2:8, the letter of James contains certainly four, and possibly six further verbal or thematic
allusions to Lev. 19:12-18. Arranged according to the order of Leviticus, and with the least
likely allusions marked with asterisks, they are:

    (1) Lev 19:12 .... James 5:12
    (2) Lev 19:13 .... James 5:4
    (3) Lev 19:15 .... James 2:1, 9
    (4) Lev 19:16 .... James 4:11
    (5) Lev 19:17b .... James 5:20*
    (6) Lev 19:18a .... James 5:9*
    (7) Lev 19:18b .... James 2:8

(Johnson, 1982, 399)

14. See Johnson's whole article, "Friendship with the World/Friendship with God: A
Study of Discipleship in James" (1985). Leo G. Perdue, however, sees things differently.

He does consider James as constituting a "withdrawal group": "By withdrawal within this *Gemeinschaft*, a different social reality is constructed and efforts are undertaken to protect it from the threat of outside worlds. A good example of this sectarian position is the Epistle of James" (1990, 26).

15. Johnson (1995, 164) makes the insightful distinction that one must understand the theology of James as grounded on "*theological* rather than *Christological* principles." For a statistical list of references to God and Jesus in the Letter of James, see Hartin 2003, 31–32.

16. Robbins says: "In previous research, verbal similarities among written versions of stories and sayings regularly have been discussed in terms of 'dependence' on written or oral sources. This terminology emerges from a presupposition that written performance of the material was guided by copying an oral or written antecedent. This language and this perception impose goals and procedures on the writers which are inaccurate, since, even if the writer recently had heard or was looking at a version of the story, the version existed in the eye, ear, and mind of the writer as a 'recitation' that should be performed anew rather than a verbal text that should be copied verbatim" (1991, 167).

Chapter Nine

1. For an overview of schemes of structuring the Apocalypse, see Humphrey 1995, 84–94. My description of Revelation has been kept as nearly neutral as possible in order to provide a foundation for the discussion of classification that follows, but it is clear in the history of the interpretation of the Apocalypse that the understanding of what it is or where it sits within a taxonomy of religions deeply conditions what interpreters understand it to be about.

2. For a fuller argument for this position, see Marshall 2001, 88–97. All translations of Revelation are taken from the RSV.

3. It should also be noted that some scholars argue that Jewish Christianity is an inappropriate description of the Apocalypse inasmuch as they consider it fully Christian. Heinrich Kraft's commentary insists that the category Jewish Christian is actually appropriate for John's opponents. According to Kraft (1974, 61), "John is not interested in the Jews, but rather in the Christians. A Synagogue of Satan is in his view a Jewish Christian group" [*Johannes ist nicht an den Juden, sondern an den Christen interessiert. Eine Satanssynagoge in seinem Sinn is eine jüdische-christliche Gruppe*]. More radically, Robert K. MacKenzie and the present author have presented diametrically opposed understandings of the Apocalypse: Mackenzie (1997) argues that the category Jewish Christianity is incorrect because the author of the Apocalypse must be understood as a Gentile and a Christian, while I have

argued that the category Jewish Christianity is incorrect because the author of the Apoca-lypse must be understood as Jewish and not Christian (Marshall 2001).

4. Sean Kelley's *Racializing Jesus* (2002, 64–88) offers an essential critical history of the racialist implications of Hegelian historiography on the Tübingen School.

5. See Engels 1957b, 173 [1882, 300]: "Dogma developed, on the one hand, in connec-tion with the legend of Jesus which was then taking shape, and, on the other hand, in the struggle between Jewish Christians and Pagan Christians" [*Die Dogmatik entwickelte sich einerseits in Verbindung mit der sich bildenden evangelischen Legende von Jesus, anderseits im Kampfe zwischen Judenchristen und Heidenchristen*].

6. Beyond the authors discussed directly below, note also Beasley-Murray 1974, 35–37; H. Kraft 1974, 15; Kümmel and Feine 1975, 472; Lohmeyer 1953, 195, 199, 203; Lohse 1979, 5; Schüssler Fiorenza 1991; 1986, 194–95; Swete 1911, cxxv.

7. For accounts, see Barton 1898, 776; Bousset 1899, col. 194; Marshall 1997, 473–83.

8. According to Völter, Cerinthus, during the reign of Vespasian, interpolated 5:10b; 11:16, 18; 12–13; 14:9-12; 15–16; and 19:11—21:8—with the exception of 12:11; 13:8; 14:10; 15:4; 16:15, 19b; and 19:13b.

9. Völter is clear in several instances (e.g., 1882, 32) that Jewish Christianity is distinct from both Judaism and Christianity.

10. According to Vischer (1886), Christian additions to the Jewish source consisted of all or most of Revelation 1–3; 5:6, 8, 9-14; 6:1, 16; 7:9-17; 9:11; 11:8, 15; 12:11, 17; 13:8, 9-10; 14.:1-5, 10, 12-13; 15:3; 16:15, 16; 17:6, 14; 18:20; 19:7, 9-10, 11, 13; 20:4, 6; 21:5-8, 9, 14, 22, 12, 27; and 22:1, 3, as well as several individual words.

11. Bousset 1906; Erbes 1891; Stade and Holtzmann 1887; Rauch 1894; Sabatier 1888; Schmidt 1891; Schoen 1887; Spitta 1889; Vischer 1886; Völter 1882; 1885; 1886; 1893; 1911 [1904]; Weizsäcker 1886; Wellhausen 1899; 1907; Weyland 1888.

12. Paul Schmidt (1891, 1) writes specifically against the notion of a Jewish Chris-tian author, conscious that by 1891 what he called the "cult" of the Tübingen School had long past, implying that its generative concept of Jewish Christianity should also recede.

13. Moses Stuart (1845, 221) used the term to describe John before Charles took it up.

14. Charles 1920, 1:xxi. The preceding pages are a preface and an annotated table of contents. The quotation is the first sentence of the introduction.

15. Beyond this, Charles also uses the term "Jewish Christian" to describe individual (and hypothetical) sources used by the Jewish Christian author of the Apocalypse. Oddly enough, Charles also describes the Jewish Christian author as using "Christian" sources.

16. Concerning Paul himself, see Rom 11:1; Phil 3:5-6; 2 Cor 11:22. Concerning Judaism, see Rom 3:1-2, 31; 9:4; 11:26; Gal 6:16. For arguments concerning the role of these passages in Paul's relations within Judaism, see Gaston 1987; Gager 2000.

17. It should be noted that Flusser is a prominent Jewish scholar, but that does not mean his view of Christian origins is unconditioned by Christianity's own narrative of self.

18. For a fuller account of what follows, see Marshall 2001, on which this section largely relies.

19. These claims depend on dating Acts, the *Didache*, and 1 Peter later than 70 or 96 CE.

20. I have in mind here the repeated positive presentation of Roman officials in Acts and the clear acceptance, and implicit endorsement, of imperial rule in 1 Pet 2:13-17.

21. "Christianity" (*christianismos* [Greek], *christianismus* [Latin]) is quite certainly a later term than "Christian." See Ignatius *Rom.* 3:3; *Phld.* 6:1; *Magn.* 10:1, 3; and *Mart. Pol.* 10:1 for the earliest instances. On the origins of *christianos,* see Peterson 1959; 1946, 355–72; Bickermann 1949, 109–24; Moreau 1949, 190–92; Mattingly 1958, 26–7; Downey 1961; Grundmann et al. 1974, 493–581; Lifshitz 1962, 65–70; and Justin Taylor 1994, 75–94. Most of these works accept the narrative of Acts at near face value, though theological and supersessionist motivations are often clear.

22. The *Oxford English Dictionary* defines "polyadic" as "[i]nvolving many (usu., three or more) quantities or elements. Hence *polyadically* adv.; *polyadicity*, the state or quality of being polyadic." It credits the first instance of the term of to C. S. Peirce in *Monist* XVI. 512 (1906): "A Predicate is either non-relative, or a monad, as is 'black'; or it is a dyadic relative, or dyad, such as 'kills', or it is a polyadic relative, such as 'gives.'"

23. This proposal for polythetic classification of religions is actually a rather wooden modification of John J. Collins's proposal for a strategy for evaluating whether individual texts should be considered members of the apocalyptic genre. Collins's original statement was as follows: "The presence or absence of a title cannot, in any case, be regarded as a decisive criterion for identifying a genre. Rather, what is at issue is whether a group of texts share a significant cluster of traits that distinguish them from other works" (1992, 25). It is interesting that, without reference to Smith or to the taxonomic theory upon which Smith drew, Collins proposed a very robust polythetic scheme for classifying literary genre with reference to the apocalyptic genre.

24. MacKenzie's (1997, 42) declaration that John displays "no interest in matters of diet and purity" seems without foundation.

25. Emphasized helpfully by Painchaud 2003, 373.28.

26. See M. Murray 2004, 73–80, for the view that John is arguing against Gentile judaizing.

27. Though see Himmelfarb (2006, 135-143), who argues that Revelation is Jewish and specifically sectarian.

28. See Rev 7:9; 10:11; 14:6. The movement that John portrays is from an initial division of Jews and Gentiles to a final division of those who dwell on earth and those who dwell in heaven. There is no indication of Jews being condemned at the end of Revelation and substantial evidence that John expects massive numbers of Gentiles to be among those who ultimately dwell in heaven. See Marshall 2001, 185–89.

Chapter Ten

1. All references to the *Didache* follow Bart Ehrman's translation in the new Loeb edition (2003) unless otherwise stated.

2. Christian apostles might be both male and female, perhaps even in partnership as with Prisca and Aquila (Schüssler Fiorenza 1989, 160–75)

Chapter Eleven

1. For a survey of modern research into the *Pseudo-Clementines*, see Jones 1993. The following presentation differs from much of past research in its appreciation of the Pseudo-Clementine novel as a self-conscious independent production (Jones 2001); it seeks to identify the author's profile. The author of *The Circuits of Peter* (elsewhere called the *Basic Writing* or the *Grundschrift*) has often been viewed, in contrast, as a literary compiler of heterogeneous materials who displays little individuality. Whereas many previous researchers thought that *The Circuits* received most of its Jewish Christian material from a source entitled *Kerygmata Petrou* (*Preachings of Peter*), this study understands the references to the previously composed books of Peter's preachings as part of the novelistic framework and does not postulate an actual source entitled *Kerygmata Petrou*.

2. This essay is concerned only with ancient Jewish Christianity. Historical descriptions of medieval, early modern, and contemporary groups will, of course, require different terminology.

3. The *Didascalia* condemns this observance, though the later church would uphold it; see Brundage 1987, 91–92, 156, 199, 242, 451–53, 508.

4. See the reconstruction, translation, and presentation of this work in Jones 2004, 190–215.

5. The thesis of a Jewish origin of the *Book of Elchasai* mars the otherwise handy collection of texts by Gerard P. Luttikhuizen (1985).

6. On direction of prayer in early Christianity, see the classic study by Dölger 1972.

7. This is the text that allows the *Book of Elchasai* to be dated to the third year after Trajan's Parthian conquests, that is, 116–117 CE.

8. For a full study and a complete translation of the Syriac and Latin, see Jones 1995. The use of Acts in this source is further explored in Jones 1997.

9. In its account of James's martyrdom, the source is dependent on Hegesippus, who wrote in the latter half of the second century; see Jones 1990. Painter (2004, 179–81) argues against this conclusion and this article especially by pointing to instances in which the first part of the *Second Apocalypse of James* is not dependent on Hegesippus. These arguments can carry no weight (regardless of how often they are repeated) because my article does not assert that the first part of the *Second Apocalypse of James* is dependent on Hegesippus (see, to the contrary, Jones 1990, 333 n. 51; 1995, 146 n. 116).

A point that I had intended but nonetheless neglected to make in my previous studies regards the elements of Jewish law on capital punishment by stoning that are supposedly present in the martyrdom in the second part of the *Second Apocalypse of James* and that supposedly demonstrate that the martyrdom is more original here than in Hegesippus. These elements are not (yet) mentioned by Painter, but others have asked about them. The most striking is the statement that "they" stretched James out, put a stone on his abdomen, and all placed their feet on him; James then digs a hole, in which he stands, and when he is covered up to his abdomen, he is stoned. Some scholars would like to change "feet" to hands in order to find a correspondence with Jewish protocol. The most remarkable element here is the first stone on the abdomen, which might correspond to a large stone that was dropped on the person condemned to stoning after the person had been pushed backwards off a ten- to twelve-foot drop (*m. Sanh.* 6:4). The correspondences are not exact, but if they are actually there, they could well be secondary additions to the account (i.e., by someone who became aware of the details of Jewish capital punishment by stoning). That, in any event, is the opinion of Armand Veilleux (1986, 180), who correctly observes the distinction between the first and second part of the *Second Apocalypse of James* and writes of the latter part: "All the account draws its inspiration fundamentally from the tradition of Hegesippus, to which many details have been added, taken from the rabbinic tradition" (*"Tout le récit s'inspire foncièrement de la tradition d'Hégésippe, à laquelle plusieurs détails ont été ajoutés, empruntés à la tradition rabbinique"*).

10. Some scholars (e.g., Painter 2004, 187–88) identify the source behind R 1 with a Jewish Christian writing entitled *The Steps* [or *Ascents*] *of James*, which is described by Epiphanius, *Panarion* 30.16.6-9, with the following words: (6) "They [the Ebionites] call other acts 'of the apostles.' In these there is much that is full of impiety. There they armed themselves against the truth in no minor way. (7) Now they set out certain steps and guides (it is true) in the *Steps of James* (*Anabathmoi Jakobou*) as if he expounds against the temple

and sacrifices and against the fire on the altar and many other things full of babble. (8) Hence, they are not ashamed of denouncing even Paul here through certain contrived falsehoods of their pseudo-apostles' villainy and deceit. They say, on the one hand, that he was a Tarsian, as he himself declares and does not deny. On the other hand, they assert that he was from the Greeks by taking a pretext in the passage spoken by him through love of the truth, 'I am a Tarsian, a citizen of no ignoble city' (Acts 21:39). (9) Then they say that he was a Greek, the child of both a Greek mother and a Greek father, that he went to Jerusalem and remained there a while, that he desired to marry a priest's daughter, that for this reason he became a proselyte and was circumcised, that when he still did not receive such a girl he became angry and wrote against circumcision and against the Sabbath and the Law." The identity of the two writings is questionable because the content described in *Panarion* 30.16.8-9 is not found in R 1, and no proponent of the identity of the two writings has yet indicated how the differences in content are to be reconciled.

BIBLIOGRAPHY

Allison, Dale C. 1985. *The End of the Ages Has Come: An Early Interpretation of the Passion and Resurrection of Jesus.* Philadelphia: Fortress Press.

———. 1997. *The Jesus Tradition in Q.* Harrisburg, Pa.: Trinity Press International.

Alon, Gedalyahu. 1980–1984. *The Jews in Their Land in the Talmudic Age (70–640 CE).* 2 vols. Translated by G. Levi. Cambridge, Mass.: Harvard University Press.

———. 1996 [1958]. "Halakah in the Teaching of the Twelve Apostles (*Didache*)." Pages 165–94 in *The Didache in Modern Research.* Edited by Jonathan A. Draper. Arbeiten zur Geschichte des antiken Judentums und des Urchristentums 37. Leiden: Brill, 1996.

Anderson, H. 1985. "4 Maccabees: A New Translation and Introduction." Pages 531–64 in vol. 2 of *The Old Testament Pseudepigrapha.* Edited by James H. Charlesworth. 2 vols. London: Darton, Longman & Todd, 1983, 1985.

Arnal, William E. 1997. "Major Episodes in the Biography of Jesus: An Assessment of the Historicity of the Narrative Tradition." *Toronto Journal of Theology* 13:201–26.

———.2001. *Jesus and the Village Scribes: Galilean Conflicts and the Setting of Q.* Minneapolis: Fortress Press.

———. 2004. "Why Q Failed: From Ideological Project to Group Formation." Pages 67–87 in *Ancient Myths and Modern Theories of Christian Origins.* Society of Biblical Literature Symposium Series 28. Edited by Ron Cameron and Merrill Miller. Atlanta: Society of Biblical Literature.

Ashton, John. 1991. *Understanding the Fourth Gospel.* Oxford: Clarendon Press.

Asiedu-Peprah, Martin. 2001. *Johannine Sabbath Conflicts as Juridical Controversy.* Wissenschaftliche Untersuchungen zum Neuen Testament 2/132. Tübingen: Mohr Siebeck.

Audet, Jean-Paul. 1958. *La Didachè: Instructions des Apôtres.* Etudes bibliques. Paris: Gabalda.

———. 1996. "Literary and Doctrinal Relationships of the 'Manual of Discipline.'" Pages 129–47 in *The Didache in Modern Research.* Edited by Jonathan A. Draper. Arbeiten zur Geschichte des antiken Judentums und des Urchristentums 37. Leiden: Brill.

Aune, David E. 1983. *Prophecy in Early Christianity and the Ancient Mediterranean World*. Grand Rapids: Eerdmans.

———. 1996. "Following the Lamb: Discipleship in the Apocalypse." Pages 269–84 in *Patterns of Discipleship in the New Testament*. McMaster New Testament Studies. Edited by R. N. Longenecker. Grand Rapids: Eerdmans.

———.1997–1998. *Revelation*. 2 vols. Word Biblical Commentary 52A–B. Dallas: Word Books.

Bagatti, Bellarmino. 1984 [1971]. *The Church from the Circumcision: History and Archaeology of the Judaeo-Christians*. Translated by Eugene Hoade. Studium Biblicum Franciscanum, Collectio Minor 2. Jerusalem: Franciscan Printing Press, 1971. Repr., 1984.

Baird, William. 1992. *History of New Testament Research*. Vol. 1, *From Deism to Tübingen*. Minneapolis: Fortress Press.

Bammel, Ernst. 1996. "Pattern and Prototype of *Didache* 16." Pages 364–72 in *The Didache in Modern Research*. Edited by Jonathan A. Draper. Arbeiten zur Geschichte des antiken Judentums und des Urchristentums 37. Leiden: Brill.

Barclay, John M. G. 1995. "Deviance and Apostasy: Some Applications of Deviance Theory to First-Century Judaism and Christianity." Pages 114–27 in *Modelling Early Christianity*. Edited by Philip Esler. London: Routledge.

———.1996. *Jews in the Mediterranean Diaspora: From Alexander to Trajan (323 BCE– 117 CE)*. Edinburgh: T & T Clark.

———.1998. "Who Was Considered an Apostate in the Jewish Diaspora?" Pages 80–98 in *Tolerance and Intolerance in Early Judaism and Christianity*. Edited by G. Stanton and G. Strousma. Cambridge: Cambridge University Press.

Barrett, C. K. 1973. *A Commentary on the Second Epistle to the Corinthians*. Harper's New Testament Commentaries. New York: Harper & Row.

Barton, George A. 1898. "The Apocalypse and Recent Criticism." *American Journal of Theology* 2:776–801.

Bauckham, Richard. 1995. "James and the Jerusalem Church." Pages 415–80 in *The Book of Acts in Its Palestinian Setting*. Edited by Richard Bauckham. Vol. 4 of *The Book of Acts in Its First Century Setting*. Edited by Bruce W. Winter. Grand Rapids: Eerdmans.

———.2003. "The Origin of the Ebionites." Pages 162–81 in *The Image of the Judaeo-Christians in Ancient Jewish and Christian Literature*. Edited by Peter J. Tomson and Doris Lambers-Petry. Wissenschaftliche Untersuchungen zum Neuen Testament 158. Tübingen: Mohr Siebeck.

Bauer, Walter. 1996. *Orthodoxy and Heresy in Earliest Christianity*. 2nd German ed., with appendices, by Georg Strecker. Translated by a team from the Philadelphia Seminar on

Christian Origins. Edited by Robert A. Kraft and Gerhard Krodel. Philadelphia: Fortress Press, 1971. Repr., Mifflintown, Pa.: Sigler.

Baur, Ferdinand Christian. 1878 [1863]. *The Church History of the First Three Centuries*. 3rd ed. Translated by Allan Menzies. 2 vols. London: Williams and Norgate. Translation of *Kirchengeschichte der drei ersten Jahrhunderte*. Tübingen: L. F. Fues, 1863.

———. 1963 [1831]. "Die Christuspartei in der korinthischen Gemeinde, der Gegensatz des petrinischen und paulinischen Christenthums in der ältesten Kirche, der Apostel Petrus in Rom." *Tübinger Zeitschrift für Theologie* (1831) 61–206. Reprinted as pages 1–146 in vol. 1 of *Ausgewählte Werke in Einzelausgaben*. Edited by Klaus Scholder. 5 vols. Stuttgart-Bad Cannstatt: F. Frommann, 1963–75.

———. 1966 [1860]. *Das Christentum und die christliche Kirche der drei ersten Jahrhunderte*. 2nd ed. Tübingen: L. F. Fues, 1860. Reprinted in vol. 3 of *Ausgewählte Werke in Einzelausgaben*. Edited by Klaus Scholder. Stuttgart-Bad Cannstatt: F. Frommann, 1963–75.

———. 2003. *Paul the Apostle of Jesus Christ: His Life and Works, His Epistles and Teaching*. 2 vols. London: Williams and Norgate, 1873-75. Repr. 2 vols. in one, Peabody, Mass.: Hendrickson.

Beasley-Murray, G. R. 1974. *The Book of Revelation*. New Century Bible. London: Oliphants.

Becker, Adam H., and Annette Yoshiko Reed. 2003. *The Ways That Never Parted: Jews and Christians in Late Antiquity and the Early Middle Ages*. Texte und Studien zum antiken Judentum 95. Tübingen: Mohr Siebeck.

Berger, Klaus. *Die Gesetzauslegung Jesu: Ihr historischer Hintergrund im Judentum und im Alten Testament*. Wissenschaftliche Monographien zum Alten und Neuen Testament 40. Neukirchen-Vluyn: Neukirchener Verlag.

Berger, Peter L., and Thomas Luckmann. 1966. *The Social Construction of Reality: A Treatise in the Sociology of Knowledge*. Garden City, N.Y.: Doubleday.

Betz, Hans Dieter. 1979. *Galatians: A Commentary on Paul's Letter to the Churches in Galatia*. Hermeneia. Philadelphia: Fortress Press.

Betz, Johannes. 1996. "The Eucharist in the *Didache*." Pages 244–75 in *The Didache in Modern Research*. Edited by Jonathan A. Draper. Arbeiten zur Geschichte des antiken Judentums und des Urchristentums 37. Leiden: Brill.

Bhabha, Homi. 1994. *Locations of Culture*. New York: Routledge.

Bickermann, Elias J. 1949. "The Name of Christians." *Harvard Theological Review* 42:109–24.

Bieringer, Reimund, and Didier Pollefeyt. 2004. "Open to Both Ways . . . ? Johannine Perspectives on Judaism in the Light of Jewish-Christian Dialogue." Pages 11–32 in *Israel und seine Heilstraditionen im Johannesevangelium: Festgabe für Johannes Beutler SJ zum 70. Geburtstag.* Edited by M. Labahn, K. Scholtissek and A. Strotmann. Paderborn: Ferdinand Schöningh.

Bieringer, Reimund, Didier Pollefeyt, and Frederique Vandecasteele-Vanneuville, eds. 2001. *Anti-Judaism and the Fourth Gospel: Papers of the Leuven Colloquium, 2000.* Jewish and Christian Heritage Series 1. Assen: Royal van Gorcum.

Binder, Donald B. 1999. *Into the Temple Courts: The Place of the Synagogues in the Second Temple Period.* Society of Biblical Literature Dissertation Series 169. Atlanta: Society of Biblical Literature.

Bird, Frederick. 2002. "Early Christianity as an Unorganized Ecumenical Movement." Pages 225–46 in *Handbook of Early Christianity: Social Scientific Approaches.* Edited by Anthony J. Blasi, Jean Duhaime, and Paul-André Turcotte. New York: AltaMira.

Blanchetière, Francois. 2001. *Enquête sur les racines juives du mouvement chrétien (30–135).* Paris: Cerf.

Bless, Herbert, Klaus Fiedler, and Fritz Strack. 2004. *Social Cognition: How Individuals Construct Social Reality.* New York: Psychology Press.

Boccaccini, Gabrielle. 1991. *Middle Judaism: Jewish Thought, 300 B.C.E. to 200 C.E.* With a foreword by James H. Charlesworth. Minneapolis: Fortress Press.

Böckenhoff, Karl. 1903. *Das apostolische Speisegesetz in den ersten fünf Jahrhunderten: Ein Beitrag zum Verständnis der quasi-levitischen Satzungen in älteren kirchlichen Rechtsquellen.* Paderborn: Ferdinand Schöningh.

Bockmuehl, Markus. 1999. "Antioch and James the Just." Pages 155–98 in *James the Just and Christian Origins.* Edited by Bruce Chilton and Craig A. Evans. Novum Testamentum Supplements 98. Leiden: Brill.

Boer, Martinus C. de. 1996. *Johannine Perspectives on the Death of Jesus.* Kampen: Pharos.

———. 1998. "The Nazoreans: Living at the Boundary of Judaism and Christianity." Pages 239–62 in *Tolerance and Intolerance in Early Judaism and Christianity.* Edited by Graham N. Stanton and Guy G. Stroumsa. Cambridge: Cambridge University Press.

———. 2001. "The Depiction of the 'Jews' in John's Gospel: Matters of Behavior and Identity." Pages 260–80 in *Anti-Judaism and the Fourth Gospel: Papers of the Leuven Colloquium, 2000.* Edited by Reimund Bieringer, Didier Pollefeyt, and Frederique Vandecasteele-Vanneuville. Jewish and Christian Heritage Series 1. Assen: Royal van Gorcum.

Boismard, Marie-Emile. 1952. "Notes sur L'Apocalypse." *Review Biblique* 59:161–181.

Boll, Franz J. 1914. *Aus der Offenbarung Johannis: Hellenistische Studien zum Weltbild der Apokalypse.* Amsterdam: A. M. Hakkert.

Bondi, Richard A. 1997. "John 8:39–47: Children of Abraham or of the Devil?" *Journal of Ecumenical Studies* 34:473–98.

Boring, M. Eugene. 1994. "The Convergence of Source Analysis, Social History, and Literary Structure in the Gospel of Matthew." In *Society of Biblical Literature Seminar Papers* 33. Atlanta: Scholars Press.

Bousset, Wilhelm. 1899. "Apocalypse." Cols. 194–212 in vol. 1 of *Encyclopaedia Biblica: A Critical Dictionary of the Literary, Political, and Religious History, the Archaeology, Geography, and Natural History of the Bible*. Edited by T. K. Cheyne and J. S. Black. 4 vols. New York: MacMillan, 1899–1903.

———. 1906. *Die Offenbarung Johannes*. Kritisch-exegetischer Kommentar über das Neue Testament. 6th ed. Göttingen: Vandenhoeck & Ruprecht.

Boyarin, Daniel. 1999. *Dying for God: Martyrdom and the Making of Christianity and Judaism*. Stanford, Calif.: Stanford University Press.

———. 2001. "The Gospel of the *Memra*: Jewish Binitarianism and the Prologue to John." *Harvard Theological Review* 94:243–84.

———. 2003. "Semantic Differences; or, 'Judaism'/'Christianity.'" Pages 65–85 in *The Ways That Never Parted: Jews and Christians in Late Antiquity and the Early Middle Ages*. Texte und Studien zum antiken Judentum 95. Edited by Adam H. Becker and Annette Yoshiko Reed. Tübingen: Mohr Siebeck.

———. 2004. *Border Lines: The Partition of Judaeo-Christianity*. Divinations: Rereading Late Ancient Religion. Philadelphia: University of Pennsylvania Press.

Bradshaw, Paul F. 1997. "Introduction: The Evolution of Early Anaphoras." Pages 1-18 in P. Bradshaw (ed.), *Essays on Early Eastern Eucharistic Prayers*. Collegeville, Minn.: Liturgical.

Brett, Mark G. 1996. "Interpreting Ethnicity: Method, Hermeneutics, Ethics." Pages 3–22 in *Ethnicity and the Bible*. Edited by Mark Brett. Leiden: Brill.

Brown, Raymond E. 1979. *The Community of the Beloved Disciple: The Life, Loves, and Hates of an Individual Church in New Testament Times*. London: Geoffrey Chapman; New York: Paulist.

———. 1983. "Not Jewish Christianity and Gentile Christianity but Types of Jewish/Gentile Christianity." *Catholic Biblical Quarterly* 45:74–79.

———. 1997. *An Introduction to the New Testament*. New York: Doubleday.

Brundage, James A. 1987. *Law, Sex, and Christian Society in Medieval Europe*. Chicago and London: University of Chicago Press.

Bruston, Charles. 1888. *Les origines de la Apocalypse de s. Jean*. Paris: Fischbacher.

Buell, Denise K., and Caroline Johnson Hodge. 2004. "The Politics of Interpretation: The Rhetoric of Race and Ethnicity in Paul." *Journal of Biblical Literature* 123:235–51.

Bultmann, Rudolf. 1955. *Theology of the New Testament*. New York: Scribner.

———. 1972. *The History of the Synoptic Tradition*. Translated by J. Marsh. Oxford: Basil Blackwell.

———. 1985. *The Second Letter to the Corinthians*. Translated by Roy A. Harrisville. Minneapolis: Augsburg.

———. 1994 [1913]. "What the Sayings Source Reveals about the Early Church." Pages 23–34 in *The Shape of Q: Signal Essays on the Sayings Gospel*. Edited and translated by John S. Kloppenborg. Minneapolis: Fortress Press.

Callahan, Allen D. 1995. "The Language of the Apocalypse." *Harvard Theological Review* 88:453–70.

Cameron, Ron. 1996. "The Anatomy of a Discourse: On 'Eschatology' as a Category for Explaining Christian Origins." *Method and Theory in the Study of Religion* 8:231–45.

Carter, Warren. 1999. "Paying the Tax to Rome as Subversive Praxis: Matthew 17:24–27." *Journal for the Study of the New Testament* 76:3–31.

———. 2000a. *Matthew and the Margins: A Sociopolitical and Religious Reading*. Maryknoll, N.Y.: Orbis Books.

———. 2000b. "Evoking Isaiah: Matthean Soteriology and an Intertextual Reading of Isaiah 7–9 in Matthew 1:23 and 4:15–16." *Journal of Biblical Literature* 119:503–20.

———. 2001. *Matthew and Empire: Initial Explorations*. Harrisburg, Pa.: Trinity Press International.

———. 2003a. "Are There Imperial Texts in the Class? Intertextual Eagles and Matthean Eschatology as 'Lights Out' Time for Imperial Rome (Matt 24:27–31)." *Journal of Biblical Literature* 122:467–87.

———. 2003b. *Pontius Pilate: Portraits of a Roman Governor*. Interfaces. Collegeville, Minn.: Liturgical Press.

———. 2004. "Matthew and the Gentiles: Individual Conversion and/or Systemic Transformation?" *Journal for the Study of the New Testament* 26:259–82.

Casey, Maurice. 1991. *From Jewish Prophet to Gentile God: The Origins and Development of New Testament Christology*. Cambridge: James Clarke; Louisville Ky.: Westminster John Knox.

Charles, R. H. 1913. *Studies in the Apocalypse*. Edinburgh: T & T Clark.

———.1920. *A Critical and Exegetical Commentary on The Revelation of St. John*. International Critical Commentary 44. New York: Scribner.

Charlesworth, James H., ed. 1983–1985. *The Old Testament Pseudepigrapha*. 2 vols. Garden City, N.Y.: Doubleday.

———. 1990. "Exploring Opportunities for Rethinking Relations among Jews and Christians." Pages 35–59 in *Jews and Christians: Exploring the Past, Present, and Future*. Edited by James H. Charlesworth. New York: Crossroad.

———, ed. 1992. *The Messiah*. Minneapolis: Fortress Press.

Chester, Andrew, and Ralph P. Martin. 1994. *The Theology of the Letters of James, Peter, and Jude*. New Testament Theology. Cambridge: Cambridge University Press.

Chevalier, Jacques M. 1997. *A Postmodern Revelation: Signs of Astrology and the Apocalypse*. Toronto: University of Toronto Press.

Chilton, Bruce. 1999. "Conclusions and Questions." Pages 251–67 in *James the Just and Christian Origins*. Edited by Bruce Chilton and Craig A. Evans. Novum Testamentum Supplements 98. Leiden: Brill.

Chilton, Bruce and Jacob Neusner. 1995. *Judaism in the New Testament: Practices and Beliefs*. London and New York: Routledge.

Cohen, Shaye J. D. 1984. "The Significance of Yavneh: Pharisees, Rabbis, and the End of Jewish Sectarianism." *Hebrew Union College Annual* 55:27–53.

———. 1989. "Crossing the Boundary and Becoming a Jew." *Harvard Theological Review* 82:13–33.

———. 1999a. "The Rabbi in Second Century Jewish Society." Pages 922–90 in *The Cambridge History of Judaism*. Vol. 3, *The Early Roman Period*. Edited by W. Horbury, W. D. Davies, and J. Sturdy. Cambridge: Cambridge University Press.

———. 1999b. *The Beginnings of Jewishness: Boundaries, Varieties, Uncertainties*. Berkeley/Los Angeles/London: University of California Press.

Collins, Adela Yarbro. 1981. "Myth and History in the Book of Revelation: The Problem of its Date." Pages 377–403 in *Traditions in Transformation*. Edited by B. Halpern. Winona Lake, Ind.: Eisenbrauns.

———. 1984a. *Crisis and Catharsis: The Power of the Apocalypse*. Philadelphia: Westminster.

———. 1984b. "Numerical Symbolism in Apocalyptic Literature." *Aufstieg und Niedergang der Romische Welt* II.21.2:1221–87.

———. 1985. "Insiders and Outsiders in the Book of Revelation and Its Social Context." Pages 187–218 in *To See Ourselves as Others See Us: Christians, Jews, and "Others" in Late Antiquity*. Scholars Press Studies in the Humanities. Edited by J. Neusner and E. S. Frerichs. Chico, Calif.: Scholars Press.

Collins, John J. 1979. "Introduction: Towards the Morphology of a Genre." *Semeia* 14:1–19.

———. 1985. "A Symbol of Otherness: Circumcision and Salvation in the First Century." Pages 163–86 in *"To See Ourselves as Others See Us": Christians, Jews, "Others" in Late Antiquity*. Edited by J. Neusner and E. S. Frerichs. Chico, Calif.: Scholars Press.

———. 1989 [1984]. *The Apocalyptic Imagination: An Introduction to the Jewish Matrix of Christianity*. New York: Crossroad.

———. 1995. *The Scepter and the Star: The Messiahs of the Dead Sea Scrolls and Other Ancient Literature*. New York: Doubleday.

———. 1997. "The Experience of the End in the Dead Sea Scrolls." Pages 74–90 in *Eschatology, Messianism, and the Dead Sea Scrolls*. Edited by C. Evans and P. W. Flint. Grand Rapids: Eerdmans.

Coneybeare, F. 1901. "The Eusebian Form of the Text of Matthew 28,29." *Zeitschrift für die Neutestamentlichen Wissenschaft* 2:275–88.

Connolly, Richard Hugh. 1932. "The Didache in Relation to the Epistle of Barnabas." *Journal of Theological Studies* 33:327–53.

Culpepper, R. Alan. 1996. "The Gospel of John as a Document of Faith in a Pluralistic Culture." Pages 107–27 in *"What is John?": Readers and Readings of the Fourth Gospel*. Edited by Fernando F. Segovia. Society of Biblical Literature Symposium Series 3. Atlanta: Scholars Press.

———. 2001. "Anti-Judaism in the Fourth Gospel as a Theological Problem for Christian Interpreters." Pages 68–91 in *Anti-Judaism and the Fourth Gospel: Papers of the Leuven Colloquium, 2000*. Edited by Reimund Bieringer, Didier Pollefeyt, and Frederique Vandecasteele-Vanneuville. Jewish and Christian Heritage Series 1. Assen: Royal van Gorcum.

Danby, Herbert. 1933. *The Mishnah: Translated from the Hebrew with Introduction and Brief Explanatory Notes*. Oxford: Oxford University Press.

Daniélou, Jean. 1964. *The Theology of Jewish Christianity*. Vol. 1 of *The Development of Christian Doctrine before the Council of Nicaea*. Translated by John A. Baker. London: Darton, Longman & Todd; Chicago: Henry Regnery.

———. 1973. *Gospel Message and Hellenistic Culture*. Vol. 2 of *The Development of Christian Doctrine before the Council of Nicaea*. Translated by John Austin Baker. London: Darton, Longman & Todd; Philadelphia: Westminster.

———. 1977. *The Origins of Latin Christianity*. Vol. 3 of *The Development of Christian Doctrine before the Council of Nicaea*. Translated by David Smith and John Austin Baker. London: Darton, Longman & Todd; Philadelphia: Westminster.

Daube, David. 1956. *The New Testament and Rabbinic Judaism*. London: University of London, Athlone.

Davids, Peter. 1982. *The Epistle of James: A Commentary on the Greek Text.* New International Greek Testament Commentary. Exeter: Paternoster.

Davies, W. D. 1999. *Christian Engagements with Judaism.* Harrisburg, Pa.: Trinity Press International.

———. 1989. *The Setting of the Sermon on the Mount.* Cambridge, England: University Press, 1964. Repr. Atlanta, Ga: Scholars Press.

Davies, W. D., and Dale Allison. 1988. *The Gospel according to Saint Matthew. Vol. 1, Introduction and Commentary on Matthew I–VII.* International Critical Commentary. Edinburgh; T & T Clark.

Del Verme, Marcello. 1993. "The Didache and Judaism: The ἀπαρχή of Didache 13:3-7." *Studia Patristica* 26:113–39.

———. 2004. *Didache and Judaism: Jewish Roots of an Ancient Christian-Jewish Work.* New York and London: T & T Clark International.

Denzy, Nicola. 2002. "The Limits of Ethnic Categories." Pages 489–507 in *Handbook of Early Christianity: Social Scientific Approaches.* Edited by Anthony J. Blasi, Jean Duhaime, Paul-André Turcotte. Walnut Creek, Calif.: AltaMira.

Destro, Adriana, and Mauro Pesce. 2001. "The Gospel of John and the Community Rule of Qumran: A Comparison of Systems." Pages 201–29 in *Judaism in Late Antiquity.* Part 5, *The Judaism of Qumran: A Systematic Reading of the Dead Sea Scrolls.* Vol. 2, *World View, Comparing Judaisms.* Edited by A. J. Avery-Peck, J. Neusner and B. D. Chilton. Handbuch der Orientalistik 1/57. Leiden: Brill.

Deutsch, Celia. 1987. *Hidden Wisdom and the Easy Yoke: Wisdom, Torah and Discipleship in Matthew 11.25-30.* Journal for the Study of the New Testament Supplement Series 18. Sheffield: JSOT Press.

Dibelius, Martin. 1935 [1919]. *From Tradition to Gospel.* Translated in collaboration with the author by Bertram Lee Woolf. New York: Charles Scribner's Sons.

———. 1975. *James: A Commentary on the Epistle of James.* Translated by Michael A. Williams. Edited by Helmut Koester. Hermeneia. Philadelphia: Fortress Press. English translation of *Der Brief des Jakobus.* 11th ed. revised by Heinrich Greeven. Göttingen: Vandenhoeck & Ruprecht, 1964.

Dibelius, Martin, and Hans Conzelmann. 1972. *The Pastoral Epistles: A Commentary on the Pastoral Epistles.* Hermeneia. Translated P. Buttolph and A. Yarbro. Philadelphia: Fortress Press.

Dihle, Albrecht. 1962. *Die goldene Regel.* Studienhefte zur Altertumswissenschaft 7. Göttingen: Vandenhoeck and Ruprecht.

Dix, Dom Gregory. 1953. *Jew and Greek: A Study in the Primitive Church.* Westminster: Dacre.

Dodd, Charles H. 1953. *The Interpretation of the Fourth Gospel.* Cambridge: Cambridge University Press.

———. 1968. "Behind a Johannine Dialogue." Pages 41–57 in *More New Testament Studies.* Manchester: Manchester University Press.

Dölger, Franz Joseph. 1972. *Sol Salutis: Gebet und Gesang im christlichen Altertum, mit besonderer Rücksicht auf die Ostung in Gebet und Liturgie.* 3rd expanded ed. Liturgiewissenschaftliche Quellen und Forschungen 16–17. Münster: Aschendorff.

Downey, Glanville. 1961. *A History of Antioch in Syria.* Princeton, N.J.: Princeton University Press.

Dozeman, Thomas B. 1980. "*Sperma Abraam* in John 8 and Related Literature: Cosmology and Judgment." *Catholic Biblical Quarterly* 42:342–58.

Draper, Jonathan A. 1983. "A Commentary on the Didache in the Light of the Dead Sea Scrolls and Related Documents." Ph.D. thesis, Cambridge University.

———. 1985. "The Jesus Tradition in the *Didache.*" Pages 269–89 in *Gospel Perspectives V: The Jesus Tradition Outside the Gospels.* Edited by D. Wenham. Sheffield: JSOT Press. Revised and reprinted in as pages 72–92 in Jonathan A. Draper, ed., *The Didache in Modern Research.* Arbeiten zur Geschichte des antiken Judentums und des Urchristentums 37. Leiden: Brill, 1996.

———. 1991a. "Torah and Troublesome Apostles in the Didache Community." *Novum Testamentum* 33:347–72. Revised and reprinted as pages 340–63 in Jonathan A. Draper, ed., *The Didache in Modern Research.* Arbeiten zur Geschichte des antiken Judentums und des Urchristentums 37. Leiden: Brill, 1996.

———. 1991b. "Korah: A Title from the Second Temple Period." Pages 150–74 in *Templum Amicitiae: Festschrift for E. Bammel.* Edited by J. A. Emerton and W. Horbury. Sheffield: JSOT Press.

———. 1992. "Christian Self-Definition against the 'Hypocrites' in Didache 8." *Society of Biblical Literature Seminar Papers* 31:362–77. Atlanta: Scholars Press. Revised and reprinted as pages 223–43 in Jonathan A. Draper, ed., *The Didache in Modern Research.* Arbeiten zur Geschichte des antiken Judentums und des Urchristentums 37. Leiden: Brill, 1996.

———. 1993. "The Development of the 'Sign of the Son of Man' in the Jesus Tradition." *New Testament Studies* 39/1:1-21.

———. 1995. "Social Ambiguity and the Production of Text: Prophets, Teachers, Bishops, and Deacons and the Development of the Jesus Tradition in the Community of the *Didache.*" Pages 284–312 in *The Didache in Context: Essays on its Text, History, and Transmission*. Edited by C. N. Jefford. Supplements to Novum Testamentum 77. Leiden: Brill.

———. 1996. *The Didache in Modern Research*. Arbeiten zur Geschichte des antiken Judentums und des Urchristentums 37. Leiden: Brill.

———. 1997. "The Role of Ritual in the Alternation of Social Universe: Jewish Christian Initiation of Gentiles in the Didache." *Listening* 37:48–67.

———. 1999. "The Genesis and Narrative Thrust of the Paraenesis in the Sermon on the Mount." *Journal for the Study of the New Testament* 75:25–48.

———. 2000a. "Ritual Process and Ritual Symbol in Didache 7–10." *Vigiliae Christianae* 54:1–38.

———. 2000b. "Holy Seed and the Return of the Diaspora in John 12:24." *Neotestamentica* 34:347–359.

———. 2003. "A Continuing Enigma: The 'Yoke of the Lord' in *Didache* 6:2-3 and Early Jewish-Christian Relations." Pages 106–23 in *The Image of Judaeo-Christians in Ancient Jewish and Christian Literature*. Edited by P. J. Tomson and D. Lambers-Petry. Tübingen: Mohr Siebeck.

———. 2005a. "Do the Didache and Matthew Reflect an 'Irrevocable Parting of the Ways' with Judaism?" Pages 131–41 in *Matthew and the Didache: Two Documents from the Same Jewish-Christian Milieu?* Edited by H. van de Sandt. Assen: Royal van Gorcum; Minneapolis: Fortress Press.

———. 2005b. "First-Fruits and the Support of Prophets, Teachers, and the Poor in *Didache* 13 in Relation to New Testament Parallels." Pages 223–43 in *Trajectories through the New Testament and the Apostolic Fathers*. Edited by A. Gregory and C. Tuckett. Oxford: Oxford University Press.

Drews, Paul. 1904. "Untersuchungen zur Didache." *Zeitschrift für die Neutestamentliche Wissenschaft* 5:53–79.

Duff, Paul B. 2000. *Who Rides the Beast? Prophetic Rivalry and the Rhetoric of Crisis in the Churches of the Apocalypse*. Oxford and New York: Oxford University Press.

Dunderberg, Ismo. 2006. *The Beloved Disciple in Conflict? Revisiting the Gospels of John and Thomas*. Oxford: Oxford University Press.

Dunn, James D. G. 1990. *Unity and Diversity in the New Testament: An Inquiry into the Character of Earliest Christianity*. 2d ed.. London: SCM; Philadelphia: Trinity Press International.

———. 1991. *The Partings of the Ways between Christianity and Judaism and Their Significance for the Character of Christianity*. London: SCM; Philadelphia: Trinity Press International.

Ehrman, Bart. 2003. *The Apostolic Fathers: I Clement, II Clement, Ignatius, Polycarp, Didache.* Loeb Classical Library. Cambridge, Mass., and London: Harvard University Press.

Eisenbaum, Pamela. 2003. "Paul as the New Abraham." Online: http://www.thepaulpage.com. Accessed January 18, 2003.

———. 2004. "A Remedy for Having Been Born of Woman: Jesus, Gentiles, and Genealogy in Romans." *Journal of Biblical Literature* 123:671–702.

Eller, David Jack. 1999. *From Culture to Ethnicity to Conflict: An Anthropological Perspective on International Ethnic Conflict.* Ann Arbor: University of Michigan Press.

Engels, Friedrich. 1882. "Bruno Bauer und das Urchristentum." *Socialdemokrat* May 4–11. Reprinted as pages 297–305 in vol. 19, 4 of Karl Marx and Friedrich Engels, *Werke.* Berlin: Dietz, 1973.

———. 1894–95. "Zur Geschichte des Urchristentums." *Die Neue Zeit* 13. Reprinted as pages 447–73 in vol. 22, 3 of Karl Marx and Friedrich Engels, *Werke.* Berlin: Dietz, 1972.

———. 1957a. "The Book of Revelation." Pages 183–89 in *Marx and Engels on Religion.* Moscow: Progress.

———. 1957b. "Bruno Bauer and Early Christianity." Pages 173–82 in *Marx and Engels on Religion.* Moscow: Progress.

Erbes, Karl. 1891. *Die Offenbarung Johannes: kritisch untersucht.* Gotha: F.A. Perthes.

Esler, Philip F. 1994. *The First Christians in Their Social Worlds: Social-Scientific Approaches to New Testament Interpretation.* London and New York: Routledge.

———. 1998. *Galatians.* New Testament Readings. London: Routledge.

———. 2003. *Conflict and Identity in Romans: The Social Setting of Paul's Letter.* Minneapolis: Fortress Press.

Fabris, Rinaldo. 1977. *Legge della liberta in Giacomo.* Supplementi alla Revista Biblica 8. Brescia: Paideia.

Farmer, William R. 1977. "Modern Developments of Griesbach's Hypothesis." *New Testament Studies* 23:275–95.

Farrer, Austin M. 1955. "On Dispensing with Q." Pages 57–88 in *Studies in the Gospels in Memory of R. H. Lightfoot.* Edited by Dennis E. Nineham. Oxford: Basil Blackwell.

Fekkes, Jan. 1994. *Isaiah and Prophetic Traditions in the Book of Revelation: Visionary Antecedents and Their Development.* Journal for the Study of New Testament Supplement Series 93. Sheffield: Sheffield Academic Press.

Finkelstein, Louis. 1930. *Some Examples of the Maccabean Halaka.* Leipzig: Officin Haag-Drugulin.

Flusser, David. 1966. "The Conclusion of Matthew in a New Jewish Christian Source." *Annual of the Swedish Theological Institute* 5:110–20.

———. 1969. "Salvation Present and Future." *Numen* 16:139–55.

———. 1996. "Paul's Jewish Christian Opponents in the *Didache*." Pages 195–211 in *The Didache in Modern Research*. Edited by Jonathan A. Draper. Arbeiten zur Geschichte des antiken Judentums und des Urchristentums 37. Leiden: Brill.

Fonrobert, Charlotte E. 2001. "The *Didascalia Apostolorum*: A Mishnah of the Disciples of Jesus." *Journal of Early Christian Studies* 9:483–509.

Ford, Josephine Massyngberde. 1975. *Revelation: Introduction, Translation, and Commentary*. Anchor Bible 38. Garden City, N.Y.: Doubleday.

Frankemölle, Hubert. 1986. "Gesetz im Jakobusbrief: Zur Tradition, contextuellen Verwendung und Rezeption eines belasteten Begiffes." Pages 175–221 in *Das Gesetz im Neuen Testament*. Questiones Disputatae 108. Edited by K. Kertelge. Freiburg: Herder.

———. 1989. "Zum Thema des Jakobusbriefes im Kontext der Rezeption von Sir 2,1-18 und 15,11-20." *Biblische Notizen* 48:21–49.

Frankenberg, Wilhelm. 1937. *Die syrischen Clementinen mit griechischem Paralleltext: Eine Vorarbeit zu dem literargeschichtlichen Problem der Sammlung*. Texte und Untersuchungen zur Geschichte der altchristlichen Literatur 48.3. Leipzig: J. C. Hinrichs.

Frankfurter, David. 2001. "Jews or Not? Reconstructing the 'Other' in Rev 2:9 and 3:9." *Harvard Theological Review* 94:403–25.

Fredricksen, Paula. 2002. "Judaism, the Circumcision of Gentiles, and Apocalyptic Hope: Another Look at Galatians 1 and 2." Pages 235–60 in *The Galatians Debate: Contemporary Issues in Rhetorical and Historical Interpretation*. Edited by Mark Nanos. Peabody, Mass.: Hendrickson.

Friedrich, Gerhardt. 1963. "Die Gegner des Paulus im 2. Korintherbrief." Pages 181–215 in *Abraham unser Vater: Juden und Christen im Gespräch über die Bibel*. Edited by O. Betz, M. Hengel, and P. Schmidt. Arbeiten zur Geschichte des Spätjudentums und Urchristentums. Leiden: Brill.

Fuller, Reginald H. 1989. "The Decalogue in the New Testament." *Interpretation* 43:243–55.

Furnish, Victor P. 1984. *II Corinthians: Translated, with Introduction, Notes, and Commentary*. Anchor Bible 32A. Garden City, N.Y.: Doubleday.

Gager, John G. 1975. *Kingdom and Community: The Social World of Early Christianity*. Prentice-Hall Studies in Religion. Englewood Cliffs, N.J.: Prentice-Hall.

———. 2000. *Reinventing Paul*. Oxford and New York: Oxford University Press.

———. 2003. "Did Jewish Christians See the Rise of Islam?" Pages 361–72 in *The WaysTthat Never Parted: Jews and Christians in Late Antiquity and the Early Middle Ages*. Texte und Studien zum antiken Judentum 95. Edited by Adam H. Becker and Annette Yoshiko Reed. Tübingen: Mohr Siebeck.

Gammie, John G. 1990. "Paraenetic Literature: Toward the Morphology of a Secondary Genre." *Semeia* 50:41–77.

Garrow, Alan John Philip. 2004. *The Gospel of Matthew's Dependence on the* Didache. Journal for the Study of the New Testament Supplements Series 254. London and New York: T & T Clark International.

Gaston, Lloyd. 1984. "Paul and Jerusalem." Pages 61–72 in *From Jesus to Paul: Studies in Honour of Francis Wright Beare*. Edited by P. Richardson and J. C. Hurd. Waterloo, Ont.: Wilfrid Laurier University Press.

———. 1987. *Paul and the Torah*. Vancouver: University of British Columbia Press.

Georgi, Dieter. 1985. "Rudolf Bultmann's *Theology of the New Testament* Revisited." Pages 75–87 in *Bultmann, Retrospect and Prospect: The Centenary Symposium at Wellesley*. Edited by Edward C. Hobbs. Harvard Theological Studies 35. Philadelphia: Fortress Press.

———. 1986 [1964]. *The Opponents of Paul in Second Corinthians*. Philadelphia: Fortress Press. Translation of *Die Gegner des Paulus im 2. Korintherbrief: Studien zur Religiösen Propaganda in der Spätantike*. Wissenschaftliche Monographien zum Alten und Neuen Testament 11. Neukirchener-Vluyn: Neukirchener Verlag, 1964.

Giet, Stanislas. 1966. "Coutume, évolution, droit canon. A Propos de deux passages de la "Didaché", *Revue de droit canonique* 16 (1966), 118-132. Reprinted in M. Nedoncelle et al. (eds.), *En Hommage à Gabriel Le Bras*. Centre de musique canadienne au Québec, 1982.

———. 1970. *L'Énigme de la Didachè*. Publications de la Faculté des lettres de l'Université de Strasbourg 149. Paris: Ophrys.

Goodacre, Mark S. 1996. *Goulder and the Gospels: An Examination of a New Paradigm*. *Journal for the Study of the New Testament Supplement Series* 133. Sheffield: JSOT Press.

Goodman, Martin. 1996. "The Function of Minim in Early Rabbinic Judaism." Pages 501–10 in *Geschichte-Tradition-Reflexion: Festschrift für Martin Hengel zum 70. Geburtstag. Band I, Judentum*. Edited by H. Cancik, H. Lichtenberger, and P. Schäfer. Tübingen: Mohr Siebeck.

Goranson, Stephen. 1992. "Nazarenes." Pages 1049–50 in vol. 4 of *Anchor Bible Dictionary*. Edited by David Noel Freedman. 6 vols. New York: Doubleday.

Goulder, Michael D. 1989. *Luke: A New Paradigm. Journal for the Study of the New Testament Supplement Series* 20. Sheffield: JSOT Press.

———. 1994. *St. Paul versus St. Peter: A Tale of Two Missions*. Louisville, Ky.: Westminster John Knox.

Gray, Rebecca. 1993. *Prophetic Figures in Late Second Temple Jewish Palestine: The Evidence from Josephus*. New York: Oxford University Press.

Green, H. Benedict. 1968. "The Command to Baptize and Other Matthean Interpolations." *Studia Evangelica* 4. *Texte und Untersuchungen* 102. Berlin: Akademie-Verlag.

Grundmann, Walter, Franz Hesse, Marinus de Jonge, and Adam Simon van der Woude. 1974. "χρίω, χριστός, αντίχριστος, χρίσμα, χριστιανίς." Pages 493–581 in vol. 9 of *Theological Dictionary of the New Testament*. Edited by G. Kittel and G. Friedrich. Translated by Geoffrey W. Bromiley. 10 vols. Grand Rapids: Eerdmans, 1964–1976.

Hagner, Donald. 1993–1995. *Matthew 1–13, 14–28*. Word Biblical Commentary 33A–B. Dallas: Word.

———. 2003. "Matthew: Apostate, Reformer, Revolutionary." *New Testament Studies* 49:193–209.

———. 2004. "Matthew: Christian Judaism or Jewish Christianity?" Pages 263–82 in *The Face of New Testament Studies: A Survey of Recent Research*. Edited by S. McKnight and G. Osborne. Grand Rapids: Baker Academic.

Häkkinen, Sakari. 1999. *Köyhät kerettiläiset: Ebionit kirkkoisien teksteissä*. [Poor Heretics: The Ebionites in Patristic Texts]. Suomalaisen teologisen kirjallisuusseuran julkaisuja 223. Helsinki: Suomalainen teologinen kirjallisuusseura. English abstract on pp. 7–8.

———. 2005. "Ebionites." Pages 247–78 in *A Companion to Second-Century Christian "Heretics."* Edited by Antti Marjanen and Petri Luomanen. *Supplements to Vigiliae Christianae* 76. Leiden: Brill.

Hakola, Raimo. 2005a. *Identity Matters: John, the Jews and Jewishness*. Novum Testamentum Supplements 118. Leiden: Brill.

———. 2005b. "The Counsel of Caiaphas and the Social Identity of the Johannine Christians (John 11:47-53)." Pages 140–63 in *Lux Humana, Lux Aeterna: Essays on Biblical and Related Themes in Honour of Lars Aejmelaeus*. Edited by A. Mustakallio in collaboration with H. Leppä and H. Räisänen. Publications of the Finnish Exegetical Society 89. Helsinki: Finnish Exegetical Society; Göttingen: Vandenhoeck and Ruprecht.

Hare, Douglas R. A. 2000. "How Jewish Is the Gospel of Matthew?" *Catholic Biblical Quarterly* 62:264–77.

Harnack, Adolf von. 1884. *Die Lehre der zwölf Apostel nebst Untersuchungen zur ältesten Geschichte der Kirchenverfassung und des Kirchenrechts*. Texte und Untersuchungen zur Geschichte der altchristlichen Literatur 2.1–2. Leipzig: Hinrichs.

———. 1908. *The Mission and Expansion of Christianity in the First Three Centuries.* 2 vols. Translated and edited by James Moffatt. 2nd enlarged and rev. ed. Theological Translation Library. London: Willams and Norgate; New York: G. P. Putnam's Sons.

———. 1961 [1896]. *History of Dogma.* Translated from the 3rd German ed. by Neil Buchanan. 7 vols. Boston: Little, Brown, 1896–1905. Repr., 7 vols. in 4, New York: Dover.

———. 1986 [1957]. *What Is Christianity?* Translated by Thomas Bailey Saunders. Introduction by Rudolf Bultmann. New York: Harper, 1957. Repr., Fortress Texts in Modern Theology, Philadelphia: Fortress Press.

Harris, Horton. 1990. *The Tübingen School.* Oxford: Clarendon, 1975. Repr. Grand Rapids, Mich: Baker.

Hartin, Patrick J. 1991. *James and the Q Sayings of Jesus.* Journal for the Study of the New Testament Supplement Series 47. Sheffield: Sheffield Academic Press.

———. 1996. "'Who is Wise and Understanding among You?' (James 3:13): An Analysis of Wisdom, Eschatology and Apocalypticism in the Epistle of James." Pages 483–503 in vol. 35 of *Society of Biblical Literature Seminar Papers.* Atlanta: Scholars Press.

———. 1999. *A Spirituality of Perfection: Faith in Action in the Letter of James.* Collegeville, Minn.: Liturgical Press.

———. 2003. *James.* Sacra Pagina 14. Collegeville, Minn.: Liturgical Press.

———. 2004. *James of Jerusalem: Heir to Jesus of Nazareth.* Interfaces. Edited by Barbara Green. Collegeville, Minn.: Liturgical Press.

Hartman, Lars. 1997. *"Into the Name of the Lord Jesus": Baptism in the Early Church.* Studies of the New Testament and Its World. Edinburgh: T & T Clark.

Hays, Richard B. 1983. *The Faith of Jesus Christ: An Investigation of the Narrative Substructure of Galatians 3:1—4:11.* Society of Biblical Literature Dissertation Series 56. Chico, Calif.: Scholars Press.

Hemer, Colin J. 1986. *The Letters to the Seven Churches of Asia in Their Local Setting.* Journal for the Study of the New Testament Supplement Series 11. Sheffield: JSOT Press.

Hengel, Martin, and R. Deines. 1995. "E. P. Sanders' 'Common Judaism,' Jesus and the Pharisees: Review Article of *Jewish Law from Jesus to Mishnah* and *Judaism: Practice and Belief* by E. P. Sanders." *Journal of Theological Studies* 46:1–70.

Hennings, Ralph. 1994. *Die Briefwechsel zwischen Augustinus und Hieronymus und ihr Streit um den Kanon des Alten Testaments und die Auslegung von Gal. 2,11–14.* Supplements to Vigiliae Christianae 21. Leiden: Brill.

Hezser, Catherine. 1997. *The Social Structure of the Rabbinic Movement in Roman Palestine.* Texte und Studien zum Antiken Judentum 66. Tübingen: Mohr Siebeck.

Hiebert, D. Edmond. 1979. "The Unifying Theme of the Epistle of James." *Bibliotheca Sacra* 135:221–31.

Hill, Craig. 1992. *Hellenists and Hebrews: Reappraising Division within the Earliest Church.* Philadelphia: Fortress Press.

———. 2002. "Restoring the Kingdom to Israel: Luke-Acts and Christian Supersessionism." Pages 185–200 in *Shadow of Glory: Reading the New Testament after the Holocaust.* Edited by Tod Linafelt. New York and London: Routledge.

Himmelfarb, Martha. 1997. "'A Kingdom of Priests': The Democritization of Priesthood in the Literature of Second Temple Judaism." *Journal of Jewish Thought and Philosophy* 6:89–104.

———. 2006. *A Kingdom of Priests: Ancestry and Merit in Ancient Judaism.* Jewish Culture and Contexts. Philadelphia: University of Pennsylvania Press.

Hoffmann, Paul. 1982. *Studien zur Theologie der Logienquelle.* 3rd ed. Neutestamentliche Abhandlungen. Münster: Aschendorff.

Hogan, Maurice. 1997. "The Law in the Epistle of James." *Studien zum Neuen Testament und seiner Umwelt. Serie A* 22:79–91.

Hogg, Michael A., and Dominic Abrams. 1988. *Social Identifications: A Social Psychology of Intergroup Relations and Group Processes.* London: Routledge.

———. 1999. "Social Identity and Social Cognition: Historical Background and Current Trends." Pages 1–25 in *Social Identity and Social Cognition.* Edited by Dominic Abrams and Michael A. Hogg. Malden, Mass.: Blackwell.

Holmberg, Bengt. 1980. *Paul and Power: The Structure of Authority in the Primitive Church as Reflected in the Pauline Epistles.* Philadelphia: Fortress Press.

———. 1998. "Jewish *Versus* Christian Identity in the Early Church?" *Revue biblique* 105:397–425.

Horbury, William. 1985. "Extirpation and Excommunication." *Vetus Testamentum* 35:13–38.

Horrell, David G. 2000. "Early Jewish Christianity." Pages 136–67 in vol. 1 of *The Early Christian World.* Edited by Philip Esler. London and New York: Routledge.

———. 2002. "'Becoming Christian': Solidifying Christian Identity and Content." Pages 309–35 in *Handbook of Early Christianity: Social Scientific Approaches.* Edited by Anthony J. Blasi, Jean Duhaime, Paul-André Turcotte. New York: AltaMira.

Horsley, Richard A. 1992. "Messianic Movements in Judaism." Pages 791–97 in vol. 4 of *Anchor Bible Dictionary.* 6 vols. Edited by David Noel Freedman. New York: Doubleday.

———. 1995a. *Galilee: History, Politics, People.* Valley Forge, Pa.: Trinity Press International.

———. 1995b. "Social Conflict in the Synoptic Sayings Source Q." Pages 37–52 in *Conflict and Invention: Literary, Rhetorical, and Social Studies on the Sayings Gospel Q*. Edited by John S. Kloppenborg. Valley Forge, Pa.: Trinity Press International.

Horsley, Richard A., and Jonathan A. Draper 1999. *Whoever Hears You Hears Me: Prophets, Performance, and Tradition in Q*. Harrisburg, Pa.: Trinity Press International.

Horsley, Richard A., and John S. Hanson. 1985. *Bandits, Prophets and Messiahs: Popular Movements at the Time of Jesus*. Minneapolis: Winston.

Hort, Fenton John Anthony. 1894. *Judaistic Christianity: A Course of Lectures*. Cambridge and London: Macmillan.

———. 1901. *Notes Introductory to the Study of the Clementine Recognitions: A Course of Lectures*. London: Macmillan.

Hultgren, Arland J. 1994. *The Rise of Normative Christianity*. Minneapolis: Fortress Press.

Humphrey, Edith M. 1995. *The Ladies and the Cities: Transformation and Apocalyptic Identity in Joseph and Aseneth, 4 Ezra, the Apocalypse and the Shepherd of Hermas*. Journal for the Study of the Pseudepigrapha Supplements Series 17. Sheffield: Sheffield Academic Press.

Hurtado, Larry W. 1999. "Pre-70 CE Jewish Opposition to Christ-Devotion." *Journal of Theological Studies* 50:35–58.

———. 2003. *Lord Jesus Christ: Devotion to Jesus in Earliest Christianity*. Grand Rapids and Cambridge: Eerdmans.

Jackson-McCabe, Matt A. 1996. "A Letter to the Twelve Tribes in the Diaspora: Wisdom and 'Apocalyptic' Eschatology in the Letter of James." Pages 504–17 in vol. 35 of *Society of Biblical Literature Seminar Papers*. Atlanta: Scholars Press.

———. 2001. *Logos and Law in the Letter of James: The Law of Nature, the Law of Moses, and the Law of Freedom*. Supplements to Novum Testamentum 100. Leiden: Brill.

———. 2003. "The Messiah Jesus in the Mythic World of James." *Journal of Biblical Literature* 122:701–30.

Jacobson, Arland D. 1992. *The First Gospel: An Introduction to Q*. Sonoma, Calif.: Polebridge.

———. 1994 [1982]. "The Literary Unity of Q." Pages 98–115 in *The Shape of Q: Signal Essays on the Sayings Gospel*. Edited by John S. Kloppenborg. Minneapolis: Fortress Press.

Jaubert, Annie. 1957. *La date de la Cène: Calendrier biblique et liturgie chrétienne*. Paris: Gabalda.

Jefford, Clayton N. 1989. *The Sayings of Jesus in the Teaching of the Twelve Apostles*. Vigiliae Christianae Supplements 11. Leiden: Brill.

———. 1995. *The Didache in Context: Essays on Its Text, History and Transmission*. Leiden: Brill.

Jeremias, Joachim. 1967. *The Prayers of Jesus*. Studies in Biblical Theology 2/6. London: SCM.

Jervell, Jacob. 1980. "The Mighty Minority." *Studia Theologica* 34:13–38.

Johnson, Luke Timothy. 1982. "The Use of Leviticus 19 in the Letter of James." *Journal of Biblical Literature* 101:391–401.

———. 1983. "James 3:13—4:10 and the Topos PERI PHTHONOU." *Novum Testamentum* 25:327–47.

———. 1985. "Friendship with the World/Friendship with God: A Study of Discipleship in James." Pages 166–83 in *Discipleship in the New Testament*. Edited by F. Segovia. Philadelphia: Fortress Press.

———. 1989. "The New Testament's Anti-Jewish Slander and the Conventions of Ancient Polemic." *Journal of Biblical Literature* 108:419–41.

———. 1995. *The Letter of James: A New Translation with Introduction and Commentary.*. Anchor Bible 37A. New York: Doubleday.

———. 1996. *The Real Jesus: The Misguided Quest for the Historical Jesus and the Truth of the Traditional Gospels.* New York: HarperCollins.

Jones, F. Stanley. 1990. The Martyrdom of James in Hegesippus, Clement of Alexandria, and Christian Apocrypha, Including Nag Hammadi: A Study of the Textual Relations." Pages 322-35 in *Society of Biblical Literature 1990 Seminar Papers*. Edited by David J. Lull. Society of Biblical Literature Seminar Papers Series 29. Atlanta, Ga.: Scholars.

———. 1993. "The Pseudo-Clementines: A History of Research." Pages 195–262 in *Literature of the Early Church*. Vol. 2 of *Studies in Early Christianity: A Collection of Scholarly Essays*. Edited by Everett Ferguson. New York and London: Garland. Originally published in *The Second Century* 2 (1982): 1–33, 63–96.

———. 1995. *An Ancient Jewish Christian Source on the History of Christianity: Pseudo-Clementine "Recognitions" 1.27–71*. Society of Biblical Literature Texts and Translations 37, Christian Apocrypha Series 2. Atlanta: Scholars Press.

———. 1996. "The Genre of the Book of Elchasai: A Primitive Church Order, Not an Apocalypse." Pages 87–104 in *Historische Wahrheit und theologische Wissenschaft: Gerd Lüdemann zum 50. Geburtstag*. Edited by Alf Özen. Frankfurt am Main: Peter Lang.

———. 1997. "An Ancient Jewish Christian Rejoinder to Luke's Acts of the Apostles: Pseudo-Clementine *Recognitions* 1.27–71." Pages 223–45 in *The Apocryphal Acts of the Apostles in Intertextual Perspectives*. Edited by Robert F. Stoops, Jr. Semeia 80. Atlanta: Scholars Press.

———. 2001. "Eros and Astrology in the *Periodoi Petrou*: The Sense of the Pseudo-Clementine Novel." *Apocrypha: Revue internationale des littératures apocryphes* 12:53–78.

———. 2004. "The *Book of Elchasai* in Its Relevance for Manichaean Institutions with a Supplement: The *Book of Elchasai* Reconstructed and Translated." *ARAM* 16:179–215.

———. 2005. "Jewish Christianity of the *Pseudo-Clementines*." Pages 315–34 in *A Companion to Second-Century Christian "Heretics."* Edited by Antti Marjanen and Petri Luomanen. Supplements to Vigiliae Christianae 76. Leiden: Brill.

Jonge, Marinus de. 1992. "Messiah." Pages 777–88 in vol. 4 of *Anchor Bible Dictionary*. 6 vols. Edited by David Noel Freedman. New York: Doubleday.

Kamlah, Ehrhard. 1964. *Die Form der katalogischen Paränese im Neuen Testament*. Wissenschaftliche Untersuchungen zum Neuen Testament 7. Tübingen: Mohr.

Kee, Howard Clark. 2002. "Sociological Insights into the Development of Christian Leadership Roles and Community Formation." Pages 337–60 in *Handbook of Early Christianity: Social Scientific Approaches*. Edited by Anthony J. Blasi, Jean Duhaime, Paul-André Turcotte. New York: AltaMira.

Kelber, Werner. 1983. *The Oral and the Written Gospel: The Hermeneutics of Speaking and Writing in the Synoptic Tradition, Mark, Paul, and Q*. Philadelphia: Fortress Press.

———. 2004. "Diversity as Function of Oral, Scribal and Typographic Dynamics: Christianity as Communications History." Unpublished paper presented to the Colloquium on Orality, Literacy and Diversity, University of Zululand, October 8–11.

Kelley, Sean. 2002. *Racializing Jesus: Race, Ideology, and the Formation of Modern Biblical Scholarship*. London and New York: Routledge.

Kelly, J. N. D. 1975. *Jerome: His Life, Writings, and Controversies*. New York: Harper & Row.

Kimelman, Reuven. 1981. "*Birkat Ha-Minim* and the Lack of Evidence for an Anti-Christian Jewish Prayer in Late Antiquity." Pages 226–44 in *Jewish and Christian Self-Definition*. Vol. 2, *Aspects of Judaism in the Greco-Roman Period*. Edited by E. P. Sanders, A. I. Baumgarten, and A. Mendelson. Philadelphia: Fortress Press.

———. 1999. "Identifying Jews and Christians in Roman Syria-Palestine." Pages 301–33 in *Galilee through the Centuries: Confluence of Cultures*. Edited by E. Meyers. Winona Lake, Ind.: Eisenbrauns.

Kirk, Alan. 1998. *The Composition of the Sayings Source: Genre, Synchrony, and Wisdom*. Supplements to Novum Testamentum 91. Leiden: Brill.

Kirk, J. A. 1969–1970. "The Meaning of Wisdom in James: Examination of a Hypothesis." *New Testament Studies* 16:24–38.

Klein, Günter. 1909. *Der Älteste Christliche Katechismus und die Jüdische Propaganda-Literatur.* Berlin: Reimer.

Klein, Martin. 1995. *Ein vollkommenes Werk: Vollkommenheit, Gesetz und Gericht als theologische Themen des Jakobusbriefes.* Stuttgart: W. Kohlhammer.

Klijn, A. F. J. 1972. "Jerome's Quotations from a Nazorean Interpretation of Isaiah." Pages 241–55 in *Judéo-Christianisme: Recherches historiques et théologiques offertes en hommage au Cardinal Jean Daniélou. Recherches de science religieuse* 60.

———. 1973–74. "The Study of Jewish Christianity." *New Testament Studies* 20:419–31.

———. 1992. *Jewish-Christian Gospel Tradition.* Supplements to Vigiliae Christianae 17. Leiden: Brill.

Klijn, A. F. J., and G. J. Reinink. 1973. *Patristic Evidence for Jewish-Christian Sects.* Novum Testamentum Supplements 36. Leiden: Brill.

Kloppenborg, John S. 1979. "Didache 16:6-8 and Special Matthean Tradition." *Zeitschrift für die Neutestamentlichen Wissenschaft* 70:54–67.

———. 1987. *The Formation of Q: Trajectories in Ancient Wisdom Collections.* Studies in Antiquity and Christianity. Philadelphia: Fortress Press.

———. 1990. "Nomos and Ethos in Q." Pages 35–48 in *Gospel Origins and Christian Beginnings: In Honor of James M. Robinson.* Edited by James Goehring, Charles W. Hedrick, Jack T. Sanders, and Hans Dieter Betz. Sonoma, Calif.: Polebridge.

Kloppenborg Verbin, John S. 2000. *Excavating Q: The History and Setting of the Sayings Gospel.* Minneapolis: Fortress Press.

Knopf, Rudolf. 1920. *Die Lehre der zwölf Apostel; Die zwei Clemensbriefe.* Handbuch zum Neuen Testament, neubearbeitung bd. 17. Tübingen: Mohr.

Koester, Helmut. 1957. *Synoptische Überlieferung bei den Apostolischen Väter.* Texte und Untersuchungen zur Geschichte der altchristlichen Literatur 65. Berlin: Akademie Verlag.

———. 1990. *Ancient Christian Gospels: Their History and Development.* Philadelphia: Trinity Press International.

Kosmala, Hans. 1965. "The Conclusion of Matthew." *Annual of the Swedish Theological Institute* 4:132–47.

Kraft, Heinrich. 1974. *Die Offenbarung des Johannes.* Tübingen: Mohr.

Kraft, Robert A. 1965. *Barnabas and the Didache.* Apostolic Fathers 3. New York: Thomas Nelson.

———. 1972. "In Search of 'Jewish Christianity' and Its 'Theology': Problems of Definition and Methodology." Pages 81–92 in *Judéo-Christianisme: Recherches historiques et théologigues offertes en hommage au Cardinal Jean Daniélou. Recherches de science religieuse* 60.

Kraft, Robert A., and George W. E. Nickelsburg, eds. 1986. *Early Judaism and Its Modern Interpreters.* Society of Biblical Literature, The Bible and Its Modern Interpreters 2. Philadelphia: Fortress Press; Atlanta: Scholars Press.

Kümmel, Werner Georg. 1972. *The New Testament: The History of the Investigation of Its Problems.* Translated by S. M. Gilmour and H. C. Kee. Nashville and New York: Abingdon.

Kümmel, Werner G., and Paul Feine. 1975. *Introduction to the New Testament.* Translated by Howard Clark Kee. Nashville: Abingdon.

Kuschel, Karl-Josef. 1995. *Abraham: Sign of Hope for Jews, Christians and Muslims.* New York: Continuum.

Laufen, Rudolf. 1980. *Die Doppelüberlieferungen der Logienquelle und des Markusevangeliums.* Bonner biblische Beiträge 54. Königstein: Peter Hanstein.

Laws, Sophie. 1980. *A Commentary on the Epistle of James.* Black's New Testament Commentaries. London: Black.

Lee, Dorothy A. 1994. *The Symbolic Narratives of the Fourth Gospel: The Interplay of Form and Meaning.* Journal for the Study of the New Testament Supplement Series 95. Sheffield: JSOT Press.

Lenski, R. C. H. 1938. *The Interpretation of the Epistle to the Hebrews and of the Epistle of James.* Columbus, Ohio: Lutheran Book Concern.

Lifshitz, Baruch. 1962. "L'origine du nom de chrétiens." *Vigiliae Christianae* 16:65–70.

Lightfoot, J. B. 1972 [1865]. *The Epistle of St. Paul to the Galatians: With Introduction, Notes and Dissertations.* Grand Rapids: Zondervan.

Lincoln, Bruce. 1999. *Theorizing Myth: Narrative, Ideology, and Scholarship.* Chicago and London: University of Chicago Press.

———. 2003. *Holy Terrors: Thinking about Religion after September 11.* Chicago and London: University of Chicago Press.

Lips, Hermann von. 1990. *Weisheitliche Traditionen im Neuen Testament.* Wissenschaftliche Monographien zum Alten und Neuen Testament 64. Neukirchen-Vluyn: Neukirchener Verlag.

Loader, William R. G. 2005. "Jesus and the Law in John." Pages 135–54 in *Theology and Christology in the Fourth Gospel: Essays by the Members of the SNTS Johannine Writings Seminar.* Edited by G. van Belle, J. G. van der Watt, and P Maritz. Bibliotheca ephemeridum theologicarum lovaniensium 184. Leuven: Leuven University Press.

Lohmeyer, Ernst. 1951. "Mir ist gegeben alle Gewalt!" Pages 22–49 in *In Memoriam Ernst Lohmeyer.* Edited by W. Schmauch. Stuttgart: Evangelisches Verlagswerk.

———. 1953. *Die Offenbarung des Johannes*. Tübingen: Mohr.

Lohse, Eduard. 1979. *Die Offenbarung des Johannes*. 12th ed. Göttingen: Vandenhoeck & Ruprecht.

Longenecker, Richard N. 1970. *The Christology of Early Jewish Christianity*. Studies in Biblical Theology, Second Series 17. Naperville, Ill.: SCM.

Luedemann, Gerd. 1989. *Opposition to Paul in Jewish Christianity*. Translated by M. Eugene Boring. Minneapolis: Fortress Press.

———. 1996. *Heretics: The Other Side of Early Christianity*. Translated by John Bowden. Louisville, Ky.: Westminster John Knox.

———. 2002. *Paul: The Founder of Christianity*. Amherst, N.Y.: Prometheus Books.

Lührmann, Dieter. 1969. *Die Redaktion der Logienquelle*. Wissenschaftliche Monographien zum Alten und Neuen Testament. Neukirchen-Vluyn: Neukirchener Verlag.

Luomanen, Petri. 2002. "The 'Sociology of Sectarianism' in Matthew: Modeling the Genesis of Early Jewish and Christian Communities." Pages 107–30 in *Fair Play: Diversity and Conflicts in Early Christianity: Essays in Honour of Heikki Räisänen*. Edited by I. Dunderberg, C. Tuckett, and K. Syreeni. Leiden: Brill.

———. 2003. "Where Did Another Rich Man Come From? The Jewish-Christian Profile of the Story about a Rich Man in the 'Gospel of the Hebrews' (Origen, *Comm. in Matth.* 15.14)." *Vigiliae Christianae* 57:243–75.

———. 2005a. "Nazarenes." Pages 279–314 in *A Companion to Second-Century Christian "Heretics."* Edited by Antti Marjanen and Petri Luomanen. Supplements to Vigiliae Christianae 76. Leiden: Brill.

———. 2005b. "Sacrifices Abolished: The Last Supper in Luke (Codex Bezae) and in the *Gospel of the Ebionites*." Pages 186–208 in *Lux Humana, Lux Aeterna: Essays on Biblical and Related Themes in Honour of Lars Aejmelaeus*. Edited by Antti Mustakallio in collaboration with Heikki Leppä and Heikki Räisänen. Publications of Finnish Exegetical Society 89. Helsinki: Finnish Exegetical Society; Göttingen: Vandenhoeck & Ruprecht.

———. 2006. "'Let Him Who Seeks Continue Seeking': The Relationship between Jewish-Christian Gospels and the *Gospel of Thomas*." Pages 119–53 in *Thomasine Traditions in Antiquity: The Social and Cultural World of the Gospel of Thomas*. Edited by Jon Ma. Asgeirsson, April DeConick, and Risto Uro. Nag Hammadi and Manichean Studies 59. Leiden: Brill.

———. Forthcoming. "The Nazarenes' Gospel and Their Commentary on Isaiah Reconsidered." In *Bringing the Underground to the Foreground: New Perspectives on Jewish and*

Christian Apocryphal Texts and Traditions. Proceedings of the Apocrypha and Pseudepigrapha Section of the Society for Biblical Literature International Meeting Held in Groningen, The Netherlands, July 25–28, 2004. Edited by Pierluigi Piovanelli. Bibliothèque de l'Ecole des hautes études, Sciences religieuses. Turnhout: Brepols.

Luttikhuizen, Gerard P. 1985. *The Revelation of Elchasai: Investigations into the Evidence for a Mesopotamian Jewish Apocalypse of the Second Century and Its Reception by Judaeo-Christian Propagandists.* Texte und Studien zum antiken Judentum 8. Tübingen: Mohr Siebeck.

———. 2005. "Elchasaites and Their Book." Pages 335–64 in *A Companion to Second-Century Christian "Heretics."* Edited by Antti Marjanen and Petri Luomanen. Supplements to Vigiliae Christianae 76. Leiden: Brill.

Luz, Ulrich. 1981. "Das Neue Testament." Pages 58–139, 149–56 in Rudolf Smend and Ulrich Luz, *Gesetz.* Biblische Konfrontationen 1015. Stuttgart: W. Kohlhammer.

———. 1989. *Matthew 1–7.* Minneapolis: Fortress Press.

Mack, Burton L. 1988. *A Myth of Innocence: Mark and Christian Origins.* Philadelphia: Fortress Press.

———. 1993. *The Lost Gospel: The Book of Q and Christian Origins.* San Francisco: HarperSanFrancisco.

MacKenzie, Robert K. 1997. *The Author of the Apocalypse: A Review of the Prevailing Hypothesis of Jewish Christian Authorship.* Lewiston, N.Y.: Mellen Biblical Press.

MacMullen, Ramsay. 1974. *Roman Social Relations 50 B.C. to A.D. 284.* New Haven and London: Yale University Press.

Malina, Bruce J. 1973. "Jewish Christianity: A Select Bibliography." *Australian Journal of Biblical Archaeology* 6:60–65.

———. 1976. "Jewish Christianity or Christian Judaism: Toward a Hypothetical Definition." *Journal for the Study of Judaism* 7:46–57.

———. 1993. *The New Testament World: Insights from Cultural Anthropology.* Revised edition. Louisville, Ky.: Westminster John Knox.

———. 1995. *On the Genre and Message of Revelation: Star Visions and Sky Journeys.* Peabody, Mass.: Hendrickson.

———. 2000. *The New Jerusalem in the Revelation of John: The City as Symbol of Life with God.* Collegeville, Minn.: Liturgical.

Malina, Bruce J., and Richard L. Rohrbaugh. 2003. *Social-Science Commentary on the Synoptic Gospels.* Minneapolis: Fortress Press.

Manson, T. W. 1955–1956. "The Lord's Prayer." *Bulletin of the John Rylands University Library of Manchester* 38:99–113.

————. 1971 [1937]. *The Sayings of Jesus*. London: SCM.

Marshall, John W. 1997. "Parables of the War: Reading the Apocalypse within Judaism and during the Judæan War." Ph.D. diss., Princeton University.

————. 2001. *Parables of War: Reading John's Jewish Apocalypse*. Waterloo, Ont.: Wilfrid Laurier University Press.

————. 2005. "The Patriarchs and the Zodiac." Pages 86–103 in *Religious Rivalries and the Struggle for Success in Sardis and Smyrna*. Edited by Richard S. Ascough. Studies in Christianity and Judaism 14. Waterloo, Ont.: Wilfrid Laurier University Press.

Martyn, J. Louis. 1978. *The Gospel of John in Christian History: Essays for Interpreters*. New York: Paulist Press.

————. 1997. *Galatians: A New Translation with Introduction and Commentary*. Anchor Bible 33A. New York: Doubleday.

————. 2003 [1968]. *History and Theology in the Fourth Gospel*. 3rd ed. New Testament Library. Louisville, Ky.: Westminster John Knox.

Massebieau, Louis. 1895. "L'Epitre de Jacques, est-elle l'oeuvre d'un Chrétien?" *Revue de l'histoire des religions* 32:249–83.

Matera, Frank J. 2003. *II Corinthians: A Commentary*. New Testament Library. Louisville, Ky.: Westminster.

Mattingly, Harold B. 1958. "The Origin of the Name Christiani." *Journal of Theological Studies* n.s. 9:26–37.

Mayor, Joseph B. 1954 [1913]. *The Epistle of St. James. The Greek Text with Introduction, Notes and Comments, and Further Studies in the Epistle of St. James*. 2nd ed. London: Macmillan, 1913. Reprint, Grand Rapids: Zondervan.

McGiffert, Arthur Cushman. 1897. *A History of Christianity in the Apostolic Age*. New York: Charles Scribner's Sons.

McKnight, Scot. 1999. "A Parting within the Way: Jesus and James on Israel and Purity." Pages 83–129 in *James the Just and Christian Origins*. Edited by Bruce Chilton and Craig A. Evans. Novum Testamentum Supplements 98. Leiden: Brill.

Meeks, Wayne A. 1975. "'Am I a Jew?'—Johannine Christianity and Judaism." Pages 163–86 in *Christianity, Judaism and Other Greco-Roman Cults: Studies for Morton Smith at Sixty. Part One*. Edited by Jacob Neusner. Studies in Judaism in Late Antiquity 12. Leiden: Brill.

Meeks, Wayne A., and Robert L. Wilken. 1978. *Jews and Christians in Antioch in the First Four Centuries of the Common Era*. Society of Biblical Literature Sources for Biblical Study 13. Missoula, Mont.: Scholars Press.

Meier, John P. 1994. *A Marginal Jew: Rethinking the Historical Jesus.* Vol. 2, *Mentor, Message, and Miracles.* New York: Doubleday.

Menken, M. J. J. 2001. "Scriptural Dispute between Jews and Christians in John: Literary Fiction or Historical Reality? John 9:13–17, 24–34 as a Test Case." Pages 445–60 in *Anti-Judaism and the Fourth Gospel: Papers of the Leuven Colloquium, 2000.* Edited by Reimund Bieringer, Didier Pollefeyt, and Frederique Vandecasteele-Vanneuville. Jewish and Christian Heritage Series 1. Assen: Royal van Gorcum.

Metzger, Bruce M. 1971. *A Textual Commentary on the Greek New Testament: A Companion Volume to the United Bible Society Greek New Testament.* United Bible Society.

Meyers, Eric M. et al. 1986. "Sepphoris, 'Ornament of All Galilee.'" *Biblical Archaeologist* 49:4-19.

Meyer, Paul Donald. 1970. "The Gentile Mission in Q." *Journal of Biblical Literature* 89:405–17.

Milavec, Aaron. 1995. "The Saving Efficacy of the Burning Process in *Didache* 16:5." Pages 131-155 in C. N. Jefford, *The Didache in Context: Essays on its Text, History, and Transmission.* Leiden: Brill.

———. 2003. *The Didache: Faith, Hope, and Life of the Earliest Christian Communities, 50-70.* New York and Mahwah, N.J.: Newman.

Miller, Patrick D., Jr. 1989. "The Place of the Decalogue in the Old Testament and Its Law." *Interpretation* 43:229–42.

Mimouni, Simon. 1992. "Pour une définition nouvelle du judéo-christianisme ancien." *New Testament Studies* 38:161–86.

———. 1998. *Le judéo-christianisme ancien: Essais historiques.* Preface by André Caquot. Paris: Les Éditions du Cerf.

Moloney, Francis J. 1996. *Signs and Shadows: Reading John 5–12.* Minneapolis: Fortress Press.

Moore, George Foot. 1958. *Judaism in the First Centuries of the Christian Era.* New York: Schocken.

Moreau, J. 1949. "Le nom des chrétiens." *La nouvelle Clio* 1/2:190–92.

Moyise, Steve. 1995. *The Old Testament in the Book of Revelation.* Journal for the Study of the New Testament Supplement Series 115. Sheffield: Sheffield Academic Press.

Muilenburg, James. 1929. "The Literary Relations of the Epistle of Barnabas and the Teaching of the Twelve Apostles." Dissertation, Marburg.

Munck, Johannes. 1959-60. "Jewish Christianity in Post-Apostolic Times." *New Testament Studies* 6:103–16.

———. 1965. "Primitive Jewish Christianity and Later Jewish Christianity: Continuation or Rupture?" Pages 77–93 in *Aspects du Judéo-Christianisme. Colloque de Strasbourg 23–25 avril 1964*. Paris: Presses Universitaires de France.

Murphy, Frederick J. 1998. *Fallen Is Babylon: The Revelation to John*. Harrisburg, Pa.: Trinity.

Murray, Michele. 2004. *Playing a Jewish Game: Gentile Christian Judaizing in the First and Second Centuries CE*. Waterloo, Ont.: Wilfrid Laurier University Press.

Murray, Robert. 1974. "Defining Judaeo-Christianity." *Heythrop Journal* 15:303–10.

———. 1982. "Jews, Hebrews and Christians: Some Needed Distinctions." *Novum Testamentum* 24:194–208.

Myllykoski, Matti. 1996. "The Social History of Q and the Jewish War." Pages 143–99 in *Symbols and Strata: Essays on the Sayings Gospel Q*. Edited by Risto Uro. Helsinki: Finnish Exegetical Society; Göttingen: Vandenhoeck & Ruprecht.

———. 2005a. "Varken judar eller kristna? Tidig kristen identitet utom och inom judendomen." *Svensk Exegetisk Årsbok* 70: 339–56.

———. 2005b. "Cerinthus." Pages 279–314 in *A Companion to Second-Century Christian "Heretics."* Edited by Antti Marjanen and Petri Luomanen. Supplements to Vigiliae Christianae 76. Leiden: Brill.

Myllykoski, Matti, and Petri Luomanen. 1999. "Varhaisen juutalaiskristillisyyden jäljillä." *Teologinen Aikakauskirja* 104: 327–48. [On the Trail of Early Judaeo Christianity in the *Finnish Journal of Theology*; English Abstract on p. 321.]

Nanos, Mark D. 1996. *The Mystery of Romans: The Jewish Context of Paul's Letter*. Minneapolis: Fortress Press.

———. 2002a. *The Irony of Galatians: Paul's Letter in First-Century Context*. Minneapolis: Fortress Press.

———. 2002b. "What was at Stake in Peter's 'Eating with Gentiles'?" Pages 282–318 in *The Galatians Debate: Contemporary Issues in Rhetorical and Historical Interpretation*. Edited by Mark Nanos. Peabody, Mass.: Hendrickson.

———. 2005. "Jewish Christianity Session Response to Papers by Sumney, Runesson, Zetterholm. Paper Presented at the Annual Meeting of Society of Biblical Literature." Philadelphia, Pa.. November 19.

Needham, Rodney. 1975. "Polythetic Classification: Convergence and Consequences." *Man* n.s. 10:349–69.

Neusner, Jacob. 1978. "Comparing Judaisms." *History of Religions* 18:177–91.

———. 1988. *Judaism: The Evidence of the Mishnah*. 2nd ed. Brown Judaic Studies 129. Atlanta: Scholars Press.

———. 2001. "What Is a 'Judaism'?" Pages 3–21 in *Judaism in Late Antiquity Part Five,* Vol. 1. Edited by A. J. Avery-Peck, J. Neusner, B. D. Chilton. Leiden: Brill.

Neyrey, Jerome H. 1987. "Jesus the Judge: Forensic Process in John 8, 21-59." *Biblica* 68:509–41.

Nickelsburg, George W. E. 1972. *Resurrection, Immortality and Eternal Life in Intertestamental Judaism.* Harvard Theological Studies 26. Cambridge: Harvard University Press.

———. 1992. "Eschatology (Early Jewish)." Pages 579–94 in vol. 2 of *Anchor Bible Dictionary.* 6 vols. Edited by D. N. Freedman. New York: Doubleday.

———. 2003. *Ancient Judaism and Christian Origins: Diversity, Continuity, and Transformation.* Minneapolis: Fortress Press.

Niederwimmer, Kurt. 1998. *The Didache: A Commentary.* Hermeneia. Minneapolis: Fortress Press.

Nissen, Andreas. 1974. *Gott und der Nächste im antiken Judentum.* Wissenschaftliche Untersuchungen zum Neuen Testament 15. Tübingen: Mohr.

Odeberg, Hugo. 1968 [1929]. *The Fourth Gospel: Interpreted in Its Relation to Contemporaneous Religious Currents in Palestine and the Hellenistic-Oriental World.* Amsterdam: B. R. Grüner.

Overman, J. Andrew. 1990. *Matthew's Gospel and Formative Judaism: The Social World of the Matthean Community.* Minneapolis: Fortress Press.

Pagels, Elaine. 1995. *The Origin of Satan.* New York: Random House.

Paget, J. Carleton. 1999. "Jewish Christianity." Pages 731–75 in *The Cambridge History of Judaism,* Vol. 3, *The Early Roman Period.* Edited by W. Horbury, W. D. Davies, and J. Sturdy. Cambridge and New York: Cambridge University Press.

Painchaud, Louis. 2003. "Review of John Marshall, *Parables of War.*" *Laval Theologique et Philosophique* 59:371–73.

Painter, John. 1993. *The Quest for the Messiah: The History, Literature and Theology of the Johannine Community.* 2nd ed. Nashville: Abingdon.

———. 2004. *Just James: The Brother of Jesus in History and Tradition.* 2nd ed. Studies on Personalities of the New Testament. Columbia, S.C.: University of South Carolina.

Pancaro, Severino. 1975. *The Law in the Fourth Gospel: The Torah and the Gospel, Moses and Jesus, Judaism and Christianity according to John.* Novum Testamentum Supplements 42. Leiden: Brill.

Park, Eung C. 2003. *Either Jew or Gentile: Paul's Unfolding Theology of Inclusiveness.* Louisville, Ky.: Westminster John Knox.

Pearson, Birger A. 2004. "A Q Community in Galilee?" *New Testament Studies* 50:476–94.

Penner, Todd C. 1996. *The Epistle of James and Eschatology: Re-reading an Ancient Christian*

Letter. Journal for the Study of the New Testament Supplement Series 121. Sheffield: Sheffield Academic Press.

Perdue, Leo G. 1990. "The Social Character of Paraenesis and Paraenetic Literature." *Semeia* 50:5–39.

Pesch, Rudolf. 1982. "Voraussetzungen und Anfänge der urchristlichen Mission." Pages 11–70 in *Mission im Neuen Testament.* Edited by Karl Kertelge. Freiburg: Herder.

Petersen, William L. 1994. *Tatian's Diatessaron: Its Creation, Dissemination, Significance and History in Scholarship.* Supplements to Vigiliae Christianae 25. Leiden: Brill.

Peterson, Erik. 1946. "Christianus." Pages 355–72 in *Miscellanea Giovanni Mercat.* Vatican: Biblioteca Apostolica Vaticana.

———. 1959. *Frühkirche, Judentum und Gnosis: Studien und Untersuchungen.* Darmstadt: Wissenschaftliche Buchgesellschaft.

Plummer, Alfred. 1915. *A Critical and Exegetical Commentary on the Second Epistle of St. Paul to the Corinthians.* International Critical Commentary. New York: Scribner.

Popkes, Wiard. 1986. *Adressaten, Situation und Form des Jakobusbriefes.* Stuttgart: Katholisches Bibelwerk.

Porter, Stanley E. 1989. "The Language of the Apocalypse in Recent Discussion." *New Testament Studies* 35:582–603.

Pritz, Ray A. 1988. *Nazarene Jewish Christianity: From the End of the New Testament Period until Its Disappearance in the Fourth Century.* Leiden: Brill.

Quispel, Gilles. 1968. "The Discussion of Judaic Christianity." *Vigiliae Christianae* 22:81–93.

Räisänen, Heikki. 1992. *Jesus, Paul and Torah: Collected Essays.* Translated by D. E. Orton. Journal for the Study of the New Testament Supplements Series 43. Sheffield: Sheffield Academic Press.

Rajak, Tessa. 2001. *The Jewish Dialogue with Greece and Rome: Studies in Cultural and Social Interaction.* Arbeiten zur Geschichte des antiken Judentums und des Urchristentums 48. Leiden: Brill.

Rauch, Christian. 1894. *Die Offenbarung des Johannes: untersucht nach ihrer Zusammensetzung und der Zeit ihrer Enstehung.* Haarlem: De Erven F. Bohn.

Rehm, Bernhard, ed. 1992. *Die Pseudoklementinen I: Homilien.* Edited by Georg Strecker. 3rd rev. ed. Die griechischen christlichen Schriftsteller der ersten Jahrhunderte 42. Berlin: Akademie.

———, ed. 1994. *Die Pseudoklementinen II: Rekognitionen in Rufins Übersetzung.* Edited by Georg Strecker. 2nd rev. ed. Die griechischen christlichen Schriftsteller der ersten Jahrhunderte 51. Berlin: Akademie.

Reiff, Stefan C. 1991. "The Early History of Jewish Worship." Pages 109-136 in P. F. Bradshaw and L. A. Hoffmann, *The Making of Jewish and Christian Worship*. Notre Dame: University of Notre Dame.

Reinhartz, Adele. 1998. "The Johannine Community and Its Jewish Neighbors: A Reappraisal." Pages 111–38 in "What Is John?" Vol. 2, *Literary and Social Readings of the Fourth Gospel*. Edited by Fernando F. Segovia. Society of Biblical Literature Symposium Series 7. Atlanta: Scholars Press.

———. 2001a. *Befriending the Beloved Disciple: A Jewish Reading of the Gospel of John*. New York: Continuum.

———. 2001b. "'Jews' and Jews in the Fourth Gospel." Pages 341–56 in *Anti-Judaism and the Fourth Gospel: Papers of the Leuven Colloquium, 2000*. Edited by Reimund Bieringer, Didier Pollefeyt, and Frederique Vandecasteele-Vanneuville. Jewish and Christian Heritage Series 1. Assen: Royal van Gorcum.

Remus, Harold. 2002. "Persecution." Pages 431–52 in *Handbook of Early Christianity: Social Scientific Approaches*. Edited by Anthony J. Blasi, Jean Duhaime, and Paul-André Turcotte. New York: AltaMira.

Rensberger, David. 1989. *Overcoming the World: Politics and Community in the Gospel of John*. London: SPCK.

Rhoads, David. 1998. "The Letter of James: Friend of God." *Currents in Theology and Mission* 25:473–86.

Riches, John K. 2000. *Conflicting Mythologies: Identity Formation in the Gospels of Mark and Matthew*. Edinburgh: T & T Clark.

Riches, John K. and David Sim, eds. 2005. *The Gospel of Matthew in its Roman Imperial Context*. London: T & T Clark.

Riegel, Stanley K. 1978. "Jewish Christianity: Definitions and Terminology." *New Testament Studies* 24:410–15.

Riggs, John W. 1984. "From Gracious Table to Sacramental Elements: The Tradition-History of Didache 9 and 10." *The Second Century* 4/2:83-101.

Ritschl, Albrecht. 1857. *Die Entstehung der altkatholischen Kirche: Eine kirchen- und dogmengeschichtliche Monographie*. 2nd ed. Bonn: Adolph Marcus.

Robbins, Vernon K. 1991. "Writing as a Rhetorical Act in Plutarch and the Gospels." Pages 142–68 in *Persuasive Artistry: Studies in New Testament Rhetoric in Honor of George A. Kennedy*. Edited by Duane F. Watson. Sheffield: JSOT Press.

Roberts, Alexander and James Donaldson, eds. 1986-89. *The Ante-Nicene Fathers: Translations of the Writings of the Fathers down to AD 325*. Reprint edition. Grand Rapids, Mich.: Eerdmanns.

Robinson, James M. 1971. "LOGOI SOPHON: On the Gattung of Q." Pages 71–113 in James M. Robinson and Helmut Koester, *Trajectories through Early Christianity*. Philadelphia: Fortress Press.

———. 2000. "History of Q Research." Pages xix–lxxi in *The Critical Edition of Q*. Edited by James M. Robinson, Paul Hoffmann, and John S. Kloppenborg. Hermeneia Supplements. Minneapolis: Fortress Press; Leuven: Peeters.

———, ed. 2002. *The Sayings of Jesus: The Sayings Gospel Q in English*. Minneapolis: Fortress Press.

Robinson, James M., Paul Hoffmann, and John S. Kloppenborg, eds. 2000. *The Critical Edition of Q*. Hermeneia Supplements. Minneapolis: Fortress Press; Leuven: Peeters.

Robinson, Joseph Armitage. 1920. *Barnabas, Hermas and the Didache: Being the Donnellan Lectures Delivered before the University of Dublin in 1920*. London. SPCK.

Roloff, Jürgen. 1993. *The Revelation of John: A Continental Commentary*. Minneapolis: Fortress Press.

Ropes, James Hardy. 1978 [1916]. *A Critical and Exegetical Commentary on the Epistle of St. James*. International Critical Commentary 41. Edited by Charles A. Briggs, Samuel R. Driver, and Alfred Plummer. Edinburgh: T & T Clark.

Rordorf, Willy. 1996. "An Aspect of the Judeo-Christian Ethic: The Two Ways." Pages 148–64 in *The Didache in Modern Research*. Edited by Jonathan A. Draper. Arbeiten zur Geschichte des antiken Judentums und des Urchristentums 37. Leiden: Brill.

———. 1997. "Die Mahlgebete in *Didache* Kap. 9-10: Ein neuer *Status Quaestionis*." *Vigiliae Christianae* 51:229-246.

Rordorf, Willy, and Andre Tuilier. 1998. *La Doctrine des Douze Apôtres (Didache)*. 2nd ed. Sources chrétiennes 248. Paris: Les Editions du Cerf.

Rowland, Christopher. 1999. "Apocalyptic: The Disclosure of Heavenly Knowledge." Pages 776–97 in vol. 3 of *The Cambridge History of Judaism*. Edited by W. Horbury, W. D. Davies, and J. Sturdy. Cambridge University Press, 1999.

Ruiz, Jean-Pierre. 1989. *Ezekiel in the Apocalypse: The Transformation of Prophetic Language in Revelation 16:17—19:10*. Frankfurt am Main: Peter Lang.

Sabatier, Auguste. 1888. *Les Origines littéraires et la composition de l'Apocalypse de Saint Jean*. Paris: Fischbacher.

Safrai, Shemuel, and Menaham Stern. 1987. *The Jewish People in the First Century: Historical Geography, Political History, Social, Cultural and Religious Life and Institutions*. Assen: Van Gorcum; Philadelphia: Fortress Press.

Saldarini, Anthony J. 1994. *Matthew's Christian-Jewish Community*. Chicago Studies in the History of Judaism. Chicago and London: University of Chicago Press.

———. 1998. "The Social World of Christian Jews and Jewish Christians." Pages 115–54 in *Religious and Ethnic Communities in Later Roman Palestine*. Edited by Hiyam Lapin. Bethesda: University of Maryland Press.

Sanders, E. P. 1976. "The Covenant as Soteriological Category and the Nature of Salvation in Palestinian and Hellenistic Judaism." Pages 11–44 in *Jews, Greeks and Christians: Religious Cultures in Late Antiquity*. Edited by Robert Hamerton-Kelly and Robin Scroggs. Leiden: Brill.

———. 1977. *Paul and Palestinian Judaism: A Comparison of Patterns of Religion*. Philadelphia: Fortress Press.

———.1994 [1992]. *Judaism: Practice & Belief, 63 BCE–66 CE*. London: SCM; Philadelphia: Trinity Press International, 1992. 2nd impression with corrections, 1994.

Sanders, Jack T. 2002. "Establishing Social Distance between Christians and Both Jews and Pagans." Pages 361–82 in *Handbook of Early Christianity: Social Scientific Approaches*. Edited by Anthony J. Blasi, Jean Duhaime, Paul-André Turcotte. New York: AltaMira.

Satlow, Michael L. 2005. "Disappearing Categories: Using Categories in the Study of Religion." *Method and Theory in the Study of Religion* 17:287–98.

Sato, Migaku. 1994 [1988]. "The Shape of the Q-Source." Pages 156–79 in *The Shape of Q*. Edited and translated by John S. Kloppenborg. Minneapolis: Fortress Press.

Schaeder, H. H. 1967. "Ναζαρηνός, Ναζωραῖος." Pages 874–79 in vol. 4 of *Theological Dictionary of the New Testament*. Edited by Gerhard Kittel and Gerhard Friedrich. Translated by Geoffrey W. Bromiley. 10 vols. Grand Rapids, Mich.: Eerdmans, 1964–1976.

Schäfer, Peter. 1975. "Die sogenannte Synode von Jabne: Zur Trennung von Juden und Christen im ersten/zweiten Jh. n. Chr." *Judaica* 31:54–64, 116–24.

Schiffmann, Lawrence H. 1985. *Who Was a Jew?* Hoboken: Ktav.

Schlatter, Adolf. 1930 [1903]. *Der Evangelist Johannes. Wie er spricht, denkt and glaubt. Ein Kommentar zum vierten Evangelium*. Stuttgart: Calwer.

Schliemann, Adolph. 1844. *Die Clementinen nebst den verwandten Schriften und der Ebionitismus*. Hamburg: Berthes.

Schmidt, Paul W. 1891. *Anmerkung über die Composition der Offenbarung Johannis*. Freiburg: Mohr.

Schmithals, Walter. 1971. *Gnosticism in Corinth: An Investigation of the Letters to the Corinthians*. Translated by John E. Seely. Nashville: Abingdon.

Schnabel, Eckhard J. 1985. *Law and Wisdom from Ben Sira to Paul: A Tradition-Historical Enquiry into the Relation of Law, Wisdom, and Ethics*. Wissenschaftliche Untersuchungen zum Neuen Testament 2/16. Tübingen: Mohr Siebeck.

Schnackenburg, Rudolf. 1971. *Das Johannesevangelium.* Herders theologischer Kommentar zum Neuen Testament 4. Freiburg: Herder.

Schoen, Henri. 1887. *L'Origine de l'Apocalypse de St. Jean.* Paris: Fischbacher.

Schoeps, Hans Joachim. 1949. *Theologie und Geschichte des Judenchristentums.* Tübingen: Mohr Siebeck.

———. 1969. *Jewish Christianity: Factional Disputes in the Early Church.* Translated by Douglas R. A. Hare. Philadelphia: Fortress Press.

Schöllgen, Georg. 1991. *Didache–Zwölf-Apostel-Lehre. Einleitung, Übersetzung und Kommentar.* Fontes Christiani 1. Freiburg: Herder.

Schultz, Siegfried. 1972. *Q: Die Spruchquelle der Evangelisten.* Zurich: Theologischer Verlag.

Schürer, Emil, Geza Vermes, Fergus Millar, and Matthew Black. 1979. *The History of the Jewish People in the Age of Jesus Christ (175 B.C.–A.D. 135).* Volume 2. Edinburgh: T & T Clark.

Schüssler Fiorenza, Elisabeth. 1986. "The Followers of the Lamb: Visionary Rhetoric and Social-Political Situation." *Semeia* 36:123–46.

———. 1991. *Revelation: Vision of a Just World.* Minneapolis: Fortress Press.

———. 1995. *In Memory of Her: A Feminist Theological Reconstruction of Christian Origins.* Second Edition. New York: Crossroad.

Seeberg, Alfred. 1903. *Der Katechismus der Urchristenheit.* Leipzig: Deichert.

———. 1906. *Die Beiden Wege und das Aposteldekret.* Leipzig: Deichert.

Seeley, David. 1991. "Blessing and Boundaries: Interpretations of Jesus' Death in Q." *Semeia* 55:131–46.

———. 1992. Jesus' Death in Q. *New Testament Studies* 38:222–34.

Segal, Alan F. 1990. *Paul the Convert: The Apostolate and Apostasy of Saul the Pharisee.* New Haven: Yale University Press.

Seidensticker, Philipp. 1959. *Die Gemeinschaftsform der religiösen Gruppen des Spätjudentums und der Urkirche.* Jerusalem: Franciscan Press.

Seitz, O. J. F. 1964. "James and the Law." *Studia Evangelica: Papers Presented to the International Congress on The Four Gospels in 1957. Studia Evangelica* 2:472–86.

Setzer, Claudia. 1994. *Jewish Responses to Early Christians: History and Polemics, 30–150 C.E.* Minneapolis: Fortress Press.

Sheppard, Gerald. 1980. *Wisdom as Hermeneutical Construct: A Study in the Sapientializing of the Old Testament.* Beihefte zur Zeitschrift für die alttestamentliche Wissenschaft 151. Berlin: Walter de Gruyter.

Sim, David. 1996. "Christianity and Ethnicity in the Gospel of Matthew." Pages 171–95 in *Ethnicity and the Bible*. Edited by M. Brett. Leiden: Brill.

———. 1998. *The Gospel of Matthew and Christian Judaism: The History and Social Setting of the Matthean Community*. Studies of the New Testament and Its World. Edinburgh: T & T Clark.

Simon, Marcel. 1965. "Problèmes du judéo-christianisme." Pages 1–17 in *Aspects du judéo-christianisme: Colloque de Strasbourg 23–25 avril 1964*. Bibliothèque des centres d'études supérieures spécialisés: Travaux du centre d'études supérieures spécialisé d'histoire des religions de Strasbourg. Paris: Presses Universitaires de France.

———. 1975. "Réflexions sur le judéo-christianisme." Pages 53–76 in vol. 2 of *Christianity, Judaism and Other Greco-Roman Cults: Studies for Morton Smith at Sixty*. 4 vols. Edited by Jacob Neusner. Studies in Judaism in Late Antiquity 12. Leiden: Brill.

———. 1996 [1986]. *Verus Israel: A Study of the Relations between Christians and Jews in the Roman Empire AD 135–425*. Translated by H. McKeating. The Littman Library of Jewish Civilization. Oxford: Oxford University Press, 1986. Repr. ed., 1996.

Six, K. 1912. *Das Aposteldekret (Act 15, 28. 29): Seine Entstehung und Geltung in den ersten vier Jahrhunderten*. Veröffentlichungen des biblisch-patristischen Seminars zu Innsbruck 5. Innsbruck: Felizian Rausch (L. Pustet).

Slee, Michelle. 2003. *The Church in Antioch in the First Century CE: Communion and Conflict*. Journal for the Study of the New Testament Supplement Series 244. London and New York: Sheffield Academic Press.

Slingerland, Dixon. 1986. "The Nature of *Nomos* (Law) within the Testaments of the Twelve Patriarchs." *Journal of Biblical Literature* 105:39–48.

Smith, Jonathan Z. 1988 [1982]. "Fences and Neighbors: Some Contours of Early Judaism." Pages 1–18 in *Imagining Religion: From Babylon to Jonestown*. Chicago: University of Chicago Press.

———. 1990. *Drudgery Divine: On the Comparison of Early Christianities and the Religions of Late Antiquity*. Chicago: University of Chicago Press.

———. 1996. "A Matter of Class: Taxonomies of Religion." *Harvard Theological Review* 89:387-403.

———. 2000. "The 'End' of Comparison: Redescription and Rectification." Pages 237–41 in *A Magic Still Dwells: Comparative Religion in the Postmodern Age*. Edited by Kimberley C. Patton and Benjamin C. Ray. Berkeley: University of California Press.

———. 2004. *Relating Religion: Essays in the Study of Religion*. Chicago: University of Chicago Press.

Smith, Thomas, Peter Peterson, and James Donaldson, trans. 1978 [1886]. "Pseudo-Clementine Literature." Pages 67–346 in *The Twelve Patriarchs, Excerpts and Epistles, the Clementina, Apocrypha, Decretals, Memoirs of Edessa and Syriac Documents, Remains of the First Ages*. Vol. 8 of *The Ante-Nicene Fathers: Translations of the Writings of the Fathers down to A.D. 325*. Edited by Alexander Roberts and James Donaldson; American reprint revised by A. Cleveland Coxe. 10 vols. Repr., Grand Rapids: Eerdmans.

Smith, Morton. 1960–61. "The Dead Sea Sect in Relation to Ancient Judaism." *New Testament Studies* 7:347–60.

Snodgrass, Klyne. 1996. "Matthew and the Law." Pages 99–127 in *Treasures Old and New: Contributions to Matthean Studies*. Edited by D. R. Bauer and M. A. Powell. Atlanta: Scholars Press.

Spickard, Paul, and W. Jeffrey Burroughs. 2000. "We Are a People." Pages 1–19 in *We Are a People: Narrative and Multiplicity in Constructing Ethnic Identity*. Edited by Paul Spickard and W. Jeffrey Burroughs. Philadelphia: Temple University Press.

Spitta, Friedrich. 1889. *Die Offenbarung des Johannes*. Halle: Verlag der Buchh. des Waisenhauses.

———. 1896. "Der Brief des Jakobus." Pages 1–239 in vol. 2 of *Zur Geschichte und Literatur des Urchristentums*. 3 vols. in 4. Göttingen: Vandenhoeck & Ruprecht, 1893–1907.

Srawley, J. H. 1949. *The Early History of the Liturgy*. Cambridge: Cambridge University Press.

Stade, Bernhard, and Oskar Holtzmann. 1887. *Geschichte des Volkes Isräel*. 2 vols. Berlin: G. Grote.

Stanton, Graham N. 1992a. *A Gospel for a New People: Studies in Matthew*. Edinburgh: T & T Clark.

———. 1992b. "Matthew's Christology and the Parting of the Ways." Pages 99–116 in *Jews and Christians: The Parting of the Ways A.D. 70 to 135*. Edited by J. D. G. Dunn. Tübingen: Mohr.

Stanton, Graham N., and Guy G. Stroumsa, eds. 1998. *Tolerance and Intolerance in Early Judaism and Christianity*. Cambridge: Cambridge University Press.

Stark, Rodney, and William Bainbridge. 1985. *The Future of Religion: Secularization, Revival, and Cult Formation*. Berkeley: University of California Press.

Steck, Odil H. 1967. *Israel und das gewaltsame Geschick der Propheten: Untersuchungen zur Überlieferung des deuteronomistischen Geschichtsbildes im Alten Testament, Spätjudentum und Urchristentum*. Wissenschaftliche Monographien zum Alten und Neuen Testament 23. Neukirchen-Vluyn: Neukirchener Verlag.

Stendahl, Krister. 1986. *Paul among Jews and Gentiles*. Philadelphia: Fortress Press.

Strack, Hermann Leberecht, and Paul Billerbeck. 1922. *Das Evangelium nach Matthäus Erläutert aus Talmud und Midrasch*. Munich: C. H. Beck'sche Verlagsbuchhandlung.

Strecker, Georg. 1988. "Judenchristentum." Pages 310–25 in vol. 17 of *Theologische Realenzyklopädie*. Edited by Horst Robert Balz, Gerhard Krause, and Gerhard Müller. Berlin and New York: de Gruyter.

———. 1996 [1971]. Appendix 1: "On the Problem of Jewish Christianity." Pages 241–85 in Walter Bauer, *Orthodoxy and Heresy in Earliest Christianity*. 2nd German ed., with appendices, by Georg Strecker. Translated by a team from the Philadelphia Seminar on Christian Origins. Edited by Robert A. Kraft and Gerhard Krodel. Philadelphia: Fortress Press, 1971. Repr., Mifflintown, Pa.: Sigler Press.

Stuart, Moses. 1845. *Commentary on the Apocalypse*. Andover, Mass.: Allen, Morrill and Wardwell.

Stuiber, Alfred. 1961. "Das ganze Joch des Herrn (Didache 6:2-3)." Pages 323–29 in *Studia Patristica IV*. Edited by F. L. Cross. Texte und Untersuchungen 79. Berlin: Akademie-Verlag.

Suggs, M. Jack. 1972. "The Christian Two Ways Tradition: Its Antiquity, Form, and Function." Pages 60–74 in *Studies in New Testament and Early Christian Literature: Essays in Honor of Allen P. Wikgren*. Edited by David E. Aune. Supplements to Novum Testamentum 33. Leiden: Brill.

Sumney, Jerry L. 1990. *Identifying Paul's Opponents: The Question of Method in 2 Corinthians*. Journal for the Study of the New Testament Supplement Series 40. Sheffield: JSOT Press.

———. 1999. *'Servants of Satan', 'False Brothers', and Other Opponents of Paul*. Journal for the Study of the New Testament Supplement Series 188. Sheffield: Sheffield Academic Press.

Swete, Henry B. 1911. *The Apocalypse of St. John: The Greek Text with Introduction, Notes and Indices*. 3rd ed. London: Macmillan.

Tajfel, Henri. 1980. *Human Groups and Social Categories: Studies in Social Psychology*. Cambridge: Cambridge University Press.

Talley, Thomas J. 1976. "From Berakah to Eucharistia: A Reopening Question." *Worship* 50/2: 115-137.

Taylor, Charles. 1886. *The Teaching of the Twelve Apostles, with illustrations from the Talmud*. Cambridge: Deighton Bell.

Taylor, Joan E. 1990. "The Phenomenon of Early Jewish-Christianity: Reality or Scholarly Invention?" *Vigiliae Christianae* 44:313–34.

Taylor, Justin. 1994. "Why Were the Disciples First Called 'Christians' at Antioch? (Acts 11, 26)." *Revue Biblique* 101:75–94.

Taylor, Nicholas H. 2002. "Conflicting Bases of Identity in Early Christianity: The Example of Paul." Pages 577–97 in *Handbook of Early Christianity: Social Scientific Approaches.* Edited by Anthony J. Blasi, Jean Duhaime, Paul-André Turcotte. New York: AltaMira.

Tellbe, Mikael. 2001. *Paul between Synagogue and State: Christians, Jews, and Civic Authorities in 1 Thessalonians, Romans, and Philippians.* Coniectanea biblica: New Testament Series 34. Stockholm: Almqvist & Wiksell.

Theissen, Gerd. 1978. *The First Followers of Jesus: A Sociological Analysis of the Earliest Christians.* Translated by John Bowden. London: SCM Press.

———. 1991. *The Gospels in Context: Social and Political History in the Synoptic Tradition.* Translated by Linda M. Maloney. Minneapolis: Fortress Press.

Theobald, Michael. 1997. "Schriftzitate im 'Lebensbrot'-Dialog Jesu (Joh 6). Ein Paradigma fur den Schriftgebrauch des vierten Evangelisten." Pages 325–66 in *The Scriptures in the Gospels.* Edited by C. M. Tuckett. Bibliotheca ephemeridum theologicarum lovaniensium 131. Leuven: Leuven University Press.

———. 2004. "Abraham – (Isaak –) Jakob: Israels Väter im Johannesevangelium." Pages 158–83 in *Israel und seine Heilstraditionen im Johannesevangelium: Festgabe für Johannes Beutler SJ zum 70. Geburtstag.* Edited by M. Labahn, K. Scholtissek and A. Strotmann. Paderborn: Ferdinand Schöningh.

Thompson, Leonard L. 1990. *The Book of Revelation: Apocalypse and Empire.* Oxford: Oxford University Press.

Tödt, Heinz Eduard. 1965 [1963]. *The Son of Man in the Synoptic Tradition.* Translated by Dorothea M. Barton. Philadelphia: Westminster Press.

Tomson, Peter J. 1986. "The Names Israel and Jew in Ancient Judaism and in the New Testament." *Bijdragen, tijdschrift voor filosofie en theologie* 47:120–40, 266–89.

———. 1990. *Paul and the Jewish Law: Halakha in the Letters of the Apostle to the Gentiles.* Assen: van Gorcum; Minneapolis: Fortress Press.

———. 2000. "'Jews' in the Gospel of John as Compared with the Palestinian Talmud, the Synoptics and Some New Testament Apocrypha." Pages 301–40 in *Anti-Judaism and the Fourth Gospel: Papers of the Leuven Colloquium, 2000.* Edited by R. Bieringer, D. Pollefeyt and F. Vandecasteele-Vanneuville. Leiden: Royal van Gorcum.

———. 2005. "The Halakhic Evidence of Didache 8 and Matthew 6 and the Didache Community's Relationship to Judaism." Pages 131–41 in *Matthew and the Didache: Two Documents from the Same Jewish-Christian Milieu?* Edited by H. van de Sandt. Assen: Royal van Gorcum; Minneapolis: Fortress Press.

Tuckett, Christopher M. 1996a. *Q and the History of Early Christianity*. Edinburgh: T & T Clark; Peabody, Mass.: Hendrikson.

Tuckett, Christopher M. 1996b [1989]. "Synoptic Tradition in the Didache." Pages 92–128 in *The Didache in Modern Research*. Edited by Jonathan A. Draper. Arbeiten zur Geschichte des antiken Judentums und des Urchristentums 37. Leiden: Brill.

Turner, Cuthbert Hamilton. 1912. "The Early Christian Ministry and the Didache." Pages 1-31 in C. H. Turner, *Studies in Early Church History*. Oxford: Oxford University Press.

Uro, Risto. 1987. *Sheep among Wolves: A Study of the Mission Instructions of Q*. Annales Academiae scientiarum fennicae. Helsinki: Suomalainen Tiedeakatemia.

Vaage, Leif E. 1994. *Galilean Upstarts: Jesus' First Followers according to Q*. Valley Forge, Pa.: Trinity Press International.

Van de Sandt, Huub. 1992. "Didache 3, 1-6: A Transformation of an Existing Jewish Hortatory Pattern." *Journal for the Study of Judaism* 23:21–41.

———, ed. 2005. *Matthew and the Didache*. Assen: Royal van Gorcum; Philadelphia: Fortress Press.

Van de Sandt, Huub, and David Flusser. 2002. *The Didache: Its Jewish Sources and its Place in Early Judaism and Christianity*. Assen: Royal van Gorcum; Minneapolis: Fortress Press.

Van Voorst, Robert. E. 1989. *The Ascents of James: History and Theology of a Jewish-Christian Community*. Society of Biblical Literature Dissertation Series 112. Atlanta: Scholars Press.

Veilleux, Armand, ed. and trans. 1986. *La Première Apocalypse de Jacques (NH V,3), La Seconde Apocalypse de Jacques (NH V,4)*. Bibliothèque Copte de Nag Hammadi, Section "Textes" 17. Sainte-Foy, Québec: Les Presses de l'Université de Laval.

Verseput, Donald, J. 1997. "Reworking the Puzzle of Faith and Deeds in James 2:14-26." *New Testament Studies* 43:97–115.

Vielhauer, Philipp, and Georg Strecker. 1991. "Jewish-Christian Gospels." Pages 134–77 in Vol. 1 of *New Testament Apocrypha*. Edited by W. Schneemelcher. English translation edited by R. McL. Wilson. 2 vols. Cambridge: James Clarke.

Vischer, Eduard. 1886. *Die Offenbarung Johan, eine jüdische Apokalypse in christlicher Bearbeitung. Mit einem Nachwort von Adolf Harnack*. Leipzig: J. C. Hinrichs.

Vokes, F. E. 1968. "The Ten Commandments in the New Testament and in First Century Judaism." *Studia Evangelica: Papers Presented to the International Congress on The Four Gospels in 1957. Studia Evangelica* 5:146–54.

Völter, Daniel. 1882. *Die Entstehung der Apokalypse: Ein Beitrag zur Geschichte des Urchristenthums*. Freiburg: Mohr.

———. 1885. *Die Entstehung der Apokalypse*. 2nd ed. Freiburg: Mohr Siebeck. ATLA Monograph Preservation Program. ATLA fiche 1986–3331.

———. 1886. *Die Offenbarung Johannis, keine Ursprünglich jüdische Apokalypse: eine Streitschrift gegen die Herren Harnack und Vischer*. Tübingen: J. J. Heckenhauer.

———. 1893. *Das Problem der Apokalypse: Nach Seinem Gegenwärtigen Stande Dargestellt und Neu Untersucht*. Freiburg: Mohr.

———. 1911 [1904]. *Die Offenbarung Johannis: Neu Untersucht und Erklärtert*. Strassburg: Heitz & Mündel. Rev. ed., 1911.

Vööbus, Arthur. 1968. *Liturgical Traditions in the Didache*. Papers of the Estonian Theological Society in Exile 16. Stockholm: ETSE.

Waanders, F. M. J. 1983. *The History of* ΤΕΛΟΣ *and* ΤΕΛΕΩ *in Ancient Greek*. Amsterdam: B.B. Grüner Publishing Co.

Wahlde, Urban C. von. 2000. "'The Jews' in the Gospel of John: Fifteen Years of Research (1983–1998)." *Ephemerides theologicae lovanienses* 76:30–55.

———. 2001. "'You Are of Your Father the Devil' in Its Context: Stereotyped Apocalyptic Polemic in John 8:38-47." Pages 418–44 in *Anti-Judaism and the Fourth Gospel: Papers of the Leuven Colloquium, 2000*. Edited by Reimund Bieringer, Didier Pollefeyt, and Frederique Vandecasteele-Vanneuville. Jewish and Christian Heritage Series 1. Assen: Royal van Gorcum.

Wall, Robert W. 1990. "James as Apocalyptic Paraenesis." *Restoration Quarterly* 32:11–22.

———. 1997. *Community of the Wise: The Letter of James*. New Testament in Context. Valley Forge, Pa.: Trinity Press International.

Weeden, Theodore J., Sr. 1979 [1971]. *Mark: Traditions in Conflict*. Philadelphia: Fortress Press.

Wegner, Uwe. 1985. *Der Hauptmann von Kafarnaum*. Wissenschaftliche Untersuchungen zum Neuen Testaement 2/14. Tübingen: Mohr.

Weiser, Arthur. 1962. *The Psalms: A Commentary*. London: SCM.

Weizsäcker, Carl Heinrich von. 1886. *Das Apostolische Zeitalter der christlichen Kirche*. Freiburg: Mohr.

Wellhausen, Julius. 1899. *Skizzen und Vorarbeiten*. Berlin: Reimer.

———. 1907. *Analyse der Offenbarung Johannis*. Berlin: Weidmann.

Wendland, Paul, ed. 1916. *Refutatio omnium haeresium*. Vol. 3 of *Hippolytus: Werke*. Die griechischen christlichen Schriftsteller der ersten drei Jahrhunderte 26. Leipzig: J. C. Hinrichs.

Wengst, Klaus. 1984. *Didache (Apostellehre), Barnabasbrief, Zweiter Klemensbrief, Schrift an Diognet*. Schriften des Urchristentums 2. Darmstadt: Wissenschaftliche Buchgesellschaft.

Weyland, Gerard J. 1888. *Om-werkings-en Compilatie-Hypothesen toegepast op de Apo-kalypse van Johannes*. Groningen.

Wilkes, A. L. 1997. *Knowledge in Minds: Individual and Collective Processes in Cognition*. New York: Psychology Press.

Williams, Frank. 1987. *The Panarion of Epiphanius of Salamis: Book I (Sects 1–46)*. Translated by Frank Williams. Nag Hammadi Studies 35. Leiden: Brill.

Williams, Michael Allen. 1996. *Rethinking "Gnosticism": An Argument for Dismantling a Dubious Category*. Princeton, N.J.: Princeton University Press.

Wilson, Bryan. 1973. *Magic and the Millennium: A Sociological Study of Religious Move-ments of Protest among Tribal and Third-World Peoples*. London: Heinemann.

Wilson, Stephen G. 1983. *Luke and the Law*. Society for New Testament Studies Monograph Series 50. Cambridge: Cambridge University Press.

———. 1995. *Related Strangers: Jews and Christians 70–170 C.E.* Minneapolis: Fortress Press.

———. 2004. "'Jew' and Related Terms in the Ancient World." *Studies in Religion/Sciences Religieuses* 33:157–71.

Witherington, Ben. 2003. *Revelation*. New York: Cambridge University Press.

Wright, R. B. 1985. "Psalms of Solomon: A New Translation and Introduction." Pages 639–70 in vol. 2 of *The Old Testament Pseudepigrapha*. Edited by James H. Charlesworth. 2 vols. London: Darton, Longman & Todd, 1983–1985.

Zahavy, Tzvee. 1990. *Studies in Jewish Prayer*. Lanham, Md: University Press of America.

Zeller, Dieter. 1984. *Kommentar zur Logienquelle*. Stuttgarter kleiner Kommentar. Stuttgart: Katholisches Bibelwerk.

Zetterholm, Magnus. 2003. *The Formation of Christianity in Antioch: A Social-Scientific Approach to the Separation Between Judaism and Christianity*. London and New York: Routledge.

———. 2005. "Jews, Christians and Gentiles: Rethinking the Categorization within the Early Jesus Movement." Paper presented at the annual meeting of Society of Biblical Litera-ture. Philadelphia, Pa. November 19.

Zumstein, Jean. 2001. "The Farewell Discourse (John 13:31–16:33) and the Problem of Anti-Judaism." Pages 461–78 in *Anti-Judaism and the Fourth Gospel: Papers of the Leuven Collo-quium, 2000*. Edited by Reimund Bieringer, Didier Pollefeyt, and Frederique Vandecasteele-Vanneuville. Jewish and Christian Heritage Series 1. Assen: Royal van Gorcum.

———. 2004. "Die Schriftrezeption in der Brotrede (Joh 6)." Pages 123–39 in *Israel und seine Heilstraditionen im Johannesevangelium: Festgabe für Johannes Beutler SJ zum 70. Geburtstag*. Edited by M. Labahn, K. Scholtissek and A. Strotmann. Paderborn: Ferdinand Schöningh.

Index of Subjects

Index of Primary Sources

11	184	4:24	105	15:19-20	90
11:51-52	198	4:27	105	15:21	50
12:42	183, 193	4:29-30	55	15:24	104
12:42-43	193	4:30	105	15:28-29	50
15:1	186	4:34-35	87, 89	15:29	90
15:1-11	273	5:17	42	18:1-3	61
15:25	183, 200	5:20	51	18:28-29	104
16:2	183	5:22-26	51	21	45
		5:31	48	21:15-26	211
Acts		5:42	51	21:20	49
1-3	41, 47	6:1	49	21:21	57
1:4	45	6:1-8:1	16	21:25	291
1:6	47	6:11-7:60	46	21:26	51
1:6-8	47	6:13	50	22:4-5	302
1:8	44	6:14	50	22:14	48
2:7-45	45	7:1	51	22:17	51
2:22	104	7:2-53	50	24:5	103, 104
2:24	105	7:37	48, 51	24:12-14	104
2:32	105	7:42	48	25:8	51
2:36	48	7:42-43	50	26:10-12	302
2:38	55	7:52	48	26:28	156, 247
2:46	51	7:53	50	26:28-29	58
3:1	51	7:57	81, 101
3:6	55	8:1-3	46	Romans	
3:12	47	8:4-7	101	1:3-4	53
3:13	49, 105	9:1	51	1:16	63, 73
3:14	48	9:1-2	302	3:1-2	63
3:15	105	10:36	48	6-8	116, 190
3:19-21	47	11:19-20	101	6:1-7	205
3:21	51	11:26	58	6:1-11	269
3:22	48	13-15	11	6:15-23	216
3:26	105	13:4-12	97	7:6-12	216
4:1	51	15	23	8:13	105
4:1-22	46	15:5	20	8:15	53
4:10	48, 105	15:6-29	43, 50	8:18	105